Further Mathematics
Statistics

Approval message from AQA

This textbook has been approved by AQA for use with our qualification. This means that we have checked that it broadly covers the specification and we are satisfied with the overall quality. Full details of our approval process can be found on our website.

We approve textbooks because we know how important it is for teachers and students to have the right resources to support their teaching and learning. However, the publisher is ultimately responsible for the editorial control and quality of this book.

Please note that when teaching the *AQA A-level Further Mathematics Statistics* course, you must refer to AQA's specification as your definitive source of information.

A wide range of other useful resources can be found on the relevant subject pages of our website: www.aqa.org.uk.

Author
John du Feu

Series editors
Roger Porkess
Catherine Berry

Contributing editor
Jonny Griffiths

Hachette UK's policy is to use papers that are natural, renewable and recyclable products and made from wood grown in sustainable forests. The logging and manufacturing processes are expected to conform to the environmental regulations of the country of origin.

Orders: please contact Bookpoint Ltd, 130 Park Drive, Milton Park, Abingdon, Oxon OX14 4SE. Telephone: (44) 01235 827720. Fax: (44) 01235 400454. Email education@bookpoint.co.uk Lines are open from 9 a.m. to 5 p.m., Monday to Saturday, with a 24-hour message answering service. You can also order through our website: www.hoddereducation.co.uk

ISBN: 978 1 5104 1465 5

© John du Feu, Roger Porkess, Catherine Berry, Jonny Griffiths and MEI 2018

First published in 2018 by

Hodder Education,
An Hachette UK Company
Carmelite House
50 Victoria Embankment
London EC4Y 0DZ

www.hoddereducation.co.uk

Impression number 10 9 8 7 6 5 4 3 2 1

Year 2022 2021 2020 2019 2018

All rights reserved. Apart from any use permitted under UK copyright law, no part of this publication may be reproduced or transmitted in any form or by any means, electronic or mechanical, including photocopying and recording, or held within any information storage and retrieval system, without permission in writing from the publisher or under licence from the Copyright Licensing Agency Limited. Further details of such licences (for reprographic reproduction) may be obtained from the Copyright Licensing Agency Limited, Saffron House, 6–10 Kirby Street, London EC1N 8TS.

Cover photo © Getty Images/iStockphoto/Thinkstock

Typeset in Bembo Std, 11/13 pts. by Integra Software Services Pvt. Ltd., Pondicherry, India

Printed in Italy

A catalogue record for this title is available from the British Library.

Contents

Getting the most from this book   iv
Prior knowledge   vi
Acknowledgements   viii

1 Statistical problem solving   1
   1.1 The problem solving cycle   2

2 Bivariate data and correlation coefficients   20
   2.1 Describing variables   22
   2.2 Interpreting scatter diagrams   23
   2.3 Pearson's product moment correlation coefficient   26
   2.4 Rank correlation   37

3 The binomial distribution   48
   3.1 The binomial distribution   49
   3.2 Hypothesis testing using the binomial distribution   52
   3.3 Critical values and critical regions   59
   3.4 One-tailed and two-tailed tests   63

4 Conditional probability   68
   4.1 Screening tests   69

Practice questions: set 1   78

5 Discrete random variables   81
   5.1 Notation and conditions for a discrete random variable   83
   5.2 Expectation and variance   87
   5.3 Expectation and variance of the uniform distribution and a linear function of a random variable   94
   5.4 The expectation and variance of functions of discrete random variables   103

6 The Poisson distribution   108
   6.1 When to use the Poisson distribution   108
   6.2 The sum of two or more Poisson distributions   116

7 The chi-squared test on a contingency table   125
   7.1 The chi-squared test on a contingency table   126

8 Continuous random variables 1   141
   8.1 Probability density function   143
   8.2 Expectation and variance   151
   8.3 The Normal distribution   156
   8.4 The distribution of sample means   161

Practice questions: set 2   169

9 Continuous random variables 2   172
   9.1 The expectation and variance of a function of X 173
   9.2 The cumulative distribution function   181

10 Confidence intervals using the Normal and t-distributions   195
   10.1 The sums and differences of Normal variables   198
   10.2 More than two independent random variables   202
   10.3 The distribution of the sample mean   206
   10.4 The theory of confidence intervals   212
   10.5 Interpreting sample data using the t-distribution   220

11 Hypothesis tests and their power   230
   11.1 Hypotheses for a test for a mean   231
   11.2 The power of a test   239

12 The rectangular and exponential distributions   251
   12.1 The continuous uniform (rectangular) distribution   252
   12.2 The exponential distribution   258

Practice questions: set 3   265

Answers   268
Index   293

Getting the most from this book

Mathematics is not only a beautiful and exciting subject in its own right but also one that underpins many other branches of learning. It is consequently fundamental to our national wellbeing.

This book covers the Statistics elements in the AQA AS and A Level Further Mathematics specifications. Students start these courses at a variety of stages. Some embark on AS Further Mathematics in Year 12, straight after GCSE, taking it alongside AS Mathematics, and so may have no prior experience of Statistics beyond GCSE. In contrast, others only begin Further Mathematics when they have completed the full A Level Mathematics and so have already met the Statistics covered in *AQA A-Level Mathematics*. Between these two extremes are the many who have covered the Statistics in AS Mathematics but no more.

This book has been written with all these users in mind. So, it provides a complete course in Statistics up to the required level. The first four chapters provide background material for the Further Mathematics course; their content will be helpful revision for some readers and new material for others.

In the AQA Further Mathematics specifications (7366 & 7367) one Statistics paper is available at AS level, and another at A level. Both are options for the applications paper. Chapter 5 to 8 of this book cover the new AS material, and 9 to 12 the remaining content for the full A level.

Between 2014 and 2016 A Level Mathematics and Further Mathematics were very substantially revised, for first teaching in 2017. Changes that particularly affect Statistics include increased emphasis on

- Problem solving
- Mathematical rigour
- Use of ICT
- Modelling.

This book embraces these ideas. A large number of exercise questions involve elements of problem solving and require rigorous logical argument.

Throughout the book the emphasis is on understanding and interpretation rather than mere routine calculations, but the various exercises do nonetheless provide plenty of scope for practising basic techniques. The exercise questions are split into three bands. Band 1 questions (indicated by a green bar) are designed to reinforce basic understanding; Band 2 questions (yellow bar) are broadly typical of what might be expected in an examination; Band 3 questions (red bar) explore around the topic and some of them are rather more demanding. In addition, extensive online support, including further questions, is available by subscription to AQA's Integral website, http://integralmaths.org.

In addition to the exercise questions, there are three sets of Practice questions. The first of these covers the background material in chapters 1 to 4; the second is based on the AS content in chapters 5 to 8 and the third set, coming at the end of the book, is drawn from the complete Further Mathematics A level.

There are places where the work depends on knowledge from earlier in the book or elsewhere and this is summarised in the statement on Prior Knowledge on page (vi). This should be seen as an invitation to those who have problems with the particular topic to revisit it. At the end of each chapter there is a list of key points covered as well as a summary of the new knowledge (learning outcomes) that readers should have gained.

Several features are used to make this book easier to follow and more informative.

- **Call-out boxes** are used to provide additional explanation particularly in the worked examples.

- **Notes** are also used for additional explanation, particularly where it involves seeing broader or deeper aspects of the topic.

- **A Caution box** is used to highlight points where it is easy to go wrong.
- **Discussion points** invite readers to talk about particular points with their fellow students and their teacher and so enhance their understanding. Short answers to discussion points are given, where appropriate, either in the text or at the back of the book.
- **Activities** are designed to help readers get into the thought processes of the new work that they are about to meet; having done an Activity, what follows will seem much easier.
- **Historical notes** provide readers with interesting information about the people who first worked on the topics, and insights into the world's cultural and intellectual development.

Answers to all exercise questions and practice questions are provided at the back of the book, and also online at www.hoddereducation.co.uk/AQAFurtherMathsStatistics

As a consequence of the changes to AS and A Level requirements in Further Mathematics, large parts of this book are new material, including sections written specifically to cover the AQA specifications. Where existing material has been used, it has typically been drawn from the well tried and tested earlier MEI books.

Catherine Berry
Roger Porkess

Prior knowledge

This book is written on the assumption that readers are familiar with the statistics in GCSE Mathematics. Thus, they should know a variety of elementary display techniques such as pictograms, tallies, pie charts, bar charts and scatter diagrams (including correlation and the use of a line of best fit). They are also expected to know summary measures, including mean, median, mode and range. Readers should also be familiar with basic probability.

Chapter 1

This chapter sets up the framework within which much of statistics is carried out in everyday life. It is about statistical problem solving, and so involves using display techniques and summary measures to shed light on real problems. Consequently, it draws on and extends the prior knowledge for the book. In particular, it introduces frequency charts and histograms, and variance and standard deviation. This chapter includes summary information about many of the terms that readers will use throughout the book, including types of data, distributions and sampling.

Chapter 2

This chapter is about correlation and association in bivariate data, and so readers will draw on their GCSE experience of scatter diagrams. This chapter includes Spearman's rank correlation coefficient and many readers will have met this in other subjects like Geography.

Chapter 3

This chapter is about the binomial distribution. It builds on ideas in Chapter 1 on variance and standard deviation, and also on the binomial theorem from Pure Mathematics. It uses the binomial distribution to introduce hypothesis testing and in doing so develops a methodology and adopts associated vocabulary that is used in the rest of the book.

Chapter 4

The title of this chapter is conditional probability. It builds on and extends readers' knowledge of probability from GCSE. The concept of conditionality underpins much of the later work in the book.

Chapter 5

This chapter focuses on discrete random variables, and so readers will build on the understanding they have gained in Chapter 3 on binomial distribution, and will go on to generalise it. Readers are also expected to be familiar with display techniques from GCSE and Chapter 1, and to have a sound knowledge of basic algebra.

Chapter 6

This chapter covers the Poisson distribution, and so it follows on from discrete random variables in Chapter 5, and exemplifies the work that readers covered there.

Chapter 7

The subject of this chapter is the chi-squared test for association. Readers are expected to be familiar with the methodology of hypothesis testing, and the associated vocabulary, as was introduced in Chapter 3.

Chapter 8

In this chapter readers are introduced to continuous random variables. This builds on their knowledge of discrete random variables from Chapter 5. A proficiency in basic calculus from Pure Mathematics is also required. In this chapter, the Normal distribution is introduced as an example of a continuous random variable and it is then used to find confidence intervals for a population mean in the simplest case, work which is taken further in Chapter 10.

Chapter 9

This chapter extends the work on continuous random variables that readers met in Chapter 8, and so is heavily dependent upon it, as well as the earlier work on discrete random variables in Chapter 5.

Chapter 10

This chapter is about confidence intervals using the Normal and t-distributions, and so evolves and formalises ideas that readers met at the end of Chapter 8.

Chapter 11

Chapter 11 discusses hypothesis tests and their power. It adds to much of the previous material in this book, particularly Chapters 3, 8 and 10.

Chapter 12

In this chapter, readers are introduced to the rectangular and exponential distributions. Both of these are continuous and so depend on knowledge and understanding from Chapters 8 and 9 on continuous random variables.

Acknowledgements

The Publishers would like to thank the following for permission to reproduce copyright material.

Practice questions have been provided by Neil Sheldon (MEI). (pp. 78–80, pp. 169–171 and pp. 265–267). Question 1 and 2 on p. 246, question 6 on p. 247 and question 14 on p. 249 have been reproduced by permission of Cambridge International Examinations. Answers to these questions are on pp. 292–293. Cambridge International Examinations bears no responsibility for the example answers to questions taken from its past question papers which are contained in this publication.

Photo credits

p.1 © Ingram Publishing Limited/General Gold Vol 1 CD 2; **p.20** © Cathy Yeulet – 123RF; **p.48** © Peter Titmuss/Shutterstock; **p.52** © Imagestate Media (John Foxx)/Vol 22 People & Emotions; **p.55** © lucato – Fotolia.com; **p.68** © Mark Atkins – Fotolia; **p.72** © Photographee.eu – Fotolia; **p.81** © DAVIPIX – Fotolia; **p.97** © Imagestate Media (John Foxx)/Store V3042; **p.108T** © Landscapes, Seascapes, Jewellery & Action Photographer/Getty Images; **p.108B** © Ingram Publishing Limited; **p.116** © rigamondis – Fotolia; **p.125** © LuckyImages/Shutterstock; **p.141** © Luciano de la Rosa Gutierrez – Fotolia.com; **p.144** © Eric Isselée – Fotolia; **p.161** © Imagestate Media (John Foxx)/Unique Images of Animals SS86; **p.172** © Shutterstock/ostill; **p.181** © Sandor Jackal – Fotolia; **p.195** © Ingram Publishing Limited/Animals Gold Vol 1 CD 3; **p.220** © Corbis, all rights reserved; **p.230** © S Curtis/Shutterstock; **p.251** © H. Mark Weidman Photography/Alamy Stock Photo

Every effort has been made to trace all copyright holders, but if any have been inadvertently overlooked, the Publishers will be pleased to make the necessary arrangements at the first opportunity.

Although every effort has been made to ensure that website addresses are correct at time of going to press, Hodder Education cannot be held responsible for the content of any website mentioned in this book. It is sometimes possible to find a relocated web page by typing in the address of the home page for a website in the URL window of your browser.

1 Statistical problem solving

A judicious man looks at statistics, not to get knowledge but to save himself from having ignorance foisted on him.
Thomas Carlyle (1795–1881)

Discussion point
Do you agree with the 'not to get knowledge' part of Carlyle's statement?

Think of one example where statistics has promoted knowledge or is currently doing so.

How would statistics have been different in Carlyle's time from now?

1 The problem solving cycle

Statistics provides a powerful set of tools for solving problems. While many of the techniques are specific to statistics they are nonetheless typically carried out within the standard cycle.

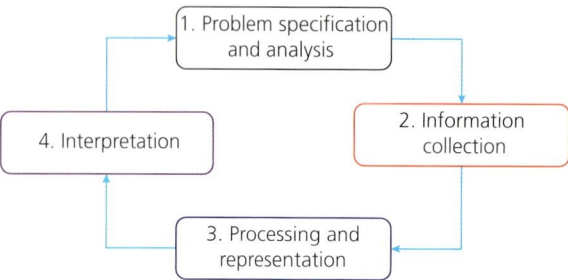

Figure 1.1

This chapter reviews the techniques that are used at the various stages, with particular emphasis on the information collection and the processing and representation elements.

Problem specification and analysis, and interpretation

The problem-solving cycle begins with a problem. That may seem like stating the obvious but it is not quite. Much of the work you do in statistics involves applying statistical techniques to statistical problems. By contrast, the problems tackled in this cycle are drawn from real life. They often require the use of statistics, but as a means to the end of providing an answer to the original problem, situation or context. Here are some examples:

- Is a particular animal in danger of extinction?
- How many coaches should a train operating company put on a particular train?
- Will a new corner shop be viable in a particular location?
- What provision of Intensive Care and High Dependency places should a hospital's neonatal unit make?

To answer questions like these you need data, but before collecting them it is essential to plan the work. Too often poor planning results in inappropriate data being collected. So, at the outset, you need to know:

- what data you are going to collect
- how you are going to collect the data
- how you are going to analyse the data
- how much data you will need
- how you are going to present the results
- what the results will mean in terms of the original problem.

Thus planning is essential and this is the work that is carried out in the first stage, problem specification and analysis, and at the end of the process interpretation is required; this includes the possible conclusion that the problem has not been addressed satisfactorily and the whole cycle must be repeated.

Both planning and interpretation depend on knowledge of how data are collected, processed and represented and so the second and third stages of the cycle are the focus of this chapter.

Information collection

The information needed in statistics is usually in the form of data so the information collection stage in the cycle is usually called **data collection**. This is an important part of statistics and this section outlines the principles involved, together with the relevant terminology and notation.

Terminology and notation

Data collection often requires you to take a sample, a set of items which are drawn from the relevant population and should be representative of it. The complete population may be too large for it to be practical, or economical, to consider every item.

A sample provides a set of data values of a random variable, drawn from all such possible values, the **parent population**. The parent population can be finite, such as all professional netball players, or infinite, such as the points where a dart can land on a dart board.

A representation of the items available to be sampled is called the **sampling frame**. This could, for example, be a list of the sheep in a flock, a map marked with a grid or an electoral register. In many situations no sampling frame exists nor is it possible to devise one, for example for the cod in the North Atlantic. The proportion of the available items that are actually sampled is called the **sampling fraction**. A 100% sample is called a **census**.

> **Note**
>
> Sampling fraction
> $= \dfrac{\text{Sample size}}{\text{Population size}}$

The term **random** is often used in connection with data collection. For a process to be described as random, each item in the population has a probability of being included in the sample. In many situations these probabilities are equal, but this is not essential. Most calculators give random numbers and these allow you to select an item from a list at random.

> **Note**
>
> Imagine you want to select a day of the year at **random**. You can number them 1 to 365. Then set your calculator to generate a three-digit number. If it is 365 or less, that gives you your day. If it is over 365, reject it and choose another number.

A parent population, often just called the population, is described in terms of its parameters, such as its mean, μ, and variance, σ^2. By convention, Greek letters are used to denote these population parameters.

A value derived from a sample is written in Roman letters, such as $\bar{x}$ and s. Such a number is the value of a sample statistic (or just statistic). When sample statistics are used to estimate the parent population parameters they are called estimates.

Thus if you take a random sample for which the mean is $\bar{x}$, you can use $\bar{x}$ to estimate the population mean, μ. Thus if in a particular sample $\bar{x} = 25.9$, you can use 25.9 as an estimate of the population mean. You would, however, expect the true value of μ to be somewhat different from 25.9.

An estimate of a parameter derived from sample data will, in general, differ from its true value. The difference is called the **sampling error**. To reduce the sampling error, you want your sample to be as representative of the parent population as you can make it. This, however, may be easier said than done.

The problem solving cycle

Sampling

There are several reasons why you might want to take a sample. These include:

- to help you understand a situation better
- as part of a pilot study to inform the design of a larger investigation
- to estimate the values of the parameters of the parent population
- to avoid the work involved in cleaning and formatting all the data in a large set
- to conduct a hypothesis test.

> This is often the situation when you are collecting data as part of the problem.

At the outset you need to consider how your sample data will be collected and the steps you can take to ensure their quality. You also need to plan how you will interpret your data. Here is a checklist of questions to ask yourself when you are taking a sample.

- Are the data relevant to the problem?
- Are the data unbiased?
- Is there any danger that the act of collection will distort the data?
- Is the person collecting the data suitable?
- Is the sample of a suitable size?
- Is a suitable sampling procedure being followed?
- Is the act of collecting the data destructive?

> **Discussion point**
> Give examples of cases where the answers to the first six questions are 'no'.

> Sample size is important. The larger the sample, the more accurate will be the information it gives you.

> For example, bringing rare deep sea creatures to the surface for examination may result in their deaths.

There are many sampling techniques. The list that follows includes the most commonly used. In considering them, remember that a key aim when taking a sample is that it should be **representative** of the parent population being investigated.

Simple random sampling

In a **simple random sampling procedure**, every possible sample of a given size is equally likely to be selected. It follows that in such a procedure every member of the parent population is equally likely to be selected. However, the converse is not true. It is possible to devise a sampling procedure in which every member is equally likely to be selected but some samples are not possible; an example occurs with **systematic sampling** which is described below.

> **Note**
> If your sample is the entire population (for example, every member of a statistics class) then you are said to be conducting a **census**.

Simple random sampling is fine when you can do it, but you must have a sampling frame. To carry out simple random sampling, the population must first be numbered, usually from 1 to n. Random numbers between 1 and n are then generated, and the corresponding members of the population are selected. If any repeats occur, more random numbers have to be generated to replace them. Note that, in order to carry out a hypothesis test or to construct a confidence interval (see Chapters 8 and 10), the sample taken should be a simple random sample and so some of the sampling methods below are not suitable for these purposes.

Example from real life

Jury selection

The first stage in selecting a jury is to take a simple random sample from the electoral roll.

Stratified sampling

Sometimes it is possible to divide the population into different groups, or strata. In **stratified sampling,** you would ensure that all strata were sampled. In **proportional stratified sampling**, the numbers selected from each of the strata are proportional to their size. The selection of the items to be sampled within each stratum is done at random, often using simple random sampling. Stratified sampling usually leads to accurate results about the entire population, and also gives useful information about the individual strata.

Example from real life

Opinion polls

Opinion polls, such as those for the outcome of an election, are often carried out online. The polling organisation collects sufficient other information to allow respondents to be placed in strata. They then use responses from the various strata in proportion to their sizes in the population.

Cluster sampling

Cluster sampling also starts with sub-groups of the population, but in this case the items are chosen from one or several of the sub-groups. The sub-groups are now called clusters. It is important that each cluster should be reasonably representative of the entire population. If, for example, you were asked to investigate the incidence of a particular parasite in the puffin population of northern Europe, it would be impossible to use simple random sampling. Rather, you would select a number of sites and then catch some puffins at each place. This is cluster sampling. Instead of selecting from the whole population you are choosing from a limited number of clusters.

Example from real life

Estimating the badger population size

An estimate of badger numbers in England, carried out between 2011 and 2013, was based on cluster sampling using 1411 1 km^2 squares from around the country. The number of badger setts in each square was counted. The clusters covered about 1% of the area of the country. There had been earlier surveys in 1985–88 and 1994–97 but with such long time intervals between them the results cannot be used to estimate the short term variability of population over a period of years rather than decades. There are two places where local populations have been monitored over many years. So the only possible estimate of short term variability would depend on just two clusters.

Systematic sampling

Systematic sampling is a method of choosing individuals from a sampling frame. If the items in the sampling frame are numbered 1 to n, you would choose a random starting point such as 38 and then every subsequent kth value, for example sample numbers 38, 138, 238 and so on. When using systematic sampling you have to beware of any cyclic patterns within the frame. For example, suppose that a school list is made up class by class, each of exactly 25 children, in order of merit, so that numbers 1, 26, 51, 76, 101, ... in the frame are those at the top of their class. If you sample every 50th child starting with number 26, you will conclude that the children in the school are very bright.

The problem solving cycle

Example from real life

Rubbish on beaches

Information was collected, using systematic sampling, about the amount and type of rubbish on the high water line along a long beach.

The beach was divided up into 1 m sections and, starting from a point near one end, data were recorded for every 50th interval.

Quota sampling

Quota sampling is the method often used by companies employing people to carry out opinion surveys. An interviewer's quota is always specified in stratified terms, for example how many males and how many females. The choice of who is sampled is then left up to the interviewer and so is definitely non-random.

Example from real life

If you regularly take part in telephone interviews, you may notice that, after learning your details, the interviewer seems to lose interest. That is probably because quota sampling is being used and the interviewer already has enough responses from people in your category.

Opportunity sampling

Opportunity sampling (also known as 'convenience sampling') is a very cheap method of choosing a sample where the sample is selected by simply choosing people who are readily available. For example, an interviewer might stand in a shopping centre and interview anybody who is willing to participate.

Example from real life

Credit card fraud

A barrister asked a mathematician to check that his argument was statistically sound in a case about credit card fraud. The mathematician wanted to find out more about the extent of suspected fraud. By chance, he was about to attend a teachers' conference and so he took the opportunity to ask delegates to fill in a short questionnaire about their relevant personal experience, if any. This gave him a rough idea of its extent and so achieved its aim.

Self-selected sampling

Self-selected sampling is a method of choosing a sample where people volunteer to be a part of the sample. The researcher advertises for volunteers, and accepts any that are suitable.

Example from real life

A medical study

Volunteers were invited to take part in a long-term medical study into the effects of particular diet supplements on heart function and other conditions. They would take a daily pill which might have an active ingredient or might be a placebo, but they would not know which they were taking. Potential participants were then screened for their suitability. At six-monthly intervals those involved were asked to fill in a questionnaire about their general health and lifestyle. The study was based on a self-selected sample of some 10 000 people.

Other sampling techniques

This is by no means a complete list of sampling techniques. Survey design and experimental design cover the formulation of the most appropriate sampling procedures in particular situations. They are major topics within statistics but beyond the scope of this book.

Processing and representation

At the start of this stage you have a set of raw data; by the end, you have worked them into forms that will allow people to see the information that this set contains, with particular emphasis on the problem in hand. Four processes are particularly important.

- Cleaning the data, which involves checking outliers, errors and missing items.
- Formatting the data so that they can be used on a spreadsheet or statistics package.
- Presenting the data using suitable diagrams, which is described below.
- Calculating summary measures, which is also described below.

Describing data

Note

In this example, the random variable happens to be discrete.

Random variables can be discrete or continuous.

The data items you collect are often values of **variables** or of **random variables**. The number of goals scored by a football team in a match is a variable because it varies from one match to another; because it does so in an unpredictable manner, it is a random variable. Rather than repeatedly using the phrase 'The number of goals scored by a football team in a match' it is usual to use an upper case letter like X to represent it. Particular values of a random variable are denoted by a lower case letter; often (but not always) the same letter is used. So if the random variable X is 'The number of goals scored by a football team in a match', for a match when the team scores 5 goals, you could say $x = 5$.

The number of times that a particular value of a random variable occurs is called its **frequency**.

When there are many possible values of the variable, it is convenient to allocate the data to groups. An example of the use of **grouped data** is the way people are allocated to age groups.

The pattern in which the values of a variable occur is called its **distribution**. This is often displayed in a diagram with the variable on the horizontal scale and a measure of frequency or probability on the vertical scale. If the diagram has one peak, the distribution is **unimodal**; if the peak is to the left of the middle, the distribution has **positive skew** and if it is to the right, it has **negative skew**. If the distribution has two distinct peaks, it is **bimodal**.

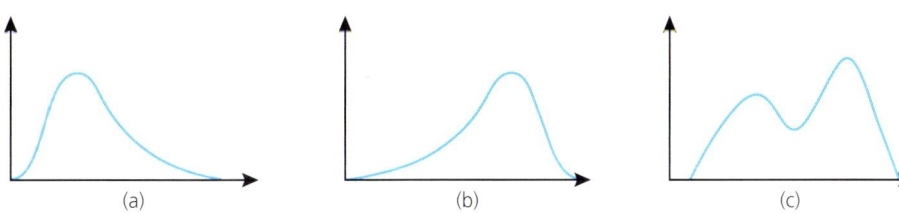

Figure 1.2 (a) Positive skew (b) negative skew (c) a bimodal distribution

The problem solving cycle

Note

Identifying outliers

There are two common tests:

- Is the item more than 2 standard deviations from the mean?
- Is the item more than 1.5 × the interquartile range beyond the nearer quartile?

A data item which is far away from the rest is called an **outlier**. An outlier may be a mistake, for example a faulty reading from an experiment, or it may be telling you something really important about the situation you are investigating. When you are cleaning your data, it is essential to look at any outliers and decide which of these is the case, and so whether to reject or accept them.

The data you collect can be of a number of different types. You always need to know what type of data you are working with as this will affect the ways you can display them and what summary measures you can use.

Categorical (or qualitative) data come in classes or categories, like types of fish or brands of toothpaste. Categorical data are also called **qualitative**, particularly if they can be described without using numbers.

Common displays for categorical data are pictograms, dot plots, tallies, pie charts and bar charts. A summary measure for the most typical item of categorical data is the modal class.

Ranked data are the positions of items within their group when they are ordered according to size, rather than their actual measurements. For example the competitors in a competition could be given their positions as 1st, 2nd, 3rd, etc. Ranked data are extensively used in the branch of statistics called **Exploratory Data Analysis**; this is beyond the scope of this book, but some of the measures and displays for ranked data are more widely used and are relevant here.

Notes

A pie chart is used for showing proportions of a total.

There should be gaps between the bars in a bar chart.

The median divides the data into two groups, those with high ranks and those with low ranks. The **lower quartile** and the **upper quartile** do the same for these two groups so, between them, the two quartiles and the median divide the data into four equal-sized groups according to their ranks. These three measures are sometimes denoted by Q_1, Q_2 and Q_3. These values, with the highest and lowest value can be used to create a box plot (or box and whisker diagram).

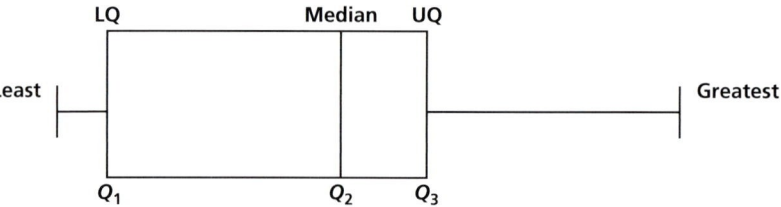

Figure 1.3 Box plot (or box and whisker diagram)

Note

You have to be aware when working out the median as to whether n is odd or even. If it is odd, for example if $n = 9$, $\frac{n+1}{2}$ works out to be a whole number but that is not so if n is even. For example if $n = 10$, $\frac{n+1}{2} = 5\frac{1}{2}$. In that case, the data set does not have a single middle value; those ranked 5 and 6 are equally spaced either side of the middle and so the median is half way between their values.

The median is a typical middle value and so is sometimes called an **average**. More formally, it is a **measure of central tendency**. It often provides a good representative value. The median is easy to work out if the data are stored on a spreadsheet since that will do the ranking for you. Notice that extreme values have little, if any, effect on the median. It is described as resistant to outliers. It is often useful when some data values are missing but can be estimated.

Interquartile range and semi interquartile range are measures of spread for ranked data, as is the range.

Drawing a stem-and-leaf diagram can be helpful when ranking data.

Numerical (or quantitative) data occur when each item has a numerical value (and not just a rank), like the number of people travelling in a car or the values of houses.

Numerical data are described as discrete if items can take certain particular numerical values but not those in between. The number of eggs a song bird lays (0, 1, 2, 3, 4, ...) the number of goals a hockey team scores in a match (0, 1, 2, 3, ...) and the sizes of women's clothes in the UK (... 8, 10, 12, 14, 16, ...) are all examples of discrete variables. If there are many possible values, it is common to group discrete data.

By contrast, **continuous** numerical data can take any appropriate value if measured accurately enough.

Distance, mass, temperature and speed are all continuous variables. You cannot list all the possible values.

If you are working with continuous data you will always need to **group** them. This includes two special cases:

> **Note**
> Sometimes a bar chart is used for grouped numerical data with the groups as categories, but you must still leave gaps between the bars.

- The variable is actually discrete but the intervals between values are very small. For example, cost in euros is a discrete variable with steps of €0.01 (i.e. 1 cent) but this is so small that the variable may be regarded as continuous.
- The underlying variable is continuous but the measurements of it are rounded (for example, to the nearest mm), making your data discrete. All measurements of continuous variables are rounded and, providing the rounding is not too coarse, the data should normally be treated as continuous. A particular case of rounding occurs with people's ages; this is a continuous variable but is usually rounded down to the nearest completed year.

> **Note**
> In frequency charts and histograms, the values of the variables go at the ends of the bars. In a bar chart, the labels are in the middle.

Displaying numerical data

Commonly used displays for discrete data include a vertical line chart and a stem-and-leaf diagram. A frequency table can be useful in recording, sorting and displaying discrete numerical data.

A frequency chart and a histogram are the commonest ways of displaying continuous data. Both have a continuous horizontal scale covering the range of values of the variable. Both have vertical bars.

> **Note**
> If you are using a frequency chart, the class intervals should all be equal. For a histogram, they don't have to be equal. So, if you have continuous data grouped into classes of unequal width, you should expect to use a histogram.

- In a frequency chart, frequency is represented by the height of a bar. The vertical scale is Frequency.
- In a histogram, frequency is represented by the area of a bar. The vertical scale is Frequency density.

Look at this frequency chart and histogram. They show the time, t minutes, that a particular train was late at its final destination in 150 journeys.

On both graphs, the interval 5–10 means $5 < t \leq 10$, and, similarly, for other intervals. A negative value of t means the train was early.

The problem solving cycle

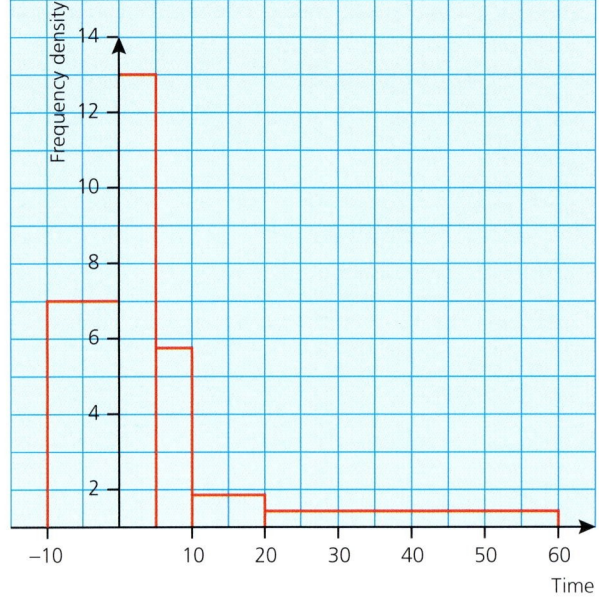

Discussion point
What is the same about the two displays and what is different?

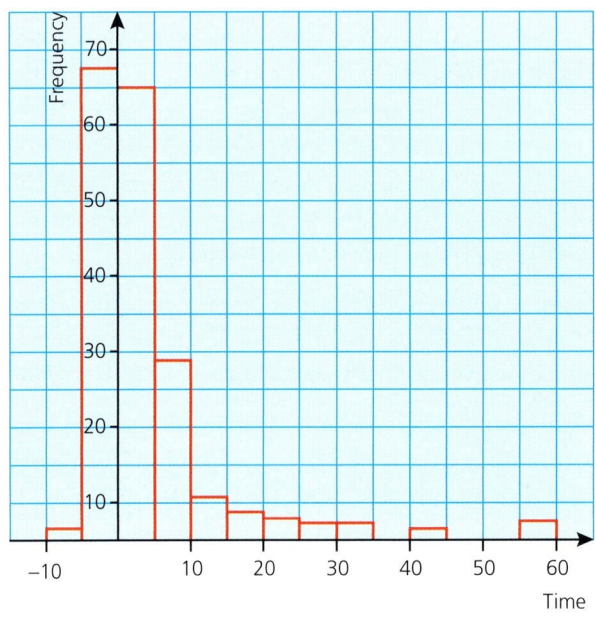

Figure 1.4

Numerical data can also be displayed on a **cumulative frequency curve**. To draw the cumulative frequency curve, you plot the cumulative frequency (vertical axis) against the upper boundary of each class interval (horizontal axis). Then you join the points with a smooth curve. This lends itself to using the median, quartiles and other percentiles as summary measures.

Summary measures for numerical data

Summary measures for both discrete and continuous numerical data include the following.

Table 1.1

Central tendency	Spread	Location in the data
Mean	Range	Lower quartile
Weighted mean	Interquartile range	Median
Mode	Standard deviation	Upper quartile
Mid-range	Variance	Percentile
Median		
Modal class (grouped data)		

Standard deviation

Standard deviation is probably the most important measure of spread in statistics. The calculation of standard deviation, and of variance, introduce important notation which you will often come across. This is explained in the example that follows.

> **Note**
> In practice, many people would just enter the data into their calculators and read off the answer. However, it is important to understand the ideas that underpin the calculation.

Example 1.1

Alice enters dance competitions in which the judges give each dance a score between 0 and 10. Here is a sample of her recent scores.

Table 1.2

| 7 | 4 | 9 | 8 | 7 | 8 | 8 | 10 | 9 | 10 |

Calculate the mean, variance and standard deviation of Alice's scores.

Solution

Alice received 10 scores, so the number of data items, $n = 10$.

In the table on the next page, her scores are denoted by $x_1, x_2, ..., x_{10}$, with the general term x_i.

The mean score is $\bar{x}$.

The problem solving cycle

Table 1.3

	x_i	$x_i - \bar{x}$	$(x_i - \bar{x})^2$	x_i^2
x_1	7	-1	1	49
x_2	4	-4	16	16
x_3	9	1	1	81
x_4	8	0	0	64
x_5	7	-1	1	49
x_6	8	0	0	64
x_7	8	0	0	64
x_8	10	2	4	100
x_9	9	1	1	81
x_{10}	10	2	4	100
Σ	80	0	28	668

The quantity $(x_i - \bar{x})$ is the **deviation** from the mean. Notice that the total of the deviations $\Sigma(x_i - \bar{x})$ is zero. It has to be so because $\bar{x}$ is the mean, but finding it gives a useful check that you haven't made a careless mistake so far.

The value of 668 for Σx_i^2 was found in the right hand column of the table.

The mean is given by $\bar{x} = \dfrac{\Sigma x_i}{n} = \dfrac{80}{10} = 8.0$.

The variance is given by $s^2 = \dfrac{S_{xx}}{n-1}$ where $S_{xx} = \Sigma(x_i - \bar{x})^2$

In this case, $S_{xx} = 28$.

So the variance is $s^2 = \dfrac{28}{10-1} = 3.111$.

The standard deviation is $s = \sqrt{\text{variance}} = \sqrt{3.111} = 1.764$.

> **Note**
>
> An **alternative** but equivalent form of S_{xx} is given by
> $S_{xx} = \Sigma x_i^2 - n\bar{x}^2$
> In this case,
> $S_{xx} = 668 - 10 \times 8^2$
> $= 668 - 640 = 28$.
> This is, as expected the same value as that found above.

ACTIVITY 1.1

Using a spreadsheet, enter the values of x in cells B2 to B11. Then, using only spreadsheet commands, and without entering any more numbers, obtain the values of $(x - \bar{x})$ in cells C2 to C11, of $(x - \bar{x})^2$ in cells D2 to D11 and of x^2 in E2 to E11. Still using only the spreadsheet commands, find the standard deviation using both of the given formulae.

Now, as a third method, use the built in functions in your spreadsheet, for example =AVERAGE and =STDEV.S to calculate the mean and standard deviation directly.

> **Note**
>
> **Bivariate data** cover two variables, such as the birth rate and life expectancy of different countries.
>
> When you are working with bivariate data you are likely to be interested in the relationship between the two variables, how this can be seen on a scatter diagram and how it can be quantified.

Notation

The notation in the example is often used with other variables. So, for example, $S_{yy} = \Sigma(y_i - \bar{y})^2 = \Sigma y_i^2 - n\bar{y}^2$. In Chapter 2, you will meet an equivalent form for bivariate data, $S_{xy} = \Sigma(x_i - \bar{x})(y_i - \bar{y}) = \Sigma x_i y_i - n\bar{x}\bar{y}$.

You can also extend the notation to cases where the data are given in frequency tables.

For example, Alice's dance scores could have been written as the frequency table below.

Table 1.4

x_i	4	7	8	9	10
f_i	1	2	3	2	2

The number of items is then given by $n = \Sigma f_i$

The mean is
$$\bar{x} = \frac{\Sigma f_i x_i}{n}$$

The sum of squared deviations is
$$S_{xx} = \Sigma f_i (x_i - \bar{x})^2 = \Sigma f_i x_i^2 - n\bar{x}^2$$

As before, the variance is
$$s^2 = \frac{S_{xx}}{n-1}$$

and the standard deviation is
$$s = \sqrt{\text{variance}} = \sqrt{\frac{S_{xx}}{n-1}}.$$

Sometimes you will be asked to use information in summary form to find the mean and standard deviation of a set of data, as in the next example.

Example 1.2

A study is being carried out on the lengths of the fingers of adult men. In a pilot study a sample of men is taken and the lengths of their forefingers, x cm, are recorded. These data are summarised as follows.

$$n = 40, \ \Sigma x = 364.4, \ \Sigma x^2 = 3442.4$$

Find the mean and standard deviation of these lengths, giving your answers to 2 significant figures.

Solution

The mean,
$$\bar{x} = \frac{\Sigma x}{n} = \frac{364.4}{40} = 9.11$$

To find the standard deviation, use $S_{xx} = \Sigma x^2 - n\bar{x}^2$

So
$$S_{xx} = \Sigma x^2 - n\bar{x}^2$$
$$= 3442.4 - 40 \times 9.11^2 = 122.716$$

The variance is
$$s^2 = \frac{S_{xx}}{n-1} = \frac{122.716}{39} = 3.146...$$

The standard deviation is $s = \sqrt{3.146...} = 1.773...$

So to 2 significant figures the mean length is 9.1 cm and the standard deviation is 1.8 cm.

Exercise 1.1

① A club secretary wishes to survey a sample of members of his club. He uses all members present at a meeting as a sample.

(i) Explain why this sample is likely to be biased.

Later the secretary decides choose a random sample of members. The club has 253 members and the secretary numbers the members from 1 to 253. He then generates random 3-digit numbers on his calculator. The first six random numbers are 156, 965, 248, 156, 073 and 181. The secretary uses each number, where possible, as the number of a member in the sample.

(ii) Find possible numbers for the first four members in the sample. [OCR]

② This stem-and-leaf diagram shows the mean GDP per person in European countries, in thousands of US$. The figures are rounded to the nearest US$ 1000.

The problem solving cycle

Table 1.5

	Europe
0	4 7 8 8 8
1	1 1 2 4 6 8 9
2	0 1 2 3 3 3 4 4 5 6 8 8
3	0 0 1 6 6 7 7 8 8
4	0 1 1 1 1 3 3 5 6
5	4 5 7
6	1 6
7	
8	0 9

> **Note**
> Key 3 | 7 = US$ 37 000

(i) The mean per capita income for the UK is US$ 37 300. What is the rank of the UK among European countries (where rank 1 = largest GDP)?

(ii) Find the median and quartiles of the data.

(iii) Use the relevant test to identify any possible outliers.

(iv) Describe the distribution.

(v) Comment on whether these data can be used as a representative sample for the GDP of all the countries in the world.

③ Debbie is a sociology student. She is interested in how many children women have during their lifetimes. She herself has one sister and no brothers. She asks the other 19 students in her class 'How many children has your mother had?' Their answers are given below; the figure for herself is included.

Table 1.6

| 1 | 1 | 2 | 3 | 1 | 4 | 2 | 1 | 2 | 2 |
| 2 | 2 | 2 | 1 | 0 | 1 | 2 | 3 | 8 | 3 |

Debbie says

'Thank you for your help. I conclude that the average woman has exactly 2.15 children.'

(i) Name the sampling method that Debbie used.

(ii) Explain how she obtained the figure 2.15.

(iii) State four things that are wrong with her method and her stated conclusion.

④ Sixty men are on a special diet, and for one day their energy intake, x kcal, is measured carefully. Their energy intakes are summarised as follows:

$$n = 60, \Sigma x = 92\,340, x^2 = 1.425 \times 10^8$$

Find the mean and standard deviation of these energy intakes, giving your answers to 3 significant figures.

⑤ A rock and soul choir has 80 members, but they do not all turn up for every rehearsal. Attendance is monitored for 30 random rehearsals, and the attendance, X people, varies between 35 and 78.

The attendance counts give $\bar{x} = 52.1, s_x = 10.3$.

Find $\Sigma x, \Sigma x^2$ for the data, giving your answers to 3 significant figures.

⑥ A supermarket chain is considering opening an out-of-town shop on a green field site. Before going any further they want to test public opinion and carry out a small pilot investigation. They employ three local students to ask people 'Would you be in favour of this development?' Each of the students is told to ask 30 adult men, 30 adult women and 40 young people who should be under 19 but may be male or female.

Their results are summarised in this table.

Table 1.7

	Men			Women			Young people		
Interviewer	Yes	No	Don't know	Yes	No	Don't know	Yes	No	Don't know
A	5	20	5	18	12	0	12	10	18
B	12	14	4	20	8	2	11	11	18
C	9	18	3	17	9	4	10	15	15

(i) Name the sampling method that has been used.

The local development manager has to give a very brief report to the company's directors and this will include his summary of the findings of the pilot survey.

(ii) List the points that he should make.

The directors decide to take the proposal to the next stage and this requires a more accurate assessment of local opinion.

(iii) What sampling method should they use?

⑦ A certain animal is regarded as a pest. There have been two surveys, eight years apart, to find out the size of the population in the UK. After the second survey a newspaper carried an article which included these words.

> **This animal is out of control. Its numbers have doubled in just 8 years.**

The graph in Figure 1.5 shows the results that would have been obtained if the population had been measured accurately every year from 1995 to 2015. The unit on the vertical scale is 100 000 animals.

The problem solving cycle

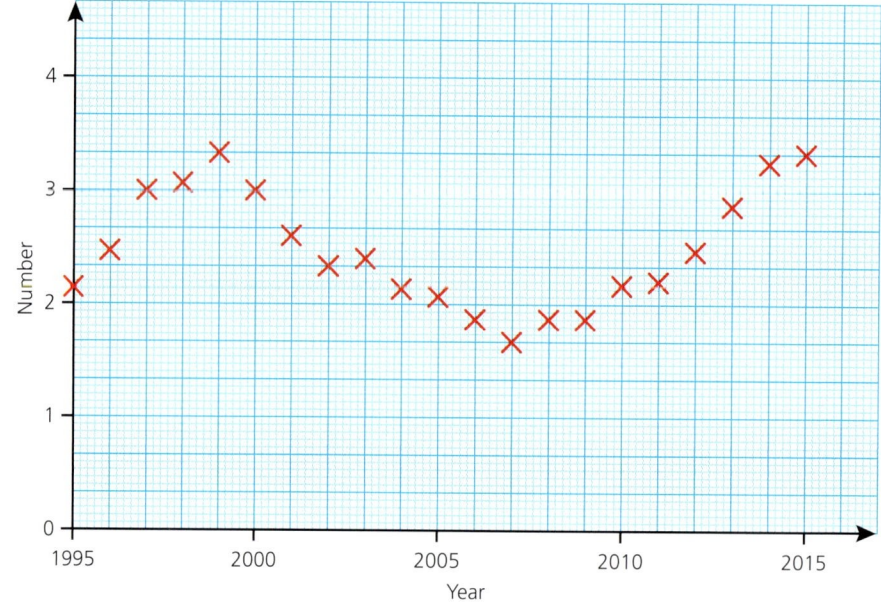

Figure 1.5 Graph of population

(i) Describe the apparent pattern of the size of the population.

(ii) In which years does it seem that the survey was carried out?

(iii) Suggest conclusions which might have been reached if the two surveys had been in (a) 1999 and 2007 (b) 1999 and 2015.

Historic data of the sale of furs of arctic mammals, such as lynx and hares, by the Hudson Bay Company indicate a 10 to 11 year cycle in their population numbers over many years.

(iv) Suppose the data are available on a spreadsheet. Describe how a systematic sample might be taken from the data on the spreadsheet. Comment on the problems that might result.

⑧ A study is conducted on the breeding success of a type of sea bird. Four islands are selected and volunteers monitor nests on them, counting the number of birds that fledge (grow up to fly away from the nest).

The results are summarised in the table below.

Table 1.8

Island	\multicolumn{5}{c}{Number of fledglings}
	0	1	2	3	>3
A	52	105	31	2	0
B	10	81	55	6	0
C	67	33	2	0	0
D	29	65	185	11	0

(i) Describe the sample that has been used.

(ii) Explain why you are unable to give an accurate value for the sampling fraction.

(iii) Estimate the mean number of fledglings per nest and explain why this figure may not be very close to that for the whole population.

(iv) Ornithologists estimate that there are about 120 000 breeding pairs of these birds. Suggest appropriate limits within which the number of fledglings might lie, showing the calculations on which your answers are based.

⑨ A health authority takes part in a national study into the health of women during pregnancy. One feature of this is that pregnant women are invited to volunteer for a fitness programme in which they exercise every day. Their general health is monitored and the days on which their babies arrive are recorded and shown on the histogram below.

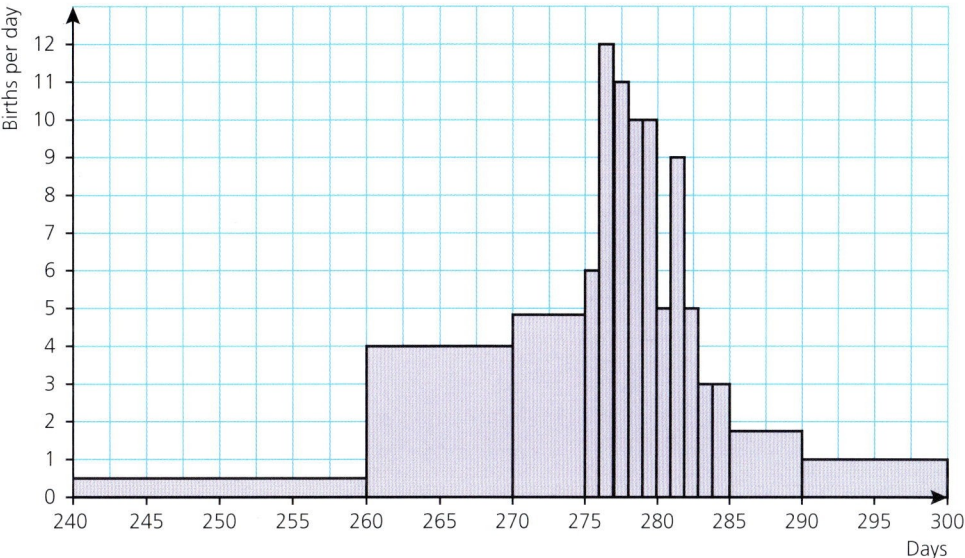

Figure 1.6

(i) The women who take part in the programme constitute a sample. What sort of sample is it?

(ii) Describe the parent population from which the sample is drawn and give one reason why it may not be completely representative. Comment on the difficulties in selecting a representative sample for this study.

(iii) Use the histogram to find how many women participated in the study.

The 'due date' of a mother to be is set at 280 days. Babies born before 260 days are described as 'pre-term'. Those born after 287 days are 'post-term'.

(iv) Give your answers to parts (a), (b) and (c) to 1 decimal place.
   (a) Find the percentage of the babies that arrived on their due dates.
   (b) Find the percentage that were pre-term.
   (c) Estimate the percentage of babies that were post-term.
   (d) Explain why your answers to parts (a), (b) and (c) do not add up to 100.

⑩ A local police force records the number of people arrested per day during January, February and March one year. The results are as follows.

Table 1.9

No of arrests	Frequency
0	55
1	24
2	6
3	2
4	0

No of arrests	Frequency
5	2
6, 7	0
8	1
>8	0

The problem solving cycle

(i) Find the mean and standard deviation of the number of arrests per day.

(ii) The figure 8 is an outlier. It was the result of a fight on a train that stopped in the area. It is suggested that the data should not include that day. What percentage changes would that make to the mean and standard deviation?

(iii) Find the percentage error if the standard deviation (with the outlier excluded) is worked out using the formula

$$s = \sqrt{\frac{S_{xx}}{n}} \text{ instead of } s = \sqrt{\frac{S_{xx}}{n-1}}.$$

(iv) The standard deviation of a sample is worked out using a divisor n instead of $(n-1)$. Find the smallest value of n for which the error in doing so is less than 1%.

KEY POINTS

1. The problem solving cycle has four stages:
   - problem specification and analysis
   - information collection
   - processing and representation
   - interpretation.
2. Information collection often involves taking a sample.
3. There are several reasons why you might wish to take a sample:
   - to help you understand a situation better
   - as part of a pilot study to inform the design of a larger investigation
   - to estimate the values of the parameters of the parent population
   - to avoid the work involved in cleaning and formatting all the data in a large set
   - to conduct a hypothesis test.
4. Sampling procedures include:
   - simple random sampling
   - stratified sampling
   - cluster sampling
   - systematic sampling
   - quota sampling
   - opportunity sampling
   - self-selected sampling.
5. For processing and representation, it is important to know the type of data you are working with i.e.:
   - categorical data
   - ranked data
   - discrete numerical data
   - continuous numerical data
   - bivariate data.
6. Display techniques and summary measures must be appropriate for the type of data.
7. Notation for mean and standard deviation.

   Mean $\quad\quad\quad\quad\quad\quad\quad\quad\quad\quad \bar{x} = \Sigma \frac{x_i}{n}$

   Sum of square deviations $\quad S_{xx} = \Sigma(x_i - \bar{x})^2 = \Sigma x_i^2 - n\bar{x}^2$

   Variance $\quad\quad\quad\quad\quad\quad\quad\quad s^2 = \frac{S_{xx}}{n-1}$

   Standard deviation $\quad\quad\quad\quad s = \sqrt{\text{variance}} = \sqrt{\frac{S_{xx}}{n-1}}.$

LEARNING OUTCOMES

When you have completed this chapter you should be able to:
- use statistics within a problem solving cycle
- explain why sampling may be necessary in order to obtain information about a population, and give desirable features of a sample, including the size of the sample
- know a variety of sampling methods, the situations in which they might be used and any problems associated with them
- explain the advantage of using a random sample when inferring properties of a population
- display sample data appropriately
- calculate and interpret summary measures for sample data.

Bivariate data and correlation coefficients

It is now proved beyond doubt that smoking is one of the leading causes of statistics.

John Peers

Discussion point

1 Across the world, countries with high life expectancy tend to have low birth rates and vice-versa. How would you describe this in mathematical language? Why do you think this happens?

2 Suggest some factors that affect the proportion of new-born babies, in one country, who have all four of their grandparents still alive.

⚠ The AQA Further Mathematics specification does not directly include bivariate data and so the material in this chapter is all either background (a review of work in A level Mathematics) or extension. Many users of this book will come across Spearman's rank correlation in their other subjects and so it is included here, marked as extension material. Ideas of bivariate data are implicit in Chapter 7, where the chi-squared test is applied to a contingency table.

The data in this table refer to the 22 American mainland countries. They cover their population in millions, birth rate per 1000 people, life expectancy in years and mean GDP per capita in thousands of US$.

Table 2.1

Country	Population	Life expectancy	Birth rate	GDP per capita
Argentina	43.0	77.51	16.88	18.6
Belize	0.3	68.49	25.14	8.8
Bolivia	10.6	68.55	23.28	5.5
Brazil	202.7	73.28	14.72	12.1
Canada	34.8	81.67	10.29	43.1
Chile	17.4	78.44	13.97	19.1
Colombia	46.2	75.25	16.73	11.1
Costa Rica	4.8	78.23	16.08	12.9
Ecuador	15.7	76.36	18.87	10.6
El Salvador	6.1	74.18	16.79	7.5
Guatemala	14.6	71.74	25.46	5.3
Guyana	0.7	67.81	15.90	8.5
Honduras	8.6	70.91	23.66	4.8
Mexico	120.3	75.43	19.02	15.6
Nicaragua	5.8	72.72	18.41	4.5
Panama	3.6	78.3	18.61	16.5
Paraguay	6.7	76.8	16.66	6.8
Peru	3.0	73.23	18.57	11.1
Suriname	0.6	71.69	16.73	12.9
United States	318.9	79.56	13.42	52.8
Uruguay	3.3	76.81	13.18	16.6
Venezuela	28.9	74.39	19.42	13.6

This is an example of a multivariate data set. For each country, the values of four variables are given.

Multivariate analysis is an important part of statistics but is beyond the scope of this book apart for the special case of bivariate data, where just two variables are considered.

Bivariate data are usually displayed on a scatter diagram like Figure 2.1. In this, life expectancy is plotted on the horizontal axis and birth rate on the vertical axis.

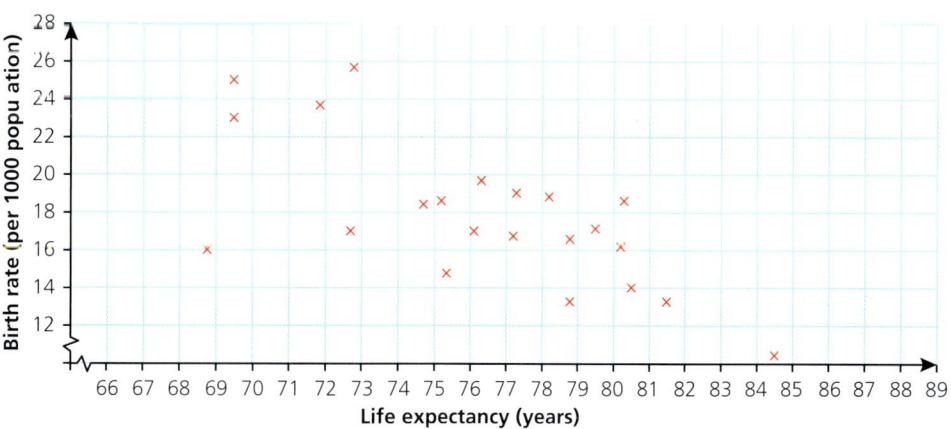

Figure 2.1

Describing variables

This diagram suggests that there is a relationship between birth rate and life expectancy. In general, such a relationship is called an **association.**

Sometimes, two special conditions apply.

- Both the variables are random.
- The relationship is linear.

> In such a case, the stronger the association, the closer the points on the scatter diagram will lie to a straight line.

Under these conditions the association is described as **correlation**. So correlation is a special case of association.

- If high values of both variables tend to occur together, and the same for low values, the correlation is **positive**.
- If, as in this example, high values of one variable are associated with low values of the other, the correlation is **negative**.

If the points on the scatter diagram lie exactly on a straight line, the correlation is described as **perfect**. However, it is much more common for the data to lie close to a straight line but not exactly on it, as in this case. The better the fit, the higher the level of correlation.

1 Describing variables

Dependent and independent variables

The scatter diagram in Figure 2.1 was drawn with the life expectancy on the horizontal axis and birth rate on the vertical axis. It could have been drawn the other way around. It is not obvious that either of the variables is dependent on the other.

By contrast, the weight of the passengers in an aeroplane is dependent on how many of them there are, but the reverse is not true; the number getting on is not determined by their weight. So, in this case, the number of passengers is described as the **independent variable** and their weight as the **dependent** variable. It is normal practice to plot the dependent variable on the vertical (y) axis and the independent variable on the horizontal (x) axis.

Here are some more examples of dependent and independent variables.

Independent variable	Dependent variable
The number of goals scored by a premier league football team in a season	The number of points the team has in the league table
The amount of rain falling on a field	The weight of a crop yielded while the crop is growing
The number of people visiting a bar	The volume of beer sold in an evening

Controlled variables

Sometimes, one or both of the variables is **controlled**, so that the variable only assumes a set of predetermined values; for example, the times at which temperature measurements are taken at a meteorological station. Controlled variables are **non-random**. Situations in which the independent variable is controlled and the dependent variable is random form the basis of **regression** analysis.

2 Interpreting scatter diagrams

You can often judge if correlation is present just by looking at a scatter diagram.

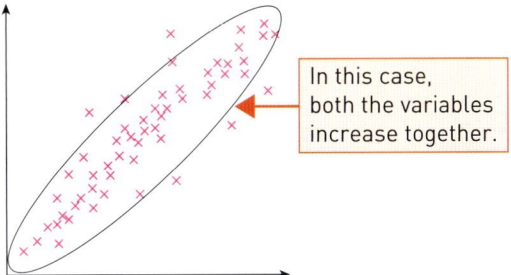

In this case, both the variables increase together.

Figure 2.2 Positive correlation

Notice that in Figure 2.2 almost all of the observation points can be contained within an ellipse. This shape often arises when both variables are random. You should look for it before going on to do a calculation of Pearson's product moment correlation coefficient (see page 26). The narrower the elliptical profile, the greater the correlation.

In this case, as one variable increases the other variable decreases.

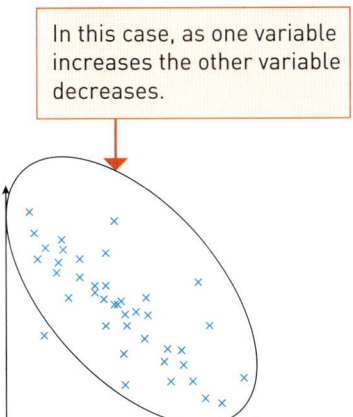

Figure 2.3 Negative correlation

In Figure 2.3 the points again fall into an elliptical profile and this time there is negative correlation. The fatter ellipse in this diagram indicates weaker correlation than in the case shown in Figure 2.2.

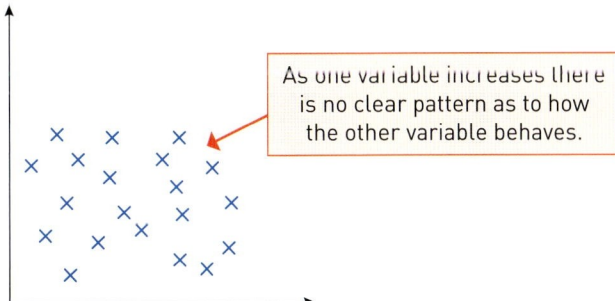

As one variable increases there is no clear pattern as to how the other variable behaves.

Figure 2.4 No correlation

Interpreting scatter diagrams

In the case illustrated in Figure 2.4, the points fall randomly in the (x, y) plane and there appears to be no association between the variables.

! You should be aware of some distributions which at first sight appear to indicate linear association, and so correlation, but in fact do not.

Notice that this distribution looks nothing like an ellipse.

This scatter diagram is probably showing two quite different groups (for example, males and females), neither of them having any correlation.

This is a small data set with no correlation.

However, the two outliers give the impression that there is positive linear association, and so correlation.

At first sight you might think you could enclose these points with an ellipse but the more you look at it the fatter the ellipse would need to be.

If you select just a few of the points on the scatter diagram you can obtain a false impression.

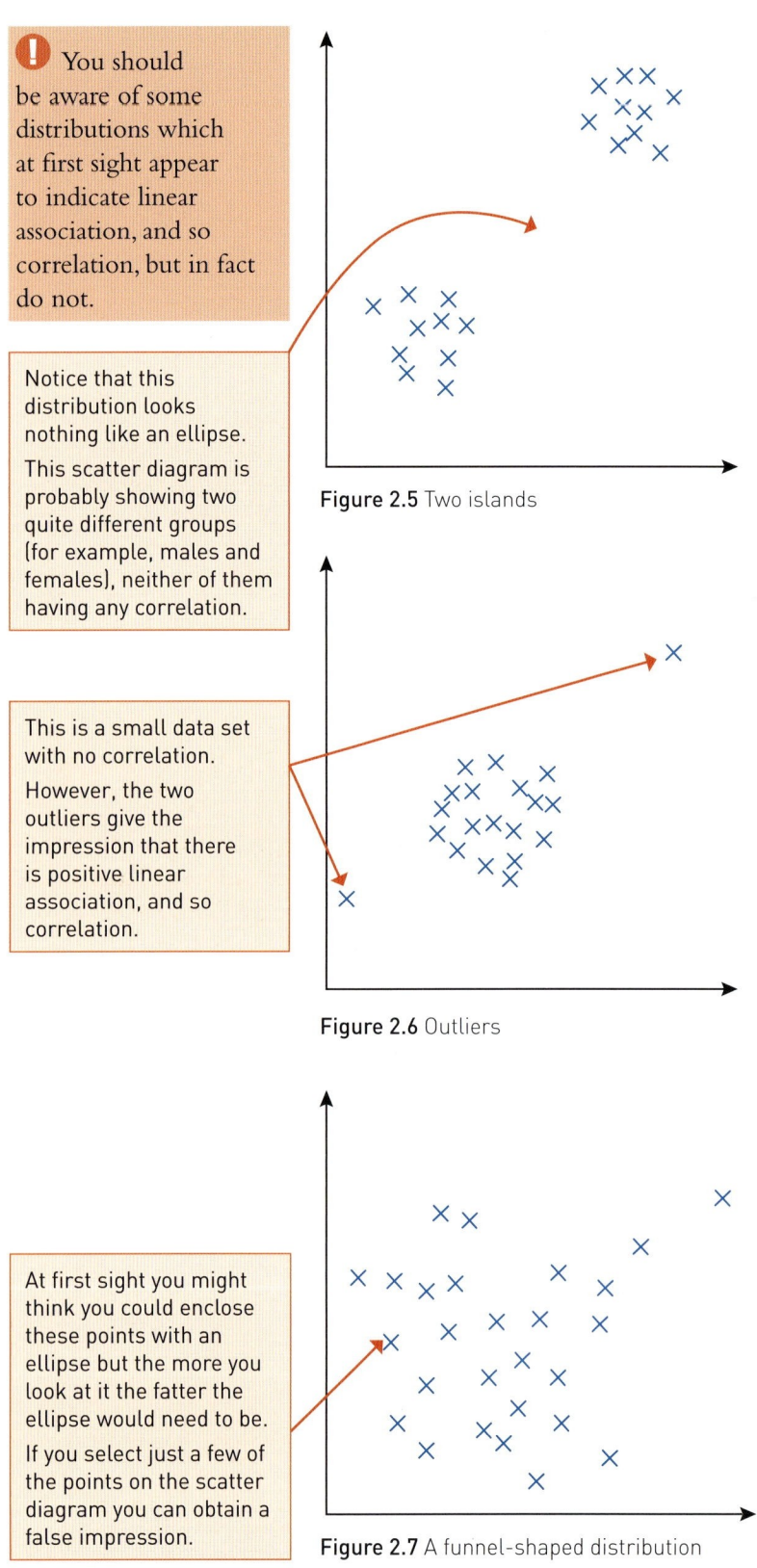

Figure 2.5 Two islands

Figure 2.6 Outliers

Figure 2.7 A funnel-shaped distribution

Here are the scatter diagrams for some of the other pairs of variables in the data for the American countries in Table 2.1 on page 21.

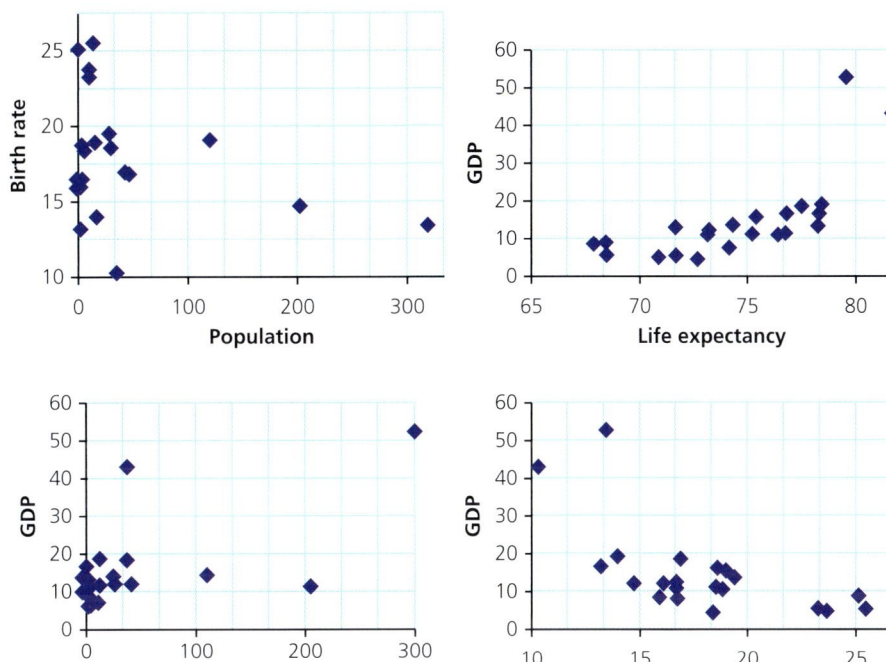

Figure 2.8

Discussion point

→ Comment on any insights the diagrams give you and the presence of outliers. Say whether they show any correlation or association.

Regression lines

When faced with a scatter diagram where the points appear to lie roughly on a straight line, you might decide to draw a line of best fit by eye. This is known as a regression line (you are in effect trying to 'regress' from the data to the underlying rule that governs it). You might go on to ask, 'Is there a way to sensibly calculate the regression line from the data, rather than guess at it?' There is: in fact, there are two such regression lines, y-on-x (used for predicting y from an x value) and x-on-y (used for predicting an x value from a y-value). If you input your data points to your calculator, it should tell you the optimum values to take for a and b in the line $y = ax + b$.

EXTENSION

If you need to carry out this calculation by hand, or without using the in-built statistical functions on your calculator, the formula

$$y - \bar{y} = \frac{S_{xy}}{S_{xx}}(x - \bar{x})$$

gives you the y-on-x version, while

$$y - \bar{y} = \frac{S_{xy}}{S_{yy}}(x - \bar{x})$$

gives you the x-on-y version, where

$$S_{xx} = \sum(x_i - \bar{x})^2, \, S_{yy} = \sum(y_i - \bar{y})^2, \, S_{xy} = \sum(x_i - \bar{x})(y_i - \bar{y}).$$

Pearson's product moment correlation coefficient

3 Pearson's product moment correlation coefficient

Pearson's product moment correlation coefficient (written as r, or the PMCC) puts a value of between -1 and 1 on the correlation for a set of bivariate data (if you find a value outside this range, there has been an error). This measures how well the points on the scatter graph fit a straight line. You will most likely calculate it using the built in functions on your calculator after entering the data, but you can see how to carry out the calculation by hand below.

EXTENSION

The value of r is given by

$$r = \frac{S_{xy}}{\sqrt{S_{xx} S_{yy}}} = \frac{\sum (x_i - \bar{x})(y_i - \bar{y})}{\sqrt{\sum (x_i - \bar{x})^2 (y_i - \bar{y})^2}}$$

$$= \frac{\sum x_i y_i - n\bar{x}\bar{y}}{\sqrt{(\sum x_i^2 - n\bar{x}^2)(\sum y_i^2 - n\bar{y}^2)}}$$

> You may use either formulation, since they are algebraically equivalent.

S_{xx} and S_{yy} must always be positive, while S_{xy} can be either positive or negative.

A value of $+1$ means perfect positive correlation; in that case, all the points on a scatter diagram would lie exactly on a straight line with positive gradient. Similarly, a value of -1 means perfect negative correlation.

> ❗ Be careful not to confuse the quantities denoted by S_{xx}, S_{yy} and S_{xy} with those denoted by s_{xx}, s_{yy} and s_{xy} and used by some other authors.
>
> In this book S_{xx} and S_{yy} are the sums of the squares and are not divided by n. Similarly, S_{xy} is the sum of the terms $(x_i - \bar{x})(y_i - \bar{y})$ and is not divided by n.

These two cases are illustrated in Figure 2.9.

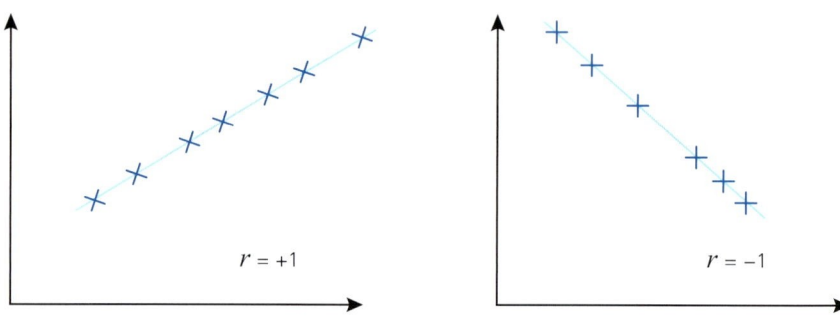

Figure 2.9 (i) Perfect positive correlation   (ii) Perfect negative correlation

In cases of little or no correlation, r takes values close to zero. The nearer the value of r is to $+1$ or -1, the stronger the correlation.

Interpreting the product moment correlation coefficient

The product moment correlation coefficient provides a measure of the correlation between the two variables. There are two different ways in which it is commonly used and interpreted: as a test statistic and as a measure of effect size.

Using r as a test statistic

When the data cover the whole of a population, the correlation coefficient tells you all that there is to be known about the level of correlation between the variables in the population. The population correlation coefficient is denoted by ρ.

> The symbol ρ is the Greek letter rho, pronounced 'row' as in 'row a boat'.

However, it is often the case that you do not know the level of correlation in a population and take a reasonably small sample to find out.

You use your sample data to calculate a value of the correlation coefficient, r. You know that if the value of r turns out to be close to +1 or −1, you can be reasonably confident that there is correlation, and that if r is close to 0 there is probably little or no correlation. What happens in a case such as $r = 0.6$?

To answer this question you have to understand what r is actually measuring. The data which you use when calculating r are actually a **sample** taken from a parent bivariate distribution, rather than the whole of a population. You have only taken a few out of a very large number of points which could, in theory, be plotted on a scatter diagram such as Figure 2.10. Each point (x_i, y_i) represents a possible pair of values corresponding to one observation of the bivariate population.

If your scatter diagram is roughly elliptical, that provides reasonable evidence that you are dealing with a bivariate Normal population, and that a hypothesis test using r is appropriate.

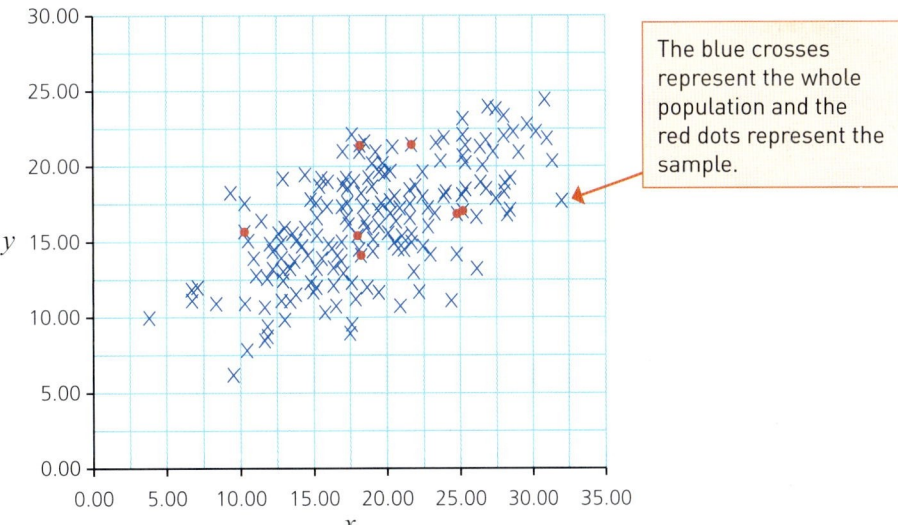

The blue crosses represent the whole population and the red dots represent the sample.

Figure 2.10 Scatter diagram showing a sample from a large bivariate population

There will be a level of correlation within the parent population and this is denoted by ρ.

The calculated value of r, which is based on the sample points, can be used as an estimate for ρ. It can also be used to carry out a hypothesis test on the value of ρ, the parent population correlation coefficient. Used in this way it is a **test statistic**.

The simplest hypothesis test which you can carry out is that there is no correlation within the parent population. This gives rise to a null hypothesis:

> **Note**
>
> It is also possible to test the null hypothesis that ρ has some other value, like 0.4, but such tests are beyond the scope of this book.

Pearson's product moment correlation coefficient

$H_0: \rho = 0$. There is no correlation between the two variables.

There are three possible alternative hypotheses, according to the sense of the situation you are investigating. These are:

1 $H_1: \rho \neq 0$. There is correlation between the variables (two-tailed test).
2 $H_1: \rho > 0$. There is positive correlation between the variables (one-tailed test).
3 $H_1: \rho < 0$. There is negative correlation between the variables (one-tailed test).

The test is carried out by comparing the value for r with the appropriate entry in a table of critical values. This will depend on the size of the sample, the significance level at which you are testing and whether your test is one-tailed or two-tailed.

Critical values

Under the null hypothesis, $H_0: \rho = 0$, i.e. when there is a complete absence of linear correlation between the variables in the *population*, it is very likely that a bivariate data set, drawn at random from the population, will produce a value of r, the *sample* product moment correlation coefficient, which is non-zero. This will be the case even if the null hypothesis is true.

The role of the significance level is that, for any sample size n, it represents the probability that the value of r will be 'further from zero' than the critical value. Three examples, using the table of critical values in Figure 2.11 (see the next page) should help you to understand this concept better.

Table 2.2

Alternative hypothesis	Sample size, n	Significance level	Meaning
$H_1: \rho > 0$	11	1%	$P(r > 0.6851) = 0.01$
$H_1: \rho < 0$	6	5%	$P(r < -0.7293) = 0.05$
$H_1: \rho \neq 0$	15	10%	$P(|r| > 0.4409) = 0.1$

Example 2.1

Are students who are good at English also good at Mathematics?

A student believes that just because you are good at English, you are no more or less likely to be good at Mathematics. He obtains the results of an English examination and a Mathematics examination for eight students in his class. He then decides to carry out a hypothesis test to investigate whether he is correct.

The results of the two examinations for eight students are as follows.

Table 2.3

English, x	74	83	61	79	41	55	42	71
Mathematics, y	73	65	67	67	58	73	25	56

Solution

The relevant hypothesis test for this situation would be

$H_0: \rho = 0$. There is no correlation between English and Mathematics scores.

$H_1: \rho \neq 0$. There is correlation between English and Mathematics scores.

The student decides to use the 5% significance level.

The critical value for $n = 8$ at the 5% significance level for a two-tailed test is found from tables to be 0.7067.

	5%	2½%	1%	½%	one-tailed test
	10%	5%	2%	1%	two-tailed test
n					
1	-	-	-	-	
2	-	-	-	-	
3	0.9877	0.9969	0.9995	0.9999	
4	0.9000	0.9500	0.9800	0.9900	
5	0.8054	0.8783	0.9343	0.9587	
6	0.7293	0.8114	0.8822	0.9172	
7	0.6694	0.7545	0.8329	0.8745	
8	0.6215	0.7067	0.7887	0.8343	
9	0.5822	0.6664	0.7498	0.7977	
10	0.5494	0.6319	0.7155	0.7646	
11	0.5214	0.6021	0.6851	0.7348	
12	0.4973	0.5760	0.6581	0.7079	
13	0.4762	0.5529	0.6339	0.6835	
14	0.4575	0.5324	0.6120	0.6614	
15	0.4409	0.5140	0.5923	0.6411	

Figure 2.11 Extract from tables of critical values for the product moment correlation coefficient, r

The calculation of the product moment correlation coefficient, r, can be set out using the Extension work on page 26.

$n = 8$

Table 2.4

x	y	x^2	y^2	xy
74	73	5476	5329	5402
83	65	6889	4225	5395
61	67	3721	4489	4087
79	67	6241	4489	5293
41	58	1681	3364	2378
55	73	3025	5329	4015
42	25	1764	625	1050
71	56	5041	3136	3976
Totals	506	484	33838	30986	31596

$$\bar{x} = \frac{\Sigma x}{n} = \frac{506}{8} = 63.25 \quad \bar{y} = \frac{\Sigma y}{n} = \frac{484}{8} = 60.5$$

$$S_{xx} = \Sigma x^2 - n\bar{x}^2 = 33838 - 8 \times 63.25^2 = 1833.5$$

$$S_{yy} = \Sigma y^2 - n\bar{y}^2 = 30986 - 8 \times 60.5^2 = 1704$$

$$S_{xy} = \Sigma xy - n\bar{x}\bar{y} = 31596 - 8 \times 63.25 \times 60.5 = 983$$

Pearson's product moment correlation coefficient

> **Note**
> This example is designed just to show you how to do the calculations, and no more. A sample of size 8 is smaller than you would usually use. Also there is no indication of how the student chose the eight people in his sample. An essential requirement for a hypothesis test is that the sample is representative and usually a random sample is taken.

$$r = \frac{S_{xy}}{\sqrt{S_{xx}S_{yy}}} = \frac{\Sigma x_i y_i - n(\bar{x})(\bar{y})}{\sqrt{(\Sigma x_i^2 - n\bar{x}^2)(\Sigma y_i^2 - n\bar{y}^2)}} = \frac{983}{\sqrt{1833.5 \times 1704}}$$

$$= 0.5561 \quad \text{(to 4 s.f.)}$$

The critical value is 0.7067. The value of r of 0.5561 is less extreme.

So there is not enough evidence to reject the null hypothesis in favour of the alternative hypothesis.

There is insufficient evidence at the 5% level to suggest that students who are good at English are any more or less likely to be good at Mathematics.

USING ICT

You can use ICT to find the correlation coefficient and also to find the p-value for the test.

Figure 2.12 shows the output from a statistical package for the data in Example 2.1. You enter the correlation coefficient, the sample size and whether the test is one- or two-tailed (and the direction if one-tailed). The software then gives you the p-value as shown in Figure 2.12.

> **Note**
> The p-value of a test is the probability of the test statistics achieving the observed value or a value more extreme than that.

From Summary Statistics — Test Correlation

First Attribute (numeric): unassigned
Second Attribute (numeric): unassigned

Sample count: 8
The observed correlation between X and Y is **0.5561**

Null hypothesis: The population correlation is 0.
Alternative hypothesis: The population correlation is not equal to 0.

The test statistic, Student's t, is **1.639**. There are 6 degrees of freedom (two less than the sample size).

If it were true that the population correlation between X and Y were equal to 0 (the null hypothesis), and the sampling process were performed repeatedly, the probability of getting a value for Student's t with an absolute value this great or greater would be **0.15**.

You can use a t test to test significance of a correlation coefficient by applying an appropriate transformation.

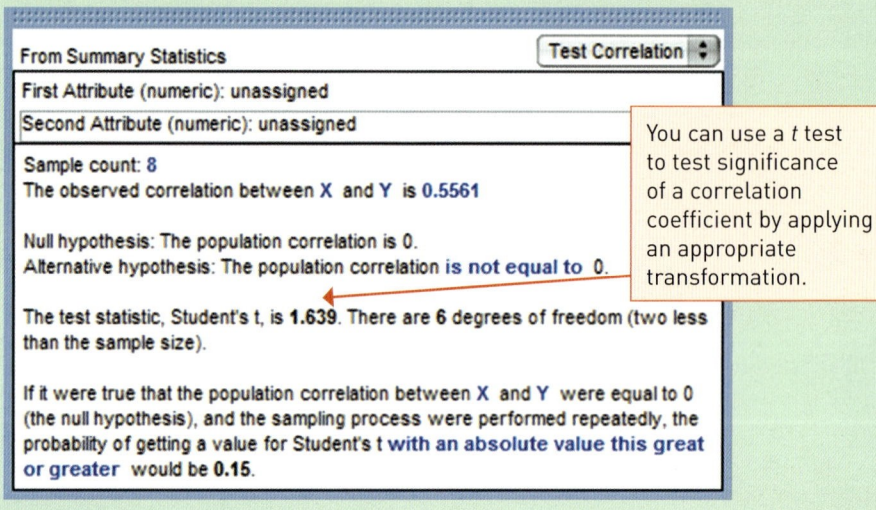

Figure 2.12

The p-value is 0.15 which is greater than 5% so there is not enough evidence to reject the null hypothesis.

Degrees of freedom

Here is an example where you have just two data points.

Table 2.5

	Sean	Iain
Height of an adult man (m)	1.70	1.90
The mortgage on his house (£)	15 000	45 000

When you plot these two points on a scatter diagram it is possible to join them with a perfect straight line and you might be tempted to conclude that taller men have larger mortgages on their houses.

This conclusion would clearly be wrong. It is based on the data from only two men so you are bound to be able to join the points on the scatter diagram with a straight line and calculate r to be either +1 or -1 (providing their heights and/or mortgages are not the same). In order to start to carry out a test you need the data for a third man, say Dafyd (height 1.75 m and mortgage £37 000). When his data are plotted on the scatter diagram in Figure 2.13 you can see how close the new point lies to the line between Sean and Iain.

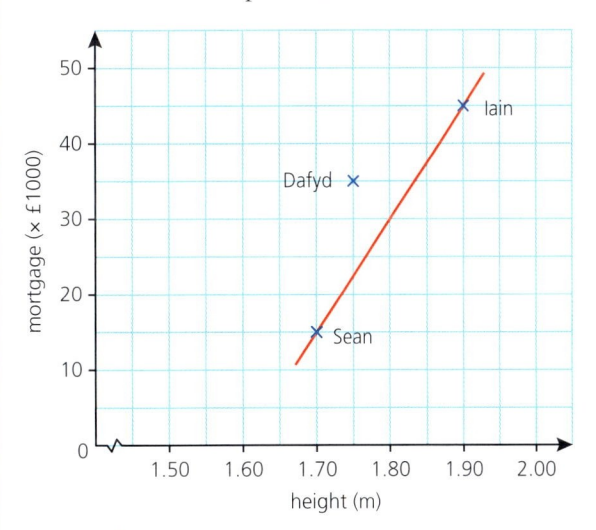

Figure 2.13

So the first two data points do not count towards a test for linear correlation. The first one to count is point number three. Similarly, if you have n points, only $n - 2$ of them count towards any test. The value $n - 2$ is called the **degrees of freedom** and denoted by υ. It is the number of free variables in the system. In this case, it is the number of points, n, less the 2 that have effectively been used to define the line of best fit.

In the case of the three men with their mortgages you would actually draw a line of best fit through all three, rather than join any particular two. So you cannot say that any two particular points have been taken out to draw the line of best fit, merely that the system as a whole has lost two.

Tables of critical values of correlation coefficients can be used without understanding the idea of degrees of freedom, but the idea is an important one throughout statistics. In general,

degrees of freedom = sample size − number of restrictions.

- Hypothesis tests using Pearson's product moment correlation coefficient require modelling assumptions that both variables are **random** and that the data are drawn from a **bivariate Normal** distribution. For large data sets this is usually the case if the scatter diagram gives an approximately elliptical distribution. If one or both of the distributions is, for example, skewed or bimodal, the procedure is likely to be inaccurate.
- The product moment correlation coefficient is a measure of correlation and so is only appropriate if the relationship between the variables is linear. For cases of non-linear association you should apply a test based on Spearman's correlation coefficient, which you will meet later in this chapter.
- The extract from the tables gives the critical value of r for various values of the significance level and the sample size, n. You will, however, find some tables where n is replaced by υ, the **degrees of freedom**. Degrees of freedom are covered in the next section.

Pearson's product moment correlation coefficient

Interpreting correlation

You need to be on your guard against drawing spurious conclusions from significant correlation coefficients.

Correlation does not imply causation

Figures for the years 1995–2005 show a high correlation between the sales of laptop computers and sales of microwave ovens. There is, of course, no direct connection between the two variables. You would be quite wrong to conclude that buying a laptop computer predisposes the buyer to buying a microwave oven.

Although there may be a high level of correlation between variables A and B it does not mean that A causes B or that B causes A. It may well be that a third variable C causes both A and B, or it may be that there is a more complicated set of relationships. In the case of laptop computers and microwaves, both are clearly caused by the advance of modern technology.

Non-linear association

A low value of r tells you that there is little or no correlation. There are, however, other forms of association, including non-linear as illustrated in Figure 2.14.

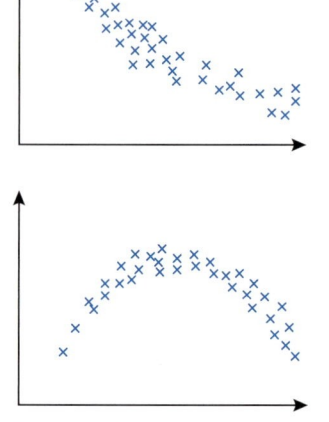

Figure 2.14 Scatter diagrams showing non-linear association

These diagrams show that there is an association between the variables, but not one that can be described as correlation.

Extrapolation

A linear relationship established over a particular domain should not be assumed to hold outside this range. For instance, there is strong correlation between the age in years and the 100 m times of female athletes between the ages of 10 and 20 years. To extend the connection, as shown in Figure 2.15, would suggest that veteran athletes are quicker than athletes who are in their prime and, if they live long enough, can even run 100 m in no time at all!

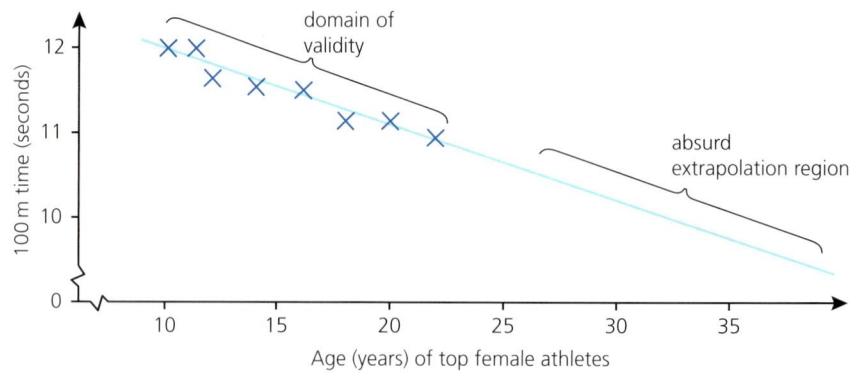

Figure 2.15

Exercise 2.1

①

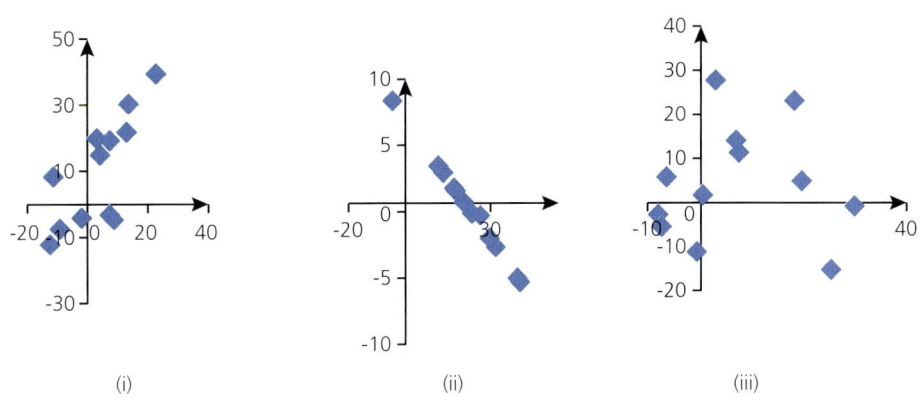

Figure 2.16

Three sets of bivariate data have been plotted on scatter diagrams, as illustrated. In each diagram the product moment correlation coefficient takes one of the values −1, −0.8, 0, 0.8, 1. Without doing any calculations, state the appropriate value of the correlation coefficient corresponding to the scatter diagrams (i), (ii) and (iii) in Figure 2.16.

② A language teacher wishes to test whether students who are good at their own language are also likely to be good at a foreign language. Accordingly, she collects the marks of eight students, all native English speakers, in their end of year examinations in English and French.

Table 2.6

Candidate	A	B	C	D	E	F	G	H
English	65	34	48	72	58	63	26	80
French	74	49	45	80	63	72	12	75

The product moment correlation coefficient is 0.913.

(i) State the null and alternative hypotheses.

(ii) Using the correlation coefficient as a test statistic, carry out the test at the 5% significance level.

③ 'You can't win without scoring goals.' So says the coach of a netball team. Jamila, who believes in solid defensive play, disagrees and sets out to prove that there is no correlation between scoring goals and winning matches. She collects the following data for the goals scored and the points gained by 12 teams in a netball league.

Table 2.7

Goals scored, x	41	50	54	47	47	49	52	61	50	29	47	35
Points gained, y	21	20	19	18	16	14	12	11	11	7	5	2

Pearson's product moment correlation coefficient

The product moment correlation coefficient is 0.380.

(i) State suitable null and alternative hypotheses, indicating whose position each represents.

(ii) Carry out the hypothesis test at the 5% significance level and comment on the result.

④ A medical student is trying to estimate the birth weight of babies using pre-natal scan images. The actual weights, x kg, and the estimated weights, y kg, of ten randomly selected babies are given in the table below. The data are plotted in the scatter diagram.

Table 2.8

x	2.61	2.73	2.87	2.96	3.05	3.14	3.17	3.24	3.76	4.10
y	3.2	2.6	3.5	3.1	2.8	2.7	3.4	3.3	4.4	4.1

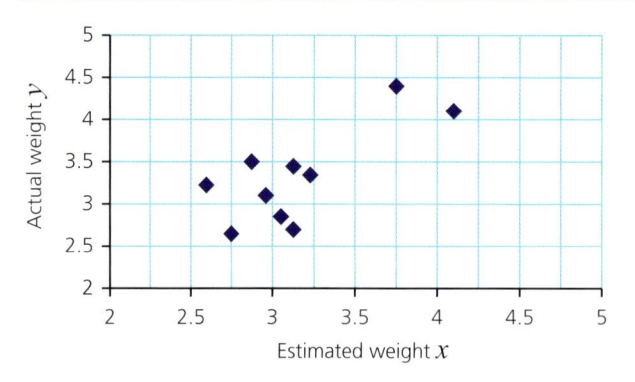

Figure 2.17

(i) The student decides to carry out a test based on the product moment correlation coefficient to investigate whether there is a positive relationship between the two variables. A friend suggests that there are two outliers so this test would not be appropriate. Explain why it may still be valid to carry out the test.

(ii) The value of the product moment correlation coefficient for these data is 0.7604. Carry out the test at the 1% significance level. [MEI]

⑤ It is widely believed that those who are good at chess are good at bridge, and vice-versa. A commentator decides to test this theory using as data the grades of a random sample of eight people who play both games.

Table 2.9

Player	A	B	C	D	E	F	G	H
Chess grade	160	187	129	162	149	151	189	158
Bridge grade	75	100	75	85	80	70	95	80

The product moment correlation coefficient is 0.850.

(i) State suitable null and alternative hypotheses.

(ii) The output in Figure 2.18 over the page comes from a statistical package. Using the p-value given at the bottom of the figure, complete the hypothesis test.

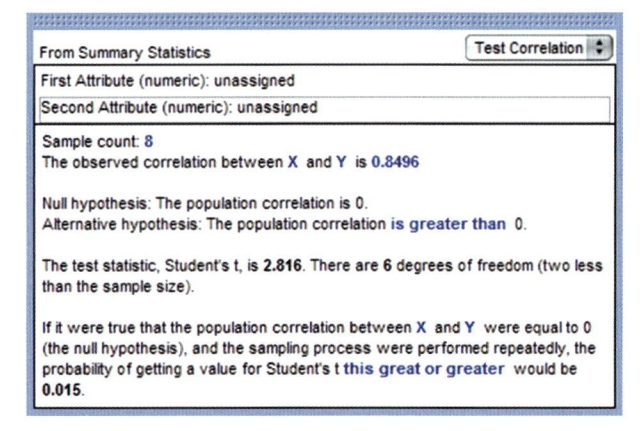

```
From Summary Statistics                    Test Correlation
First Attribute (numeric): unassigned
Second Attribute (numeric): unassigned

Sample count: 8
The observed correlation between X and Y is 0.8496

Null hypothesis: The population correlation is 0.
Alternative hypothesis: The population correlation is greater than 0.

The test statistic, Student's t, is 2.816. There are 6 degrees of freedom (two less
than the sample size).

If it were true that the population correlation between X and Y were equal to 0
(the null hypothesis), and the sampling process were performed repeatedly, the
probability of getting a value for Student's t this great or greater would be
0.015.
```

Figure 2.18

(6) A biologist believes that a particular type of fish develops black spots on its scales in water that is polluted by certain agricultural fertilisers. She catches a number of fish; for each one she counts the number of black spots on its scales and measures the concentration of the pollutant in the water it was swimming in. She uses these data to test for positive linear correlation between the number of spots and the level of pollution.

Table 2.10

Fish	A	B	C	D	E	F	G	H	I	J
Pollutant concentration (parts per million)	124	59	78	79	150	12	23	45	91	68
Number of black spots	15	8	7	8	14	0	4	5	8	8

The product moment correlation coefficient is 0.946.

(i) State suitable null and alternative hypotheses.

(ii) Carry out the hypothesis test at the 2% significance level. What can the biologist conclude?

(7) Andrew claims that the older you get, the slower is your reaction time. His mother disagrees, saying the two are unrelated. They decide that the only way to settle the discussion is to carry out a proper test. A few days later they are having a small party and so ask their 12 guests to take a test that measures their reaction times. The results are as follows.

Table 2.11

Age	Reaction time (s)	Age	Reaction time (s)
78	0.8	35	0.5
72	0.6	30	0.3
60	0.7	28	0.4
56	0.5	20	0.4
41	0.5	19	0.3
39	0.4	10	0.3

Pearson's product moment correlation coefficient

The product moment correlation coefficient is 0.901.

Carry out the test at the 5% significance level, stating the null and alternative hypotheses. Who won the argument, Andrew or his mother?

⑧ The teachers at a school have a discussion as to whether girls, in general, run faster or slower as they get older. They decide to collect data for a random sample of girls the next time the school cross country race is held (which everybody has to take part in). They collect the following data, with the times given in minutes and the ages in years (the conversion from months to decimal parts of a year has already been carried out).

Table 2.12

Age	Time	Age	Time	Age	Time
11.6	23.1	18.2	45.	13.9	29.1
15.0	24.0	15.4	23.2	18.1	21.2
18.8	45.0	14.4	26.1	13.4	23.9
16.0	25.2	16.1	29.4	16.2	26.0
12.8	26.4	14.6	28.1	17.5	23.4
17.6	22.9	18.7	45.0	17.0	25.0
17.4	27.1	15.4	27.0	12.5	26.3
13.2	25.2	11.8	25.4	12.7	24.2
14.5	26.8				

(i) State suitable null and alternative hypotheses and decide on an appropriate significance level for the test.

(ii) The product moment correlation coefficient is 0.491. State the conclusion from the test.

(iii) Plot the data on a scatter diagram and identify any outliers. Explain how they could have arisen.

(iv) Comment on the validity of the test.

⑨ A random sample of students who are shortly to sit an examination are asked to keep a record of how long they spend revising, in order to investigate whether more revision time is associated with a higher mark. The data are given below, with x hours being the revision time (correct to the nearest half hour) and y% being the mark scored in the examination.

Table 2.13

x	0	3	4.5	3.5	7	5.5	5	6.5	6	10.5	2
y	36	52	52	57	60	61	63	63	64	70	89

The product moment correlation coefficient is 0.3377.

(i) Specify appropriate null and alternative hypotheses, and carry out a suitable test at the 5% level of significance.

(ii) Without further calculation, state the effect of the data $x = 2$, $y = 89$ on the value of the product moment correlation coefficient. Explain whether or not this point should be excluded when carrying out the hypothesis test.

[MEI]

⑩ The table below gives the heights, *h*, of six male Olympic 100m sprint winners together with the times, *t*, they took.

Table 2.14

h	1.80	1.83	1.87	1.88	1.85	1.76
t	10.00	9.95	10.06	9.99	9.84	9.87

(i) Draw a scatter diagram to illustrate the data.

The product moment correlation coefficient is 0.4386.

(ii) Carry out a suitable hypothesis test, at a suitable level of significance, to determine whether or not it is reasonable to suppose that the heights and times are positively correlated.

(iii) Rewrite the table giving just the rank of each data value, using a rank of 1 for the lowest value and 6 for the highest value. For example the rank associated with a height of 1.88 m would be 6 since it is the height of the tallest person. The rank associated with a time of 9.87 s would be 2 since it is the second lowest time.

(iv) Calculate the product moment correlation coefficient of the ranked data.

(v) Comment on the difference between the two correlation coefficients.

4 Rank correlation

Dance competition dispute

In the dance competition at the local fete last Saturday, the two judges differed so much in their rankings of the ten competitors that initially nobody could be declared the winner. In the end, competitor C was declared the winner as the total of her ranks was the lowest (and so the best) but several of the other entrants felt that it was totally unfair.

The judgements that caused all the trouble were as follows.

Table 2.15

Competitor	A	B	C	D	E	F	G	H	I	J
Judge 1	1	9	7	2	3	10	6	5	4	8
Judge 2	8	3	1	10	9	4	7	6	5	2
Total	9	12	⑧	12	12	14	13	11	9	10

Winner

You will see that both judges ranked the ten entrants, 1st, 2nd, 3rd, ... , 10th. The winner, C, was placed 7th by one judge and 1st by the other. Their rankings look different so perhaps they were using different criteria on which to assess them. How can you use these data to decide whether that was or was not the case?

One way would be to calculate a correlation coefficient and use it to carry out a hypothesis test. However, the data you have are of a different type from any that you have used before for calculating correlation coefficients. In the point (1, 8), corresponding to competitor A, the numbers 1 and 8 are **ranks** and not scores (like marks in an examination or measurements). It is, however, possible to calculate a **rank correlation coefficient** in the same way as before. Rank

Rank correlation

correlation may be used in circumstances where ordinary correlation would not be appropriate and so is described as testing **association** rather than correlation.

The hypotheses for this particular test are stated as follows:

H_0: there is no association.

H_1: there is positive association.

The null hypothesis, H_0, represents the idea that the judges are using completely different unrelated criteria to judge the competitors. The alternative hypothesis represents the idea that the judges are using similar criteria to judge the competitors.

> **EXTENSION**
>
> ## ACTIVITY 2.1
>
> Show that the product moment correlation coefficient of the ranks in Table 2.15 is −0.794.
>
> Although you can carry out the calculation in the same way as you did in Example 2.1, it is usually done a different way.
> Denoting the two sets of ranks by $x_1, x_2, \ldots, x_n$ and $y_1, y_2, \ldots, y_n$, the coefficient of association is given by
>
> $$r_s = 1 - \frac{6\Sigma d_i^2}{n(n^2 - 1)}$$
>
> Where
>
> - r_s is called Spearman's rank correlation coefficient
> - d_i is the difference in the ranks for a general data item (x_i, y_i); $d_i = x_i - y_i$
> - n is the number of items of data.
>
> The calculation of Σd_i^2 can then be set out in a table like this.
>
> Table 2.16
>
> | Competitor | Judge 1, x_i | Judge 2, y_i | $d_i = x_i - y_i$ | d_i^2 |
> |---|---|---|---|---|
> | A | 1 | 8 | −7 | 49 |
> | B | 9 | 3 | 6 | 36 |
> | C | 7 | 1 | 6 | 36 |
> | D | 2 | 10 | −8 | 64 |
> | E | 3 | 9 | −6 | 36 |
> | F | 10 | 4 | 6 | 36 |
> | G | 6 | 7 | −1 | 1 |
> | H | 5 | 6 | −1 | 1 |
> | I | 4 | 5 | −1 | 1 |
> | J | 8 | 2 | 6 | 36 |
> | | | | Σd_i^2 | 296 |
>
> The value of n is 10, so $r_s = 1 - \dfrac{6 \times 296}{10(10^2 - 1)} = -0.794$
>
> You will see that this is the same answer as before, but the working is much shorter. It is not difficult to prove that the two methods are equivalent.

> **Note**
>
> If several items are ranked equally you give them the mean of the ranks they would have had if they had been slightly different from each other.

Hypothesis tests using Spearman's rank correlation coefficient

Spearman's rank correlation coefficient is often used as a test statistic for a hypothesis test of

H_0: there is no association between the variables

against one of three possible alternative hypotheses:

either H_1: there is association between the variables (two-tailed test)

or H_1: there is positive association between the variables (one-tailed test)

or H_1: there is negative association between the variables (one-tailed test).

The test is carried out by comparing the value of r_s with the appropriate critical value. This depends on the sample size, the significance level of the test and whether it is one-tailed or two-tailed. Critical values can be found from statistical software or tables.

Once you have found the value of r_s, this test follows the same procedure as that for correlation. However, the tables of critical values are not the same and so you need to be careful that you are using the right one.

The calculation is often carried out with the data across the page rather than in columns and this is shown in the next example.

Example 2.2

During their course two trainee tennis coaches, Rachael and Leroy, were shown videos of seven people, A, B, C, ... , G, doing a top-spin service and were asked to rank them in order according to the quality of their style. They placed them as follows.

Table 2.17

Rank order	1	2	3	4	5	6	7
Rachael	B	G	F	D	A	C	E
Leroy	F	B	D	E	G	A	C

Spearman's coefficient of rank correlation is 0.54 (2 s.f.).

Use it to test whether there is evidence, at the 5% level, of positive association between their judgements.

Solution

H_0: there is no association between their rankings.
H_1: there is positive association between their rankings.
Significance level: 5%
One-tailed test.

From tables, the critical value of r_s for a one-tailed test at this significance level for $n = 7$ is 0.7143.

0.54 < 0.7143 so H_0 is not rejected.

Rank correlation

There is insufficient evidence to claim positive association between Rachael's and Leroy's rankings.

	5%	2½%	1%	½%	one-tailed test
	10%	5%	2%	1%	two-tailed test
n					
1	-	-	-	-	
2	-	-	-	-	
3	-	-	-	-	
4	1.0000	-	-	-	
5	0.9000	1.0000	1.0000	-	
6	0.8286	0.8857	0.9429	1.0000	
7	0.7143	0.7857	0.8929	0.9286	
8	0.6429	0.7381	0.8333	0.8810	
9	0.6000	0.7000	0.7833	0.8333	
10	0.5636	0.6485	0.7455	0.7939	

Figure 2.19 Extract from table of critical values for Spearman's rank correlation coefficient, r_s

USING ICT

You can use ICT to find the correlation coefficient and also to find the *p*-value for the test.

Figure 2.20 shows the output from a statistical package for the data in Example 2.2. You enter the data and the software produces the output shown below.

This is Spearman's rank correlation coefficient.

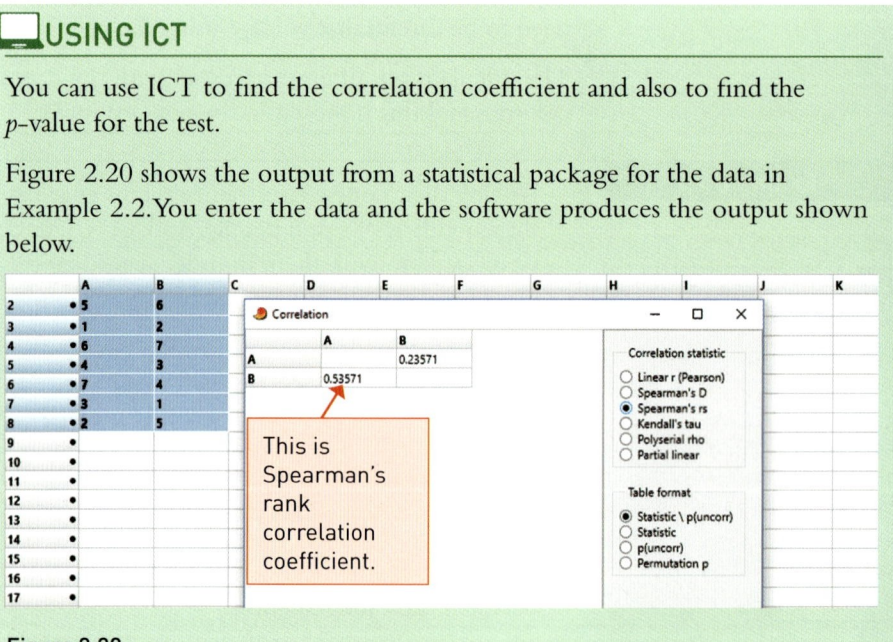

Figure 2.20

The *p*-value is 0.23571. However, because the test is one-tailed you have to divide this by 2 before comparing with the significance level. This gives approximately 0.118 which is greater than 0.05 or 5% so there is not enough evidence to reject the null hypothesis.

When to use rank correlation

Sometimes your data will be available in two forms, as values of variables or in rank order. If you have the choice you will usually work out the correlation coefficient from the variable values rather than the ranks.

It may well be the case, however, that only ranked data are available to you and, in that case, you have no choice but to use them. It may also be that, while you could collect variable values as well, it would not be worth the time, trouble or expense to do so.

Pearson's product moment correlation coefficient is a measure of correlation and so is not appropriate for non-linear data like those illustrated in the scatter diagram in Figure 2.21. You may, however, use rank correlation to investigate whether one variable generally increases (or decreases) as the other increases. The term **association** describes such a relationship.

> **Note**
>
> Spearman's rank correlation coefficient provides one among many statistical tests that can be carried out on ranks rather than variable values. Such tests are examples of **non-parametric tests**. A non-parametric test is a test on some aspect of a distribution which is not specified by its defining parameters.

> **Note**
>
> It makes no assumptions about the population.

Figure 2.21 Non-linear data with a high degree of rank correlation

You should, however, always look at the sense of your data before deciding which is the more appropriate form of correlation to use.

If the value of r_s is close to 1 then in general the rankings are in agreement. If the value of r_s is close to −1 then in general the rankings are in **disagreement** – low rankings in one set correspond to high rankings in the other, and vice versa. If the value of r_s is close to 0 then the rankings have little relationship – there is neither agreement nor disagreement.

Historical note

Karl Pearson was one of the founders of modern statistics. Born in 1857, he was a man of varied interests and practised law for three years before being appointed Professor of Applied Mathematics and Mechanics at University College, London in 1884. Pearson made contributions to various branches of mathematics but is particularly remembered for his work on the application of statistics to biological problems in heredity and evolution. He died in 1936.

Charles Spearman was born in London in 1863. After serving 14 years in the army as a cavalry officer, he went to Leipzig to study psychology. On completing his doctorate there he became a lecturer, and soon afterwards a professor also at University College, London. He pioneered the application of statistical techniques within psychology and developed the technique known as factor analysis in order to analyse different aspects of human ability. He died in 1945.

Rank correlation

Exercise 2.2

① In a driving competition, there were eight contestants and two judges who placed them in rank order, as shown in the table below.

Table 2.18

Competitor	A	B	C	D	E	F	G	H
Judge X	2	5	6	1	8	4	7	3
Judge Y	1	6	8	3	7	2	4	5

Spearman's coefficient of rank correlation for the data is 0.6667.

Stating suitable null and alternative hypotheses, carry out a hypothesis test on the level of agreement of these two judges.

② A coach wanted to test his theory that, although athletes have specialisms, it is still true that those who run fast at one distance are also likely to run fast at another distance. He selected six athletes at random to take part in a test and invited them to compete over 100 m and over 1500 m.

The times and places of the six athletes were as follows.

Table 2.19

Athlete	100 m time	100 m rank	1500 m time	1500 m rank
Allotey	9.8 s	1	3 m 42 s	1
Chell	10.9 s	6	4 m 11 s	2
Giles	10.4 s	2	4 m 19 s	6
Mason	10.5 s	3	4 m 18 s	5
O'Hara	10.7 s	5	4 m 12 s	3
Stuart	10.6 s	4	4 m 16 s	4

(i) The values of r and r_s are calculated to be $r = 0.766$, $r_s = -0.143$. Comment on these values.

(ii) State suitable null and alternative hypotheses and carry out hypothesis tests on these data.

(iii) State which you consider to be the more appropriate correlation coefficient in this situation, giving your reasons.

③ At the end of a word-processing course, the trainees are given a document to type. They are assessed on the time taken and on the quality of their work. For a random sample of 12 trainees, the following results were obtained.

Table 2.20

Trainee	A	B	C	D	E	F	G	H	I	J	K	L
Quality (%)	97	96	94	91	90	87	86	83	82	80	77	71
Time (s)	210	230	198	204	213	206	200	186	192	202	191	199

(i) Spearman's coefficient of rank correlation for the data is 0.636. Explain what the sign of your association coefficient indicates about the data.

(ii) Carry out a test, at the 5% level of significance, of whether or not there is any association between time taken and quality of work for trainees who have attended this word-processing course. State clearly the null and alternative hypotheses under test and the conclusion reached. [MEI]

④ A school holds an election for parent governors. Candidates are invited to write brief autobiographies and these are sent out at the same time as the voting papers.

After the election, one of the candidates, Mr Smith, says that the more words you wrote about yourself the more votes you got. He sets out to 'prove this statistically' by calculating the product moment correlation between the number of words and the number of votes.

Table 2.21

Candidate	A	B	C	D	E	F	G
Number of words	70	101	106	232	150	102	98
Number of votes	99	108	97	144	94	54	87

The product moment correlation coefficient is 0.680.

Mr Smith claims that this proves his point at the 5% significance level.

(i) State his null and alternative hypotheses and show how he came to his conclusion.

Spearman's rank correlation coefficient for these data is 0.214.

(ii) Explain the difference in the two correlation coefficients and criticise the procedure Mr Smith used in coming to his conclusion.

⑤ To test the belief that milder winters are followed by warmer summers, meteorological records are obtained for a random sample of ten years. For each year, the mean temperatures are found for January and July. The data, in °C, are given below.

Table 2.22

January	8.3	7.1	9.0	1.8	3.5	4.7	5.8	6.0	2.7	2.1
July	16.2	13.1	16.7	11.2	14.9	15.1	17.7	17.3	12.3	13.4

Spearman's rank correlation coefficient is 0.636.

(i) Test, at the 2.5% level of significance, the belief that milder winters are followed by warmer summers. State clearly the null and alternative hypotheses under test.

(ii) Would it be more appropriate, less appropriate or equally appropriate to use the product moment correlation coefficient to analyse these data? Briefly explain why. [MEI]

⑥ In a random sample of eight areas, residents were asked to express their approval or disapproval of the services provided by the local authority. A score of zero represented complete dissatisfaction, and ten represented complete satisfaction. The table below shows the mean score for each local authority together with the authority's level of community charge.

Table 2.23

Authority	A	B	C	D	E	F	G	H
Community charge (£)	485	490	378	451	384	352	420	212
Approval rating	3.0	4.0	5.0	4.6	4.1	5.5	5.8	6.1

Spearman's rank correlation coefficient for the data is −0.7857.

(i) State appropriate null and alternative hypotheses for a test to investigate whether there is any association between level of community charge and approval rating.

Rank correlation

(ii) The output in Figure 2.22 below comes from a statistical package. Using the *p*-value given in the table headed 'Correlation', carry out a hypothesis test at the 5% significance level.

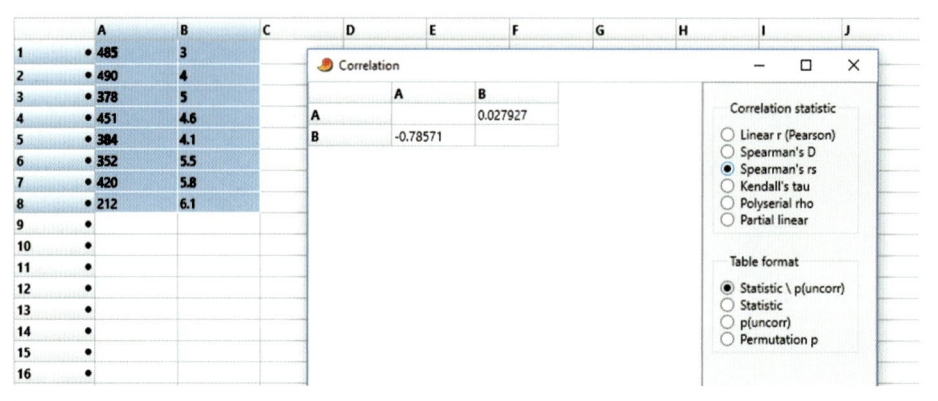

	A	B	C	D	E	F	G	H	I	J
1	485	3								
2	490	4		Correlation						
3	378	5			A	B			Correlation statistic	
4	451	4.6		A		0.027927			○ Linear r (Pearson)	
5	384	4.1		B	−0.78571				○ Spearman's D	
6	352	5.5							● Spearman's rs	
7	420	5.8							○ Kendall's tau	
8	212	6.1							○ Polyserial rho	
9									○ Partial linear	
10									Table format	
11									● Statistic \ p(uncorr)	
12									○ Statistic	
13									○ p(uncorr)	
14									○ Permutation p	
15										
16										

Figure 2.22

[MEI]

⑦ A fertiliser additive is claimed to enhance the growth of marrows. To test the claim statistically, a random sample of ten marrows is treated with varying levels of additive. The amounts of additive (in ounces) and the eventual weights of the marrows (in pounds) are given in the table.

Table 2.24

Amount of additive	8.2	3.5	8.8	1.6	1.9	9.9	5.8	5.5	4.4	3.9
Weight of marrow	6.6	7.2	8.4	4.7	7.4	8.7	7.5	7.3	5.9	7.0

Spearman's coefficient of rank correlation is 0.612.

(i) State appropriate null and alternative hypotheses for the test. Justify the alternative hypothesis you have given.

(ii) Carry out the test using a 5% level of significance. State clearly the conclusion reached.

(iii) Suppose it is discovered that the figures for the amounts of additive shown in the table were weights in grams rather than ounces. State, with reasons, whether this does or does not invalidate your answer. [MEI]

⑧ In order to assess whether increased expenditure in schools produces better examination results, a survey of all the secondary schools in England was conducted. Data on a random sample of 12 of these schools are shown below. The score shown is a measure of academic performance, a higher score indicating a higher success rate in examinations; expenditure is measured in thousands of pounds per student per year.

Table 2.25

Score	1.54	1.50	1.49	1.22	1.19	1.11	1.09	1.06	1.05	0.97	0.88	0.68
Expenditure	1.70	3.95	2.75	1.95	2.35	1.45	2.40	2.05	2.15	2.30	1.75	2.10

Spearman's rank correlation coefficient for the data is 0.1608.

(i) Perform an appropriate test at the 5% level, making clear what your hypotheses are. State clearly the conclusions to be drawn from the test.

Now suppose that the value of Spearman's rank correlation coefficient, calculated for *all* the secondary schools in England, is 0.15.

(ii) What conclusion would you now reach about any association between expenditure per student and examination success, and why? [MEI]

9. In a national survey into whether low death rates are associated with greater prosperity, a random sample of 14 areas was taken. The areas, arranged in order of their prosperity, are shown in the table below together with their death rates. (The death rates are on a scale for which 100 is the national average.)

Table 2.26

most prosperous   least prosperous

Area	A	B	C	D	E	F	G	H	I	J	K	L	M	N
Death rate	66	76	84	83	102	78	100	110	105	112	122	131	165	138

(i) Spearman's coefficient of rank correlation for the data is 0.952. Use it to test, at the 5% level of significance, whether or not there is such an association. State your hypotheses and your conclusion carefully.

(ii) A newspaper carried this story under the headline 'Poverty causes increased deaths'. Explain carefully whether or not the data justify this headline.

(iii) The data include no information on the age distributions in the different areas. Explain why such additional information would be relevant. [MEI]

10. The following data, referring to the ordering of perceived risk of 25 activities and technologies and actual fatality estimates, were obtained in a study in the United States. Use these data to test at the 5% significance level for positive correlation between

(i) the League of Women Voters and college students ($r = 0.881$)

(ii) experts and actual fatality estimates ($r = 0.888$)

(iii) college students and experts ($r = 0.622$).

Comment on your results and identify any outliers in the three sets of bivariate data you have just used.

Table 2.27

	League of Women Voters	College students	Experts	Actual fatalities (estimates)
Nuclear power	1	1	18	16
Motor vehicles	2	4	1	3
Handguns	3	2	4	4
Smoking	4	3	2	1
Motorcycles	5	5	6	6
Alcoholic beverages	6	6	3	2
General (private) aviation	7	12	11	11
Police work	8	7	15	18
Surgery	9	10	5	8
Fire fighting	10	9	16	17
Large construction	11	11	12	12
Hunting	12	15	20	14
Mountain climbing	13	17	24	21
Bicycles	14	19	13	13
Commercial aviation	15	13	14	20
Electric power (non-nuclear)	16	16	8	5

Rank correlation

	League of Women Voters	College students	Experts	Actual fatalities (estimates)
Swimming	17	25	9	7
Contraceptives	18	8	10	19
Skiing	19	20	25	24
X-rays	20	14	7	9
High school & college football	21	21	22	23
Railroads	22	18	17	10
Power mowers	23	23	23	22
Home appliances	24	22	19	15
Vaccinations	25	24	21	25

Source: Shwing and Albers, *Societal Risk Assessment,* Plenum

11. A population analyst wishes to test how death rates and birth rates are correlated in European countries.

   (i) State appropriate null and alternative hypotheses for the test. Justify the alternative hypothesis you have given.

   A random sample of ten countries from Europe was taken and their death rates (x) and birth rates (y), each per 1000 population for 1997, were noted.

   Table 2.28

x	9	9	7	12	11	10	7	13	8	7
y	14	9	13	13	10	11	16	9	16	12

   (ii) Represent the data graphically.

   The product moment correlation coefficient is −0.574.

   (iii) Carry out the hypothesis test at the 5% level of significance. State clearly the conclusion reached.

   In fact, the value of the product moment correlation coefficient for *all* the countries in Europe in 1997 was −0.555.

   (iv) What does this tell you about the relationship between death rates and birth rates in European countries?

   (v) State, giving a reason, whether your conclusion in part (iii) is still valid.
   [MEI]

12. Bird abundance may be assessed in several ways. In one long-term study in a nature reserve, two independent surveys (A and B) are carried out. The data show the number of wren territories recorded (survey A) and the numbers of adult wrens trapped in a fine mesh net (survey B) over a number of years.

   Table 2.29

Survey A	16	19	27	50	60	70	79	79	84	85	97
Survey B	11	12	15	18	22	35	35	71	46	53	52

   (i) Plot a scatter diagram to compare results for the two surveys.

   Spearman's coefficent of rank correlation for the data is 0.916.

   (ii) Perform a significance test, at the 5% level, to determine whether there is any association between the results of the two surveys. Explain what your conclusion means in practical terms.

(iii) Would it be more appropriate, less appropriate or equally appropriate to use the product moment correlation coefficient to analyse these data? Explain briefly why.

⑬ Two people are interviewing eight candidates for a job. Each of the interviewers ranks each of the candidates in order, with 1 being the most preferable and 8 the least. The ranks given to each of the candidates are as follows.

Table 2.30

| Interviewer A | 3 | 7 | 1 | 2 | 4 | 8 | 5 | 6 |
| Interviewer B | 2 | 4 | 3 | 7 | 8 | 5 | 1 | 6 |

(i) Represent the data graphically.

Spearman's coefficient of rank correlation for the data is 0.0476.

(ii) Explain why it would not be appropriate to carry out a hypothesis on these data using the critical values for the product moment correlation coefficient.

KEY POINTS

1 A scatter diagram is a graph to illustrate bivariate data.

2 Hypothesis testing based on Pearson's product moment correlation coefficient

$H_0: \rho = 0$

$H_1: \rho > 0$ or $\rho < 0$ (one-tailed test) or $\rho \neq 0$ (two-tailed test).

Test the sample value, r, against the critical value, which depends on the number of pairs in the bivariate sample, n, and the significance level.

3 Hypothesis testing based on Spearman's coefficient of rank correlation

H_0: no association

H_1: positive association or negative association (one-tailed test) or some association (two-tailed test).

Test the sample value, r_s, against the critical value, which depends on the number of pairs in the bivariate sample, n, and the significance level.

LEARNING OUTCOMES

When you have completed this chapter you should:

► understand what bivariate data are and know the conventions for choice of axis for variables in a scatter diagram
► be able to use and interpret a scatter diagram
► interpret a scatter diagram produced by software
► know when it is appropriate to carry out a hypothesis test using Pearson's product moment correlation coefficient
► be able to carry out hypothesis tests using the Pearson's product moment correlation coefficient and tables of critical values or the p-value from software
► be able to carry out hypothesis tests using Spearman's rank correlation coefficient and tables of critical values or the output from software
► decide whether a test based on r or r_s may be more appropriate, or whether neither is appropriate.

3 The binomial distribution

Doublethink means the power of holding two contradictory beliefs in one's mind simultaneously, and accepting both of them.

George Orwell

A learner driver has done no revision for the driving theory test. He decides to guess each answer. There are 50 questions in the test and four answers to each question. Exactly one of these answers is correct. He answers all of them.

> ### Discussion point
> How many questions on average would you expect the learner driver to get correct?

1 The binomial distribution

> For example the student could get the first r questions correct and the remaining ones wrong, or the first $r-1$ correct as well as the last one and the rest wrong. In all the number of possibilities is $^{50}C_r$, where ^nC_r is the number of ways of choosing r things from n things.

- The probability of getting a question correct is clearly 0.25 as there are four responses of which one is correct.
- The probability of getting a question wrong is therefore 0.75.
- If the student gets r questions correct out of 50 then he must get the remaining $50 - r$ wrong.
- You might think that the probability of getting r questions correct out of 50 is $0.25^r \times 0.75^{50-r}$.
- However, there are many possible combinations, in fact $^{50}C_r$ of them, so you need to multiply the above term by $^{50}C_r$.

So the probability of getting r questions correct out of 50 is equal to $^{50}C_r \times 0.25^r \times 0.75^{50-r}$.

This situation is an example of the binomial distribution. For a binomial distribution to be appropriate, the following conditions must apply.

> In this example, the possible outcomes are **correct** (success) and **wrong** (failure).

- You are conducting trials on random samples of a certain size, denoted by n.
- On each trial, the outcomes can be classified as either **success** or **failure**.

In addition, the following assumptions are needed if the binomial distribution is to be a good model and give reliable answers.

> This is particularly true when, in contrast to answering a question involving coins, dice, cards etc., you are modelling a situation drawn from real life.

- The outcome of each trial is independent of the outcome of any other trial.
- The probability of success is the same on each trial.

The probability that the number of success, X, has the value r, is given by

$$P(X = r) = {^nC_r}\, p^r q^{n-r} \text{ for } r = 0, 1, \ldots, n$$

$$P(X = r) = 0 \text{ otherwise.}$$

You can either use this formula to find binomial probabilities or you can find them directly from your calculator without using the formula.

> The probability of success is usually denoted by p and that of failure by q, so $p + q = 1$.

The notation $B(n, p)$ is often used to mean that the distribution is binomial, with n trials each with probability of success p.

In a set of n trials, each with probability p of success, the mean number of success is np. This is also called the average number of successes or, more formally, the expectation.

When faced with a situation where you think the binomial distribution is in operation, you should check that the above criteria are fulfilled.

Example 3.1

On average, 5% of patients do not turn up for their appointment at a dental clinic. There are 30 appointments per day.

(i) Find the probability that on a random chosen day

　(a) everybody turns up,

　(b) exactly two people do not turn up,

　(c) at least three people do not turn up.

(ii) What modelling assumption do you have to make to answer the questions in part (i)? Do you think that this assumption is reasonable?

(iii) What is the mean number of people not turning up on a day?

49

The binomial distribution

> **Note**
>
> The distribution which you need to use is B(30, 0.05).

Solution

(i) The probabilities, to 4 s.f., are

(a) $0.95^{30} = 0.2146$

(b) $^{30}C_2 \times 0.05^2 \times 0.95^{28} = 0.2586$

(c) $1 - {^{30}C_2} \times 0.05^2 \times 0.95^{28} - {^{30}C_1} \times 0.05^1 \times 0.95^{29} - 0.95^{30} = 0.1878$

(ii) You have to assume that the people who miss appointments do so independently of each other. It may not be true, as perhaps two members of the same family may both have an appointment and so would probably either both attend or neither. Also fewer people may attend when the weather is bad.

(iii) Mean $= np = 30 \times 0.05 = 1.5$

The mean number of people not turning up is 1.5

> **USING ICT**
>
> Notice that you can find the answers to all three parts of this example directly from your calculator without using the formula.

Example 3.2

Using ICT

You can use a spreadsheet to check these formulae for a particular binomial distribution, for example B(6, 0.25). Note that using the formulae, the mean $= np = 6 \times 0.25 = 1.5$ and the variance $= npq = 6 \times 0.25 \times 0.75 = 1.125$

In order to check these results, take the following steps:

1. Enter the values of X into cells B1 to H1.

2. Enter the formula provided by your spreadsheet to find $P(X = 0)$, for example =BINOM.DIST(B1,6,0.25,FALSE) into cell B2.

3. Copy this formula into cells C2 to H2 to find $P(X = 1)$ to $P(X = 6)$.

> The number in cell G2 should come out to be 0.0044. Check that you have got this right before continuing.

	A	B	C	D	E	F	G	H	I
1	r	0	1	2	3	4	5	6	SUM
2	$P(X=r)$	0.1780	0.3560						

Figure 3.1

4. Enter the formula = B1*B2 into cell B3 to calculate $0 \times P(X = 0)$.

5. Copy this formula into cells C3 to H3 to calculate $r \times P(X = r)$ for the remaining cells.

	A	B	C	D	E	F	G	H	I
1	r	0	1	2	3	4	5	6	SUM
2	$P(X=r)$	0.1780	0.3560						
3	$r \times P(X=r)$	0.0000	0.3560						

Figure 3.2

6. Enter the formula = B1^2*B2 into cell B4 to calculate $0^2 \times P(X = 0)$.

7. Copy this formula into cells C4 to H4 to calculate $r^2 \times P(X = r)$ for the remaining cells.

	A	B	C	D	E	F	G	H	I
1	r	0	1	2	3	4	5	6	SUM
2	$P(X=r)$	0.1780	0.3560						
3	$r \times P(X=r)$	0.0000	0.3560						
4	$r^2 \times P(X=r)$	0.0000	0.3560						

Figure 3.3

8 Use the SUM function to sum the values in each of rows 2, 3 and 4. Note that the sum of row 2 should be 1 (as you would expect).

9 Enter the formula = I3 into cell B6 to find the mean (which is simply the sum of the cells B3 to H3). If you have done it correctly the answer should be 1.5.

10 Enter the formula = I4 − I3^2 into cell B7 to calculate the variance. This answer should be 1.125.

ACTIVITY 3.1
Use a spreadsheet to confirm that, for B(8, 0.625), the procedures used in the example above give the same answers as the standard binomial formulae for the mean (*np*) and variance (*npq*).

Exercise 3.1

1 A fair coin is spun ten times.
   (i)   State the distribution of the number of heads that occur.
   (ii) Find the probability of exactly four heads occurring.
   (iii) Find the probability of at least five heads occurring.

2 The random variable $X \sim B(15, 0.4)$
   (i)   Find $E(X)$.
   (ii) Find $P(X = 3)$.
   (iii) Find $P(X > 3)$.

3 In an airport departure lounge a stall offers the chance to win a sports car. The game is to draw a card at random from each of four normal packs. If all four cards are aces, then the car is won.
   (i)   What is the probability of winning the car?
   (ii) How many goes would be expected before the car was won?
   (iii) The stall charges £5 per go and the car costs £35 000. What is the expected profit per go?

4 A pottery company manufactures bowls in batches of 100. The probability of a bowl being faulty is known to be 0.03.
   (i)   What is the probability that in a batch of bowls there are less than five faulty bowls?
   (ii) What is the probability that in two batches of bowls there are at most eight faulty bowls?
   (iii) What is the probability that in each of two batches of bowls there are at most four faulty bowls?
   (iv) Explain why your answer to part (ii) is different from your answer to part (iii).

5 Mark travels to work by bus each morning. The probability of his bus being late is 0.25.
   (i)   What is the probability that his bus is late twice in a five-day working week?
   (ii) What is the probability that it is late at most once in a five-day working week?

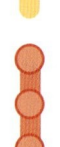

(iii) Fred buys a quarterly ticket which allows him to travel for 13 weeks. How many times would he expect the bus to be late in this thirteen-week period?

6. The random variable $X \sim B(n, p)$. The values of the mean and variance are 24 and 14.4, respectively.
   (i) Find $P(X = 30)$.
   (ii) Find $P(X > 30)$.

2 Hypothesis testing using the binomial distribution

THE AVONFORD STAR

Earlier in the year, Meg Green was appointed Captain of The Speckled Fox's pub cricket team. And luck has been with her. In her first 8 matches she has won the toss all 8 times.

'My mother always told me I am naturally lucky,' says Meg. 'Even when I was just a little girl, I could usually tell whether a coin was going to land heads or tails, and this has stayed with me. So it is no surprise to me that I keep winning the toss.'

I asked Meg what she did to stay lucky. She gave me an enchanting smile. 'It helps when other people are kind to me, like buying me a drink at the bar.'

So I bought her a glass of wine. Good luck, Meg!

Table 3.1

Win	Lose	Probability
0	8	$\frac{1}{256}$
1	7	$\frac{8}{256}$
2	6	$\frac{28}{256}$
3	5	$\frac{56}{256}$
4	4	$\frac{70}{256}$
5	3	$\frac{56}{256}$
6	2	$\frac{28}{256}$
7	1	$\frac{8}{256}$
8	0	$\frac{1}{256}$

What do you think?

Is Meg naturally lucky or is her good fortune just by chance?

Of course you can win the toss 8 times out of 8, or even 100 times out of 100, but how likely is it?

The toss at the start of each match can be thought of as a trial. Success is winning the toss, and on any occasion the probability of doing so is $\frac{1}{2}$; similarly failure is losing the toss and the probability of this is also $\frac{1}{2}$. So you can model the number of wins among 8 tosses by the binomial distribution $B(8, \frac{1}{2})$.

This gives these probabilities, shown in Table 3.1 and Figure 3.4.

Figure 3.4

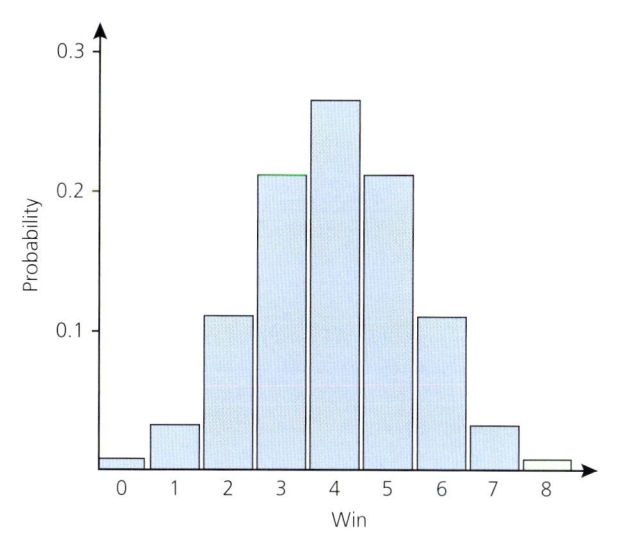

So the probability of 8 wins out of 8 is $\dfrac{1}{256}$ (shaded in Figure 3.4).

This is unlikely but by no means impossible.

Defining terms

In this example Meg's claim to be lucky is investigated by comparing it to the usual situation, the unexceptional. If you use p for the probability that you win the toss, the normal state of affairs can be stated as

$$p = 0.5.$$

This is called the **null hypothesis**, denoted by H_0.

Meg's claim (made, she says, long ago when she was still a little girl) was that

$$p > 0.5$$

and this is called the **alternative hypothesis**, H_1.

The word hypothesis (plural **hypotheses**) means a theory which is put forward either for the sake of argument or because it is believed or suspected to be true. An investigation like this is usually conducted in the form of a test, called a **hypothesis** test. There are many different sorts of hypothesis test used in statistics; in this chapter you meet only one of them but a few of the others are covered later in the book.

It is never possible to prove something statistically in the sense that, for example, you can prove that the angle at the centre of a circle is twice the angle at the circumference. Even if you tossed a coin a million times and it came down heads every single time, it is still possible that the coin is unbiased and just happened to land that way. What you can say is that it is very unlikely; the probability of it happening that way is $(0.5)^{1\,000\,000}$ which is a decimal that starts with over 300 000 zeros. This is so tiny that you would feel quite confident in declaring the coin biased.

There comes a point when the probability is so small that you say 'That's good enough for me. I am satisfied that it hasn't happened that way by chance.'

Hypothesis testing using the binomial distribution

The probability at which you make that decision is called the **significance level** of the test. Significance levels are usually given as percentages; 0.05 is written as 5%, 0.01 as 1% and so on.

So in the case of Meg Green, the question could have been worded as follows.

Meg Green's claim is that she is more likely than not to win the toss.

Null hypothesis, H_0: $p = 0.5$ Meg is equally likely to win or lose the toss.

Alternative hypothesis, H_1: $p > 0.5$ Meg is more likely to win the toss than to lose it.

Significance level: 1%

Probability of 8 wins from 8 tosses $= \dfrac{1}{256} = 0.0039 = 0.39\%$.

Since $0.39\% < 1\%$, we reject the null hypothesis and accept the alternative hypothesis. So the evidence supports Meg's claim.

This example also illustrates some of the problems associated with hypothesis testing. Here is a list of points you should be considering.

Hypothesis testing checklist

1 Was the test set up before or after the data were known?

Ideally the test should be set up before the data are collected. This was not the case for the test on Meg's winning the toss. A better test would involve making a prediction about the outcomes of, say, the next 8 tosses she is involved in.

2 Was the sample involved random?

The sample for Meg's data was not random but it was reasonably representative. The toss at the start of one game is much the same as that at the start of another.

3 Were the data independent?

The answer to this is yes. The outcome of one toss does not affect the outcome of another.

4 Is the statistical procedure actually testing the original claim?

The claim is that Meg can often win a toss. The statistical procedure is testing the alternative hypothesis that $p > 0.5$. The two are essentially the same so there is no problem in this case.

Carrying out a hypothesis test

This example shows the steps involved in carrying out a hypothesis test and the order in which you would take them.

1. Analyse the situation or problem and decide what variables are involved.
2. Establish the null and alternative hypotheses.
3. Decide on the significance level.
4. Collect suitable data using a sampling procedure that ensures the items are representative and independent.

> This will usually involve a random sample

5 Conduct the test, doing the necessary calculations.
6 Interpret the result in terms of the original claim, theory or problem.

Choosing the significance level

In the test involving Meg, the significance level was set at 1%. You will notice that if instead it had been set at 0.1% the result would have been different; the alternative hypothesis would have been rejected and you would have said something like 'There is not enough evidence to support Meg's claim to be more likely to win the toss than to lose it.'

In general the lower the percentage of the significance level, the more stringent is the test.

The significance level you choose involves a balanced judgement. Imagine that you are testing the sleepers on a railway line for possible faults. In this situation the null hypothesis would be that the sleepers are good and the alternative hypothesis that they are faulty. Setting a small significance level, say 0.1%, means that you will only declare the sleepers to be faulty if you are very certain that is the case, and so run the risk of allowing trains to run over unsafe track; this would involve accepting the null hypothesis when it is in fact false. By contrast, if you set a high figure for the significance level, like 10%, you risk declaring the sleepers faulty when they actually good, and so causing the expense of unnecessary replacement work; in this case you would be rejecting a true null hypothesis.

Rejecting a true null hypothesis is called a Type I error. So the probability of making a Type I error is the significance level of the test.

Accepting a false alternative hypothesis is called a Type II error. You will meet examples of calculating the probability of a Type II error in Chapter 11.

> **Note**
> Notice the cautious wording. Despite the test result it is still quite possible that Meg is no more likely than anyone else to win the toss and this is just a freak result.

Example 3.3

Here is another example. Cover up the solution and then, as you work your way through it, see if you can predict the next step at each stage.

Dave is a keen angler and enters a competition for 6 people. Each person is assigned a different site at random; the sites are numbered 1, 2, 3, 4, 5 and 6. Dave is given Site 1. At the end of the competition Dave has caught more fish than any of the other entrants and so is declared the winner. However, one of the other anglers complains that there are more fish at Site 1 and so it is not fair.

The management say that they have used the same sites for many years and no one has complained before. Nonetheless they will look at the outcomes for the previous 20 competitions and carry out a statistical analysis. The winning sites were as follows.

1	6	6	2	3
4	2	4	1	1
3	5	4	1	4
1	3	1	1	3

Carry out a suitable hypothesis test at the 5% significance level and state whether Dave should remain the winner.

Hypothesis testing using the binomial distribution

Solution

Let p be the probability of Site 1 winning in any competition.

Null hypothesis, H_0: $p = \dfrac{1}{6}$ Site 1 is no more likely to win than the others (on average).

Alternative hypothesis, H_1: $p > \dfrac{1}{6}$ Site 1 is more likely to win than the others (on average).

Significance level: 5%

The results may be summarised as follows.

Table 3.2

Site	1	2	3	4	5	6
Frequency	7	2	4	4	1	2

Under the null hypothesis, the wins for Site 1 is modelled by the binomial distribution, $B\left(20, \dfrac{1}{6}\right)$ which gives these probabilities:

Table 3.3

Site 1 wins frequency	Expression	Probability (4 d.p.)
0	$\left(\dfrac{5}{6}\right)^{20}$	0.0261
1	$^{20}C_1 \left(\dfrac{5}{6}\right)^{19}\left(\dfrac{1}{6}\right)$	0.1043
2	$^{20}C_2 \left(\dfrac{5}{6}\right)^{18}\left(\dfrac{1}{6}\right)^2$	0.1982
3	$^{20}C_3 \left(\dfrac{5}{6}\right)^{17}\left(\dfrac{1}{6}\right)^3$	0.2379
4	$^{20}C_4 \left(\dfrac{5}{6}\right)^{16}\left(\dfrac{1}{6}\right)^4$	0.2022
5	$^{20}C_5 \left(\dfrac{5}{6}\right)^{15}\left(\dfrac{1}{6}\right)^5$	0.1294
6	$^{20}C_6 \left(\dfrac{5}{6}\right)^{14}\left(\dfrac{1}{6}\right)^6$	0.0647
7	$^{20}C_7 \left(\dfrac{5}{6}\right)^{13}\left(\dfrac{1}{6}\right)^7$	0.0259
8	$^{20}C_8 \left(\dfrac{5}{6}\right)^{12}\left(\dfrac{1}{6}\right)^8$	0.0084
⋮	⋮	⋮
20	$\left(\dfrac{1}{6}\right)^{20}$	0.0000

> The probability of 1 coming up between 0 and 6 times is found by adding these probabilities to get 0.9628.

> If you worked out all these and added them you would get the probability that the number of 1s is 7 or more (up to a possible 20). It is much quicker, however, to find this as 1 − 0.9628 (the answer above) = 0.0372.

Calling X the number of 1s occurring when a die is rolled 20 times, the probability of seven or more 1s is given by

$$P(X \geq 7) = 1 - P(X \leq 6) = 1 - 0.9628 = 0.0372$$

So, if the null hypothesis is true, the probability of 7 or more wins at Site 1 is 0.0372, or 3.72%.

The significance level is 5% and since 3.72% < 5%, the null hypothesis is rejected.

The evidence does indeed suggest that Site 1 is likely to be the winning site.

(The organisers allowed Dave to keep his winner's medal but agreed to find new sites for future competitions.)

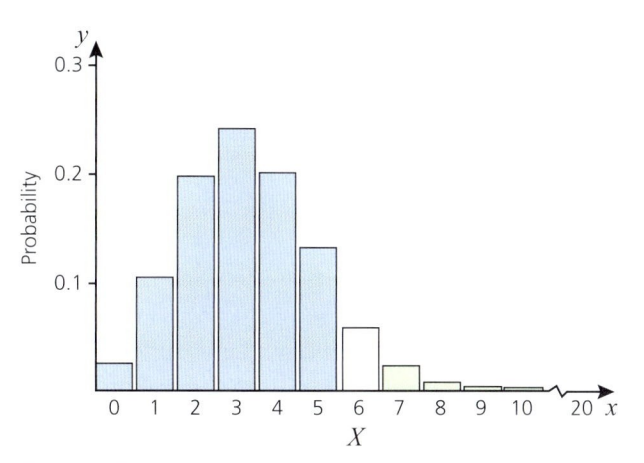

Figure 3.5

Other methods

You could have found the probability of up to 6 wins at Site 1 using cumulative binomial probability tables, either in your Formula book or on a calculator. These give $P(X \leq x)$ when X B(n, p) for $x = 0, 1, 2, \ldots, n$ and values of p from 0.05 to 0.95 at intervals of 0.05 plus $\frac{1}{6}, \frac{1}{3}, \frac{2}{3}, \frac{5}{6}$. There is a separate table for each value of n from 1 to 20.

In this case $p = \frac{1}{6}$ so the probability of up to 6 wins at Site 1 is found to be 0.9629, the same result as before apart from the last figure where there is a difference of 1 from rounding. You can obtain the same figures from many calculators and once you have learnt what keys to press, this is the most efficient method.

Hypothesis testing using the binomial distribution

Exercise 3.2

Many calculators have the cumulative probabilities for a binomial distributions built in. This can save you much time when compared with using tables.

In all these questions you should apply this checklist to the hypothesis test.

(a) Was the test set up before or after the data were known?

(b) Was the sample used for the test chosen at random and are the data independent?

(c) Is the statistical procedure actually testing the original claim?

You should also comment critically on whether these steps have been followed.

(a) Establish the null and alternative hypotheses.

(b) Decide on the significance level.

(c) Collect suitable data using a random sampling procedure that ensures the items are independent.

(d) Conduct the test, doing the necessary calculations.

(e) Interpret the result in terms of the original claim, theory or problem.

① Mrs da Silva is running for President. She claims to have 60% of the population supporting her.

She is suspected of overestimating her support and a random sample of 20 people are asked whom they support. Only nine say Mrs da Silva.

Test, at the 5% significance level, the hypothesis that she has overestimated her support.

② A company developed synthetic coffee and claim that coffee drinkers could not distinguish it from the real product. A number of coffee drinkers challenged the company's claim, saying that the synthetic coffee tasted synthetic. In a test, carried out by an independent consumer protection body, 20 people were given a mug of coffee. Ten had the synthetic brand and ten the natural, but they were not told which they had been given.

Out of the ten given the synthetic brand, eight said it was synthetic and two said it was natural. Use this information to test the coffee drinkers' claim (as against the null hypothesis of the company's claim), at the 5% significance level.

③ A group of 18 students decides to investigate the truth of the saying that if you drop a piece of toast it is more likely to land butter-side down.

They each take one piece of toast, butter it on one side and throw it in the air. Eleven land butter-side down, the rest butter-side up. Use their results to carry out a hypothesis test at the 10% significance level, stating clearly your null and alternative hypotheses.

④ On average 70% of people pass their driving test first time. There are complaints that Mr McTaggart is too harsh and so, unknown to himself, his work is monitored. It is found that he fails 10 out of 20 candidates. Are the complaints justified at the 5% significance level?

⑤ A machine makes bottles. In normal running 5% of the bottles are expected to be cracked, but if the machine needs servicing this proportion will increase. As part of a routine check, 50 bottles are inspected and 5 are found to be unsatisfactory. Does this provide evidence, at the 5% significance level, that the machine needs servicing?

⑥ A firm producing mugs has a quality control scheme in which a random sample of 10 mugs from each batch is inspected. For 50 such samples, the numbers of defective mugs are as follows.

Table 3.4

Number of defective mugs	0	1	2	3	4	5	6+
Number of samples	5	13	15	12	4	1	0

(i) Find the mean and standard deviation of the number of defective mugs per sample.

(ii) Show that a reasonable estimate for p, the probability that a mug is defective, is 0.2. Use this figure to calculate the probability that a randomly chosen sample will contain exactly two defective mugs. Comment on the agreement between this value and the observed data.

The management is not satisfied with 20% of mugs being defective and introduces a new process to reduce the proportion of defective mugs.

(iii) A random sample of 20 mugs, produced by the new process, contains just one which is defective. Test, at the 5% level, whether it is reasonable to suppose that the proportion of defective mugs has been reduced, stating your null and alternative hypotheses clearly.

(iv) What would the conclusion have been if the management had chosen to conduct the test at the 10% level? [MEI]

⑦ An annual mathematics contest contains 15 questions, 5 short and 10 long.

The probability that I get a short question right is 0.9.

The probability that I get a long question right is 0.5.

My performances on questions are independent of each other. Find the probability of the following:

(i) I get all the 5 short questions right

(ii) I get exactly 8 of the 10 long questions right

(iii) I get exactly 3 of the short questions and all of the long questions right

(iv) I get exactly 13 of the 15 questions right.

After some practice, I hope that my performance on the long questions will improve this year. I intend to carry out an appropriate hypothesis test.

(v) State suitable null and alternative hypotheses for the test.

In this year's contest I get exactly 8 of the 10 long questions right.

(vi) Is there sufficient evidence, at the 5% significance level, that my performance on long questions has improved?

3 Critical values and critical regions

In Example 3.3, Site 1 came up seven times, and this was enough to conclude that it was likely to be an advantageous place to fish. What is the largest number of times Site 1 could come up for the opposite conclusion to be reached?

You again use X to denote the number of times Site 1 comes up in the 20 competitions, and so $X = 6$ means that Site 1 comes up six times.

Critical values and critical regions

You know from your earlier work that the probability $X \geq 7 = 0.0372 < 5\%$. You also know from the binomial distribution that

$$P(X = 6) = {}^{20}C_6 \left(\frac{5}{6}\right)^{14} \left(\frac{1}{6}\right)^6 = 0.0647.$$

This tells you that $P(X \geq 6) = 0.1019 > 10\%$.

These figures tell you that six wins for Site 1 would not be enough to lead you to conclude that it was an advantageous place to fish, whether your test was at the 5%, or even the 10% level. The value 7 is the smallest score that would lead you to do that.

You might feel that concluding one thing for the value 6 and another for the value 7 is a bit harsh. Sometimes tests are designed so that if the result falls within a certain region further trials are recommended.

In this example, the number 7 is the **critical value** (at the 5% significance level), which is the value at which you change from accepting the null hypothesis to rejecting it. The range of values for which you reject the null hypothesis, in this case, $X \geq 7$, is called the **critical region**.

It is sometimes easier in hypothesis testing to find the critical region and see if your value lies in it, rather than working out the probability of a value at least as extreme as the one you have, which is the procedure used so far.

The quality control department of a factory tests a random sample of 20 items from each batch produced. A batch is rejected (or perhaps subject to further tests) if the number of faulty items in the sample, X, is more than 2.

This means that the critical region is $X \geq 3$.

It is much simpler for the operator carrying out the test to be told the critical region (determined in advance by the person designing the procedure) than to have to work out a probability for each test result.

> **Test procedure**
>
> **Take 20 pistons**
>
> **If 3 or more are faulty, REJECT the batch**

Example 3.4

World wide, 25% of men are colour-blind but it is believed that the condition is less widespread among a group of remote hill tribes. An anthropologist plans to test this by sending field workers to visit villages in that area. In each village, 30 men are to be tested for colour-blindness. Find the critical region for the test at the 5% level of significance.

Solution

Let p be the probability that a man in that area is colour-blind.

Null hypothesis, H_0: $p = 0.25$

Alternative hypothesis, H_1: $p < 0.25$ (Less colour-blindness in this area.)

Significance level: 5%

With the hypothesis H_0, if the number of colour-blind men in a sample of 30 is X, then $X \sim B(30, 0.25)$.

The critical region is the region $X \leq k$, where

$$P(X \leq k) \leq 0.05 \quad \text{and} \quad P(X \leq k + 1) > 0.05.$$

Since $n = 30$ is too large for the available tables, we have to calculate the probabilities:

$P(X = 0) = (0.75)^{30} = 0.00018$

$P(X = 1) = 30(0.75)^{29}(0.25) = 0.000179$

$P(X = 2) = (0.75)^{28}(0.25)^2 = 0.00863$

$P(X = 3) = (0.75)^{27}(0.25)^3 = 0.02685$

$P(X = 4) = (0.75)^{28}(0.25)^4 = 0.06042$

So $P(X \leq 3) = 0.00018 + 0.00179 + 0.00863 + 0.02685 \approx 0.0375 \leq 0.05$

But $P(X \leq 4) = 0.0929 > 0.05$

Therefore the critical region is $X \leq 3$.

Discussion point
What is the critical region at the 10% significance level?

EXPERIMENTS

Mind reading

Here is a simple experiment to see if you can read the mind of a friend whom you know well. The two of you face each other across a table on which is placed a coin. Your friend takes the coin and puts it in one or other hand under the table. You have to guess which one.
Play this game at least 20 times and test at the 10% significance level whether you can read your friend's mind.

Smarties

Get a large box of Smarties and taste the different colours. Choose the colour, C, which you think has the most distinctive flavour.
Now close your eyes and get a friend to feed you Smarties. Taste each one and say if it is your chosen colour or not. Do this for at least 20 Smarties and test at the 10% significance level whether you can pick out those with colour C by taste.

Left and right

It is said that if people are following a route which brings them to a T-junction where they have a free choice between turning left and right the majority will turn right. Design and carry out an experiment to test this hypothesis.

Note
This is taken very seriously by companies choosing stands at exhibitions. It is considered worth paying extra for a location immediately to the right of one of the entrances.

Critical values and critical regions

Exercise 3.3

① A leaflet from the Department of Health recently claimed that 70% of businesses operate a no smoking policy on their premises. A member of the public who believed the true figure to be lower than 70% rang a random sample of 19 businesses to ask whether or not they operated a no smoking policy. She then carried out a hypothesis test.

  (i) Write down the null and alternative hypotheses under test.

  (ii) Of the 19 businesses, k say that they do operate a no smoking policy. Use tables to write down the critical region for a 10% test. (That is, write down the values of k for which the null hypothesis would be rejected at the 10% level of significance.)

  (iii) A second person decided to carry out a similar test, also at the 10% level, but sampled only four businesses. Write down the critical region in this case.

  (iv) Find, for each test, the probability that the null hypothesis is rejected if the true figure is 65%. Hence state which of the two tests is preferable and explain why. [MEI]

② In a certain country, 90% of letters are delivered the day after posting.

A resident posts eight letters on a certain day. Find the probability that

  (i) all eight letters are delivered the next day

  (ii) at least six letters are delivered the next day

  (iii) exactly half the letters are delivered the next day.

  It is later suspected that the service has deteriorated as a result of mechanisation. To test this, 17 letters are posted and it is found that only 13 of them arrive the next day. Let p denote the probability that, after mechanisation, a letter is delivered the next day.

  (iv) Write down suitable null and alternative hypotheses for the value of p.

  (v) Carry out the hypothesis test, at the 5% level of significance, stating your results clearly.

  (vi) Write down the critical region for the test, giving a reason for your choice. [MEI]

③ For most small birds, the ratio of males to females may be expected to be about 1:1. In one ornithological study, birds are trapped by setting fine-mesh nets. The trapped birds are counted and then released. The catch may be regarded as a random sample of the birds in the area.

The ornithologists want to test whether there are more male blackbirds than females.

  (i) Assuming that the sex ratio of blackbirds is 1:1, find the probability that a random sample of 6 blackbirds contains

    (a) 2 males

    (b) at least 2 males.

  (ii) State the null and alternative hypotheses the ornithologists should use.

  In one sample of 16 blackbirds there are 12 males and 4 females.

  (iii) Carry out a suitable test using these data at the 5% significance level, stating your conclusion clearly. Find the critical region for the test.

(iv) Another ornithologist points out that, because female birds spend much time sitting on the nest, females are less likely to be caught than males.

Explain how this would affect your conclusions. [MEI]

4 A seed supplier advertises that, on average, 80% of a certain type of seed will germinate. Suppose that 18 of these seeds, chosen at random, are planted.

(i) Find the probability that 17 or more seeds will germinate if

(a) the supplier's claim is correct

(b) the supplier is incorrect and 82% of the seeds, on average, germinate.

Mr Brewer is the advertising manager for the seed supplier. He thinks that the germination rate may be higher than 80% and he decides to carry out a hypothesis test at the 10% level of significance. He plants 18 seeds.

(ii) Write down the null and alternative hypotheses for Mr Brewer's test, explaining why the alternative hypothesis takes the form it does.

(iii) Find the critical region for Mr Brewer's test. Explain your reasoning.

(iv) Determine the probability that Mr Brewer will reach the *wrong* conclusion if

(a) the true germination rate is 80%

(b) the true germination rate is 82%. [MEI]

4 One-tailed and two-tailed tests

Think back to the two examples in the first part of this chapter.

What would Meg have said if she had lost her last eight tosses?

What would Dave have said if Site 1 had not been the site for any previous winning angler?

In both the examples the claim was not only that something was unusual but that it was so in a particular direction. So you looked only at one side of the distributions when working out the probabilities, as you can see in Figure 3.4 on page 53 and Figure 3.5 on page 57. In both cases we applied one-tailed tests. (The word tail refers to the shaded part at the end of the distribution.)

Suppose that someone claims that Meg has been using a biased coin, but does not specify whether it is in the direction of heads or tails. The next eight tosses of the coin are observed to be all heads. You would then have to work out the probability of a result as extreme on either side of the distribution, in this case eight heads or eight tails, and you would then apply a two-tailed test.

Here is an example of a two-tailed test.

Example 3.5

The producer of a television programme claims that it is politically unbiased.

'If you take somebody off the street it is 50:50 whether he or she will say the programme favours the government or the opposition', she says.

However, when ten people, selected at random, are asked the question 'Does the programme support the government or the opposition?', nine say it supports the government.

Does this constitute evidence, at the 5% significance level, that the producer's claim is inaccurate?

One-tailed and two-tailed tests

Solution

Read the last sentence carefully and you will see that it does not say in which direction the bias must be. It does not ask if the programme is favouring the government or the opposition, only if the producer's claim is inaccurate. So you must consider both ends of the distribution, working out the probability of such an extreme result either way; 9 or 10 saying it favours the government, or 9 or 10 the opposition. This is a two-tailed test.

If p is the probability that somebody believes the programme supports the government, you have

Null hypothesis, H_0: $p = 0.5$ (Claim accurate)

Alternative hypothesis, H_1: $p \neq 0.5$ (Claim inaccurate)

Significance level: 5%

                               Two-tailed test

The situation is modelled by the binomial distribution B(10, 0.5) and is shown in Figure 3.6.

> **Note**
>
> You have to look carefully at the way a test is worded to decide if it should be one-tailed or two-tailed.
>
> Meg claimed she could successfully predict the result of a coin toss; this requires a one-tailed test.
>
> Dave was considering whether Site 1 was an advantageous place to fish; again, this is a one-tailed test.
>
> The test of the television producer's claim was for inaccuracy in either direction and so a two-tailed test was needed.

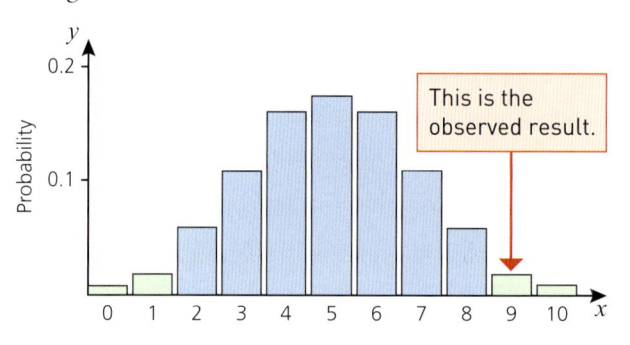

Figure 3.6

This gives

$$P(X = 0) = \frac{1}{1024} \qquad P(X = 1) = \frac{10}{1024}$$

$$P(X = 10) = \frac{1}{1024} \qquad P(X = 9) = \frac{10}{1024}$$

where X is the number of people saying the programme favours the government.

Thus the total probability for the two green tails is $\frac{22}{1024}$ or 2.15%.

Since 2.15% < 5%, the null hypothesis is rejected in favour of the alternative, that the producer's claim is inaccurate.

Asymmetrical cases

In the example above, the distribution was symmetrical and so the two-tailed test was quite simple to apply. In the next case, the distribution is not symmetrical and the test has to be carried out by finding out the critical regions at each tail.

Example 3.6

Pepper moths occur in two varieties, light and dark. The proportion of dark moths increases with certain types of atmospheric pollution.

In a particular village, 25% of the moths are dark, the rest light. A biologist wants to use them as a pollution indicator. She traps samples of 15 moths and counts how many of them are dark.

For what numbers of dark moths among the 15 can she say, at the 10% significance level, that the pollution level is changing?

What is the probability of a Type I error in this test?

Solution

In this question you are asked to find the critical region for the test:

$H_0: p = 0.25$ (The proportion of dark moths is 25%)

$H_1: p \neq 0.25$ (The proportion is no longer 25%)

Significance level: 10%

Two-tailed test

where p is the probability that a moth selected at random is dark.

You want to find each tail to be as nearly as possible 5% but both must be less than 5%, something that is easiest done using cumulative binomial distribution tables (or you can use a calculator).

Look under $n = 15$, for $p = 0.25$.

Table 3.5

n	p \ x	0.050	0.100	0.150	$\frac{1}{6}$	0.200	0.250	0.300	$\frac{1}{3}$	0.350	0.400
15	0	0.4633	0.2059	0.0874	0.0649	0.0352	0.0134	0.0047	0.0023	0.0016	0.0005
	1	0.8290	0.5490	0.3186	0.2596	0.1671	0.0802	0.0353	0.0194	0.0142	0.0052
	2	0.9638	0.8159	0.6042	0.5322	0.3980	0.2361	0.1268	0.0794	0.0617	0.0271
	3	0.9945	0.9444	0.8227	0.7685	0.6482	0.4613	0.2969	0.2092	0.1727	0.0905
	4	0.9994	0.9873	0.9383	0.9102	0.8358	0.6865	0.5155	0.4041	0.3519	0.2173
	5	0.9999	0.9978	0.9832	0.9726	0.9389	0.8516	0.7216	0.6184	0.5643	0.4032
	6	1.0000	0.9997	0.9964	0.9934	0.9819	0.9434	0.8689	0.7970	0.7548	0.6098
	7		1.0000	0.9994	0.9987	0.9958	0.9827	0.9500	0.9118	0.8868	0.7869
	8			0.9999	0.9998	0.9992	0.9958	0.9848	0.9692	0.9578	0.9050
	9			1.0000	1.0000	0.9999	0.9992	0.9963	0.9915	0.9876	0.9662
	10					1.0000	0.9999	0.9993	0.9982	0.9972	0.9907
	11						1.0000	0.9999	0.9997	0.9965	0.9981
	12							1.0000	1.0000	0.9999	0.9997
	13									1.0000	1.0000
	14										
	15										

From this you can see that the left-hand tail includes 0 but not 1 or more; the right-hand tail is 8 and above but not 7.

So the critical regions are less than 1 and more than 7 dark moths in the 15. For these values she would claim the pollution level is changing.

P(Type I error) = P(reject H_0 when true)

= P(result is in critical region when $p = 0.25$)

= 0.0134 + 0.0173 = 0.0307

> **Note**
>
> This is really quite a crude test. The left-hand tail is 1.34%, the right-hand is 1 − 0.9827 or 1.73%. Neither is close to 5%. This situation would be improved if you were to increase the sample size; 15 is a small number of moths on which to base your findings. However, for large samples you would expect to use either the Normal or the Poisson approximation to the binomial distribution; you will meet the second of these in Chapter 6.

One-tailed and two-tailed tests

Exercise 3.4

1. To test the claim that a coin is biased, it is tossed 20 times. It comes down heads 7 times. Test at the 10% significance level whether this claim is justified.

2. A biologist discovers a colony of a previously unknown type of bird nesting in a cave. Out of the 36 chicks which hatch during his period of investigation, 13 are female. Test at the 5% significance level whether this supports the view that the sex ratio for the chicks differs from 1:1.

3. People entering an exhibition have to choose whether to turn left or right. Out of the first twelve people, nine turn left and three turn right. Test at the 5% significance level whether people are more likely to turn one way than another.

4. Weather records for a certain seaside resort show that on average one day in four in April is wet, but local people write to their newspaper complaining that the climate is changing.

    A reporter on the paper records the weather for the next 20 days in April and finds that 10 of them are wet.

    Do you think the complaint is justified? (Assume a 10% significance level.)

5. In a fruit machine there are five drums which rotate independently to show one out of six types of fruit each (lemon, apple, orange, melon, banana and pear). You win a prize if all five stop showing the same fruit. A customer claims that the machine is fixed; the lemon in the first place is not showing the right number of times. The manager runs the machine 20 times and the lemon shows 6 times in the first place. Is the customer's complaint justified at the 10% significance level?

6. A boy is losing in a game of cards and claims that his opponent is cheating.

    Out of the last 18 times he shuffled and dealt the cards, the first card to be laid down was a spade on only one occasion. Can he justify his claim at

    (i) the 10% significance level

    (ii) the 5% significance level?

7. A small colony of 20 individuals of a previously unknown animal is discovered. It is believed it might be the same species as one described by early explorers who said that one-quarter of them were male, the rest female.

    What numbers of males and females would lead you to believe, at the 5% significance level, that they are not the same species?

8. A multiple choice test has 20 questions, with the answer for each allowing four options, A, B, C and D. All the students in a class tell their teacher that they guessed all 20 answers. The teacher does not believe them. Devise a two-tailed test at the 10% significance level to apply to a student's mark to test the hypothesis that the answers were not selected at random.

9. When a certain language is written down, 15% of the letters are Z. Use this information to devise a test at the 10% significance level which somebody who does not know the language could apply to a short passage, 50 letters long, to determine whether it is written in the same language.

⑩ A seed firm states on the packets of bean seeds that the germination rate is 80%. Each packet contains 25 seeds.

(i) How many seeds would you expect to germinate out of one packet?

(ii) What is the probability of exactly 17 germinating?

A man buys a packet and only 2 germinate.

(iii) Is he justified in complaining?

KEY POINTS

Binomial distribution

1 The binomial distribution may be used to model situations in which these conditions hold.
   - You are conducting trials on random samples of a certain size, n.
   - On each trial the outcomes can be classified as either success or failure.

   For the binomial distribution to be a good model, these assumptions are required.
   - The outcome of each trial is independent of the outcome of any other trial.
   - The probability of success, p, is the same on each trial.

2 For a binomial random variable X, where $X \sim B(n, p)$
   - $P(X = r) = {}^nC_r q^{n-r} p^r$ for $r = 0, 1, 2, ..., n$, where $q = 1 - p$

3 For $X \sim B(n, p)$
   - $E(X) = np$
   - $Var(X) = npq$.

4 Hypothesis testing using the binomial distribution.

   (i) This tests the null hypothesis H_0 that $p = k$ against an alternative hypothesis H_1.

   (ii) H_1 could be of the form $p < k$ or $p > k$, both of which lead to a one-tailed test, or $p \neq k$, which gives a two-tailed test.

   (iii) The significance level of the test is the probability that you reject the null hypothesis when it is true.

   (iv) There will be a critical value (or two critical values) where you will reject H_0 if your test statistic (which in the case of a binomial test is the number of successes recorded) is more extreme than this (is in the critical region).

   (v) The region within which the test statistic must fall for you to accept the null hypothesis is called the acceptance region.

   (vi) The p-value of a test is the probability of the test statistic achieving the observed value or a value more extreme than that. It will be compared with the significance level of the test to allow you to make your decision.

LEARNING OUTCOMES

When you have completed this chapter you should be able to:

▶ recognise situations under which the binomial distribution is likely to be an appropriate model

▶ calculate probabilities using a binomial distribution

▶ know and be able to use the mean and variance of a binomial distribution

▶ carry out a hypothesis test on a binomial distribution, which may be one-tailed or two-tailed

▶ understand the vocabulary associated with a hypothesis test

4 Conditional probability

The consequences of an act affect the probability of its occurring again.
B.F. Skinner

This picture shows a tropical lightning storm.

Typically, about two people die per year in the UK from being struck by lightning.

Discussion point
How would you estimate the probability that a particular person will be killed by lightning strike in the UK on Wednesday next week?

You might give an argument along these lines.

There are about 60 million people in the UK.

So the probability of any individual being killed by lightning strike in the next year is

$$\frac{2}{60\,000\,000}$$

There are 365 days in a year so the probability of this happening on any particular day is

$$\frac{2}{60\,000\,000} \times \frac{1}{365} \approx 9 \times 10^{-11}$$

or a little under 1 in 10 billion.

The problem with this argument is that it assumes that all people are equally likely to be victims of lightning strike and that it is equally likely to happen on any day of the year. Neither of these is true.

- Lightning is much more common over the summer months.
- Relevant data show that men are much more likely to be the victims than women.

So the figure of 1 in 10 billion is actually fairly meaningless. The probability is conditional upon other circumstances such as the time of year and the gender and lifestyle of the person.

This chapter is about **conditional probability**.

Notation

In standard notation

- A and B are events.
- The event *not-A* is denoted by A'. $P(A') = 1 - P(A)$.
- $P(A|B)$ means the probability of event A occurring, given that event B has occurred.

You can see the meaning of $P(A|B)$ in this Venn diagram. The fact that event B has already occurred restricts the possibilities to the red region. If event A also occurs the event must be in the overlap region $A \cap B$.

So the probability is given by

$$P(A|B) = \frac{P(A \cap B)}{P(B)}$$

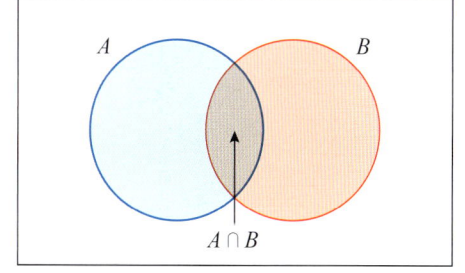

Figure 4.1 Venn diagram

This is a fundamental result in conditional probability.

> **Note**
>
> Important probability results include that:
>
> - A and B are mutually exclusive if and only if they never happen together ($P(A|B) = 0$), which is if and only if $P(A \cap B) = 0$
> - A and B are independent if and only if $P(A|B) = P(A)$, which is if and only if $P(A \cap B) = P(A) \times P(B)$.

> **Note**
>
> A false positive occurs when a person tests positive but has not got the condition. A false negative occurs when a person tests negative but has actually got the condition.

1 Screening tests

Another example of conditional probability arises with medical screening tests.

For many medical conditions, a **screening test** is given to large parts of the population to check if they have the condition. These tests are never 100% reliable and it is often the case that the test suggests that a person has the

Screening tests

condition being screened for when in fact they do not. Such a case is called a **false positive**. On other occasions, the test suggests that a person does not have the condition when in fact they do have it. This type of case is known as a **false negative**. It may at first seem strange that screening tests do not give the correct result 100% of the time, but the human body is a very complex system and screening tests are useful. They provide early diagnosis of conditions that would later become difficult or impossible to treat.

Example 4.1

This contingency table shows the probabilities for the outcomes of a screening test for a medical condition on a randomly selected person.

The following letters describe the sets involved.

C Has the condition C' Does not have the condition

Y Tests positive N Tests negative

Table 4.1

	C	C'
Y	0.20	0.15
N	0.05	0.60

(i) Copy the table and add in the marginal totals.

(ii) Find the probabilities that a randomly selected person

(a) has the condition and tests positive, (b) has the condition, (c) tests positive.

Use set notation as well as giving the values of your answers.

(iii) Find the probability that a person who has the condition tests positive.

(iv) Find the percentages of false positives and false negatives given by the test. Hence state the percentage of incorrect results it gives.

Discussion point

In this example, set notation was used to describe most of the events. You will find it helpful to relate these to a Venn diagram below.

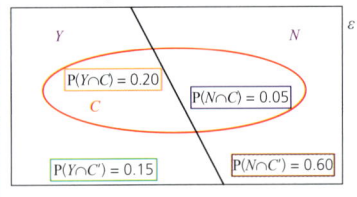

Figure 4.2

What sets do the various regions represent? What probabilities are associated with them?

Solution

(i) The marginal totals are given in **red**.

Table 4.2

	C	C'	
Y	0.20	0.15	0.35
N	0.05	0.60	0.65
	0.25	0.75	1

(ii) (a) $P(C \cap Y) = 0.20$ (b) $P(C) = 0.25$ (c) $P(Y) = 0.35$.

(iii) $P(Y|C) = \dfrac{P(Y \cap C)}{P(C)} = \dfrac{0.2}{0.25} = 0.8$.

(iv) False positives $P(C' \cap Y) = 0.15 = 15\%$

False negatives $P(C \cap N) = 0.05 = 5\%$

Incorrect results $15\% + 5\% = 20\%$

Another way to represent conditional probabilities is to use a tree diagram, as in the next example.

Example 4.2

This contingency table, together with the marginal totals, shows the probabilities for the outcomes of a screening test for a medical condition on a randomly selected person.

Table 4.3

	C	C'	
Y	0.20	0.15	**0.35**
N	0.05	0.60	**0.65**
	0.25	**0.75**	**1**

> This is the same table as in Example 4.1.

(i) Draw a tree diagram to illustrate the same information, marking in all the relevant probabilities.

(ii) Using appropriate notation, describe the numbers that appear vertically above and below each other in the tree diagram.

(iii) Show that $P(Y) = P(Y|C) \times P(C) + P(Y|C') \times P(C')$.

> **Discussion point**
> Identify which of the numbers in the table in the question feature in the tree diagram, and where they appear.
> State which numbers in the table do not feature in the tree diagram.
> Would your answers be the same if you drew the tree diagram with Y and N for the left-hand branches and C and C' for the right-hand branches?

Solution

(i)

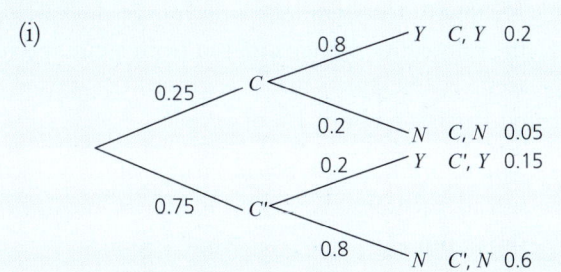

```
                  0.8   Y   C, Y   0.2
           0.25  /
               C
                \
                  0.2   N   C, N   0.05
                  0.2   Y   C', Y  0.15
           0.75  /
               C'
                \
                  0.8   N   C', N  0.6
```

Figure 4.3

(ii) Left-hand branches $0.25 = P(C), 0.75 = P(C')$

Right-hand branches $0.8 = P(Y|C), 0.2 = P(N|C)$

$0.2 = P(Y|C'), 0.8 = P(N|C')$

Right-hand line $0.2 = P(C \cap Y), 0.05 = P(C \cap N),$

$0.15 = P(C' \cap Y), 0.6 = P(C' \cap N)$

(iii) In numbers $P(Y) = 0.25 \times 0.8 + 0.75 \times 0.2$

> Multiplying along the branches and adding the two cases where Y occurs.

In symbols $P(Y) = P(C) \times P(Y|C) + P(C') \times P(Y|C')$
$= P(Y|C) \times P(C) + P(Y|C') \times P(C')$

as required.

> **Note**
> This result can be written for events A and B as
> $P(B) = P(B|A) \times P(A) + P(B|A') \times P(A')$.

The next example shows how important it is to specify the prior conditions correctly when using conditional probability.

Screening tests

Figure 4.4

Example 4.3

A robbery has taken place on one of the UK's islands. When carrying out the crime, the robber suffered from a cut and left a sample of blood at the scene. A test shows that it is group AB–; this is the rarest group in the UK, occurring in about 1% of people.

The police have the blood groups of a few of the island's 800 residents on record, including Tom who is AB– . On this evidence alone, he is arrested for the crime.

- The arresting officer says 'The national figures for this blood group mean that the probability that you are innocent is 1% and so that you are guilty is 99%'.
- Tom's solicitor says 'About eight people on the island will have this blood group, so, in the absence of any other evidence, the probability that my client is guilty is only $12\frac{1}{2}$% and that he is innocent is $87\frac{1}{2}$%'.

(i) Which one of these two statements is correct?

(ii) How would you explain the fault in the other statement?

> **Note**
>
> Explaining why the other statement is wrong requires some thought. The arresting officer has, in fact, made a well-known error called **the prosecutor's fallacy**.
>
> In order to use probability in the analysis of a situation like this, you have to be very careful to ask the right question.

Solution

(i) The solicitor's statement is correct.

The expected number of people on the island with AB– blood is $800 \times 1\% = 8$.

So the probability that the blood is from Tom is $\frac{1}{8} = 0.125$ or 12.5%.

> **Discussion point**
> This example was set on an island with a small population. This allowed the solicitor's statement to be fairly obviously correct. If it had been set in, say, somewhere in London it would not have been possible to quantify the probability that the accused person was innocent and so the prosecutor's fallacy might have seemed more plausible, even though it was still completely false.
>
> Is there a danger of the prosecutor's fallacy being used in cases where identification is carried out on the basis of DNA?

(ii) There are three relevant events.

R A blood sample selected at random is AB−,

T The blood sample came from Tom,

I Tom is innocent.

The arresting officer asked

'What is the probability that a random blood sample is AB−?'

i.e. 'What is the value of P(R)?'

The officer has made the reasonable assumption that people's criminal tendencies and their blood groups are independent. So the question he asked is equivalent to

'What is the probability that an innocent person has blood group AB−?'

i.e. 'What is the value of P($R\,|\,I$)?'

However, this is the wrong question because it is known that event R has occurred but it is not known that event I has occurred.

The correct question is

'Given that an AB− sample has been found, what is the probability that it came from Tom?'

i.e. 'What is the value of P($T\,|\,R$)?'

The sample came from Tom if and only if he is guilty. So the probability that he is innocent is given by

P(I) = 1 − P($T\,|\,R$).

The last example involved the prosecutor's fallacy. It showed that, without clear thinking, it is all too easy to go wrong with conditional probability, with potentially serious consequences. This is illustrated in the next example.

Example 4.4

A screening test for a particular condition is not 100% reliable. In fact, the probability that a person who has the condition tests positive is 0.97. The probability that a person who does not have the condition tests positive is 0.01. The proportion of the population which has the condition is 1.5%.

A person is selected at random and tested for the condition.

(i) Using A for the event that the person does not have the condition and B for the event that the person tests positive, illustrate this situation on a tree diagram.

(ii) Find the probability that the person tests positive.

(iii) The person tests positive. Find the probability that the person does not have the condition.

(iv) In the light of your answer to part (iii), comment briefly on the effectiveness of the test.

Screening tests

Solution

(i)

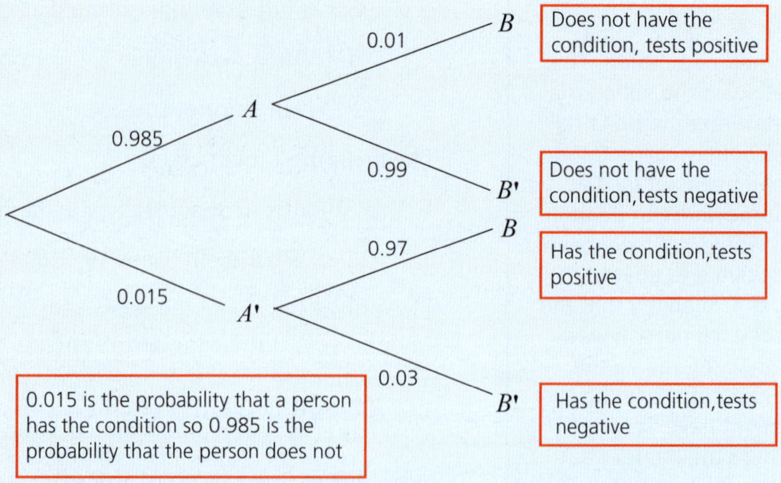

```
                            0.01      B   Does not have the
                         ┌──────                 condition, tests positive
              0.985   A ─┤
           ┌────────────  0.99     B'  Does not have the
           │             └──────        condition, tests negative
           │                      B    Has the condition, tests
           │             ┌0.97─────     positive
           │   0.015  A'─┤
           └────────────  0.03    B'  Has the condition, tests
                         └──────       negative
```

> 0.015 is the probability that a person has the condition so 0.985 is the probability that the person does not

Figure 4.5

> To find the probability that the person tests positive, you need to include both those who have the condition and those who do not.

(ii) $P(B) = 0.985 \times 0.01 + 0.015 \times 0.97$

$ = 0.00985 + 0.01455$

$ = 0.0244$

(iii) To find the probability that someone who tested positive (event B) does not have the condition (event A), use the conditional probability formula

$$P(A \mid B) = \frac{P(A \cap B)}{P(B)}.$$

From part (ii) you know that $P(B) = 0.0244$.

From the tree diagram $P(A \cap B) = 0.985 \times 0.01 = 0.00985$

> $P(A \cap B)$ is the probability that the person does not have the condition and tests positive.
>
> You can find this by multiplying along the A and B branches of the tree diagram.

So $P(A' \mid B) = \dfrac{0.00985}{0.0244} = 0.404$.

(iv) The test has a false positive rate of just over 40%. This does seem rather high. The false positives would need further tests to determine whether they actually have the condition and would be unnecessarily worried. On the other hand, under 1% of the population would be in this situation so the screening test may still be worthwhile. Also over half of the positives would actually have the condition.

> **Note**
>
> The event $A \mid B$ is an example of a false positive

Exercise 4.1

1. It is given that P(A) = 0.25, P(B) = 0.13 and P($A \cap B$) = 0.05.
   (i) Find P($A \cup B$).
   (ii) Find P($A\,|\,B$).
   (iii) Find P($B\,|\,A$).

2. Steve is going on holiday. The probability that he is delayed on his outward flight is 0.3. The probability that he is delayed on his return flight is 0.2, independently of whether or not he is delayed on the outward flight.
   (i) Find the probability that Steve is delayed on his outward flight but not on his return flight.
   (ii) Find the probability that he is delayed on at least one of the two flights.
   (iii) Given that he is delayed on at least one flight, find the probability that he is delayed on both flights. [MEI]

3. In the 2001 census, people living in Wales were asked whether or not they could speak Welsh. A resident of Wales is selected at random.
   - W is the event that this person speaks Welsh.
   - C is the event that this person is a child.

   You are given that P(W) = 0.20, P(C) = 0.17 and P($W \cap C$) = 0.06.
   (i) Determine whether the events W and C are independent.
   (ii) Draw a Venn diagram, showing the events W and C, and mark in the probability corresponding to each region of your diagram.
   (iii) Find P($W\,|\,C$).
   (iv) Given that P($W\,|\,C'$) = 0.169, use this information and your answer to part (iii) to comment very briefly on how the ability to speak Welsh differs between children and adults. [MEI]

4. When it is reasonably dry, I cycle to work. Otherwise I take the bus. On one day in ten, on average, it is too wet for me to cycle. If I cycle, the probability that I am late for work is 0.02. If I take the bus, the probability that I am late for work is 0.15.
   (i) Find the probability that I am late on a randomly chosen day.
   (ii) Given that I am late, find the probability that I cycled.

5. A screening test for a particular disease has a probability of 0.99 of giving a positive result for somebody who has the disease and of 0.05 for somebody who does not have the disease. It is thought that 0.35% of the population have the disease.
   (i) Find the probability that a randomly selected person tests positive.
   (ii) Find the probability that a randomly selected person has the disease given that they test positive.
   (iii) Write down the probability that a randomly selected person does not have the disease given that they test positive.
   (iv) In the light of your answers to parts (ii) and (iii), comment briefly on the effectiveness of the test.

Screening tests

6. A machine which makes gear wheels has two settings, fast and slow. On the fast setting, 10% of the gear wheels are faulty. On the slow setting, 1% of them are faulty. One day, 1000 gear wheels are made using the fast setting and 500 using the slow setting.
   (i) Find the probability that a randomly selected gear wheel from the day's production is faulty.
   (ii) Given that a gear wheel is faulty, find the probability that the machine was on the slow setting when it was manufactured.

7. Two thirds of the trains which I catch on my local railway line have four coaches and the rest have eight coaches (the eight coach trains are run during busy periods). If I catch a four coach train, the probability of me getting a seat is 0.7. If I catch an eight coach train, the probability of me getting a seat is 0.9. Given that I get a seat on a train, find the probability that it is a train with four coaches.

8. A company which runs a large fleet of HGVs (heavy goods vehicles) regularly tests its employees for consumption of illegal drugs. The test is not 100% reliable, so if somebody is found to be positive, further testing is carried out. The false positive rate is 0.5% and the false negative rate is 3%. You should assume that 1% of employees have taken drugs preceding the test.
   (i) Find the probability that a randomly selected person tests positive.
   (ii) Find the probability that a randomly selected person has consumed illegal drugs, given that they test positive.

9. Three machines, A, B and C are used to make dress fabric. Machine A makes 50% of the fabric, Machine B makes 30% and Machine C makes the remainder. Each piece of fabric is checked for defects. The percentages of defective fabric for Machines A, B and C are 2, 4 and 1.5, respectively.
   (i) Find the probability that a randomly selected piece of fabric is defective.
   (ii) Given that a piece of fabric is defective, find the probability that it was produced on Machine A.

10. Onions often suffer from a disease called white rot. This disease stays in the soil for several years, and when onions are planted in infected ground, they can get the disease. A gardener grows onions in four separate plots Q, R, S and T, so that there is less risk of most of her onions getting white rot. She grows an equal number of onions in each plot.

    The percentages of onions in each plot which get white rot are as follows
    - Plot Q 2%
    - Plot R 3%
    - Plot S 60%
    - Plot T 8%.

    (i) Find the probability that a randomly selected onion has white rot.
    (ii) Given that a randomly selected onion has white rot, find the probability that it came from plot S.

KEY POINTS

1 The conditional probability of event A given the event B has occurred is given by

$$P(A|B) = \frac{P(A \cap B)}{P(B)}$$

2 It is often helpful to use a tree diagram or a contingency table to illustrate a situation involving conditional probability.
3 In contexts such as a medical screening test:
   - a false positive occurs when a person tests positive but has not got the condition
   - a false negative occurs when a person tests negative but actually has got the condition.

LEARNING OUTCOMES

When you have completed this chapter you should be able to:
➤ understand and use the notation associated with conditional probability
➤ use tree diagrams and contingency tables to illustrate situations involving conditional probability
➤ solve problems involving conditional probability.

Practice questions: set 1

① The Highways Authority proposes to impose new parking restrictions on a small town. The Town Council fear that it will be bad for trade, and so for the town's prosperity. They plan to object, but first they need data so that they can estimate the cost to the town.

The council call a special meeting. Their room can only take 20 more people (in addition to the councillors) and they invite

    8 of the 41 shops

    7 of the 33 restaurants and cafes

    5 of the 27 hotels and bed and breakfasts.

(i) Describe the sort of sample they have selected. Explain how they decided on the numbers from the various groups. [3 marks]

(ii) They use a random selection procedure to describe who actually gets invited. Describe two possible ways they might do this. [2 marks]

(iii) Explain why those selected are not a simple random sample. [1 mark]

At the meeting, those present are asked to estimate the annual cost, to the nearest £1000, to their businesses if the parking restrictions go ahead. Their replies, in thousands of pounds, are given in the table below.

Table 1

Shops	2	1	5	0	12	10	8	3
Restaurants and cafes	1	2	2	1	3	2	1	-
Hotels and B&B	15	0	0	10	1	-	-	-

(iv) Use these figures to estimate the total cost of the parking restrictions to the town. [3 marks]

(v) Comment on the likely accuracy of the estimate and suggest measures that might be taken to improve it. [2 marks]

② Given that X has a binomial distribution in which $n = 15$ and $p = 0.5$, find the probability of each of the following events.

(i) $X = 4$ [1 mark]

(ii) $X \leq 4$ [1 mark]

(iii) $X = 4$ or $X = 11$ [1 mark]

(iv) $X \leq 4$ or $X \geq 11$ [1 mark]

A large company is considering introducing a new selection procedure for job applicants. The selection procedure is intended to result over a long period in equal numbers of men and women being offered jobs. The new procedure is tried with a random sample of applicants and 5 of them, 1 woman and 4 men, are offered jobs.

(v) Carry out a suitable test at the 5% level of significance to determine whether it is reasonable to suppose that the selection procedure is performing as intended. You should state the null and alternative hypothesis under test and explain carefully how you arrive at your conclusions. [6 marks]

③ The scatter diagrams below were constructed from data on 248 adult patients at a clinic in the United States. Weights are in kg, heights are in cm and ages are completed in years.

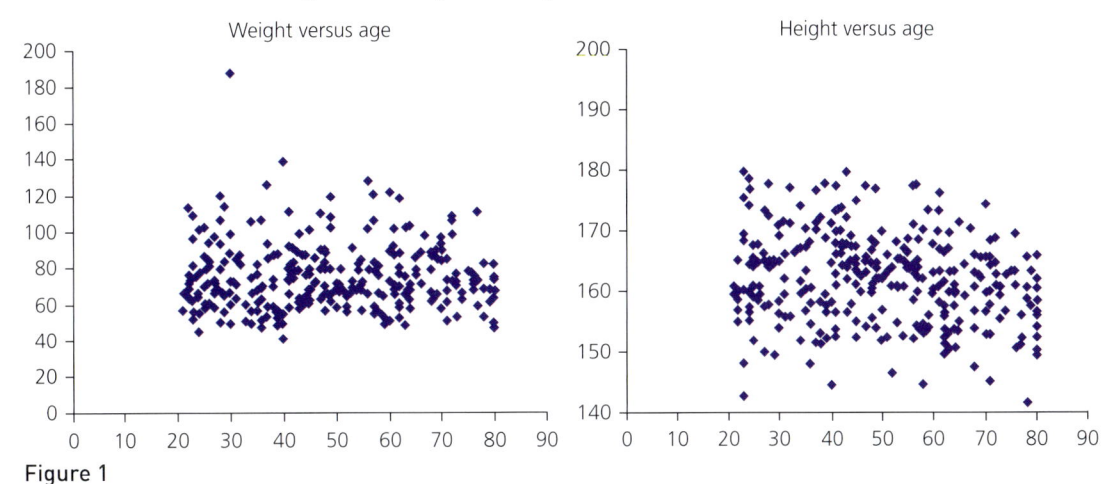

Weight versus age

Height versus age

Figure 1

(i) Aster says that the average weight is much the same for patients of all ages, but the spread of weights is less for older patients. State what features of the weight versus age scatter diagrams support these conclusions.

Comment in similar terms on the relationship between height and age for these patients. [4 marks]

(ii) Estimate the mean weight and mean height for these patients. Hence, given that all the patients are of the same sex, state with a reason whether they are men or women. [4 marks]

(iii) For these data it is possible to calculate three product moment correlation coefficients: weight and age, height and age, weight and height. The values of these three coefficients, in random order, are −0.17, −0.05, and 0.31. State, with justification, which correlation has the value of 0.31. [2 marks]

(iv) Explain why, without further information, it would not be advisable to regard these data as representative of the population in the area where the clinic is situated. [2 marks]

④ Births, deaths and marriages are listed for England and Wales (and separately for other parts of the UK). As part of a pilot study, three research students, A, B and C, selected samples of the ages of women who died in 2016 from the list, using random numbers.

Summary data for their samples are:

Table 2

A	$n = 25$,	$\Sigma x = 2038$,	$\Sigma x^2 = 168\,545$
B	$n = 40$,	$\Sigma x = 2720$,	$\Sigma x^2 = 214\,893$
C	$n = 40$,	$\Sigma x = 3230$,	$\Sigma x^2 = 214\,893$

(i) Describe the samples that the research students took. [1 mark]

(ii) Find the mean and standard deviation for each of the samples. Explain why they are not all the same. [4 marks]

(iii) Find the mean and standard deviation when the three samples are put together. Comment on the likely accuracy of your answer. [3 marks]

Practice questions: set 1

5 Esperanza buys a large number of Premium Bonds. These bonds are entered into a monthly draw and may win a prize. Esperanza calculates that her probability of winning one or more prizes in any month is 0.4.

(i) Find the probability that Esperanza wins

   (A) her first prize in the third month [1 mark]

   (B) no prizes in the first six months [1 mark]

   (C) no prizes in the first six months but at least one prize in the first year [2 marks]

   (D) something in exactly two months of the first six. [2 marks]

(ii) Esperanza wonders if her chance of winning one or more prizes in any month is actually less than 0.4. She decides to conduct a hypothesis test at the 5% level. In the next year, there are 2 months in which she wins something.

What should her conclusion be? [6 marks]

6 It is sometimes claimed that the height of most humans is about equal to their arm span. In order to investigate this, data were obtained from the *CensusAtSchool* website. A random sample of 50 sixth form students was taken. The data, in cm and sorted by arm span, start and finish as in the table on the left.

(i) Explain why I would be sensible to eliminate the first three data points from the sample. What seems to have happened here? [2 marks]

It seems likely that the fourth data point is an error too, and there is some doubt about the fifth. So the subsequent investigation is based on just 45 data points. Two students analyse the data.

(ii) Annabel finds that the PMCC for the data is 0.85 and she states that this provides strong evidence that the height and arm span are almost equal. Explain why Annabel is wrong. [2 marks]

(iii) Boris finds the regression line of height (y) on the arm span (x) to be as follows.

$$y = 1.017x - 3.989$$

Discuss briefly whether or not Boris could argue that height and arm span are nearly equal. [3 marks]

[60 marks]

	A	B
1	Height	Arm span
2	170	50
3	170	50
4	164	67
5	165	100
6	162	132
7	158	151
8	164	152
9	153	153
10	167	154
42	180	175
43	173	177
44	178	178
45	173	179
46	174	183
47	181	183
48	183	183
49	187	189
50	190	196
51	205	207

Figure 2

5 Discrete random variables

Probability theory is nothing but common sense reduced to calculation.
Pierre Simon Laplace

An archery competition is held each month. In the first round of the competition, each competitor has five tries at hitting a small target. Those who hit the target at least three times get through to the next round. In April, there are 250 competitors in the first round. The frequencies of the different numbers of possible successes are as follows.

Table 5.1

Number of successes	0	1	2	3	4	5
Frequency	65	89	48	21	11	16

The numbers of successes are necessarily discrete. A discrete frequency distribution is best illustrated by a vertical line chart, as in Figure 5.1. This shows you that the distribution has positive skew, with the bulk of the data at the lower end of the distribution.

Discrete random variables

Figure 5.1

The survey involved 250 competitors. This is a reasonably large sample and so it is reasonable to use the results to estimate the **probabilities** of the various possible outcomes: 0, 1, 2, 3, 4, 5 successes. You divide each frequency by 250 to obtain the **relative frequency**, or probability, of each outcome (number of successes).

Table 5.2

Outcome (Number of successes)	0	1	2	3	4	5
Probability	0.260	0.356	0.192	0.084	0.044	0.064

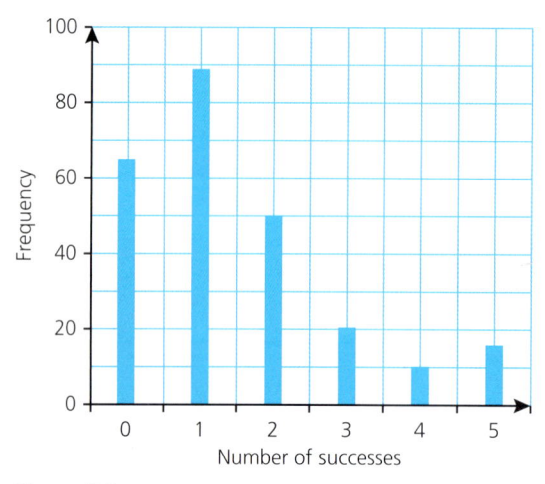

> **Note**
> You can draw a diagram to show this **probability distribution**. It is identical in shape to Figure 5.1 but with probability rather than frequency on the vertical axis.

You now have a **mathematical model** to describe a particular situation. In statistics, you are often looking for models to describe and explain the data you find in the real world. In this chapter, you are introduced to some of the techniques for working with models for discrete data. Such models are called **discrete random variables**.

> For example: the number of rolls to get a six on a die.

The number of successes is a **random variable** since the actual value of the outcome is variable and can only be predicted with a given probability, i.e. the outcomes occur at random. The random variable is **discrete** since the number of successes is an integer (between 0 and 5).

In the archery competition, the maximum number of successes is five so the variable is **finite**, and so, for example, if each competitor had ten tries, then the maximum would be ten. In this case, there would be eleven possible outcomes (including zero). Two well-known examples of a finite discrete random variable are the **binomial distribution** (which you met in Chapter 3) and the **uniform distribution** (which you will meet later in this chapter).

By contrast, if you considered the number of times you need to roll a pair of dice to get a double six, there is no theoretical maximum, and so the distribution is **infinite**. A well-known example of an infinite discrete random variable is the Poisson distribution, which you will meet in Chapter 6.

1 Notation and conditions for a discrete random variable

- A random variable is denoted by an upper case letter, such as X, Y, or Z.
- The particular values that the random variable takes are denoted by lower case letters, such as x, y, z and r.
- In the case of a discrete variable these are sometimes given suffixes such as $r_1, r_2, r_3, \ldots$
- Thus $P(X = r_1)$ means the probability that the random variable X takes a particular value r_1.
- If a finite discrete random variable can take n distinct values $r_1, r_2, \ldots, r_n$, with associated probabilities $p_1, p_2, \ldots, p_n$, then the sum of the probabilities must equal 1.
- In that case, $p_1 + p_2 + \ldots + p_n = 1$.
- This can be written more formally as

$$\sum_{k=1}^{n} p_k = \sum_{k=1}^{n} P(X = r_k) = 1.$$

- If there is no ambiguity, then

$$\sum_{k=1}^{n} P(X = r_k)$$

is often abbreviated to

$$\sum P(X = r).$$

> **Note**
> You will often see the expression $P(X = r)$ in a table heading.

> The various outcomes cover all possibilities; they are **exhaustive**.

Example 5.1

The probability distribution of a random variable X is given by

$P(X = r) = kr^2$ for $r = 3, 4, 5$

$P(X = r) = 0$ otherwise.

(i) Find the value of the constant k.

(ii) Illustrate the distribution and describe the shape of the distribution.

(iii) Two successive values of X are generated independently of each other. Find the probability that

  (a) both values of X are the same

  (b) the total of the two values of X is greater than 8.

Notation and conditions for a discrete random variable

Solution

(i) Tabulating the probability distribution for X gives:

Table 5.3

r	3	4	5
$P(X = r)$	$9k$	$16k$	$25k$

Since X is a random variable,

$$\Sigma(P(X = r)) = 1$$
$$9k + 16k + 25k = 1$$
$$50k = 1$$
$$k = 0.02$$

Hence $P(X = r) = 0.02r^2$ for $r = 3, 4, 5$ which gives the following probability distribution.

Table 5.4

r	3	4	5
$P(X = r)$	0.18	0.32	0.50

(ii) The vertical line chart in Figure 5.2 illustrates this distribution. It has negative skew.

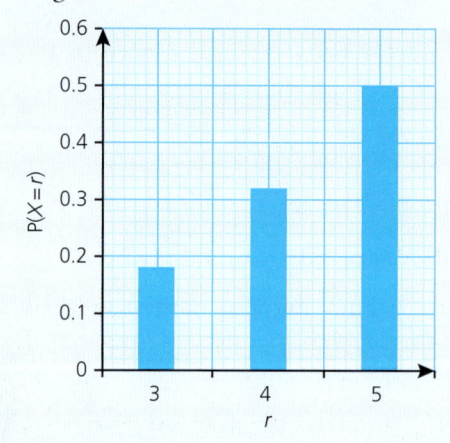

Figure 5.2

(iii) (a) P(both values of X are the same)

$$= (0.18)^2 + (0.32)^2 + (0.5)^2$$
$$= 0.0324 + 0.1024 + 0.25$$
$$= 0.3848$$

> The ways of getting a total greater than 8 are: 4 and 5, 5 and 4, 5 and 5

(b) P(total of the two values is greater than 8)

$$= 0.32 \times 0.5 + 0.5 \times 0.32 + 0.5 \times 0.5$$
$$= 0.16 + 0.16 + 0.25$$
$$= 0.57$$

Exercise 5.1

① A fair five-sided spinner has faces labelled 1, 2, 3, 4, 5. The random variable X represents the score when the spinner is spun.

(i) Copy and complete the table below to show the probability distribution of X.

Table 5.5

r	1	2	3		
P(X = r)	0.2				

(ii) Illustrate the distribution.

(iii) Find the values of
  (a) $P(X > 2)$
  (b) $P(X \text{ is even})$
  (c) $P(X > 5)$.

② The probability distribution of a discrete random variable X is given by
$P(X = r) = kr$ for $r = 1, 2, 3, 4$
$P(X = r) = 0$ otherwise.

(i) Copy and complete the table below to show the probability distribution of X in terms of k.

Table 5.6

r	1	2	3	
P(X = r)				4k

(ii) Use the fact that the sum of the probabilities is equal to 1 to find the value of k.

(iii) Find the values of
  (a) $P(X = 4)$
  (b) $P(X < 4)$.

③ A fair three-sided spinner has faces labelled 1, 2 and 3. The random variable X is given by the sum of the scores when the spinner is spun three times.

(i) Find the probability distribution of X.

(ii) Illustrate the distribution and describe the shape of the distribution.

(iii) Find the values of
  (a) $P(X > 6)$
  (b) $P(X \text{ is odd})$
  (c) $P(|X - 4| < 2)$.

④ The random variable Y is given by the absolute difference when the spinner in Question 1 is spun twice.

(i) Find the probability distribution of Y.

(ii) Illustrate the distribution and describe the shape of the distribution.

(iii) Find the values of
  (a) $P(Y < 2)$
  (b) $P(Y \text{ is even})$.

Notation and conditions for a discrete random variable

5. Two ordinary dice are thrown. The random variable X is the product of the numbers shown on the dice.
   (i) Find the probability distribution of X.
   (ii) What is the probability that any throw of the two dice results in a value of X which is an even number?

6. The probability distribution of a discrete random variable X is given by
   $$P(X = r) = \frac{kr}{4} \text{ for } r = 2, 3, 4, 5$$
   $P(X = r) = 0$ otherwise.
   (i) Find the value of k and tabulate the probability distribution.
   (ii) If two successive values of X are generated independently find the probability that
      (a) the two values are equal
      (b) the first value is less than the second value.

7. A curiously-shaped five-faced spinner produces scores, X, for which the probability distribution is given by
   $$P(X = r) = k(r^2 + 2r + 10) \text{ for } r = 0, 1, 2, 3, 4$$
   $P(X = r) = 0$ otherwise.
   (i) Find the value of k and illustrate the distribution.
   (ii) Show that, when this spinner is spun twice, the probability of obtaining one non-zero score which is exactly twice the other is very nearly 0.18.

8. Four fair coins are tossed.
   (i) By considering the set of possible outcomes, HHHH, HHHT, etc., tabulate the probability distribution of X, the number of heads occurring.
   (ii) Illustrate the distribution and describe the shape of the distribution.
   (iii) Find the probability that there are more heads than tails.
   (iv) Without further calculation, state whether your answer to part (iii) would be the same if five fair coins were tossed. Give a reason for your answer.

9. A doctor is investigating the numbers of children, X, which women have in a country. She notes that the probability that a woman has more than five children is negligible. She suggests the following model for X.
   $P(X = 0) = 0.3$
   $P(X = r) = k(12 + 3r - r^2)$ for $r = 1, 2, 3, 4, 5$
   $P(X = r) = 0$ otherwise.
   (i) Find the value of k and write the probability distribution as a table.
   (ii) Find the probability that two women chosen at random both have more than three children.

10. A motoring magazine correspondent conducts a survey of the numbers of people per car travelling along a stretch of motorway. He denotes the number by the random variable X which he finds to have the following probability distribution.

    Table 5.7

r	1	2	3	4	5	6+
$P(X = r)$	0.57	0.28	a	0.04	0.01	negligible

(i) Find the value of *a*.

He wants to find an algebraic model for the distribution and suggests the following model.

$P(X = r) = k(2^{-r})$ for $r = 1, 2, 3, 4, 5$

$P(X = r) = 0$ otherwise.

(ii) Find the value of *k* for this model.

(iii) Compare the algebraic model with the probabilities he found, illustrating both distributions on one diagram. Do you think it is a good model?

⑪ A box contains six black pens and four red pens. Three pens are taken at random from the box.

(i) Illustrate the various outcomes on a probability tree diagram.

(ii) The random variable *X* represents the number of black pens obtained. Find the probability distribution of *X*.

2 Expectation and variance

The next round of the archery competition is held in May. In this month's competition there are 200 competitors altogether. The organisers of the competition would like to increase the number of people getting through to the next round, without changing the rules. They decide to give each of the competitors a relaxation session before their attempt. The number of successes for each competitor this time is as follows.

> **Discussion point**
>
> How would you compare the results in the competitions?

Table 5.8

Number of successes	0	1	2	3	4	5
Frequency	36	54	60	19	15	16

The competition involves 200 people. This is again a reasonably large sample and so, once again, it is reasonable to use the results to estimate the probabilities of the various possible outcomes: 0, 1, 2, 3, 4, 5 successes, as before.

Table 5.9

Outcome (Number of successes)	0	1	2	3	4	5
Probability (Relative frequency)	0.18	0.27	0.30	0.095	0.075	0.08

> **Note**
>
> The mode, or modal value of a DRV *X* is the value of *X* that has the highest probability associated with it.
>
> The median value of a DRV is the value of *X* that is 'halfway through the probability'. More formally, the median of *X* is the smallest value of *s* (where *r* and *s* are consecutive values of *X* in the table) so that both $P(X \le r) < 0.5$ and $P(X \le s) \ge 0.5$.
>
> If the first value *r* of *X* is such that $P(X \le r) \ge 0.5$, then *r* is the median.

One way to compare the two probability distributions, in April and in May, is to calculate a measure of central tendency and a measure of spread.

You can see from Table 5.9 that the mode is 2 since this has the highest probability. You can also work out the median.

The probability that $X < 2$ is $0.18 + 0.27 = 0.45$ and the probability that $X > 2$ is $0.095 + 0.075 + 0.08 = 0.25$.

Since both of these are less than 0.5, the median must be at $X = 2$.

Just as you can calculate the mean and variance of a frequency distribution, you can also do something very similar for a probability distribution.

- The most useful measure of central tendency for a probability distribution is the **mean** or **expectation** of the random variable. This is denoted by μ.

Expectation and variance

- The most useful measure of spread for a probability distribution is the **variance**, σ^2, or its square root the **standard deviation**, σ.

The expectation is given by $E(X) = \mu = \Sigma r P(X = r)$. Its calculation is shown below using the probability distribution for the archers in May (after the relaxation session) as an example.

Table 5.10

r	P(X = r)	rP(X = r)
0	0.18	0
1	0.27	0.27
2	0.30	0.60
3	0.095	0.285
4	0.075	0.30
5	0.08	0.4
Totals	1	1.855

> **Note**
> You will find it helpful to set your work out systematically in a table like this.

In this case:
$$E(X) = \mu = \Sigma r P(X = r)$$
$$= 0 \times 0.18 + 1 \times 0.27 + 2 \times 0.30 + 3 \times 0.095 + 4 \times 0.075 + 5 \times 0.08$$
$$= \mathbf{1.855}$$

There are two common ways of giving the variance.

Either $\text{Var}(X) = \sigma^2 = E(X^2) - [E(X)]^2$

or $E(X - \mu)^2 = \Sigma(r - \mu)^2 P(X = r)$

> This version can be remembered as 'The expectation of the squares minus the square of the expectation'. It can also be written as $E(X^2) - \mu^2$.

To see how variance is calculated the same probability distribution is used as an example.

> **Note**
> You will use these statistics later to compare the distribution of numbers of successes with and without the relaxation session.

The table below shows the working for the variance in May after the relaxation session, using both of the methods above.

Table 5.11

r	P(X = r)	r²P(X = r)
0	0.18	0
1	0.27	0.27
2	0.30	1.2
3	0.095	0.855
4	0.075	1.2
5	0.08	2
Totals	1	**5.525**

r	P(X = r)	$(r-\mu)^2 P(X = r)$
0	0.18	0.6194
1	0.27	0.1974
2	0.30	0.0063
3	0.095	0.1245
4	0.075	0.3451
5	0.08	0.7913
Totals	1	**2.0840**

> The mean, μ, was found above. It is **1.855**.

> **Discussion point**
> Using these two statistics, judge the success or otherwise of the relaxation session.

(a) $\text{Var}(X) = \Sigma r^2 P(X=r) - [\Sigma r P(X=r)]^2$
$= 5.525 - 1.855^2$
$= 2.084$

(b) $\text{Var}(X) = \Sigma(r-\mu)^2 P(X=r)$
$= 2.084$

The standard deviation of X is therefore $\sqrt{2.084} = 1.44$

In practice, the computation is usually easier in Method (a), especially when the expectation is not a whole number.

ACTIVITY 5.1
Show that the expectation and variance of the probability distribution in April (without the relaxation session) are 1.49 and 1.97, respectively.

Example 5.2

The discrete random variable X has the following probability distribution:

Table 5.12

r	0	1	2	3
$P(X=r)$	0.2	0.3	0.4	0.1

Find

(i) $E(X)$

(ii) $\text{Var}(X)$ using (a) $E(X^2) - \mu^2$ (b) $E[(X-\mu)^2]$.

Solution

(i) Table 5.13

r	$P(X=r)$	$rP(X=r)$
0	0.2	0
1	0.3	0.3
2	0.4	0.8
3	0.1	0.3
Totals	1	1.4

> To find $E(X)$ you simply multiply each value of r by its probability and then add.

$E(X) = \mu = \Sigma r P(X=r)$
$= 0 \times 0.2 + 1 \times 0.3 + 2 \times 0.4 + 3 \times 0.1$
$= 1.4$

Expectation and variance

> **Discussion point**
> Look carefully at both methods for calculating the variance. Are there any situations where one method might be preferred to the other?

(ii)
Table 5.14

r	$P(X = r)$	$r^2 P(X = r)$
0	0.2	0
1	0.3	0.3
2	0.4	1.6
3	0.1	0.9
Totals	1	2.8

r	$P(X = r)$	$(r - \mu)^2 P(X = r)$
0	0.2	0.392
1	0.3	0.048
2	0.4	0.144
3	0.1	0.256
Totals	1	0.84

(a) $\text{Var}(X) = \sigma^2 = E(X^2) - \mu^2$
$= 2.8 - 1.4^2$
$= 0.84$

(b) $\text{Var}(X) = \sigma^2 = E\left([X - \mu]^2\right)$
$= \Sigma (r - \mu)^2 P(X = r)$
$= 0.84$

Notice that the two methods of calculating the variance in part (ii) give the same result, since one formula is just an algebraic rearrangement of the other. In practice, you would not need to use both methods and so only either the left-hand or the right-hand table would be needed to calculate the variance, according to which method you are using.

ACTIVITY 5.2

Use a spreadsheet to find the variance of X for the following probability distribution.

Table 5.15

r	1	2	3	4
$P(X = r)$	0.25	0.22	0.08	0.45

You should use both methods of calculating the variance and check that they give the same result.

As well as being able to carry out calculations for the expectation and variance, you often need to solve problems in context. The following example illustrates this idea.

Example 5.3

Laura has one pint of milk on three days out of every four and none on the fourth day. A pint of milk costs 40 p. Let X represent her weekly milk bill.

(i) Find the probability distribution of her weekly milk bill.

(ii) Find the mean (μ) and standard deviation (σ) of her weekly milk bill.

(iii) Find

(a) $P(X > \mu + \sigma)$

(b) $P(X < \mu - \sigma)$.

Solution

(i) The delivery pattern repeats every four weeks.

Table 5.16

M	Tu	W	T	F	Sa	Su	Number of pints	Milk bill
✓	✓	✓	✗	✓	✓	✓	6	£2.40
✗	✓	✓	✓	✗	✓	✓	5	£2.00
✓	✗	✓	✓	✓	✗	✓	5	£2.00
✓	✓	✗	✓	✓	✓	✗	5	£2.00

Tabulating the probability distribution for X gives the following.

Table 5.17

r (£)	2.00	2.40
$P(X = r)$	0.75	0.25

(ii) $E(X) = \mu = \Sigma r\, P(X = r)$

$ = 2 \times 0.75 + 2.4 \times 0.25$

$ = 2.1$

$Var(X) = \sigma^2 = E(X^2) - \mu^2$

$ = 4 \times 0.75 + 5.76 \times 0.25 - 2.1^2$

$ = 0.03$

$\Rightarrow \sigma = \sqrt{0.03} = 0.1732$

Hence her mean weekly milk bill is £2.10, with a standard deviation of about 17 p.

(iii) (a) $P(X > \mu + \sigma) = P(X > 2.27) = 0.25$

(b) $P(X < \mu - \sigma) = P(X < 1.93) = 0$

EXTENSION

Expectation and variance of the binomial distribution

> **Note**
>
> The results are:
> $E(X_1 + X_2) = E(X_1) + E(X_2)$
> (always true) and
> $Var(X_1 + X_2) = Var(X_1) + Var(X_2)$
> (if X_1 and X_2 are independent)
> Note that these results can be extended to any number of random variables.

In order to find the expectation and variance of X, you can sum a series, involving binomial coefficients but this is fairly awkward. However, you can instead think of X as the sum of n independent variables $X_1, X_2, \ldots, X_n$. Each of these variables is a binomial random variable which takes the value 1 with probability p and the value 0 with probability $1 - p$. To find the expectation and variance of X, you first find the expectation and variance of one of these binomial random variables. You can then use the results from the previous chapter (see note) to find the expectation and variance of X.

$E(X_i) = 0 \times (1 - p) + 1 \times p = p$

$E(X_i^2) = 0^2 \times (1 - p) + 1^2 \times p = p$

$Var(X_i) = E(X_i^2) - [E(X_i)]^2 = p - p^2 = p(1 - p) = pq$ where $q = 1 - p$

Expectation and variance

You now use the results that

$$E(X_1 + X_2 + \cdots + X_n) = E(X_1) + E(X_2) + \cdots + E(X_n)$$
$$= p + p + \cdots + p = np \text{ and}$$

$$\text{Var}(X_1 + X_2 + \cdots + X_n) = \text{Var}(X_1) + \text{Var}(X_2) + \cdots + \text{Var}(X_n)$$
$$= p(1-p) + p(1-p) + \cdots + p(1-p)$$
$$= np(1-p) = npq$$

Thus if $X \sim B(n, p)$
$E(X) = \mu = np$ and
$\text{Var}(X) = \sigma^2 = np(1-p) = npq$

Exercise 5.2

① Find by calculation the expectation of the outcome with the following probability distribution.

Table 5.18

Outcome	1	2	3	4	5
Probability	0.1	0.2	0.4	0.2	0.1

How otherwise might you have arrived at your answer?

② The spreadsheet shows part of a discrete probability distribution, together with some calculations of $r \times P(X = r)$ and $r^2 \times P(X = r)$. Using only spreadsheet commands, and without entering any more numbers, obtain the remaining values in columns B, C and D. Hence find the mean and variance of this distribution.

	A	B	C	D
1	r	$P(X=r)$	$r \times P(X=r)$	$r^2 \times P(X=r)$
2	1	0.20		
3	2	0.30		
4	3	0.10	0.30	
5	4	0.05		
6	5	0.20		5.00
7	6			
8	SUM			

Figure 5.3

③ The probability distribution of the discrete random variable X is given by

$P(X = r) = \dfrac{2r - 1}{16}$ for $r = 1, 2, 3, 4$

$P(X = r) = 0$ otherwise.

(i) Find $E(X) = \mu$.

(ii) Find $P(X < \mu)$.

④ The random variable $X \sim B(4, 0.3)$. Show that the mean and variance of X are 1.2 and 0.84, respectively.

⑤ (i) A discrete random variable X can take only the values 4 and 5, and has expectation 4.2.

By letting $P(X = 4) = p$ and $P(X = 5) = 1 - p$, solve an equation in p and so find the probability distribution of X.

(ii) A discrete random variable Y can take only the values 50 and 100. Given that $E(Y) = 80$, write out the probability distribution of Y.

⑥ The random variable Y is given by the absolute difference between the scores when two ordinary dice are thrown.

(i) Find $E(Y)$ and $\text{Var}(Y)$.

(ii) Find the values of the following.
  (a) $P(Y > \mu)$ (b) $P(Y > \mu + 2\sigma)$

7 Three fair coins are tossed. Let X represent the number of tails.
  (i) Find $E(X)$.
    Show that this is equivalent to $3 \times \frac{1}{2}$.
  (ii) Find $Var(X)$.
    Show that this is equivalent to $3 \times \frac{1}{4}$.
  If instead ten fair coins are tossed, let Y represent the number of tails.
  (iii) Write down the values of $E(Y)$ and $Var(Y)$.

8 An unbiased tetrahedral die has faces labelled 2, 4, 6 and 8. If the die lands on the face marked 2, the player has to pay £5. If it lands on the face marked with a 4 or a 6, the player wins £2. If it lands on the face labelled 8, then no money changes hands.

  Let X represent the amount 'won' each time the player throws the die. (A loss is represented by a negative X value.)

  (i) Complete the following probability distribution for X.

   Table 5.19

r	−5	0	2
$P(X = r)$			

  (ii) Find $E(X)$ and $Var(X)$.
    What does the sign of $E(X)$ indicate?
  (iii) How much less would the player have to pay, when the die lands on the face marked 2, so that he would break even in the long run?

9 85% of first-class mail arrives the day after being posted, the rest takes one day longer.

  For second class mail the corresponding figures are 10% and 40%, while a further 35% take three days and the remainder four days.

  Two out of every five letters go by first class mail.

  Let X represent the delivery time for letters.

  (i) Explain why $P(X = 1) = 0.4$.
  (ii) Complete the following probability distribution for X.

   Table 5.20

r	1	2	3	4
$P(X = r)$	0.4			

  (iii) Calculate $E(X)$ and $Var(X)$.

10 (i) A discrete random variable X can take only the values 3, 4 and 5, has expectation 4 and variance 0.6.
    By letting $P(X = 3) = p$, $P(X = 4) = q$ and $P(X = 5) = 1 - p - q$, set up and solve a pair of simultaneous equations in p and q and so find the probability distribution of X.
  (ii) A discrete random variable Y can take only the values 20, 50 and 100. Given that $E(Y) = 34$ and $Var(Y) = 624$, write out the probability distribution of Y.

11. Two dice are thrown. The random variable X is the higher of the two scores (or the score on either if they are both the same).
    (i) Show the probability distribution of X in a table.
    (ii) State which of these terms best describes the distribution: symmetrical, bimodal, positively skewed, or negatively skewed.
    (iii) Write down the mode of X and find the mean and median.

12. A traffic surveyor is investigating the lengths of queues at a particular set of traffic lights during the daytime, but outside rush hours. He counts the number of cars, X, stopped and waiting when the lights turn green on 100 occasions, with the following results.

    Table 5.21

X	0	1	2	3	4	5	6	7	8	9+
f	3	10	13	16	18	17	12	9	2	0

    (i) Use these figures to estimate the probability distribution of the number of cars waiting when the lights turn green.
    (ii) Use your probability distribution to estimate the expectation and variance of X.

    A colleague of the surveyor suggests that the probability distribution might be modelled by the expression
    $P(X = r) = kr(8 - r)$ for $r = 0, 1, 2, 3, 4, 5, 6, 7, 8$
    $P(X = r) = 0$ otherwise.

    (iii) Find the value of k.
    (iv) Find the expectation and variance of X given by this model.
    (v) State, with reasons, whether it is a good model.

3 Expectation and variance of the uniform distribution and a linear function of a random variable

The uniform (discrete) distribution

When fair six-sided dice are thrown, there are only six outcomes for each of the dice, all equally likely. You can write the probability distribution for each of them formally as

$$P(X = r) = \frac{1}{6} \quad \text{for } r = 1, 2, 3, 4, 5, 6$$
$$P(X = r) = 0 \quad \text{otherwise,}$$

where X represents the score on one of the dice.

Tabulating the probability distribution for X gives

Table 5.22

r	1	2	3	4	5	6
P(X = r)	$\frac{1}{6}$	$\frac{1}{6}$	$\frac{1}{6}$	$\frac{1}{6}$	$\frac{1}{6}$	$\frac{1}{6}$

The vertical line chart in Figure 5.4 illustrates this distribution.

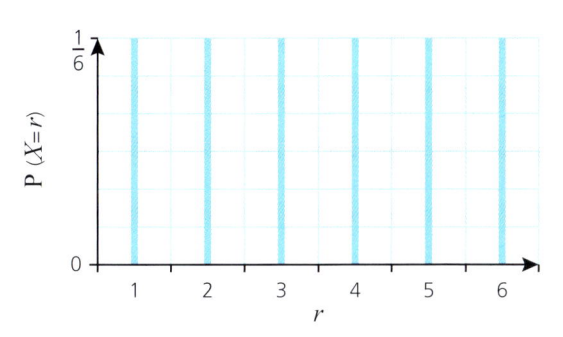

Figure 5.4

This is an example of the uniform probability distribution.

In general, the uniform probability distribution over the values {1, 2, ..., n} is defined as follows:

$$P(X = r) = \frac{1}{n} \quad \text{for } r = 1, 2, ..., n$$

$$P(X = r) = 0 \quad \text{otherwise.}$$

However, the lowest value may be k rather than 1 in which case the distribution over the n values {k, k + 1, ..., n + k − 1} is as follows:

$$P(X = r) = \frac{1}{n} \quad \text{for } r = k, k + 1, ..., n + k - 1$$

$$P(X = r) = 0 \quad \text{otherwise.}$$

Expectation and variance of the uniform distribution

You can find the expectation and variance of the score X on one of the fair dice, using the formulae which you met in Chapter 5.

$$E(X) = \mu = \Sigma r P(X = r)$$

$$= 1 \times \frac{1}{6} + 2 \times \frac{1}{6} + \cdots + 6 \times \frac{1}{6}$$

$$= 21 \times \frac{1}{6} = \frac{21}{6} = \frac{7}{2}$$

$$\text{Var}(X) = \sigma^2 = E(X^2) - \mu^2$$

$$= 1^2 \times \frac{1}{6} + 2^2 \times \frac{1}{6} + \cdots + 6^2 \times \frac{1}{6} - \left(\frac{7}{2}\right)^2$$

$$= (1 + 4 + 9 + 16 + 25 + 36) \times \frac{1}{6} - \left(\frac{7}{2}\right)^2$$

$$= \frac{91}{6} - \frac{49}{4} = \frac{35}{12}$$

Expectation and variance of the uniform distribution

These results can be generalised for a uniform random variable X taking the values $1, 2, \ldots, n$.

> Note that you are using the formula $\sum_{r=1}^{n} r = \frac{n(n+1)}{2}$.

$$E(X) = \sum_{r=1}^{n} r P(X=r)$$
$$= \sum_{r=1}^{n}\left(r \times \frac{1}{n}\right)$$
$$= \frac{1}{n} \sum_{r=1}^{n} r$$
$$= \frac{1}{n} \times \frac{n(n+1)}{2}$$
$$= \frac{n+1}{2}$$

To find the variance, you use the formula $\text{Var}(X) = E(X^2) - [E(X)]^2$

> Note that you are using the formula $\sum_{r=1}^{n} r^2 = \frac{1}{6} n(n+1)(2n+1)$.

$$E(X^2) = \sum_{r=1}^{n} r^2 P(X=r)$$
$$= \sum_{r=1}^{n} r^2 \frac{1}{n}$$
$$= \frac{1}{n} \sum_{r=1}^{n} r^2$$
$$= \frac{1}{n} \times \frac{1}{6} n(n+1)(2n+1)$$
$$= \frac{1}{6}(n+1)(2n+1)$$

$$\text{Var}(X) = E(X^2) - [E(X)]^2$$
$$= \frac{1}{6}(n+1)(2n+1) - \left(\frac{n+1}{2}\right)^2$$
$$= \frac{n+1}{12}[2(2n+1) - 3(n+1)]$$
$$= \frac{n+1}{12}(4n+2-3n-3)$$
$$= \frac{(n+1)(n-1)}{12}$$
$$= \frac{n^2 - 1}{12}$$

> **Note**
> For a discrete uniform distribution,
> $E(X) = \frac{n+1}{2}$,
> $\text{Var}(X) = \frac{n^2 - 1}{12}$.

Example 5.4

A five-sided fair spinner has faces labelled 10, 11, 12, 13, 14. The score on the spinner when it is rolled once is denoted by Z.

(i) Prove that $E(Z) = 12$.

(ii) Prove that $\text{Var}(Z) = 2$.

> **Note**
> Although it may seem obvious by symmetry that $E(Z) = 12$, the question asks for a proof. You therefore need to use the formula for expectation $E(X) = \sum r P(X=r)$.

Solution

(i) $E(Z) = \sum_{r=10}^{14} r P(Z=r)$.
$$= \sum_{10}^{14}\left(r \times \frac{1}{n}\right)$$
$$= 10 \times \frac{1}{5} + 11 \times \frac{1}{5} + 12 \times \frac{1}{5} + 13 \times \frac{1}{5} + 14 \times \frac{1}{5}$$
$$= 60 \times \frac{1}{5}$$
$$= 12$$

(ii) $$E(Z^2) = \sum_{r=1}^{n} r^2 P(Z=r)$$
$$= 100 \times \frac{1}{5} + 121 \times \frac{1}{5} + 144 \times \frac{1}{5} + 169 \times \frac{1}{5} + 196 \times \frac{1}{5}$$
$$= (100 + 121 + 144 + 169 + 196) \times \frac{1}{5}$$
$$= 730 \times \frac{1}{5}$$
$$= 146$$
$$\text{Var}(X) = E(X^2) - [E(X)]^2$$
$$= 146 - 144$$
$$= 2$$

Expectation and variance of a linear function of a random variable

Sometimes you need to find the expectation and variance of a linear function of a random variable $E(aX + b)$ and $\text{Var}(aX + b)$.

Example 5.5

Figure 5.5

Kiara is an employee at an estate agency. The number of properties that she sells during a month is denoted by the random variable X. The probability distribution of X is as follows.

Table 5.23

Number of houses	0	1	2	3	4	5+
Probability	0.07	0.33	0.4	0.12	0.08	0

(i) Calculate $E(X)$.

Kiara earns £750 per month plus £400 for each house that she sells. The random variable Y is the amount (in £) that Kiara earns each month.

(ii) Show that $Y = 400X + 750$. Draw up a probability table for Y.

(iii) Calculate $E(Y)$.

(iv) Calculate $400E(X) + 750$ and comment on your result.

Solution

(i) $E(X) = 0 \times 0.07 + 1 \times 0.33 + 2 \times 0.4 + 3 \times 0.12 + 4 \times 0.08 = 1.81$

(ii) Table 5.24

Earnings Y	750	1150	1550	1950	2350
Probability	0.07	0.33	0.4	0.12	0.08

(iii) $E(Y) = 750 \times 0.07 + 1150 \times 0.33 + 1550 \times 0.4$
$\qquad + 1950 \times 0.12 + 2350 \times 0.08$
$\quad = 1474$

(iv) $400E(X) + 750 = 400 \times 1.81 + 750 = 1474$

Clearly $E(Y) = 400E(X) + 750$, both having the value 1474.

Expectation and variance of the uniform distribution

Expectation: general results

In Example 5.5 on the previous page you found that $E(Y) = E(400X + 750)$
$= 400E(X) + 750$.

The working was numerical, showing that both expressions came out to be 1474. In fact, the following rules for expectation apply to any random variable X where a, b, c and d are constants.

> **Note**
> These are very similar to the rules for the mean of a frequency distribution.

- $E(aX + b) = aE(X) + b$
- $E(cX) = cE(X)$
- $E(d) = d$

Example 5.6

The random variable X has the following probability distribution.

Table 5.25

r	1	2	3	4
$P(X = r)$	0.6	0.2	0.1	0.1

(i) Find $\text{Var}(X)$ and the standard deviation of X.

(ii) Find $\text{Var}(3X)$ and the standard deviation of $3X$. Comment on the relationship between $\text{Var}(3X)$ and $\text{Var}(X)$ and likewise for the standard deviations.

(iii) Find $\text{Var}(3X + 7)$ and compare this with your answer to part (ii).

Solution

(i) $E(X) = 1 \times 0.6 + 2 \times 0.2 + 3 \times 0.1 + 4 \times 0.1$
$= 1.7$

$E(X^2) = 1 \times 0.6 + 4 \times 0.2 + 9 \times 0.1 + 16 \times 0.1$
$= 3.9$

$\text{Var}(X) = E(X^2) - [E(X)]^2$
$= 3.9 - 1.7^2$
$= 1.01$

The standard deviation of $X = \sqrt{1.01} = 1.005$

> You can use the formula for $E(aX + b)$ above to rewrite $E(9X^2)$ as $9E(X^2)$ and likewise for $E(3X)$

(ii) $\text{Var}(3X) = E[(3X)^2] - \mu^2$
$= E(9X^2) - [E(3X)]^2$
$= 9E(X^2) - [3E(X)]^2$
$= 9 \times 3.9 - (3 \times 1.7)^2$
$= 35.1 - 26.01$
$= 9.09$

This shows that $\text{Var}(3X) = 9 \times \text{Var}(X)$ ← Note that $9 = 3^2$.

The standard deviation of $3X = \sqrt{9.09} = 3.015 = 3 \times$ s.d. of X

> **Note**
> Notice that $E(9X^2 + 42X + 49)$ is written as $E(9X^2) + E(42X) + E(49)$. This illustrates the general rule that
> $E(X_1 + X_2 + \cdots)$
> $= E(X_1) + E(X_2) + \cdots$

(iii) $\quad \text{Var}(3X+7) = \text{E}\left[(3X+7)^2\right] - \left[\text{E}(3X+7)\right]^2$
$= \text{E}(9X^2 + 42X + 49) - [3\text{E}(X) + 7]^2$
$= \text{E}(9X^2) + \text{E}(42X) + \text{E}(49) - [3 \times 1.7 + 7]^2$
$= 9\text{E}(X^2) + 42\text{E}(X) + 49 - 12.1^2$
$= 9 \times 3.9 + 42 \times 1.7 + 49 - 146.41$
$= 9.09$

This has the same value as $\text{Var}(3X)$ so is also equal to $9 \times \text{Var}(X)$

Variance: general results

In Example 5.6 above you found that $\text{Var}(3X+7) = \text{Var}(3X) = 9 \times \text{Var}(X)$

As with expectation, the working was numerical, showing that both expressions came out to be 9.09. In fact, the following rules for variance apply to any random variable X where a, b, and c are constants.

- $\text{Var}(aX) = a^2\text{Var}(X)$
- $\text{Var}(aX + b) = a^2\text{Var}(X)$
- $\text{Var}(c) = 0$

> Notice that the variance of a constant is zero. It can only take one value so there is no spread.

It may seem surprising that $\text{Var}(aX) = a^2\text{Var}(X)$ rather than simply $a\text{Var}(X)$, but the former relationship then gives the result that the standard deviation of aX is equal to $a \times$ the standard deviation of X, as you would expect from common sense.

Notice also that adding a constant does not make any difference to the variance, which is again as you would expect.

Finally, the variance of a constant is zero. This result is obvious – a constant does not have any variation.

Sums and differences of random variables

Sometimes you may need to add or subtract a number of independent random variables. This process is illustrated in the next example.

Example 5.7

A cricket bat manufacturer makes the blades and the handles separately. The blades are made in five lengths (in cm), with a uniform discrete distribution:

38, 40, 42, 44, 46.

The lengths (in cm) of the handles of cricket bats also form a discrete uniform distribution:

22, 24, 26.

Expectation and variance of the uniform distribution

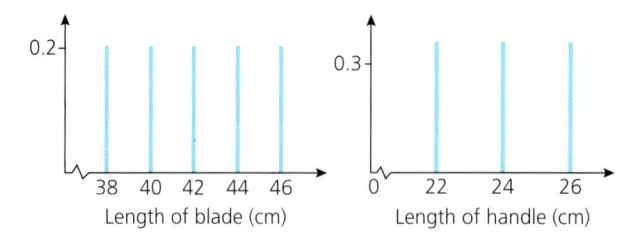

Figure 5.6

The blades and handles can be joined together to make bats of various lengths, and it may be assumed that the lengths of the two sections are independent. The different combinations occur with equal probabilities.

(i) How many different (total) bat lengths are possible?

(ii) Work out the mean and variance of random variable X_1, the length (in cm) of the blades.

(iii) Work out the mean and variance of random variable X_2, the length (in cm) of the handles.

(iv) Work out the mean and variance of random variable $X_1 + X_2$, the total length of the bats.

(v) Verify that
$$E(X_1 + X_2) = E(X_1) + E(X_2)$$
and $\text{Var}(X_1 + X_2) = \text{Var}(X_1) + \text{Var}(X_2)$.

Solution

(i) The number of different bat lengths is 7. This can be seen from the sample space diagram below.

Length of handle (cm) \ Length of blade (cm)	38	40	42	44	46
26	64	66	68	70	72
24	62	64	66	68	70
22	60	62	64	66	68

total length of bats

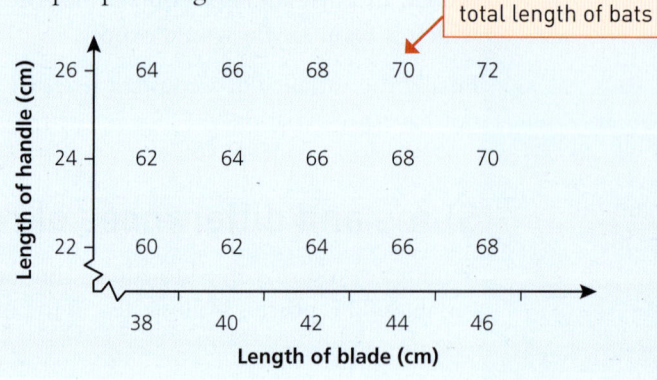

Figure 5.7

(ii) **Table 5.26**

Length of blade (cm)	38	40	42	44	46
Probability	0.2	0.2	0.2	0.2	0.2

$$E(X_1) = \mu_1 = \Sigma xp = (38 \times 0.2) + (40 \times 0.2) + (42 \times 0.2)$$
$$+ (44 \times 0.2) + (46 \times 0.2)$$
$$= 42 \text{ cm}$$
$$\text{Var}(X_1) = E(X_1^2) - \mu_1^2$$
$$E(X_1^2) = (38^2 \times 0.2) + (40^2 \times 0.2) + (42^2 \times 0.2)$$
$$+ (44^2 \times 0.2) + (46^2 \times 0.2)$$
$$= 1772$$
$$\text{Var}(X_1) = 1772 - 42^2 = 8$$

(iii)
Table 5.27

Length of handle (cm)	22	24	26
Probability	$\frac{1}{3}$	$\frac{1}{3}$	$\frac{1}{3}$

$$E(X_2) = \mu_2 = 22 \times \frac{1}{3} + 24 \times \frac{1}{3} + 26 \times \frac{1}{3} = 24 \text{ cm}$$
$$\text{Var}(X_2) = E(X_2^2) - \mu_2^2$$
$$E(X_2^2) = \left(22^2 \times \frac{1}{3}\right) + \left(24^2 \times \frac{1}{3}\right) + \left(26^2 \times \frac{1}{3}\right) = 578.667 \text{ to 3 d.p.}$$
$$\text{Var}(X_2) = 578.667 - 24^2 = 2.667 \text{ to 3 d.p.}$$

(iv) The probability distribution of $X_1 + X_2$ can be obtained from Figure 5.7.

Table 5.28

Total length of cricket bat (cm)	60	62	64	66	68	70	72
Probability	$\frac{1}{15}$	$\frac{2}{15}$	$\frac{3}{15}$	$\frac{3}{15}$	$\frac{3}{15}$	$\frac{2}{15}$	$\frac{1}{15}$

> **Note**
> Notice that the standard deviations of X_1 and X_2 do not add up to the standard deviation of $X_1 + X_2$.
> i.e. $\sqrt{8} + \sqrt{2.667} \neq \sqrt{10.667}$
> or $2.828 + 1.633 \neq 3.266$

$$E(X_1 + X_2) = \left(60 \times \frac{1}{15}\right) + \left(62 \times \frac{2}{15}\right) + \left(64 \times \frac{3}{15}\right) + \left(66 \times \frac{3}{15}\right)$$
$$+ \left(68 \times \frac{3}{15}\right) + \left(70 \times \frac{2}{15}\right) + \left(72 \times \frac{1}{15}\right)$$
$$= 66 \text{ cm}$$
$$\text{Var}(X_1 + X_2) = E\left[(X_1 + X_2)^2\right] - 66^2$$
$$E\left[(X_1 + X_2)^2\right] = \left(60^2 \times \frac{1}{15}\right) + \left(62^2 \times \frac{2}{15}\right) + \left(64^2 \times \frac{3}{15}\right) + \left(66^2 \times \frac{3}{15}\right)$$
$$+ \left(68^2 \times \frac{3}{15}\right) + \left(70^2 \times \frac{2}{15}\right) + \left(72^2 \times \frac{1}{15}\right)$$
$$= \frac{65500}{15} = 4366.667 \text{ to 3 d.p.}$$
$$\text{Var}(X_1 + X_2) = 4366.667 - 66^2 = 10.667 \text{ to 3 d.p.}$$

(v) $E(X_1 + X_2) = 66 = 42 + 24 = E(X_1) + E(X_2)$, as required.

$\text{Var}(X_1 + X_2) = 10.667 = 8 + 2.667 = \text{Var}(X_1) + \text{Var}(X_2)$, as required.

Expectation and variance of the uniform distribution

General results

Example 5.7 has illustrated the following general results for the sums and differences of random variables.

For any two random variables X_1 and X_2

- $E(X_1 + X_2) = E(X_1) + E(X_2)$
- $E(X_1 - X_2) = E(X_1) - E(X_2)$

If the variables X_1 and X_2 are independent

- $\text{Var}(X_1 + X_2) = \text{Var}(X_1) + \text{Var}(X_2)$
- $\text{Var}(X_1 - X_2) = \text{Var}(X_1) + \text{Var}(X_2)$

Note that if X_1 and X_2 are not independent, then the relationship between $\text{Var}(X_1 + X_2) = \text{Var}(X_1) + \text{Var}(X_2)$ does not hold. In this case, the relationship between $\text{Var}(X_1 + X_2) \ldots X_2$ is beyond the scope of this book.

These results can be extended to n random variables, $X_1 + X_2 + \ldots + X_n$.

> Replacing X_2 by $-X_2$ in this result gives
> $E(X_1 + (-X_2))$
> $= E(X_1) + E(-X_2)$
> $= E(X_1) - E(X_2)$.

> $\text{Var}(X_1 - X_2)$
> $= \text{Var}(X_1 + (-X_2))$
> $= \text{Var}(X_1) + \text{Var}(-X_2)$
> $= \text{Var}(X_1) + (-1)^2 \text{Var}(X_2)$
> $= \text{Var}(X_1) + \text{Var}(X_2)$

Linear combinations of two or more independent random variables

> A 'linear combination' of random variables is an expression of the form $a_1 X_1 + a_2 X_2 + \cdots + a_n X_n$.

These results can also be generalised to include linear combinations of random variables.

For any random variables X and Y

$$E(aX + bY) = aE(X) + bE(Y)$$

where a and b are constants.

If X and Y are independent

$$\text{Var}(aX + bY) = a^2 \text{Var}(X) + b^2 \text{Var}(Y)$$

These results may be extended to any number of random variables.

Exercise 5.3

1. Two fair six-sided dice are rolled.
   (i) Find the probability that the score on the first die is at least 5.
   (ii) Find the probability that the score on at least one of the two die is at least 5.

2. A fair four-sided spinner has sectors labelled 2, 3, 4 and 5. The score on the spinner when it is spun once is denoted by X.
   (i) Find $P(X > 3)$.
   (ii) Find $E(X)$.
   (iii) Find $\text{Var}(X)$.

3. Five fair six-sided dice are each rolled once.
   (i) Find the expectation and variance of the score on one of the dice.
   (ii) Find the expectation and variance of the total score on the five dice.

4. A fair seven-sided spinner has sectors labelled 7, 8, …12 and 13. Find the expectation and variance of the score on the spinner.

⑤ The random variable X denotes the score on a fair three-sided spinner which has sectors labelled 1, 2 and 3. The random variable Y denotes the score on a fair three-sided spinner which has sectors labelled 10, 20 and 30.

(i) Find $E(X)$ and $Var(X)$.

(ii) Find $E(Y)$ and $Var(Y)$.

(iii) The spinner with sectors labelled 1, 2 and 3 is spun ten times. Find the expectation and variance of the total score.

(iv) Compare your answers to parts (ii) and (iii).

4 The expectation and variance of functions of discrete random variables

!!! This is A-level only content

You may wish to find the expectation and variance of a function of a discrete random variable X. You know that $E(X) = \Sigma p_i x_i$ and that $Var(X) = E(X^2) - (E(X))^2$. These results can be extended to give, for any well-defined function g,

$$E(g(X)) = \Sigma p_i g(x_i) \text{ and } Var(g(X)) = E((g(X))^2) - (E(g(X)))^2$$

Example 5.8

Find $E(5X^3)$ and $Var(5X^3)$, where X is the score when a single fair die is thrown.

Solution

You know from your work on the uniform distribution above that

$$E(X) = \sum p_i x_i = 3.5, \text{ and } Var(X) = \frac{35}{12}.$$

Since X is distributed uniformly, with $n = 6$ and $p_i = \frac{1}{6}$,

$$E(5X^3) = \sum \frac{1}{6} 5x_i^3 = \frac{5}{6}(1^3 + 2^3 + 3^3 + 4^3 + 5^3 + 6^3) = 367.5$$

Similarly, $E((5X^3)^2) = \sum p_i (5x_i^3)^2 = E(25X^6)$

$$= \sum \frac{1}{6} 25 x_i^6 = \frac{25}{6}(1^6 + 2^6 + 3^6 + 4^6 + 5^6 + 6^6)$$

$$= 279879.2$$

$Var(5X^3) = E((5X^3)^2) - (E((5X^3)))^2 = 279879.2 - 367.5^2 = 144822.9$

The standard deviation of $5X^3$ is $\sqrt{144822.9} = 380.6$.

Notice that $E(5X^3) = 367.5 \neq 5(E(X))^3 = 214.375$.

Similarly $Var(5X^3) \neq 25(Var(X))^3$.

If g is not a linear function, there are no shortcuts of this kind that you can take to find $E(g(X))$ and $Var(g(X))$.

The expectation and variance of functions

Exercise 5.4

① The probability distribution of random variable X is as follows.

Table 5.29

x	1	2	3	4	5
$P(X = x)$	0.1	0.2	0.3	0.3	0.1

(i) Find (a) $E(X)$ (b) $Var(X)$.

(ii) Verify that $Var(2X) = 4Var(X)$.

② The probability distribution of a random variable X is as follows.

Table 5.30

x	0	1	2
$P(X = x)$	0.5	0.3	0.2

(i) Find (a) $E(X)$ (b) $Var(X)$

(ii) Verify that $Var(5X + 2) = 25Var(X)$.

③ The expectations and variances of independent random variables A, B and C are 35 and 9, 30 and 8 and 25 and 6, respectively. Write down the expectations and variances of

(i) $A + B + C$

(ii) $5A + 4B$

(iii) $A + 2B + 3C$

(iv) $4A - B - 5C$.

④ Prove that $Var(aX - b) = a^2 Var(X)$, where a and b are constants.

⑤ A coin is biased so that the probability of obtaining a tail is 0.75. The coin is tossed four times and the random variable X is the number of tails obtained.

Find

(i) $E(2X)$

(ii) $Var(3X)$.

⑥ A game at a charity fair costs £1 to play. The player rolls two fair dice and receives in return 10p plus 25 times the lower of the scores on the dice.

(i) Find the probability distribution of X, the lower of the scores.

(ii) Find the expectation and the variance of the players winnings in one go at the game.

(iii) In the long run, will the game make or lose money for the charity?

⑦ The probability distributions of two independent random variables X and Y are as follows.

Table 5.31

x	1	2	3	4
$P(X = x)$	0.2	0.4	0.3	0.1

Table 5.32

y	0	1	2
$P(Y = y)$	0.2	0.3	0.5

(i) Find (a) $E(X)$ (b) $E(Y)$ (c) $Var(X)$ (d) $Var(Y)$.

(ii) Show the probability distribution of $Z = X + Y$ in a table.

(iii) Using your table, verify that
    (a) $E(Z) = E(X) + E(Y)$ (b) $\text{Var}(Z) = \text{Var}(X) + \text{Var}(Y)$
(iv) Show the probability distribution of $W = X - Y$ in a table.
(v) Using your table, verify that
    (a) $E(W) = E(X) - E(Y)$ (b) $\text{Var}(W) = \text{Var}(X) + \text{Var}(Y)$

⑧ In a game at a charity fair, three coins are spun and a die is thrown. The game costs one pound to play. The amount in pence that the player wins is ten times the score on the die plus 20 times the number of heads that occur. Find the expectation and variance of the amount won by the player.

⑨ The random variable X represents the number of tails which occur when two fair coins are spun.
(i) Find $E(X)$ and $\text{Var}(X)$.
(ii) Find $E(10X - 5)$ and $\text{Var}(10X - 5)$.
(iii) Find the expectation and variance of the total of 50 observations of X.
(iv) Explain the similarities and differences between your answers to part (iii) and $E(50X)$ and $\text{Var}(50X)$.
(v) Find $E(X^3)$ and $\text{Var}(X^3)$.

⑩ A family eats a lot of bread. Most days, at least one loaf of bread is bought by the family. The random variable X represents the number of loaves bought by the family on a day. The probability distribution of X is shown in the table.

Table 5.33

r	0	1	2
P(X = r)	0.3	0.35	0.35

(i) Find $E(X)$ and $\text{Var}(X)$.

The number of loaves bought on any day depends on the number of loaves bought on the previous day. The table below shows the joint distribution of the numbers of loaves X_1 and X_2 bought on two successive days.

Table 5.34

		Second day X_2			
		0	1	2	Total
First day X_1	0	0	0.05	0.25	0.3
	1	0.05	0.2	0.1	0.35
	2	0.25	0.1	0	0.35
	Total	0.3	0.35	0.35	1

(ii) Complete the following probability distribution for $Y = X_1 + X_2$, the total number bought on the two days.

Table 5.35

R	0	1	2	3	4
P(Y = r)	0	0.1	0.7		

(iii) Find $E(Y)$, and show that $\text{Var}(Y) = 0.29$.
(iv) Explain why $\text{Var}(Y)$ is not equal to $\text{Var}(X_1) + \text{Var}(X_2)$.

The expectation and variance of functions

⑪ Two three-sided spinners bearing the numbers 1, 2 and 3 are spun. The resulting score X is taken to be the sum divided by 4.
Find

(i) $E(3X^2 - 4)$ (ii) $\text{Var}(3X^2 - 4)$

KEY POINTS

1 For a discrete random variable, X, which can take only the values $r_1, r_2, ..., r_n$, with probabilities $p_1, p_2, ..., p_n$, respectively:

- $p_1 + p_2 + \cdots + p_n = \sum_{n=1}^{n=k} p_k = \sum_{1}^{n} P(X = r_k) = 1$ where $p_k \geq 0$

2 A discrete probability distribution is best illustrated by a *vertical line chart*.

- The expectation $= E(X) = \mu = \Sigma r P(x = r)$.
- The variance $= \text{Var}(X) = \sigma^2$
  $= E(X - \mu)^2 = \Sigma(r - \mu)^2 P(X = r)$
  or $E(X^2) - [E(X)]^2 = \Sigma r^2 P(X = r) - [\Sigma r P(X = r)]^2$.

3 **Uniform distribution (discrete)**
  1 The uniform distribution may be used to model situations in which:
     - all outcomes are equally likely.
  2 For a uniform random variable X taking n different values
     - $P(X = r) = \dfrac{1}{n}$ for $r = 1, 2, ..., n$.
  3 For a uniform random variable X taking values 1 to n inclusive
     - $E(X) = \dfrac{n+1}{2}$
     - $\text{Var}(X) = \dfrac{n^2 - 1}{12}$.

4 For any random variables X and Y and constants a, b and c:
  - $E(c) = c$
  - $E(aX) = aE(X)$
  - $E(aX + c) = aE(X) + c$
  - $E(X \pm Y) = E(X) \pm E(Y)$
  - $E(aX + bY) = aE(X) + bE(Y)$.

5 For two random variables X and Y, and constants a, b and c:
  - $\text{Var}(c) = 0$
  - $\text{Var}(aX) = a^2 \text{Var}(X)$
  - $\text{Var}(aX + c) = a^2 \text{Var}(X)$.

  and, if X and Y are independent,
  - $\text{Var}(X \pm Y) = \text{Var}(X) + \text{Var}(Y)$
  - $\text{Var}(aX + bY) = a^2 \text{Var}(X) + b^2 \text{Var}(Y)$.

LEARNING OUTCOMES

When you have completed this chapter you should be able to:
- use probability functions, given algebraically or in tables
- calculate the numerical probabilities for a simple distribution
- draw and interpret graphs representing probability distributions
- calculate the expectation (mean), $E(X)$, and understand its meaning
- calculate the variance, $Var(X)$, and understand its meaning
- understand where the uniform distribution is a good model
- know how to calculate the value of the expectation for a uniform distribution
- know how to calculate the value of the variance for a uniform distribution
- use the result $E(aX+b) = aE(X)+b$ and understand its meaning
- use the result $Var(aX+b) = a^2 Var(X)$ and understand its meaning
- find the mean of any linear combination of random variables and the variance of any linear combination of independent random variables.

6 The Poisson distribution

If something can go wrong, sooner or later it will go wrong.

Murphy's Law

1 When to use the Poisson distribution

Electrics Express – next day delivery

Since the new website went live, with next day delivery for all items, the number of orders has increased dramatically. We have taken on more staff to cope with the demand for our products. Orders come in from all over the place. It seems impossible to predict the pattern of demand, but one thing we do know is that currently we receive an average of 150 orders per hour.

The appearance of this update on the Electrics Express website prompted a statistician to contact Electrics Express. She offered to analyse the data and see what suggestions she could come up with.

For her detailed investigation, she considered the distribution of the number of orders per minute. For a random sample of 1000 single-minute intervals during the last month, she collected the following data.

> There were five occasions on which there were more than seven orders. These were grouped into a single category and treated as if all five of them were eight.

Table 6.1

Number of orders per minute	0	1	2	3	4	5	6	7	> 7
Frequency	70	215	265	205	125	75	30	10	5

Summary statistics for this frequency distribution are as follows.

$$n = 1000, \quad \Sigma xf = 2525 \quad \text{and} \quad \Sigma x^2 f = 8885$$
$$\Rightarrow \bar{x} = 2.525, s^2 = 2.5119 \quad \text{and} \quad s = 1.58 \text{ (to 3 s.f.)}$$

She also noted that:

- orders made on the website appear at random and independently of each other
- the average number of orders per minute is about 2.5 which is equivalent to 150 per hour.

She suggested that the appropriate probability distribution to model the number of orders was the Poisson distribution.

The particular Poisson distribution, with an average number of 2.5 orders per minute, is defined as an **infinite** discrete random variable given by

$$P(X = r) = e^{-2.5} \times \frac{2.5^r}{r!} \quad \text{for } r = 0, 1, 2, 3, 4, \ldots$$

where

- X represents the random variable 'number of orders per minute'
- e is the mathematical constant 2.718 ...
- $e^{-2.5}$ can be found from your calculator as 0.082
- $r!$ means r **factorial**, for example $5! = 5 \times 4 \times 3 \times 2 \times 1 = 120$.

> **USING ICT**
>
> You can find Poisson probabilities directly from your calculator, without using this formula.

You can use the formula to calculate the values of the corresponding probability distribution, together with the expected frequencies it would generate. For example,

$$P(X = 4) = e^{-2.5} \times \frac{2.5^4}{4!}$$
$$= 0.13360\ldots$$
$$= 0.134 \text{ (to 3 s.f.)}$$

The table shows the observed frequencies for the orders on the website, together with the expected frequencies for a Poisson distribution with a mean of 2.5.

Table 6.2

Number of orders per minute (r)	0	1	2	3	4	5	6	7	> 7
Observed frequency	70	215	265	205	125	75	30	10	5
$P(X = r)$	0.082	0.205	0.257	0.214	0.134	0.067	0.028	0.010	0.004
Expected frequency	82	205	257	214	134	67	28	10	4

When to use the Poisson distribution

> **Note**
> Note that the final probability is found by subtracting the other probabilities from 1.
> Note also that the total of the expected frequencies is 1001 due to rounding.

The closeness of the observed and expected frequencies (see Figure 3.1) implies that the Poisson distribution is indeed a suitable model in this instance.

Note also that the sample mean, $\bar{x} = 2.525$ is very close to the sample variance, $s^2 = 2.512$ (to 4 s.f.). You will see later that, for a Poisson distribution, the expectation and variance are the same. So the closeness of these two summary statistics provides further evidence that the Poisson distribution is a suitable model.

> **Note**
> As with the discrete random variables you met in Chapter 2, the Poisson distribution may be illustrated by a vertical line chart.

Figure 6.1

This is an example of the Poisson distribution. When you learnt about the binomial distribution, you needed to consider whether certain conditions and certain modelling assumptions were applied in the situation you were investigating. The same is true for the Poisson distribution.

The following **conditions** are needed for the Poisson distribution to apply.

- The variable is the frequency of events that occur in a fixed interval of time or space. *(So the variable takes values 0, 1, 2, 3, ...)*
- The events occur randomly. *(That is, events do not occur at regular or predictable intervals.)*

There is rarely any doubt as to whether these conditions are satisfied. However, for the Poisson distribution to be a good model the following are also needed.

- Events occur independently of one another. *(Whether or not one event occurs does not affect the probability of whether another event occurs.)*
- The mean number of events occurring in each interval of the same size is the same. *(The rate per interval (or the mean number of events per interval) is often denoted by λ (pronounced 'lambda'). λ is the only parameter of the Poisson distribution. So the probability of an event occurring in an interval of a given size is the same. This condition can also be written as 'events occur at a constant average rate'.)*

There will often be doubt as to whether either or both of these are satisfied, and often the best you can say is that you must assume them to be true. So they will usually be modelling assumptions.

So if X represents the number of events in a given interval, then

$$P(X = r) = e^{-\lambda} \times \frac{\lambda^r}{r!} \quad \text{for } r = 0, 1, 2, 3, 4, \ldots$$

The Poisson distribution has an infinite number of outcomes, so only part of the distribution can be illustrated. The shape of the Poisson distribution depends on the value of the parameter λ. If λ is small, the distribution has positive skew, but as λ increases the distribution becomes progressively more symmetrical. Three typical Poisson distributions are illustrated in Figure 6.2.

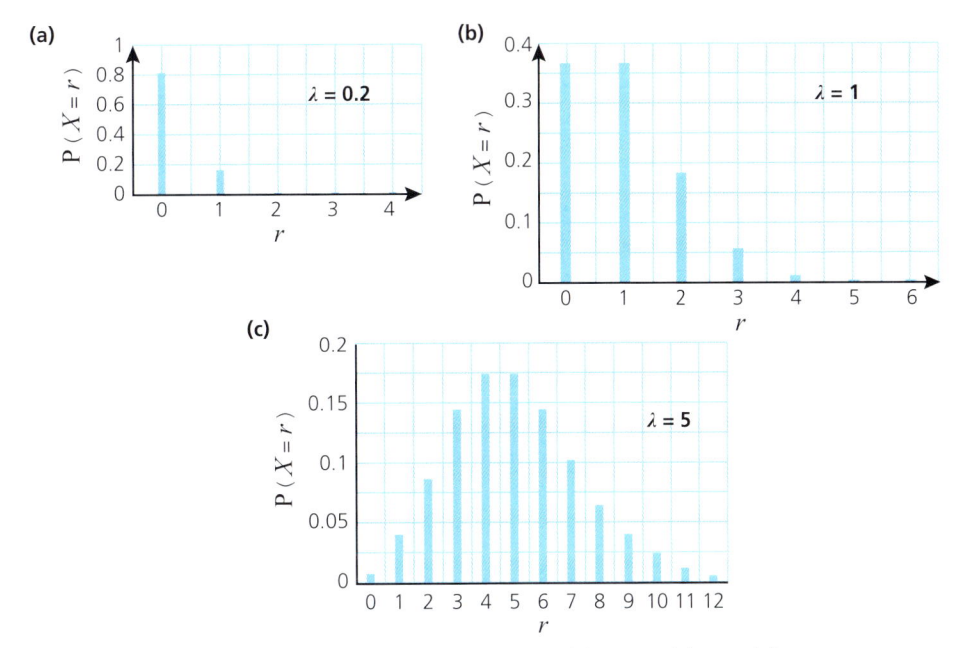

Figure 6.2 The shape of the Poisson distribution for (a) $\lambda = 0.2$ (b) $\lambda = 1$ (c) $\lambda = 5$

There are many situations in which events happen singly and the average number of occurrences per given interval of time or space is uniform and is known or can be easily found. Such events might include:

- the number of goals scored by a team in a football match
- the number of telephone calls received per minute at a call centre
- the number of accidents in a factory per week
- the number of particles emitted in a minute by a radioactive substance
- the number of typing errors per page in a document
- the number of flaws per metre in a roll of cloth
- the number of micro-organisms in 1 ml of pond water.

Modelling with the Poisson distribution

Often you will not be able to say that the conditions and assumptions for a Poisson distribution are met exactly, but you will nevertheless be able to get useful probabilities from the Poisson distribution. Sometimes it will be clear that some or all of the conditions and assumptions at not satisfied, and so you can confidently say that the Poisson distribution is not a good model.

Example 6.1

Discuss whether the Poisson distribution provides a good probability model for the variable X in each of the following scenarios.

(i) X is the number of cars that pass a point in the grandstand in a Formula 1 motor race in an interval of 3 minutes.

(ii) X is the number of coins found in $1\,m^3$ of earth during the investigation of an archaeological site.

(iii) X is the number of cars that pass a given point on a main road in a ten second period between 6 am and noon on a weekday.

(iv) X is the number of separate incidents reported to a Fire Brigade control room in a 1-hour period.

When to use the Poisson distribution

Solution

> Cars pass at a roughly constant rate, but this is not the same as 'constant average rate'. 'Constant rate' implies no variation.

(i) Cars in a Formula 1 race will pass the grandstand at fairly regular and predictable intervals, so the 'random' condition does not hold and a Poisson distribution is almost certainly not a good model.

(ii) It is quite likely that coins will be found in groups, or even in a hoard, and in this case the independence condition would not hold. If on the other hand you are in part of the site where single coins might have been lost on an occasional basis then independence could be assumed and the Poisson distribution might be a good model.

(iii) It is likely that the mean number of cars passing during rush hours would not be the same as the mean number passing at other times, so the 'constant average rate' assumption is unlikely to hold. This may mean that the Poisson distribution is not a good model.

(iv) In general, incidents such as these are likely to occur independently and at a uniform rate, at least within a relatively short time interval. However, circumstances might exist which negate this, for instance in the case of a series of deliberate attacks.

Discussion point

The managers of the new Avonford maternity hospital need to know how many beds are needed. At a meeting, one of the managers suggests that the number of births per day in the region covered by the hospital could be modelled by a Poisson distribution.

(i) What assumptions are needed for the Poisson distribution to be a good model?
(ii) Are these assumptions likely to hold?
(iii) What else would the managers need to consider when planning the number of beds?

Note

For a Poisson distribution with parameter λ,
$$\text{mean} = E(X) = \lambda,$$
$$\text{variance} = \text{Var}(X) = \lambda$$

The mean and variance of the Poisson distribution are both equal to the parameter λ.

You can see these results in the example about Electrics Express. The Poisson parameter was $\lambda = 2.5$, the mean of the number of orders placed per minute on the website was 2.525 and the variance was 2.512.

When modelling data with a Poisson distribution, the closeness of the mean and variance is one indication that the model fits the data well.

When you have collected the data, go through the following steps in order to check whether the data may be modelled by a Poisson distribution.

- Work out the mean and variance and check that they are roughly equal.
- Use the sample mean to work out the Poisson probability distribution and a suitable set of expected frequencies.
- Compare these expected frequencies with your observations.

Example 6.2

The number of defects in a wire cable can be modelled by the Poisson distribution with a uniform rate of 1.5 defects per kilometre.

Find the probability that

(i) a single kilometre of wire will have exactly three defects.

(ii) a single kilometre of wire will have at least five defects.

Solution

> You are told that defects occur with a uniform rate of 1.5 defects per kilometre. From this, you can infer that the value of the mean, λ, is 1.5.

Let X represent the number of defects per kilometre.

$$P(X = r) = e^{-1.5} \times \frac{1.5^r}{r!} \quad \text{for } r = 0, 1, 2, 3, 4, \ldots$$

(i) $P(X = 3) = e^{-1.5} \times \frac{1.5^3}{3!}$

$= 0.125510\ldots$

$= 0.126$ (to 3 s.f.)

(ii) $P(X \geq 5) = 1 - P(X \leq 4)$

$= 1 - 0.98142\ldots$

$= 0.0186$

You can use the term you have obtained to work out the next one. Although calculators can work out every term, sometimes you might still find it useful to understand this process. For the Poisson distribution with parameter λ

$P(X = 0) = e^{-\lambda}$

$P(X = 1) = \lambda e^{-\lambda} = \lambda P(X = 0)$ Multiply the previous term by λ

$P(X = 2) = e^{-\lambda} \times \frac{\lambda^2}{2!} = \frac{\lambda}{2} P(X = 1)$ Multiply the previous term by $\frac{\lambda}{2}$

$P(X = 3) = e^{-\lambda} \times \frac{\lambda^3}{3!} = \frac{\lambda}{3} P(X = 2)$ Multiply the previous term by $\frac{\lambda}{3}$

In general, you can find $P(X = r)$ by multiplying your previous probability, $P(X = r - 1)$, by $\frac{\lambda}{r}$.

> **Note**
>
> The process of finding the next term from the previous one can be described as a **recurrence relation**.

Example 6.3

Jasmit is considering buying a telephone answering machine. He has one for five days' free trial and finds that 22 messages are left on it. Assuming that this is typical of the use it will get if he buys it, find:

(i) the mean number of messages per day

(ii) the probability that on one particular day there will be exactly six messages

(iii) the probability that on one particular day there will be more than six messages.

When to use the Poisson distribution

Solution

(i) Converting the total for five days to the mean for a single day gives

$$\text{daily mean} = \frac{22}{5} = 4.4 \text{ messages per day}$$

(ii) Calling X the number of messages per day

$$P(X = 6) = e^{-4.4} \times \frac{4.4^6}{6!}$$

$$= 0.124 \text{ (3 s.f.)}$$

(iii) $P(X \leq 6) = 0.8436$

and so

$P(X > 6) = 1 - 0.8436$

$= 0.156$ (3 s.f.)

Hypothesis testing using the Poisson distribution

It is possible to carry out a hypothesis test on the mean of a Poisson distribution in much the same way as with the proportion of the binomial distribution. The null hypothesis is that the mean $\lambda = k$, for some value k, and the alternative hypothesis is that either $\lambda < k$ or $\lambda > k$ (in which case, it is a one-tailed test) or $\lambda \neq k$ (in which case, it is a two-tailed test).

Example 6.4

Farmers are required to report a rare birth defect among sheep. Over many years the mean number reported per year has been 2.4.

(i) State the conditions needed for the Poisson distribution to provide a good model for this situation and comment on them.
There is, however, a suggestion that the number of defects has increased, and the authorities decide to carry out a hypothesis test to judge if there is cause for concern. The next year, 7 lambs were born with the defect.

(ii) State the null and alternative hypotheses for such a test.

(iii) Carry out the test at the 5% significance level, using the Poisson distribution as a model.

(iv) State and interpret the outcome of the test.

(v) What is the probability of a Type I error in this test?

> Notice that this part of the question is asking about the probability of this test in general giving a Type I error. It is not asking whether the result in this particular case is wrong.

Solution

(i) If events occur randomly, singly, independently and uniformly, then a Poisson model is likely to be appropriate. These conditions appear to hold in this case (unless it is likely that if one twin lamb has the defect, then the other twin will too).

(ii) We have that H_0 is $\lambda = 2.4$, while H_1 is $\lambda > 2.4$.

(iii) Let X be the number of lambs with the defect in one year. Assuming H_0 is true, the $X \sim Po(2.4)$, and $P(X \geq 7) = 0.01159... < 5\%$. (The critical region is in fact $\{X \geq 6\}$, as shown in the diagram on the next page).

114

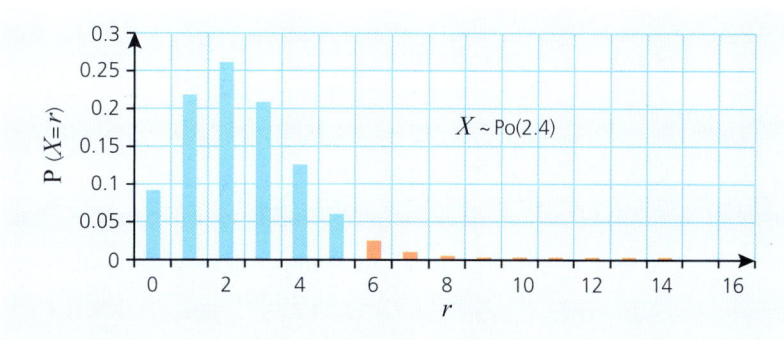

Figure 6.3

(iv) Thus the test suggests that there is significant evidence that the number of defects has increased.

(v) If H_0 is true, the probability of a result in the critical region of $X \geq 6$ is 0.0357, and this is the probability of a Type I error.

You say here that the **p-value** of your result is $P(X \geq 7) = 0.01159\ldots$ The p-value of a result is the probability, assuming that the null hypothesis is true, of achieving a result at least as extreme as the observed result.

Exercise 6.1

① If $X \sim \text{Po}(1.75)$, calculate
   (i) $P(X = 2)$ (ii) $P(X > 0)$.

② If $X \sim \text{Po}(3.1)$, calculate
   (i) $P(X = 3)$ (ii) $P(X < 2)$ (iii) $P(X \leq 2)$.

③ The number of cars passing a house in a residential road between 10 a.m. and 11 a.m. on a weekday is a random variable, X. Give a condition under which X may be modelled by a Poisson distribution.

Suppose that $X \sim \text{Po}(3.4)$. Calculate $P(X \geq 4)$.

④ The number of wombats that are killed on a particular stretch of road in Australia in any one day can be modelled by a $\text{Po}(0.42)$ random variable.
   (i) Calculate the probability that exactly two wombats are killed on a given day on this stretch of road.
   (ii) Find the probability that exactly four wombats are killed over a five-day period on this stretch of road.

⑤ A typesetter makes 1500 mistakes in a book of 500 pages. On how many pages would you expect to find (i) 0, (ii) 1, (iii) 2, (iv) 3 or more mistakes? State any assumptions in your workings.

⑥ In which of the following scenarios is it likely that X can be well modelled by a Poisson distribution? For those scenarios where X is probably not a good model, give a reason.
   (i) X is the number of aeroplanes landing at Heathrow Airport in a randomly chosen period of 1 hour.
   (ii) X is the number of foxes that live in a randomly chosen urban region of area 1 km².
   (iii) X is the number of tables booked at a restaurant on a randomly chosen evening.
   (iv) X is the number of particles emitted by a radioactive substance in a period of 1 minute.

The sum of two or more Poisson distributions

7. A ferry takes cars on a short journey from an island to the mainland. On a representative sample of weekday mornings, the numbers of vehicles, X, on the 8 a.m. sailing were as follows.

   20 24 24 22 23 21 20 22 23 22
   21 21 22 21 23 22 20 22 20 24

   (i) Show that X is unlikely to be well modelled by a Poisson distribution.

   In fact 20 of the vehicles belong to commuters who use that sailing of the ferry every weekday morning. The random variable Y is the number of vehicles other than that arrive wishing to use the ferry.

   (ii) Investigate whether Y may reasonably be modelled by a Poisson distribution.

   The ferry can take 25 vehicles on any journey.

   (iii) On what proportion of days would you expect at least one vehicle to be unable to travel on this particular sailing of the ferry because there was no room left and so have to wait for the next one?

8. Weak spots occur at random in the manufacture of a certain cable at an average rate of 1 per 120 metres.

   (i) If X represents the number of weak spots in 120 m of cable, write down the distribution of X.

   Lengths of this cable are wound on to drums. Each drum carries 60 m of cable.

   (ii) Find the probability that a drum will have three or more weak spots.

   (iii) A contractor buys six such drums. Find the probability that two have just one weak spot each and the other four have none.

   (iv) A different make of cable is suspected to have more than one weak spot per 120 m. One cable is checked, and 2400 m of cable reveals 30 weak spots. Carry out a hypothesis test at the 5% level.

2 The sum of two or more Poisson distributions

New crossing near leisure centre?

A recent traffic survey has revealed that the number of vehicles using the main road near the leisure centre has reached levels where crossing the road has become hazardous.

The survey, carried out by a leisure centre staff member, suggested that the numbers of vehicles travelling in both directions along the main road has increased so much during the past year that pedestrians are almost taking their lives into their own hands when crossing the road.

Between 2 p.m. and 3 p.m., usually one of the quietest periods of the day, the average number of vehicles travelling into town is 3.5 per minute and the average number of vehicles travelling out of town is 5.7 per minute. A new crossing is a must.

If it can be shown that there is a greater than 1 in 4 chance of more than ten vehicles passing per minute, then there is a good chance of getting a pelican crossing.

Assuming that the flows of vehicles, into and out of town, can be modelled by independent Poisson distributions, you can model the flow of vehicles in both directions as follows.

Let X represent the number of vehicles travelling into town between 2 p.m. and 3 p.m. then $X \sim \text{Po}(3.5)$.

Let Y represent the number of vehicles travelling out of town between 2 p.m. and 3 p.m. then $Y \sim \text{Po}(5.7)$.

Let T represent the number of vehicles travelling in either direction between 2 p.m. and 3 p.m. then $T = X + Y$.

You can find the probability distribution for T as follows.

$$P(T=0) = P(X=0) \times P(Y=0)$$
$$= 0.0302 \times 0.0033$$
$$= 0.0001$$

> There are two ways of getting a total of 1. They are 0 and 1, 1 and 0.

$$P(T=1) = P(X=0) \times P(Y=1) + P(X=1) \times P(Y=0)$$
$$= 0.0302 \times 0.0191 + 0.1057 \times 0.0033$$
$$= 0.0009$$

> There are three ways of getting a total of 2. They are 0 and 2, 1 and 1, 2 and 0.

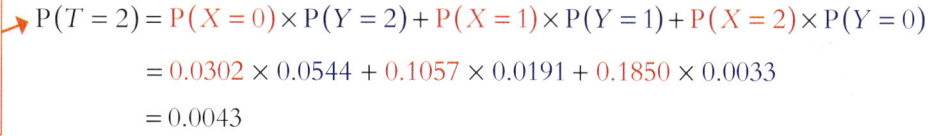

$$P(T=2) = P(X=0) \times P(Y=2) + P(X=1) \times P(Y=1) + P(X=2) \times P(Y=0)$$
$$= 0.0302 \times 0.0544 + 0.1057 \times 0.0191 + 0.1850 \times 0.0033$$
$$= 0.0043$$

and so on.

> **Note**
>
> $X \sim \text{Po}(\lambda)$ and $Y \sim \text{Po}(\mu)$
> $\Rightarrow X + Y \sim \text{Po}(\lambda + \mu)$
> if X and Y are independent

You can see that this process is very time consuming. Fortunately, you can make life a lot easier by using the fact that if X and Y are two independent Poisson random variables, with means λ and μ, respectively, then if $T = X + Y$, T is a Poisson random variable with mean $\lambda + \mu$.

Using $T \sim \text{Po}(9.2)$ gives the required probabilities straight away.

$$P(T=0) = 0.0001$$
$$P(T=1) = 0.0009$$
$$P(T=2) = 0.0043$$

You can now use the distribution for T to find the probability that the total traffic flow exceeds ten vehicles per minute.

$$P(T>10) = 1 - P(T \leq 10)$$
$$= 1 - 0.6820$$
$$= 0.318$$

Since there is a greater than 25% chance of more than ten vehicles passing per minute, the case for the pelican crossing has been made, based on the Poisson probability models.

The sum of two or more Poisson distributions

Example 6.5

A rare disease causes the death, on average, of 3.8 people per year in England, 0.8 in Scotland and 0.5 in Wales. As far as is known, the disease strikes at random and cases are independent of one another.

What is the probability of 7 or more deaths from the disease on the British mainland (i.e. England, Scotland and Wales together) in any year?

Solution

Notice first that:

- $P(7 \text{ or more deaths}) = 1 - P(6 \text{ or fewer deaths})$
- each of the three distributions fulfils the conditions for it to be modelled by the Poisson distribution.

You can therefore add the three distributions together and treat the result as a single Poisson distribution.

The overall mean is given by $\quad 3.8 \quad + \quad 0.8 \quad + \quad 0.5 \quad = \quad 5.1$

$\qquad\qquad\qquad\qquad\qquad\qquad$ England $\quad$ Scotland $\quad$ Wales $\quad$ Total

giving an overall distribution of Po(5.1).

The probability of 6 or fewer deaths is 0.7474.

So the probability of 7 or more deaths is given by $1 - 0.7474 = 0.2526$.

> **Note**
> You may add Poisson distributions in this way if they are independent of each other.

Example 6.6

On a lonely Highland road in Scotland, cars are observed passing at the rate of six per day and lorries at the rate of two per day. On the road, there is an old cattle grid which will soon need repair. The local works department decide that if the probability of more than 15 vehicles per day passing is less than 1%, then the repairs to the cattle grid can wait until next spring; otherwise it will have to be repaired before the winter.

When will the cattle grid have to be repaired?

Solution

Let C be the number of cars per day, L be the number of lorries per day and V be the number of vehicles per day.

Assuming that a car or a lorry passing along the road is a random event and that the two are independent

$$C \sim \text{Po}(6), L \sim \text{Po}(2)$$
$$\text{and so } V \sim \text{Po}(6 + 2)$$
$$\Rightarrow V \sim \text{Po}(8).$$
$$P(V \leq 15) = 0.9918.$$

The required probability is $P(V > 15) = 1 - P(V \leq 15)$
$$= 1 - 0.9918$$
$$= 0.0082$$

This is just less than 1% and so the repairs are left until spring.

EXTENSION

Link between binomial and Poisson distributions

In certain circumstances, you can use either the binomial distribution or the Poisson distribution as a model to calculate the probabilities you need. The example below illustrates this.

Example 6.7

It is known that, nationally, one person in a thousand is allergic to a particular chemical used in making a wood preservative. A firm that makes this wood preservative employs 500 people in one of its factories.

(i) Use the binomial distribution to estimate the probability that more than two people at the factory are allergic to the chemical.

(ii) What assumption are you making?

(iii) Using the fact that the mean of a binomial distribution is np, find the Poisson probability $P(Y > 2)$ where $Y \sim \text{Po}(np)$.

Solution

(i) Let X be the number of people in a random sample of 500 who are allergic to the chemical.

$$X \sim B(500, 0.001)$$
$$P(X > 2) = 1 - P(X \leq 2)$$
$$= 1 - 0.985669\ldots$$
$$= 0.0143$$

(ii) The assumption made is that people with the allergy are just as likely to work in the factory as those without the allergy. In practice, this seems rather unlikely: you would not stay in a job that made you unwell.

(iii) The mean of the binomial is $np = 500 \times 0.001 = 0.5$.

Using $Y \sim \text{Poisson}(0.5)$

$$P(Y > 2) = 1 - P(Y \leq 2)$$
$$= 1 - 0.985612\ldots$$
$$= 0.0144.$$

These two probabilities are very similar, so this suggests that sometimes the Poisson distribution and the binomial distribution give similar results. Four comparisons of binomial and Poisson probabilities are illustrated in Figure 6.4. In each case, the binomial probabilities are shown in blue and the Poisson probabilities in red.

Examining these four charts, it seems that whatever the value of n, the value of p must be small for the two distributions to give similar results. In fact, when n is reasonably large and p is small, the binomial and Poisson probabilities are similar. The smaller the value of p and the larger the value of n, the better the two distributions agree.

If p is small, $q \approx 1$, so $np \approx npq$ and the mean and variance are roughly equal, as required by a Poisson distribution.

> **Note**
>
> Note that if the binomial parameters are n and p then the corresponding Poisson distribution has parameter $\lambda = np$.

The sum of two or more Poisson distributions

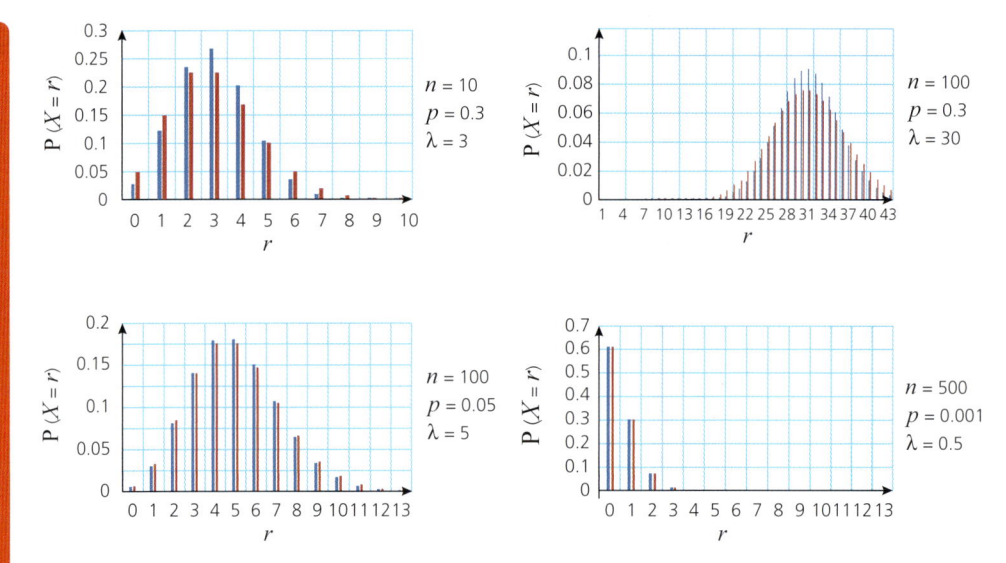

Figure 6.4 Comparison between the Poisson and binomial distributions for various values of n and p.

Exercise 6.2

1. You are given that $X \sim B(200, 0.04)$.

   (i) Find $P(X = 5)$.

   (ii) State the mean of a Poisson distribution which is likely to give a similar result to the probability found in part (i).

   (iii) Use this mean to find the corresponding Poisson probability and compare it with your answer to part (i).

2. The spreadsheet below shows two distributions, $B(10, 0.5)$ and $Poisson(\lambda)$.

	A	B	C	D	E	F	G	H	I	J	K	L
1	r	0	1	2	3	4	5	6	7	8	9	10
2	Probability B(10, 0.5)	0.0010	0.0098	0.0439	0.1172	0.2051	0.2461	0.2051	0.1172	0.0439	0.0098	0.0010
3	Probability Poisson(λ)	0.0067	0.0337	0.0842	0.1404	0.1755	0.1755	0.1462	0.1044	0.0653	0.0363	0.0181

Figure 6.5

   (i) The Poisson(λ) distribution is used to approximate the $B(10, 0.5)$ distribution. Write down the value of λ.

   (ii) Plot a vertical line chart to compare the $B(10, 0.5)$ and the Poisson(λ) distributions.

   (iii) Comment on whether the Poisson distribution (λ) is a good approximation to the $B(10, 0.5)$ distribution.

   The spreadsheet shows two other distributions, $B(100, 0.05)$ and Poisson(μ).

	A	B	C	D	E	F	G	H	I	J	K	L
1	r	0	1	2	3	4	5	6	7	8	9	10
2	Probability B(100, 0.05)	0.0059	0.0312	0.0812	0.1396	0.1781	0.1800	0.1500	0.1060	0.0649	0.0349	0.0167
3	Probability Poisson(μ)	0.0067	0.0337	0.0842	0.1404	0.1755	0.1755	0.1462	0.1044	0.0653	0.0363	0.0181

Figure 6.6

   (iv) The Poisson(μ) distribution is used to approximate the $B(100, 0.05)$ distribution. Write down the value of μ.

   (v) Figure 4.7 shows a vertical line chart comparing the $B(100, 0.05)$ and the Poisson(μ) distributions. Compare this with the vertical line chart with the one which you have drawn for $B(10, 0.5)$ and Poisson(λ) and comment on the differences.

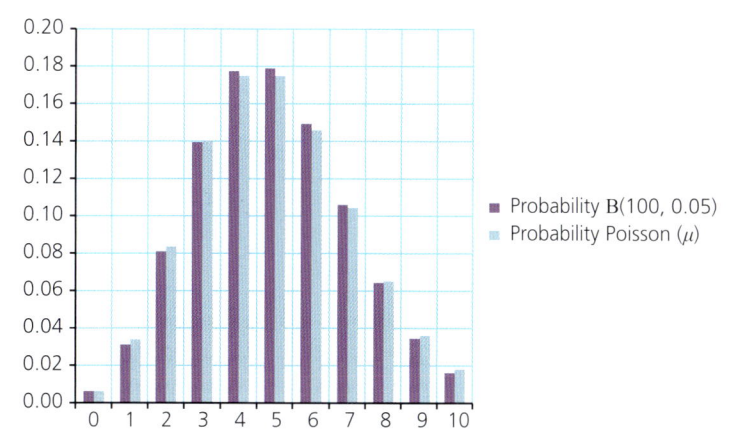

Figure 6.7

③ It is known that 0.3% of items produced by a certain process are defective. A random sample of 2000 items is selected.

(i) Use a binomial distribution to find the probability that there are at least five defective items in the sample.

(ii) Use a Poisson distribution to find the probability that there are at least five defective items in the sample.

(iii) Explain why your answers are similar although you are using two different distributions.

④ At a coffee shop both hot and cold drinks are sold. The number of hot drinks sold per minute may be assumed to be a Poisson variable with mean 0.7 and the number of cold drinks sold per minute may be assumed to be an independent Poisson variable with mean 0.4.

(i) Calculate the probability that in a given one-minute period exactly one hot drink and one cold drink are sold.

(ii) Calculate the probability that in a given three-minute period fewer than three drinks altogether are sold.

(iii) In a given one-minute period exactly three drinks are sold. Calculate the probability that these are all hot drinks.

⑤ The numbers of lorry drivers and car drivers visiting an all-night transport cafe between 2 a.m. and 3 a.m. on a Sunday morning have independent Poisson distributions with means 5.1 and 3.6, respectively. Find the probabilities that between 2 a.m. and 3 a.m. on any Sunday

(i) exactly five lorry drivers visit the cafe

(ii) at least one car driver visits the cafe

(iii) exactly five lorry drivers and exactly two car drivers visit the cafe.

(iv) By using the distribution of the total number of drivers visiting the cafe, find the probability that exactly seven drivers visit the cafe between 2 a.m. and 3 a.m. on any Sunday.

(v) Given that exactly seven drivers visit the cafe between 2 a.m. and 3 a.m. on one Sunday, find the probability that exactly five of them are driving lorries. [MEI]

⑥ Telephone calls reach a departmental administrator independently and at random, internal ones at a mean rate of two in any five-minute period, and external ones at a mean rate of one in any five-minute period.

The sum of two or more Poisson distributions

   (i) Find the probability that, in a five-minute period, the administrator receives
      (a) exactly three internal calls
      (b) at least two external calls
      (c) at most five calls in total.
   (ii) Given that the administrator receives a total of four calls in a five-minute period, find the probability that exactly two were internal calls.
   (iii) Find the probability that in any one-minute interval no calls are received.

7 During a weekday, cars pass a census point on a quiet side road independently and at random times. The mean rate for westward travelling cars is two in any five-minute period, and for eastward travelling cars is three in any five-minute period.

Find the probability

   (i) that there will be no cars passing the census point in a given two-minute period
   (ii) that at least one car from each direction will pass the census point in a given two-minute period
   (iii) that there will be exactly ten cars passing the census point in a given ten-minute period.

8 A ferry company has two small ferries, A and B, that run across a river. The number of times per week that ferry A needs maintenance in a week has a Poisson distribution with mean 0.5, while, independently, the number of times that ferry B needs maintenance in a week has a Poisson distribution with mean 0.3.

Find, to three decimal places, the probability that in the next three weeks

   (i) ferry A will not need maintenance at all
   (ii) each ferry will need maintenance exactly once
   (iii) there will be a total of two occasions when one or other of the two ferries will need maintenance.

9 Two random variables, X and Y, have independent Poisson distributions given by $X \sim \text{Po}(1.4)$ and $Y \sim \text{Po}(3.6)$, respectively.

   (i) Using the distributions of X and Y only, calculate
      (a) $P(X+Y=0)$
      (b) $P(X+Y=1)$
      (c) $P(X+Y=2)$.

The random variable T is defined by $T = X + Y$.

   (ii) Write down the distribution of T.
   (iii) Use your distribution from part (ii) to check your results in part (i).

10 The numbers of emissions per minute from two radioactive substances, A and B, are independent and can be modelled by Poisson distributions with means 2.8 and 3.25, respectively.

Find the probabilities that in a period of one minute there will be

   (i) at least three emissions from substance A
   (ii) one emission from one of the two substances and two emissions from the other substance
   (iii) a total of five emissions.

11. The number of cats rescued by an animal shelter each day may be modelled by a Poisson distribution with parameter 2.5, while the number of dogs rescued each day may be modelled by an independent Poisson distribution with parameter 3.2.

    (i) Calculate the probability that on a randomly chosen day the shelter rescues

       (a) exactly two cats   (b) exactly three dogs

       (c) exactly five cats and dogs in total.

    (ii) Given that one day exactly five cats and dogs were rescued, find the conditional probability that exactly two of these animals were cats.

12. A sociologist claims that only 3% of all suitably qualified students from inner city schools go on to university. The sociologist selects a random sample of 200 of these students. Use a Poisson distribution to estimate the probability that

    (i) exactly five go to university

    (ii) more than five go to university.

    (iii) If there is at most a 5% chance that more than n of the 200 students go to university, find the lowest possible value of n.

    Another group of 100 students from inner city schools is also chosen. Estimate the probability that

    (iv) exactly five of each group go to university

    (v) exactly ten of all the chosen students go to university.

KEY POINTS

Poisson distribution

1. The Poisson distribution may be used in situations in which:
   - the variable is the frequency of events occurring in fixed intervals of time or space.

2. For the Poisson distribution to be a good model:
   - events occur randomly
   - events occur independently
   - events occur at a uniform average rate.

3. For a Poisson random variable X, where $X \sim \text{Poisson}(\lambda)$
   - $P(X = r) = e^{-\lambda} \times \dfrac{\lambda^r}{r!}$ for $r = 0, 1, 2, \ldots$

4. For $X \sim \text{Poisson}(\lambda)$
   - $E(X) = \lambda$
   - $\text{Var}(X) = \lambda$.

5. The sum of two independent Poisson distributions
   - If $X \sim \text{Poisson}(\lambda)$ and $Y \sim \text{Poisson}(\mu)$, then $X + Y \sim \text{Poisson}(\lambda + \mu)$.

6. Hypothesis testing using the Poisson distribution
   - This tests the null hypothesis H_0 that $\lambda = k$ against an alternative hypothesis H_1.
   - H_1 could be of the form $p < k$ or $p > k$, both of which lead to a one-tailed test, or $p \neq k$, which gives a two-tailed test.

The sum of two or more Poisson distributions

LEARNING OUTCOMES

When you have completed this chapter you should be able to:

- recognise situations under which the Poisson distribution is likely to be an appropriate model
- calculate probabilities using a Poisson distribution
- know and be able to use the mean and variance of a Poisson distribution
- know that the sum of two or more independent Poisson distributions is also a Poisson distribution
- recognise situations in which both the Poisson distribution and the binomial distribution might be appropriate models
- carry out a hypothesis test on the mean of a Poisson distribution using a single observation

7 The chi-squared test on a contingency table

The fact that the criterion which we happen to use has a fine ancestry of statistical theorems does not justify its use. Such justification must come from empirical evidence that it works.

W. A. Shewhart

What kind of films do you enjoy?

To help it decide when to show trailers for future programmes, the management of a cinema asks a sample of its customers to fill in a brief questionnaire saying which type of film they enjoy. It wants to know whether there is any relationship between people's enjoyment of horror films and action movies.

Discussion point
How do you think the management should select the sample of customers?

The chi-squared test on a contingency table

1 The chi-squared test on a contingency table

The management of the cinema takes 150 randomly selected questionnaires and records whether those patrons enjoyed or did not enjoy horror films and action movies.

Table 7.1

Observed frequency f_o	Enjoyed horror films	Did not enjoy horror films
Enjoyed action movies	51	41
Did not enjoy action movies	15	43

This method of presenting data is called a 2 × 2 **contingency table**. It is used where two variables (here 'attitude to horror films' and 'attitude to action movies') have been measured on a sample, and each variable can take two different values ('enjoy' or 'not enjoy').

The values of the variables fall into one or other of two categories. You want to determine the extent to which the variables are **related**.

It is conventional, and useful, to add the row and column totals in a contingency table: these are called the **marginal totals** of the table.

Table 7.2

Observed frequency f_o	Enjoyed horror films	Did not enjoy horror films	Total
Enjoyed action movies	51	41	92
Did not enjoy action movies	15	43	58
Total	66	84	150

> **Note**
> You will meet larger contingency tables later in this chapter.

A formal version of the cinema management's question is, 'Is enjoyment of horror films independent of enjoyment of action movies?'. You can use the sample data to investigate this question.

You can estimate the probability that a randomly chosen cinema-goer will enjoy horror films as follows. The number of cinema-goers in the sample who enjoyed horror films is 51 + 15 = 66.

So the proportion of cinema-goers who enjoyed horror films is $\frac{66}{150}$.

In a similar way, you can estimate the probability that a randomly chosen cinema-goer will enjoy action movies. The number of cinema-goers in the sample who enjoyed action movies is 51 + 41 = 92.

So the proportion of cinema-goers who enjoyed action movies is $\frac{92}{150}$.

> Notice how you use the marginal totals 66 and 92 which were calculated previously.

If people enjoyed horror films and action movies independently with the probabilities you have just estimated, then you would expect to find, for instance:

Number of people enjoying both types

= 150 × P(a random person enjoying both types)

= 150 × P(enjoying horror) × P(enjoying action)

$$= 150 \times \frac{66}{150} \times \frac{92}{150}$$

$$= \frac{6072}{150}$$

$$= 40.48$$

In the same way, you can calculate the number of people you would expect to correspond to each cell in the table.

Table 7.3

Expected frequency f_e	Enjoyed horror films	Did not enjoy horror films	Total
Enjoyed action movies	$150 \times \frac{66}{150} \times \frac{92}{150} = 40.48$	$150 \times \frac{84}{150} \times \frac{92}{150} = 51.52$	92
Did not enjoy action movies	$150 \times \frac{66}{150} \times \frac{58}{150} = 25.52$	$150 \times \frac{84}{150} \times \frac{58}{150} = 32.48$	58
Total	66	84	150

Note that it is an inevitable consequence of this calculation that these expected figures have the same marginal totals as the sample data.

You are now in a position to test the original hypotheses, which you can state formally as:

H_0: enjoyment of the two types of film is independent.

H_1: enjoyment of the two types of film is not independent.

The expected frequencies were calculated assuming the null hypothesis is true. You know the actual sample frequencies and the aim is to decide whether those from the sample are so different from those calculated theoretically that the null hypothesis should be rejected.

A statistic which measures how far apart a set of observed frequencies is from the set expected under the null hypothesis is the χ^2 (chi-squared) statistic. It is given by the formula:

> The value of the χ^2 test statistic is denoted by X^2.

$$X^2 = \sum \frac{(f_o - f_e)^2}{f_e} = \sum \frac{(\text{observed frequency} - \text{expected frequency})^2}{\text{expected frequency}}$$

You can use this here: the observed and expected frequencies are summarised below.

Table 7.4

Observed frequency f_o	Enjoyed horror	Did not enjoy horror
Enjoyed action	51	41
Did not enjoy action	15	43

Expected frequency f_e	Enjoyed horror	Did not enjoy horror
Enjoyed action	40.48	51.52
Did not enjoy action	25.52	32.48

The chi-squared test on a contingency table

The χ^2 statistic is:

$$X^2 = \Sigma \frac{(f_o - f_e)^2}{f_e} = \frac{(51 - 40.48)^2}{40.48} + \frac{(41 - 51.52)^2}{51.52} + \frac{(15 - 25.52)^2}{25.52} + \frac{(43 - 32.48)^2}{32.48}$$

$$= \frac{(10.52)^2}{40.48} + \frac{(10.52)^2}{51.52} + \frac{(10.52)^2}{25.52} + \frac{(10.52)^2}{32.48} = 12.626$$

> Note that the four numbers on the top lines (numerators) in this calculation are equal. This is not by chance; it will always happen with a 2 × 2 table. It provides you with a useful check and short cut when you are working out X^2.

Following the usual hypothesis-testing methodology, you want to know whether a value for this statistic at least as large as 12.626 is likely to occur by chance when the null hypothesis is true. The critical value at the 10% significance level for this test statistic is 2.706.

> You will see how to find critical values for a χ^2 test later in this chapter.

Since $12.626 > 2.706$, you reject the null hypothesis, H_0, and conclude that people's enjoyment of the two types of film is not independent or that the enjoyment of the two is *associated*.

The diagram below shows you the relevant χ^2 distribution for this example, the critical region and the test statistic.

Note

Notice that you cannot conclude that attending one session or the other causes people to enjoy one type of film in preference to another. The test is whether enjoyment of the two types is associated. It could be that audiences for the different sessions are dominated, for instance, by different age groups, but you do not know. The test tells you nothing about causality.

> The critical region at the 10% level is shaded in grey
>
> The test statistic $X^2 = 12.626$ is inside the critical region

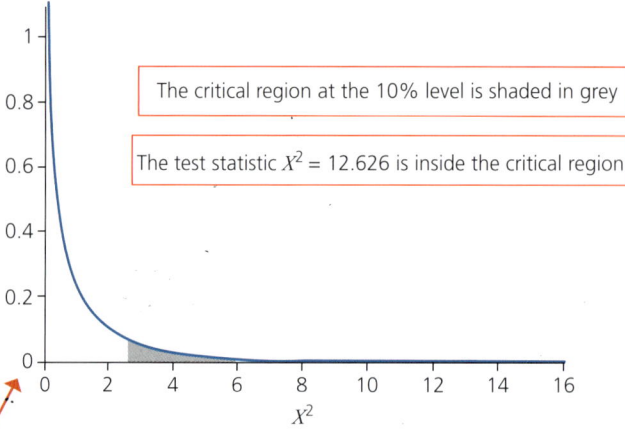

Figure 7.1

> Equation of graph is
> $y = \dfrac{2e^{\frac{-x}{2}}}{\sqrt[5]{x}}$

> The information about the χ^2 distribution is for your interest – you do not need to use it to carry out the tests in this chapter.
>
> A standard Normal variable is drawn from a Normal population with mean 0 and variance 1.

The chi-squared distribution

The χ^2 distribution with n degrees of freedom is the distribution of the sum of the squares of n independent standard Normal random variables.

You can use it to test how well a set of data matches a given distribution. Many examples of such tests are covered in this chapter.

These tests include that used in the example of the cinema-goers: that is, whether the two classifications used in a contingency table are independent of one another. The hypotheses for such a test are:

H_0: The two variables whose values are being measured are independent in the population.

H_1: The two variables whose values are being measured are not independent in the population.

In order to carry out this test, you need to know more about the χ^2 distribution.

Figure 7.1 is an example of a χ^2 distribution. The shape of the χ^2 distribution curve depends on the number of free variables involved, the degrees of freedom, υ. To find the value for υ in this case, you start off with the number of cells which must be filled and then subtract one degree of freedom for each restriction, derived from the data, which is placed on the frequencies. In the cinema example above, you are imposing the requirements that the total of the frequencies must be 150, and that the overall proportions of people enjoying horror films and action movies are $\frac{66}{150}$ and $\frac{92}{150}$, respectively.

Hence $\upsilon = 4$ (number of cells)

$\qquad - 1$ (total of frequencies is fixed by the data)

$\qquad - 2$ (proportions of people enjoying each type are estimated from the data)

$\qquad = 1$

So Figure 7.1 shows the shape of the χ^2 distribution for 1 degree of freedom.

In general, for an $m \times n$ contingency table, the degrees of freedom is:

$\upsilon = m \times n$ (number of cells)

$\qquad - (m + n - 1)$ (row and column totals are fixed but row totals and column totals have the same sum)

$\qquad = mn - m - n + 1$

$\qquad = (m - 1)(n - 1)$

As you will see later in the chapter, the calculation of the degrees of freedom varies from one χ^2 test to another.

Figure 7.2 shows the shape of the chi-squared distribution for $\upsilon = 1, 2, 3, 5$ and 10 degrees of freedom.

> **Note**
>
> As you can see, the shape of the chi-squared distribution depends very much on the number of degrees of freedom. So the critical region also depends on the number of degrees of freedom.

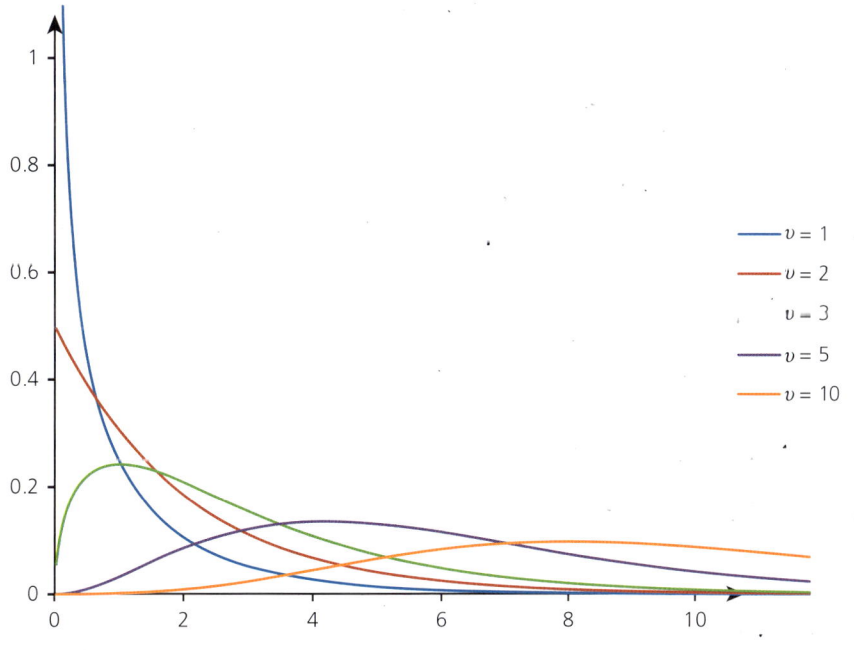

Figure 7.2

The chi-squared test on a contingency table

You can see in Figure 7.3 a typical χ^2 distribution curve together with the critical region for a significance level of $p\%$. An extract from a table of critical values of the χ^2 distribution for various degrees of freedom is also shown.

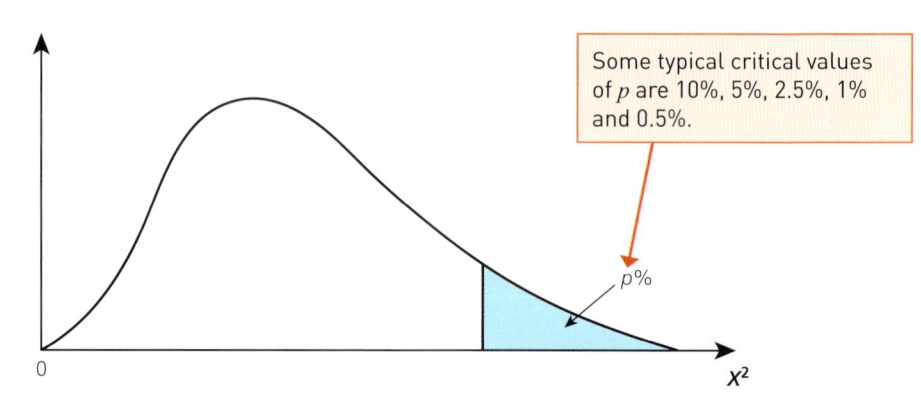

Some typical critical values of p are 10%, 5%, 2.5%, 1% and 0.5%.

$p\%$	99	97.5	95	90	10	5.0	2.5	1.0	0.5
$v = 1$	.0001	.0010	.0039	.0158	2.706	3.841	5.024	6.635	7.879
2	.0201	.0506	0.103	0.211	4.605	5.991	7.378	9.210	10.60
3	0.115	0.216	0.352	0.584	6.521	7.815	9.348	11.34	12.84
4	0.297	0.484	0.711	1.064	7.779	9.488	11.14	13.28	14.86
5	0.554	0.831	1.145	1.610	9.236	11.07	12.83	15.09	16.75
6	0.872	1.237	1.635	2.204	10.64	12.59	14.45	16.81	18.55
7	1.239	1.690	2.167	2.833	12.02	14.07	16.01	18.48	20.28
8	1.646	2.180	2.733	3.490	13.36	15.51	17.53	20.09	21.95
9	2.088	2.700	3.325	4.168	14.68	16.92	19.02	21.67	23.59

Figure 7.3

EXTENSION

> **Note**
>
> The figures on the left hand side of the table, covering probabilities for 99% to 90%, can be used to investigate whether a match is too good to be credible.

Yates' correction

> ! This is A-level only content

The statistic $\Sigma \dfrac{(f_o - f_e)^2}{f_e}$ does have a distribution that is approximately that of the chi-squared distribution, but this is only approximate, and the difference tends to increase the probability of rejecting H_0. This bias is most exaggerated in the case of a 2-by-2 contingency tables. Yates' correction is an attempt to make the approximation more exact. It involves tweaking the chi-squared statistic into

$$X^2_{Yates} = \Sigma \dfrac{(|f_o - f_e| - 0.5)^2}{f_e}.$$

Clearly this change has the effect in almost all cases of reducing the size of the chi-squared statistic, and so it makes it less likely that the null hypothesis will be rejected.

Yates' correction is needed

- when the total number of observations is low (less than 20)
- for a 2-by-2 contingency table.

To see Yates' correction in action, return now to the example that began this chapter, concerning people's enjoyment of horror and action movies.

Table 7.5

Observed frequency f_o	Enjoyed horror	Did not enjoy horror
Enjoyed action	51	41
Did not enjoy action	15	43

Expected frequency f_e	Enjoyed horror	Did not enjoy horror
Enjoyed action	40.48	51.52
Did not enjoy action	25.52	32.48

The chi-squared statistic for this table when not using Yates is 12.626.

If we use Yates, we get instead
$$\frac{(|51 - 40.48| - 0.5)^2}{40.48} + \frac{(|41 - 51.52| - 0.5)^2}{51.52}$$
$$+ \frac{(|15 - 25.52| - 0.5)^2}{25.52} + \frac{(|43 - 32.48| - 0.5)^2}{32.48}$$

which gives us the value 11.454.

The critical value here at the 10% level is 2.706, so the result of the test remains the same (we reject H_0). But you can see that if the critical value had been 12.000, the result of the test would have been different.

Properties of the test statistic X^2

You have seen the test statistic is given by

$$X^2 = \sum_{\text{All classes}} \frac{(f_o - f_e)^2}{f_e}$$

Here are some points to notice.

- It is clear that as the difference between the expected values and the observed values increases then so will the value of this test statistic. Squaring the top gives due weight to any particularly large differences. It also means that all values are positive.
- Dividing $(f_e - f_o)^2$ by f_e has the effect of standardising that element, allowing for the fact that, the larger the expected frequency within a class, the larger will be the difference between the observed and the expected.
- The usual convention in statistics is to use a Greek letter for a parent population parameter and the corresponding Roman letter for the equivalent sample statistic. Unfortunately, when it comes to χ^2, there is no Roman equivalent to the Greek letter χ, since it translates into 'CH'. Since X looks rather like χ a sample statistic from a χ^2 population is denoted by X^2. (In the same way Christmas is abbreviated to χmas but written Xmas.)

> **Note**
> An alternative notation which is often used is to call the expected frequency in the ith class E_i and the observed frequency in the ith class O_i.
> In this notation
> $$X^2 = \sum_i \frac{(O_i - E_i)^2}{F_i}$$

For example:
Population parameters	Sample statistics
Greek letters	Roman letters
μ	$\bar{x}$
σ	s
ρ	r

The chi-squared test on a contingency table

Continuing with tests on contingency tables

Example 7.1

The 4 × 3 contingency table below shows the type of car (saloon, sports, hatchback or SUV) owned by 360 randomly chosen people, and the age category (under 30, 30–60, over 60) into which the owners fall.

Table 7.6

Observed frequency f_o	Age of driver – under 30	Age of driver – 30–60	Age of driver – over 60	Total
Saloon	10	67	57	134
Sports car	19	14	3	36
Hatchback	32	47	34	113
SUV	7	56	14	77
Total	68	184	108	360

> **Note**
> The marginal totals are not essential in a contingency table, but it is conventional – and convenient – to add them. They are very helpful for subsequent calculations.

(i) Write down appropriate hypotheses for a test to investigate whether type of car and owner's age are independent.

(ii) Calculate expected frequencies assuming that the null hypothesis is true.

(iii) Calculate the value of the test statistic X^2.

(iv) Find the critical value at the 5% significance level.

(v) Complete the test.

(vi) Comment on how the ownership of different types of car depends on the age of the owner.

Solution

(i) H_0: Car type is independent of owner's age.

H_1: Car type is not independent of owner's age.

(ii) Table 7.7

Expected frequency f_e	Age of driver – under 30	Age of driver – 30–60	Age of driver – over 60	Total
Saloon	25.311	68.489	40.200	134
Sports car	6.800	18.400	10.800	36
Hatchback	21.344	57.756	33.900	113
SUV	14.544	39.356	23.100	77
Total	68	184	108	360

> You need to calculate the expected frequencies in the table assuming that the null hypothesis is true.
> Use the probability estimates given by the marginal totals.
> For instance the expected frequency for hatchback and owner's age is over 60 is given by
> $$360 \times \frac{113}{360} \times \frac{108}{360}$$
> $$= \frac{113 \times 108}{360} = 33.900$$

> **Note**
> You need to check that all the frequencies are large enough to make the χ^2 distribution a good approximation to the distribution of the X^2 statistic. The usual rule of thumb is to require all the expected frequencies to be greater than 5.
>
> This requirement is (just) satisfied here. However, you might be cautious in your conclusions if the X^2 statistic is very near the relevant critical value. If some of the cells have small expected frequencies, you should either collect more data or amalgamate some of the categories if it makes sense to do so. For instance, two adjacent age ranges could reasonably be combined, but two car types probably could not.

> **Note**
> You reject the null hypothesis if the test statistic is *greater* than the critical value.

> **Note**
> This illustrates the general result for contingency tables:
> Expected frequency for a cell
> $= \dfrac{\text{product of marginal totals for that cell}}{\text{total number of observations}}$

(iii) The value of the X^2 statistic is $X^2 = \sum \dfrac{(f_o - f_e)^2}{f_e}$

The contributions of the various cells to this are shown in the table below.

Table 7.8

Contribution to test statistic	Age of driver		
	under 30	30–60	over 60
Saloon	9.262	0.032	7.021
Sports car	21.888	1.052	5.633
Hatchback	5.319	2.003	0.000
SUV	3.913	7.039	3.585

An example of the calculation is
$\dfrac{(10 - 25.311)^2}{25.311} = 9.262$
for the top left cell.

Total = 9.262 + 0.032 + 7.021 + 21.888 + ⋯ + 3.585

$X^2 = 66.749$

(iv) The degrees of freedom are given by $v = (m-1)(n-1)$.

$v = (4-1) \times (3-1) = 6$

The number of rows, m, is 4
The number of columns, n, is 3

From the χ^2 tables, the critical value at the 5% level with six degrees of freedom is 12.59.

(v) The observed X^2 statistic of 66.749 is greater than the critical value of 12.59. So the null hypothesis is rejected and the alternative hypothesis is accepted at the 5% significance level:

that car type is not independent of owner's age,

or that car type and owner's age are associated.

(vi) In this case, the under-30 age group own fewer saloon cars and SUVs, more hatchbacks and many more sports cars than expected. Other cells with relatively large contributions to the X^2 statistic correspond to SUVs being owned more often than expected by 30–60-year-olds, and less often than expected by older or younger drivers, and over-60s owning more saloon cars and fewer sports cars than expected.

> **Note**
> You should always refer to the size of the contributions when commenting on the way that one variable is associated with the other (assuming, of course, that the conclusion to your test is that there is association).

The chi-squared test on a contingency table

USING ICT

Statistical software

You can use statistical software to carry out a χ^2 test for a contingency table.

In order for the software to process the test, you need to input the information in the table of observed frequencies. This consists of category names and the observed frequencies, so, in this case, it is the information in this table.

Table 7.9

Observed frequency f_o	Age of driver		
	under 30	30–60	over 60
Saloon	10	67	57
Sports car	19	14	3
Hatchback	32	47	34
SUV	7	56	14

The software then carries out all the calculations. Here is a typical output.

ChiSquared test

	under 30	30–60	over 60
Saloon	25.3111 9.2619 10	68.4889 0.0324 67	40.2 7.0209 57
Sports car	6.8 21.8882 19	18.4 1.0522 14	10.8 5.633 3
Hatchback	21.3444 5.3195 32	57.7556 2.003 47	33.9 0.0003 34
SUV	14.5444 3.9134 7	39.3556 7.0394 56	23.1 3.5848 14

Result
ChiSquared test
df 6
X^2 .... 66.7493
p 0.0000

Figure 7.4

Notice that the *p*-value is stated to be 0.0000. This requires some interpretation.
- The other output figures are given either to 4 decimal places or as whole numbers.
- So you can conclude that *p* = 0.0000 to 4 decimal places and therefore that *p* < 0.000 05.
- So the result is significant even at the 0.01% significance level.

> **Discussion points**
>
> The output includes the following information:
> → the expected frequencies
> → the contributions to the X^2 statistic
> → the degrees of freedom
> → the value of the X^2 statistic
> → the *p*-value for the test
>
> Identify where each piece of information is displayed.
>
> What other information is contained in the output box?

A spreadsheet

You can also use a spreadsheet to do the final stages of this test. To set it up, you would need to take the following steps.

- Enter the same information as before: the variable categories and the observed frequencies.
- Use a suitable formula to calculate the expected frequencies.
- Combine classes as necessary if any expected frequencies are below 5.
- Use a suitable formula to calculate the contributions to the test statistic.

- Find the sum of the contributions.
- Find the *p*-value using the formula provided with the spreadsheet, for example =CHISQ.DIST.RT(H1,6).

Cell H1 contains the value of the test statistic, X^2.

There are 6 degrees of freedom.

In this case, a typical spreadsheet gives the value of *p* as 1.894E-12, ie 1.894×10^{-12}, so much less than the upper bound of 0.000 05 inferred from the statistical software.

Exercise 7.1

① A group of 330 students, some aged 13 and the rest aged 16 is asked 'What is your usual method of transport from home to school?' The frequencies of each method of transport are shown in the table.

Table 7.10

	Age 13	Age 16
Walk	43	35
Cycle	24	42
Bus	64	49
Car	41	32

(i) Find the total of each row and each column.

A student is going to carry out a test to determine whether method of transport is independent of age.

(ii) Show that the expected frequency for age 16 students who walk is 37.35.

(iii) Show that the expected frequency for age 13 students who cycle is 34.40.

(iv) Would you expect the method of transport to be independent of age?

② A random sample of 80 students studying for a first aid exam was selected. The students were asked how many hours of revision they had done for the exam. The results are shown in the table, together with whether or not they passed the exam.

Table 7.11

	Pass	Fail
Less than 10 hours	13	18
At least 10 hours	42	7

(i) Find the expected frequency for each cell for a test to determine whether the number of hours of revision is independent of passing or failing.

(ii) Find the corresponding contributions to the chi-squared test statistic, including the use of Yates' correction.

The chi-squared test on a contingency table

3 A group of 281 voters is asked to rate how good a job they think the Prime Minister is doing. Each is also asked for the highest educational qualifications they have achieved. The frequencies with which responses occurred are shown in the table.

Table 7.12

Rating of PM	Highest qualifications achieved			
	None	GCSE or equivalent	A-level or equivalent	Degree or equivalent
Very poor	11	37	13	6
Poor	12	17	22	8
Moderate	7	11	25	10
Good	10	17	17	9
Very good	19	16	8	6

Use these figures to test whether there is an association between rating of the Prime Minister and highest educational qualification achieved.

4 A medical insurance company office is the largest employer in a small town. When 37 randomly chosen people living in the town were asked where they worked and whether they belonged to the town's health club, 21 were found to work for the insurance company, of whom 15 also belonged to the health club, while 7 of the 16 not working for the insurance company belonged to the health club.

Test the hypothesis that health club membership is independent of employment by the medical insurance company.

5 In a random sample of 163 adult males, 37 suffer from hay-fever and 51 from asthma, both figures including 14 men who suffer from both. Test whether the two conditions are associated.

6 In a survey of 184 London residents brought up outside the south-east of England, respondents were asked whether, job and family permitting, they would like to return to their area of origin. Their responses are shown in the table.

Table 7.13

Region of origin	Would like to return to	Would not like to return to
South-west	16	28
Midlands	22	35
North	15	31
Wales	8	6
Scotland	14	9

Test the hypothesis that desire to return is independent of region of origin.

7 A sample of 80 men and 150 women selected at random are tested for colour-blindness. Twelve of the men and five of the women are found to be colour-blind. Is there evidence at the 1% level that colour-blindness is gender-related?

⑧ Depressive illness is categorised as Type I, II or III. In a group of depressive psychiatric patients, the length of time for which their symptoms are apparent is observed. The results are shown below.

Table 7.14

Length of depressive episode	Type of symptoms		
	I	II	III
Brief	15	22	12
Average	30	19	26
Extended	7	13	21
Semi-permanent	6	9	11

Is the length of the depressive episode independent of the type of symptoms?

⑨ The personnel manager of a large firm is investigating whether there is any association between the length of service of the employees and the type of training they receive from the firm. A random sample of 200 employee records is taken from the last few years and is classified according to these criteria. Length of service is classified as short (meaning less than 1 year), medium (1–3 years) and long (more than 3 years). Type of training is classified as being merely an initial 'induction course', proper initial on the job training but little, if any, more, and regular and continuous training. The data are as follows.

Table 7.15

Type of training	Length of service		
	Short	Medium	Long
Induction course	14	23	13
Initial on-the-job	12	7	13
Continuous	28	32	58

The output from a statistical package for these data is shown below.

ChiSquared test

	Short	Medium	Long
Induction course	13.5000 0.018519 14	15.500 3.6290 23	21.000 3.0476 13
Initial on-the-job	8.6400 1.3067 12	9.9200 0.85952 7	13.440 0.01440 13
Continuous	313.860 0.46766 28	36.580 0.57344 32	49.560 1.4373 58

Result

ChiSquared test

df 4
X^2 .... 11.354
p 0.022859

Figure 7.5

The chi-squared test on a contingency table

Use the output to examine at the 5% level of significance whether these data provide evidence of association between length of service and type of training, stating clearly your null and alternative hypotheses.

Discuss your conclusions.

⑩ Public health officers are monitoring air quality over a large area. Air quality measurements using mobile instruments are made frequently by officers touring the area. The air quality is classified as poor, reasonable, good or excellent. The measurement sites are classified as being in residential areas, industrial areas, commercial areas or rural areas. The table shows a sample of frequencies over an extended period. The row and column totals and the grand total are also shown.

Table 7.16

Measurement site	Air quality				Row totals
	Poor	Reasonable	Good	Excellent	
Residential	107	177	94	22	400
Industrial	87	128	74	19	308
Commercial	133	228	148	51	560
Rural	21	71	24	16	132
Column totals	348	604	340	108	1400

Examine at the 5% level of significance whether or not there is any association between measurement site and air quality, stating carefully the null and alternative hypotheses you are testing. Report briefly on your conclusions.

⑪ The bank manager at a large branch was investigating the incidence of bad debts. Many loans had been made during the past year; the manager inspected the records of a random sample of 100 loans, and broadly classified them as satisfactory or unsatisfactory loans and as having been made to private individuals, small businesses or large businesses. The data were as follows.

Table 7.17

	Satisfactory	Unsatisfactory
Private individual	22	5
Small business	34	11
Large business	21	3

(i) Discuss any problems which could occur in carrying out a χ^2 test to examine if there is any association between whether or not the loan was satisfactory and the type of customer to whom the loan was made.

(ii) State suitable null and alternative hypotheses for the test described in part (i).

(iii) Carry out a test at the 5% level of significance without combining any groups.

(iv) Explain which groups it might be best to combine and carry out the test again with these groups combined.

⑫ A survey of a random sample of 44 people is carried out. Their musical preferences are categorised as pop, classical or jazz. Their ages are categorised as under 20, 20 to 39, 40 to 59 and 60 or over. A test is to be carried out to examine whether there is any association between musical preference and age group. The results are as follows.

Table 7.18

		Musical preference		
		Pop	Classical	Jazz
Age group	Under 20	8	4	1
	20–39	3	3	0
	40–59	2	4	3
	60 or over	1	7	8

(i) Calculate the expected frequencies for 'Under 20' and '60 or over' for pop music.

(ii) Explain why the test would not be valid using these four age categories.

(iii) State which categories it would be best to combine in order to carry out the test.

(iv) Using this combination, carry out the test at the 5% significance level.

(v) Discuss briefly how musical preferences vary between the combined age groups, as shown by the contributions to the test statistic.

[MEI ADAPTED]

KEY POINTS

1 Contingency tables

To test whether the variables in an $m \times n$ contingency table are independent the steps are as follows.

(i) The null hypothesis is that the variables are independent, the alternative is that they are not.

(ii) Calculate the marginal (row and column) totals for the table.

(iii) Calculate the expected frequency in each cell.

(iv) The χ^2 statistic is given by $X^2 = \sum \frac{(f_o - f_e)^2}{f_e}$ where f_o is the observed frequency and f_e is the expected frequency in each cell.

(v) Yates' correction for a 2-by-2 contingency table uses the statistic

$$X^2_{Yates} = \sum \frac{(|f_o - f_e| - 0.5)^2}{f_e}.$$

(vi) The number of degrees of freedom, v, for the test is $(m-1)(n-1)$ for an $m \times n$ table.

(vii) Read the critical value from the χ^2 tables (alternatively, use suitable software) for the appropriate degrees of freedom and significance level. If X^2 is less than the critical value, the null hypothesis is accepted; otherwise it is rejected.

(viii) If two variables are not independent, you say that there is an association between them.

The chi-squared test on a contingency table

LEARNING OUTCOMES

When you have completed this chapter you should be able to:
- interpret bivariate categorical data in a contingency table
- apply the χ^2 test to a contingency table
- apply Yates' correction for a 2-by-2 contingency table
- interpret the results of a χ^2 test using tables of critical values or the output from software.

8 Continuous random variables 1

A theory is a good theory if it satisfies two requirements: It must accurately describe a large class of observations on the basis of a model that contains only a few arbitrary elements, and it must make definite predictions about the results of future observations.

Stephen Hawking,
A Brief History of Time

Lucky escape for local fisherman

Local fisherman George Sutherland stared death in the face yesterday as he was plucked from the deck of his 56 ft boat, the *Belle Star*, by a freak wave. Only the quick thinking of his brother James, who grabbed hold of his legs, saved George from a watery grave.

'It was a bad day and suddenly this lump of water came down on us,' said George. 'It was a wave in a million, higher than the mast of the boat, and it caught me off guard'.

Hero James is a man of few words. 'All in a day's work' was his only comment.

Continuous random variables 1

> **Note**
> The data are historical. The last weather ship, the Polarfront, was withdrawn from service in 2010.

Freak waves do occur and they can have serious consequences in terms of damage to shipping, oil rigs and coastal defences, sometimes resulting in loss of life. It is important to estimate how often they will occur, and how high they will be. Was George Sutherland's one in a million estimate for a wave higher than the mast of the boat (11 m) at all accurate?

Before you can answer this question, you need to know the **probability density** of the heights of waves at that time of the year in the area where the *Belle Star* was fishing. The graph in Figure 8.1 shows this sort of information; it was collected in the same season of the year as the Sutherland incident by the Offshore Weather Ship *Juliet* in the North Atlantic.

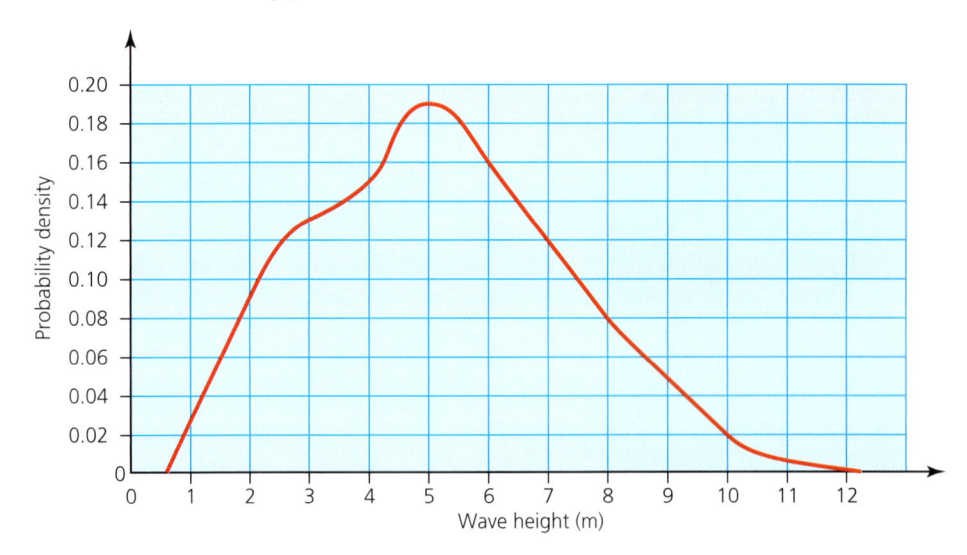

Figure 8.1

To obtain Figure 8.1 a very large amount of wave data had to be collected. This allowed the class interval widths of the wave heights to be sufficiently small for the outline of the curve to acquire this shape. It also ensured that the sample data were truly representative of the population of waves at that time of the year.

In a graph such as Figure 8.1, the vertical scale is a measure of probability density. Probabilities are found by estimating the area under the curve. The total area is 1.0, meaning that, effectively, all waves at this place have heights between 0.6 and 12.0 m (see Figure 8.2).

If this had been the place where the *Belle Star* was situated, the probability of encountering a wave at least 11 m high would have been 0.003, about 1 in 300. Clearly, George's description of it as 'a wave in a million' was not justified purely by its height. The fact that he called it a 'lump of water' suggests that perhaps it may have been more remarkable for its steep sides than its height.

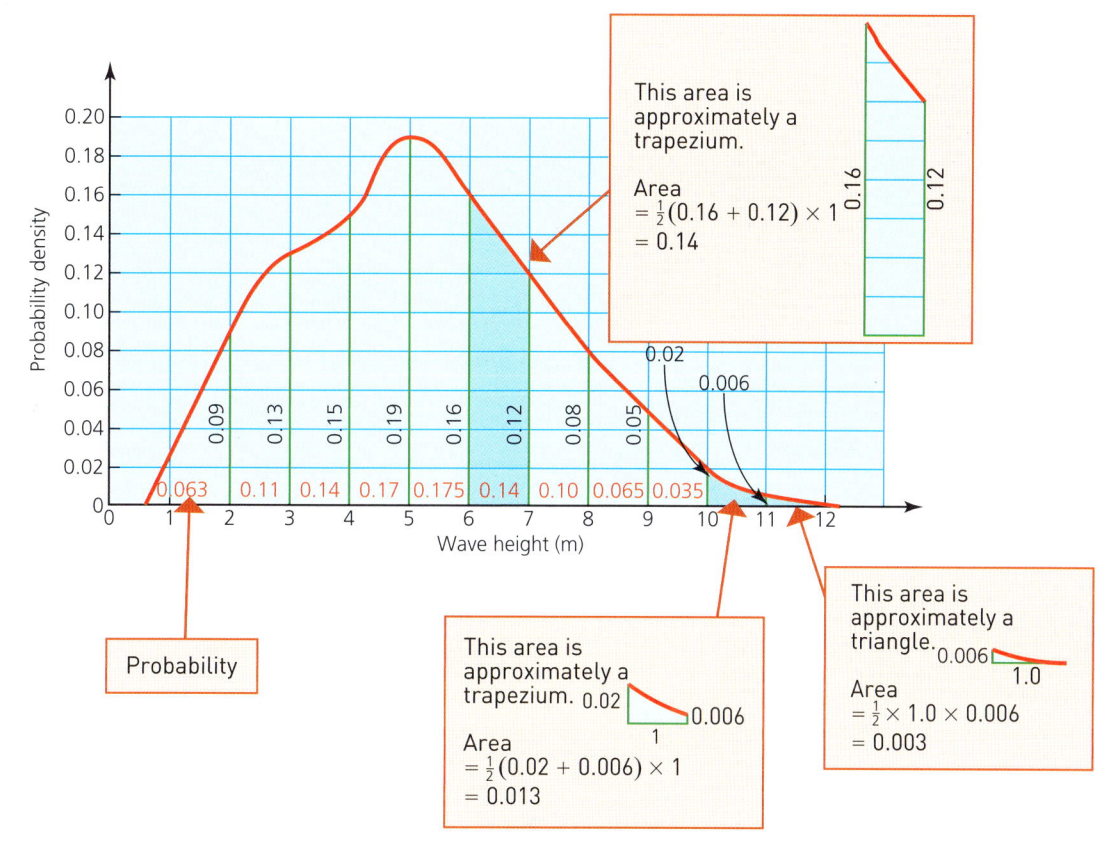

Figure 8.2

Discussion point

Is it reasonable to describe the height of a wave as *random*?

1 Probability density function

In the wave height example, the curve was determined experimentally, using equipment on board the Offshore Weather Ship *Juliet*. The curve is continuous because the random variable, the wave height, is continuous and not discrete. The possible heights of waves are not restricted to particular steps (say every 0.5 m), but may take any value within a range.

A function represented by a curve of this type is called a **probability density function**, often abbreviated to p.d.f. The probability density function of a continuous random variable, X, is usually denoted by $f(x)$. If $f(x)$ is a p.d.f. it follows that:

- $f(x) \geq 0$ for all x You cannot have negative probabilities.
- $\int_{\text{All values of } x} f(x)\,dx = 1$ The total area under the curve is 1.

Note

In the wave heights example, the probability density function has quite a complicated curve and so it is not possible to find a simple algebraic expression with which to model it.

For a continuous random variable with probability density function $f(x)$, the probability that X lies in the interval $[a, b]$ is given by

$$P(a \leq X \leq b) = \int_a^b f(x)\,dx$$

Probability density function

Note: Class boundaries

If you were to ask the question *'What is the probability of a randomly selected wave being exactly 2 m high?'* the answer would be zero. If you measured a likely looking wave to enough decimal places (assuming you could do so), you would eventually come to a figure which was not zero. The wave height might be 2.01...m or 2.000 003...m but the probability of it being exactly 2 m is infinitesimally small. Consequently, in theory, it makes no difference whether you describe the class interval from 2 to 2.5 m as $2 < h < 2.5$ or as $2 \leqslant h \leqslant 2.5$.

However, in practice, measurements are always rounded to some extent. The reality of measuring a wave's height means that you would probably be quite happy to record it to the nearest 0.1 m and get on with the next wave. So, in practice, measurements of 2.0 m and 2.5 m probably will be recorded, and intervals have to be defined so that it is clear which class they belong to. You would normally expect < at one end of the interval and ⩽ at the other: either $2 \leqslant h < 2.5$ or $2 < h \leqslant 2.5$. In either case, the probability of the wave being within the interval would be given by $\int_{2}^{2.5} f(x)dx$

Most of the techniques in this chapter assume that you do, in fact, have a convenient algebraic expression with which to work. However, the methods are still valid if this is not the case, but you would need to use numerical, rather than algebraic, techniques for integration and differentiation. In the high-wave incident, the areas corresponding to wave heights of less than 2 m and of at least 11 m were estimated by treating the shape as a triangle: other areas were approximated by trapezia.

Rufus foils council office break-in

Somewhere an empty-pocketed thief is nursing a sore leg and regretting the loss of a pair of trousers. Council porter Fred Lamming, and Rufus, a wiry haired Jack Russell, were doing a late-night check round the Council head office when they came upon the intruder on the ground floor. 'I didn't need to say anything,' Fred told me; 'Rufus went straight for him and grabbed him by the leg.' After a tussle, the man's trousers tore, leaving Rufus with a mouthful of material while the man made good his escape out of a window.

Following the incident, the local Council are looking at an electronic security system. 'Rufus won't live for ever,' explained Council leader Sandra Martin.

Example 8.1

The local Council are thinking of fitting an electronic security system inside head office. They have been told by manufacturers that the lifetime, X years, of the system they have in mind has the p.d.f.:

$$f(x) = \frac{3x(20-x)}{4000} \quad \text{for } 0 \leqslant x \leqslant 20.$$

and $f(x) = 0$ otherwise.

(i) Show that the manufacturers' statement is consistent with $f(x)$ being a probability density function.

(ii) Find the probability that:
  (a) it fails in the first year
  (b) it lasts ten years but then fails in the next year.

Solution

(i) The condition $f(x) \geqslant 0$ for all values of x between 0 and 20 is satisfied, as shown by the graph of $f(x)$, Figure 8.3.

> **Note**
> The general rule is:
> $F(x) = P(X \leq x) \int_{-\infty}^{x} f(u)\,du$.
> However, in practice the lower limit of the integral is replaced by the lower limit of the non-zero part of the probability density function (except when this is itself equal to $-\infty$).

This area gives the probability it fails in the first year, part **(ii)(a)**

This area gives the probability that it lasts 10 years but then fails in the next year, part **(ii)(b)**

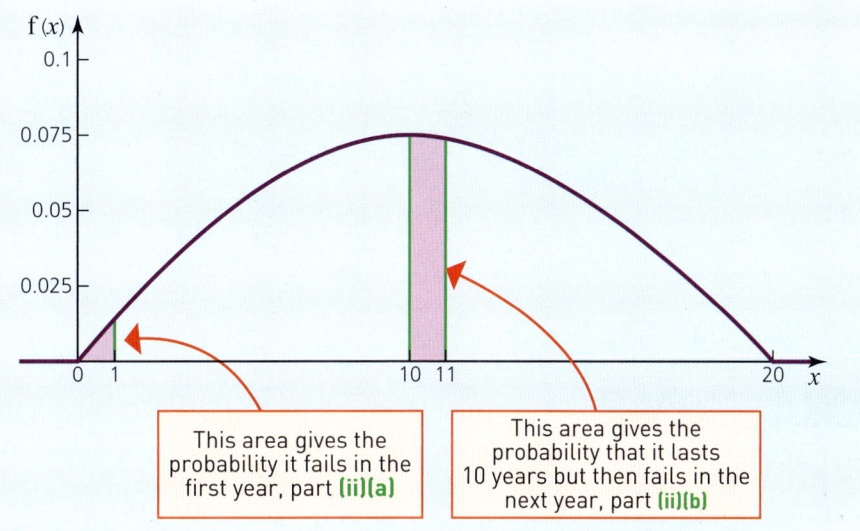

Figure 8.3

The other condition is that the area under the curve is 1.

$$\text{Area} = \int_{-\infty}^{\infty} f(x)\,dx = \int_{0}^{20} \frac{3x(20-x)}{4000}\,dx$$

$$= \frac{3}{4000} \int_{0}^{20} (20x - x^2)\,dx$$

$$= \frac{3}{4000} \left[10x^2 - \frac{x^3}{3}\right]_{0}^{20}$$

$$= \frac{3}{4000} \left[10 \times 20^2 - \frac{20^3}{3}\right]$$

$$= 1, \text{ as required.}$$

(a) *It fails in the first year.*

This is given by $P(X < 1) = \int_{0}^{1} \frac{3x(20-x)}{4000}\,dx$

$$= \frac{3}{4000} \int_{0}^{1} (20x - x^2)\,dx$$

$$= \frac{3}{4000} \left[10x^2 - \frac{x^3}{3}\right]_{0}^{1}$$

$$= \frac{3}{4000} \left(10 \times 1^2 - \frac{1^3}{3}\right)$$

$$= 0.00725$$

(b) *It fails in the 11th year.*

This is given by $P(10 \leq X < 11)$

Probability density function

$$= \int_{10}^{11} \frac{3x(20-x)}{4000} dx$$

$$= \frac{3}{4000}\left[10x^2 - \frac{1}{3}x^3\right]_{10}^{11}$$

$$= \frac{3}{4000}\left(10\times 11^2 - \frac{1}{3}\times 11^3\right) - \frac{3}{4000}\left(10\times 10^2 - \frac{1}{3}\times 10^3\right)$$

$$= 0.07475$$

Example 8.2

The continuous random variable X represents the amount of sunshine in hours between noon and 4 p.m. at a skiing resort in the high season. The probability density function, f(x), of X is modelled by

$$f(x) = \begin{cases} kx^2 & \text{for } 0 \leq x \leq 4 \\ 0 & \text{otherwise.} \end{cases}$$

(i) Find the value of k.

(ii) Find the probability that on a particular day in the high season there are more than two hours of sunshine between noon and 4 p.m.

Solution

(i) To find the value of k you must use the fact that the area under the graph of f(x) is equal to 1.

$$\int_{-\infty}^{\infty} f(x) \, dx = \int_0^4 kx^2 \, dx = 1$$

Therefore $\left[\frac{kx^3}{3}\right]_0^4 = 1$

$$\frac{64k}{3} = 1$$

So $k = \frac{3}{64}$

(ii)

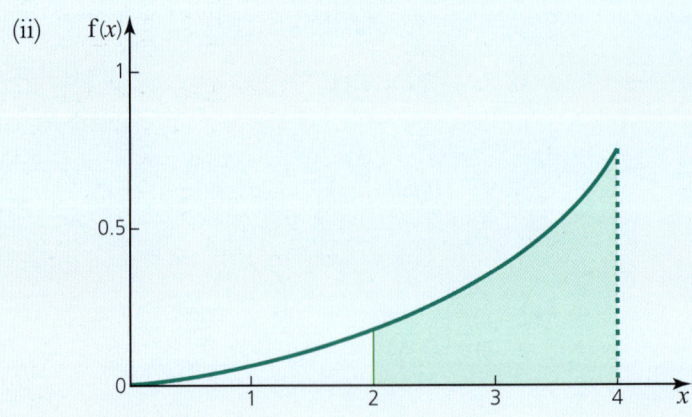

Figure 8.4

The probability of more than 2 hours of sunshine is given by

$$P(X > 2) = \int_2^\infty f(x)\,dx = \int_2^4 \frac{3x^2}{64}\,dx$$

$$= \left[\frac{x^3}{64}\right]_2^4$$

$$= \frac{64 - 8}{64}$$

$$= \frac{56}{64}$$

$$= 0.875$$

Example 8.3

The number of hours Darren spends each day working in his garden is modelled by the continuous random variable X, with p.d.f. $f(x)$ defined by

$$f(x) = \begin{cases} kx & \text{for } 0 \leq x < 3 \\ k(6-x) & \text{for } 3 \leq x < 6 \\ 0 & \text{otherwise.} \end{cases}$$

(i) Find the value of k.

(ii) Sketch the graph of $f(x)$.

(iii) Find the probability that Darren will work between 2 and 5 hours in his garden on a randomly selected day.

Solution

(i) To find the value of k you must use the fact that the area under the graph of $f(x)$ is equal to 1. You may find the area by integration, as shown below.

$$\int_{-\infty}^\infty f(x)\,dx = \int_0^3 kx\,dx + \int_3^6 k(6-x)\,dx = 1$$

$$\left[\frac{kx^2}{2}\right]_0^3 + \left[6kx - \frac{kx^2}{2}\right]_3^6 = 1$$

Therefore $\quad \frac{9k}{2} + (36k - 18k) - \left(18k - \frac{9k}{2}\right) = 1$

$$9k = 1$$

So $k = \frac{1}{9}$

Probability density function

> In this case, you could have found k without integration because the graph of the p.d.f. is a triangle, with area given by ½ × base × height, resulting in the equation
>
> $$\frac{1}{2} \times 6 \times k(6-3) = 1$$
>
> hence $9k = 1$
>
> and $k = \frac{1}{9}$.

(ii) Sketch the graph of f(x).

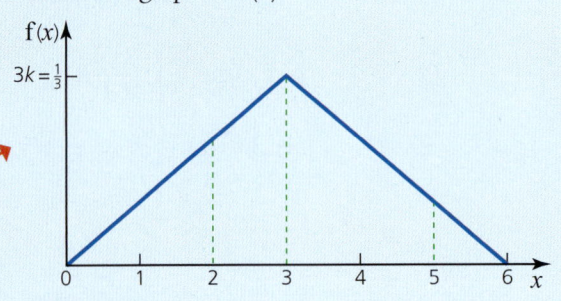

Figure 8.5

(iii) To find $P(2 \leqslant X \leqslant 5)$, you need to find both $P(2 \leqslant X < 3)$ and $P(3 \leqslant X \leqslant 5)$ because there is a different expression for each part.

$$P(2 \leqslant X \leqslant 5) = P(2 \leqslant X < 3) + P(3 \leqslant X \leqslant 5)$$

$$= \int_2^3 \frac{1}{9}x\,dx + \int_3^5 \frac{1}{9}(6-x)\,dx$$

$$= \left[\frac{x^2}{18}\right]_2^3 + \left[\frac{2x}{3} - \frac{x^2}{18}\right]_3^5$$

$$= \frac{9}{18} - \frac{4}{18} + \left(\frac{10}{3} - \frac{25}{18}\right) - \left(2 - \frac{1}{2}\right)$$

$$= 0.72 \quad \text{to two decimal places.}$$

The probability that Darren works between 2 and 5 hours in his garden on a randomly selected day is 0.72.

Exercise 8.1

① The continuous random variable X has probability density function f(x) where

$$f(x) = \begin{cases} kx & \text{for } 1 \leqslant x < 6 \\ 0 & \text{otherwise.} \end{cases}$$

  (i) Find the value of the constant k.
  (ii) Sketch $y = f(x)$.
  (iii) Find $P(X > 5)$.
  (iv) Find $P(2 \leqslant X \leqslant 3)$.

② The continuous random variable X has p.d.f. f(x) where

$$f(x) = \begin{cases} k(5-x) & \text{for } 0 \leqslant x \leqslant 4 \\ 0 & \text{otherwise.} \end{cases}$$

  (i) Find the value of the constant k.
  (ii) Sketch $y = f(x)$.
  (iii) Find $P(1.5 \leqslant X \leqslant 2.3)$.

③ The continuous random variable X has p.d.f. f(x) where

$$f(x) = \begin{cases} c & \text{for } -3 \leqslant x \leqslant 5 \\ 0 & \text{otherwise.} \end{cases}$$

(i) Find c.
(ii) Sketch $y = f(x)$.
(iii) Find $P(X < -1)$.
(iv) Find $P(X > 2)$.

④ The continuous random variable X has p.d.f. $f(x)$ where

$$f(x) = \begin{cases} kx & \text{for } 0 \leq x \leq 2 \\ 4k - kx & \text{for } 2 < x \leq 4 \\ 0 & \text{otherwise.} \end{cases}$$

(i) Find the value of the constant k.
(ii) Sketch $y = f(x)$.
(iii) Find $P(1 \leq X \leq 3.5)$.

⑤ The continuous random variable X has p.d.f. $f(x)$ where

$$f(x) = \begin{cases} ax^3 & \text{for } 0 \leq x \leq 3 \\ 0 & \text{otherwise.} \end{cases}$$

(i) Find the value of the constant a.
(ii) Sketch $y = f(x)$.
(iii) Find $P(X \leq 2)$.

⑥ A continuous random variable X has p.d.f.

$$f(x) = \begin{cases} k(x-1)(6-x) & \text{for } 1 \leq x \leq 6 \\ 0 & \text{otherwise.} \end{cases}$$

(i) Find the value of k.
(ii) Sketch $y = f(x)$.
(iii) Find $P(2 \leq X \leq 3)$.

⑦ A random variable X has p.d.f.

$$f(x) = \begin{cases} (x-1)(2-x) & \text{for } 1 \leq x < 2 \\ a & \text{for } 2 \leq x < 4 \\ 0 & \text{otherwise.} \end{cases}$$

(i) Find the value of the constant a.
(ii) Sketch $y = f(x)$.
(iii) Find $P(1.5 \leq X \leq 2.5)$.
(iv) Find $P(|X - 2| < 1)$.

⑧ A random variable X has p.d.f.

$$f(x) = \begin{cases} kx(3-x) & \text{for } 0 \leq x \leq 3 \\ 0 & \text{otherwise.} \end{cases}$$

(i) Find the value of k.
(ii) The lifetime (in years) of an electronic component is modelled by this distribution. Two such components are fitted in a radio which will only function if both devices are working. Find the probability that the radio will still function after two years, assuming that their failures are independent.

Probability density function

⑨ The planning officer in a council needs information about how long cars stay in the car park, and asks the attendant to do a check on the times of arrival and departure of 100 cars. The attendant provides the following data.

Table 8.1

Length of stay	Under 1 hour	1–2 hours	2–4 hours	4–10 hours	More than 10 hours
Number of cars	20	14	32	34	0

The planning officer suggests that the length of stay in hours may be modelled by the continuous random variable X with probability density function of the form

$$f(x) = \begin{cases} k(20 - 2x) & \text{for } 0 \leq x \leq 10 \\ 0 & \text{otherwise.} \end{cases}$$

(i) Find the value of k.
(ii) Sketch the graph of $f(x)$.
(iii) According to this model, how many of the 100 cars would be expected to fall into each of the four categories?
(iv) Do you think the model fits the data well?
(v) Are there any obvious weaknesses in the model? If you were the planning officer, would you be prepared to accept the model as it is, or would you want any further information?

⑩ During a war, the crew of an aeroplane has to destroy an enemy railway line by dropping bombs. The distance between the railway line and where the bomb hits the ground is X m, where X has the following p.d.f.

$$f(x) = \begin{cases} 10^{-4}(a + x) & \text{for } -a \leq x < 0 \\ 10^{-4}(a - x) & \text{for } 0 \leq x \leq a \\ 0 & \text{otherwise.} \end{cases}$$

(i) Find the value of a.
(ii) Find $P(50 \leq X \leq 60)$.
(iii) Find $P(|X| < 20)$. [MEI]

⑪ This graph shows the probability distribution function, f(x), for the heights, X, of waves at the point with Latitude 44°N Longitude 41°W.

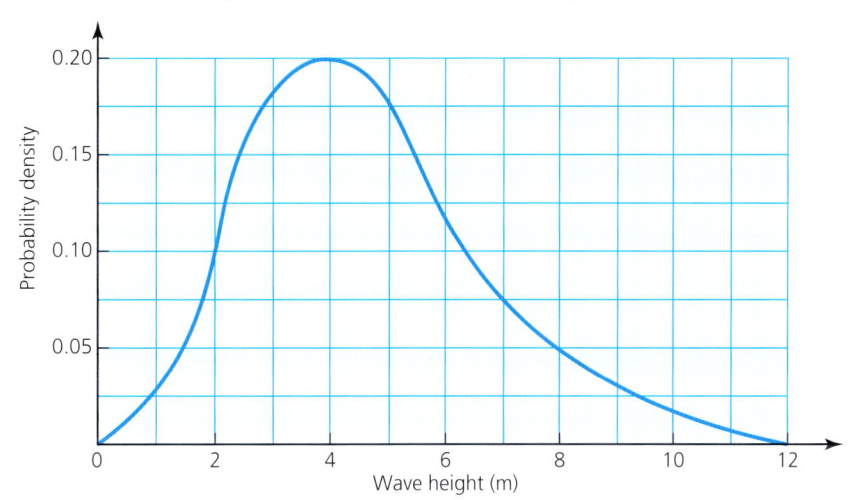

Figure 8.6

(i) Write down the values of f(x) when x = 0, 2, 4, ... , 12.

(ii) Hence estimate the probability that the height of a randomly selected wave is in the interval

　(a)　0–2 m　　(b)　2–4 m　　(c)　4–6 m
　(d)　6–8 m　　(e)　8–10 m　　(f)　10–12 m.

A model is proposed in which

$$f(x) = \begin{cases} kx(12-x)^2 & \text{for } 0 \leq x \leq 12 \\ 0 & \text{otherwise.} \end{cases}$$

(iii) Find the value of k.

(iv) Find, according to this model, the probability that a randomly selected wave is in the interval

　(a)　0–2 m　　(b)　2–4 m　　(c)　4–6 m
　(d)　6–8 m　　(e)　8–10 m　　(f)　10–12 m.

(v) By comparing the figures from the model with the real data, state whether you think it is a good model or not.

2 Expectation and variance

You will recall that, for a discrete random variable, expectation and variance are given by:

$$E(X) = \sum_i x_i p_i$$

$$\text{Var}(X) = \sum_i (x_i - \mu)^2 p_i = \sum_i x_i^2 p_i - [E(X)]^2$$

where μ is the mean and p_i is the probability of the outcome x_i for $i = 1, 2, 3, \ldots$, with the various outcomes covering all possibilities.

> **Note**
>
> You met these formulae in Chapter 5.
>
> Recall that p_i is another way of writing $P(X = x_i)$.

151

Expectation and variance

The expressions for the expectation and variance of a continuous random variable are equivalent, but with summation replaced by integration.

$$E(X) = \int_{\text{All values of } x} x f(x) \, dx$$

$\int_{\text{All values of } x}$ can also be written as $\int_{-\infty}^{\infty}$

$$\text{Var}(X) = \int_{\text{All values of } x} (x - \mu)^2 f(x) \, dx = \int_{\text{All values of } x} x^2 f(x) \, dx - [E(X)]^2$$

$E(X)$ is the same as the population mean, μ, and is often called the mean of X.

Example 8.4

The response time, in seconds, for a contestant in a general knowledge quiz is modelled by a continuous random variable X whose p.d.f. is

$$f(x) = \frac{x}{50} \quad \text{for } 0 < x \leq 10.$$

The rules state that a contestant who makes no answer is disqualified from the whole competition. This has the consequence that everybody gives an answer, if only a guess, to every question. Find

(i) the mean time in seconds for a contestant to respond to a particular question

(ii) the standard deviation of the time taken.

The organiser estimates the proportion of contestants who are guessing by assuming that they are those whose time is at least one standard deviation greater than the mean.

(iii) Using this assumption, estimate the probability that a randomly selected response is a guess.

Solution

(i) Mean time:

$$E(X) = \int_0^{10} x \frac{x}{50} \, dx$$

$$= \left[\frac{x^3}{150} \right]_0^{10} = \frac{1000}{150} = \frac{20}{3}$$

$$= 6 \frac{2}{3}$$

(ii) Variance:

$$\text{Var}(X) = \int_0^{10} x^2 f(x) \, dx - [E(X)]^2$$

$$= \int_0^{10} \frac{x^3}{50} \, dx - \left(6 \frac{2}{3} \right)^2$$

$$= \left[\frac{x^4}{200} \right]_0^{10} - \left(6 \frac{2}{3} \right)^2$$

$$= 5 \frac{5}{9}$$

Standard deviation $= \sqrt{\text{variance}} = \sqrt{5 \frac{5}{9}} = 2.357\ldots$

The standard deviation of the times is 2.36 (to 3 s.f.).

(iii) All those with response times greater than 6.667 + 2.357 = 9.024 seconds are taken to be guessing. The longest possible time is 10 seconds.

The probability that a randomly selected response is a guess is given by

$$= \int_{9.024}^{10} \frac{x}{50} dx$$

$$= \left[\frac{x^2}{100}\right]_{9.024}^{10}$$

$$= 0.185$$

so just under 1 in 5 answers are deemed to be guesses.

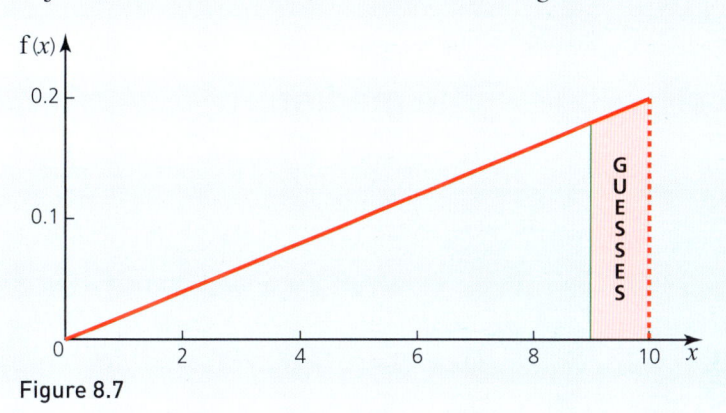

> **Note**
> Although the intermediate answers have been given rounded to three decimal places, more figures have been carried forward into subsequent calculations.

Figure 8.7

Example 8.5

The number of hours per day that Darren spends in his garden is modelled by the continuous random variable X, the p.d.f. of which is

$$f(x) = \begin{cases} \frac{1}{9}x & \text{for } 0 \leq x \leq 3 \\ \frac{6-x}{9} & \text{for } 3 < x \leq 6 \\ 0 & \text{otherwise.} \end{cases}$$

This is a continuation of Example 8.3.

Find $E(X)$, the mean number of hours per day that Darren spends in his garden.

Solution

$$E(X) = \int_{-\infty}^{\infty} x f(x) dx$$

$$= \int_0^3 x \frac{1}{9} x \, dx + \int_3^6 x \frac{6-x}{9} dx$$

$$= \left[\frac{x^3}{27}\right]_0^3 + \left[\frac{x^2}{3} - \frac{x^3}{27}\right]_3^6$$

$$= 1 - 0 + (12 - 8) - (3 - 1)$$

$$= 3$$

Darren spends a mean of 3 hours per day in his garden.

Expectation and variance

> **Note**
>
> Notice that, in this case, E(X) can be found from the line of symmetry of the graph of f(x). This situation often arises and you should be alert to the possibility of finding E(X) by symmetry as shown in Figure 8.8.

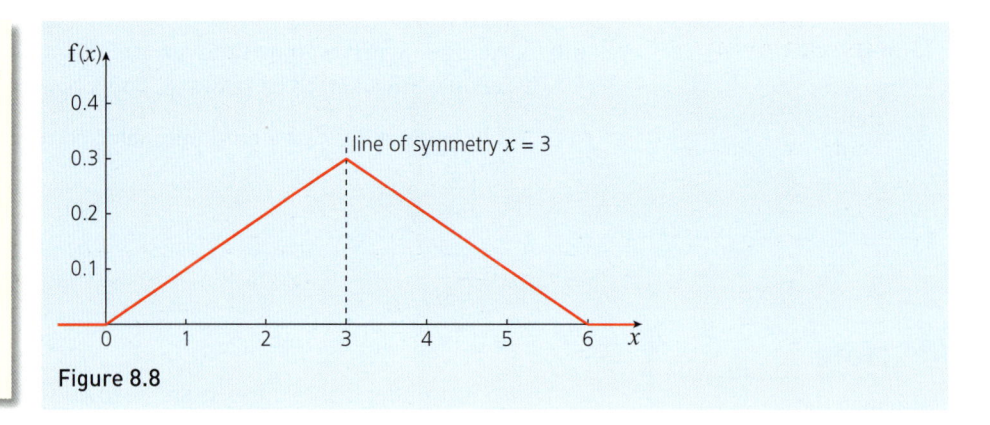

Figure 8.8

The median

The median value of a continuous random variable X with p.d.f. f(x) is the value m for which

$$P(X < m) = P(X > m) = 0.5.$$

Consequently, $\int_{-\infty}^{m} f(x)\,dx = 0.5$ and $\int_{m}^{\infty} f(x)\,dx = 0.5.$

The median is the value m such that the line $x = m$ divides the area under the curve f(x) into two equal parts. In Figure 8.9, a is the smallest possible value of X, b the largest. The line $x = m$ divides the shaded region into two regions A and B, both with area 0.5.

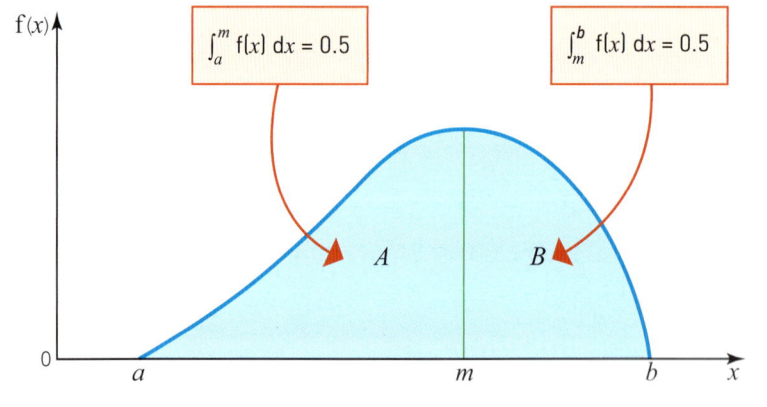

> ⚠ In general, the *mean* does not divide the area into two equal parts but it will do so if the curve is symmetrical about it because, in that case, it is equal to the median.

Figure 8.9

The mode

The mode of a continuous random variable X whose p.d.f. is f(x) is the value for which f(x) has the greatest value. Thus the mode is the value of X where the curve is at its highest.

If the mode is at a local maximum of f(x), then it may often be found by differentiating f(x) and solving the equation

$$f'(x) = 0.$$

> **Discussion point**
> For which of the distributions in Figure 8.10 could the mode be found by differentiating the p.d.f.?

(a) The exponential distribution $f(x) = \lambda e^{-\lambda x}$

(b) A distribution with negative skew

(c) A triangular distribution

(d) A bimodal distribution

(e) Pascal's distribution $f(x) = \frac{1}{2} e^{-|x|}$

(f) A uniform (rectangular) distribution

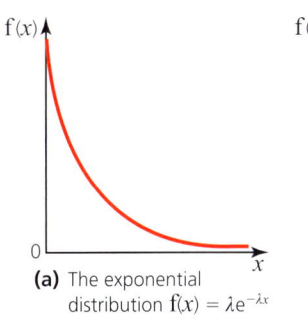

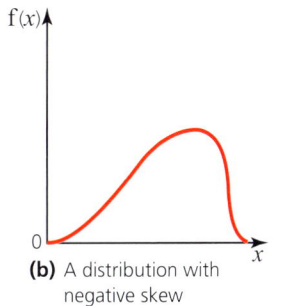

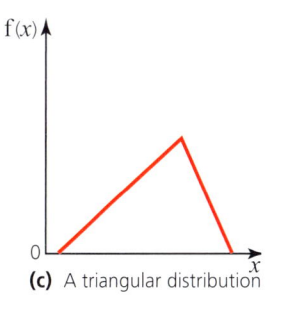

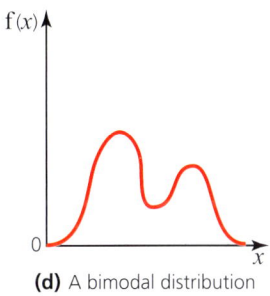

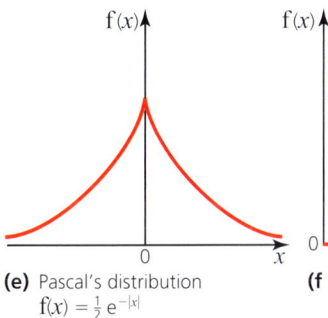

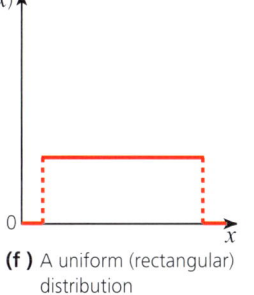

Figure 8.10

Example 8.6

The continuous random variable X has p.d.f. $f(x)$ where

$$f(x) = \begin{cases} 4x(1-x^2) & \text{for } 0 \leq x \leq 1 \\ 0 & \text{otherwise.} \end{cases}$$

Find

(i) the mode

(ii) the median.

Solution

(i) The mode is found by differentiating $f(x) = 4x - 4x^3$

$$f'(x) = 4 - 12x^2$$

Solving $f'(x) = 0$

$$x = \frac{1}{\sqrt{3}} = 0.577 \text{ to 3 decimal places.}$$

> $x = -0.577$ is also a root of $f'(x) = 0$ but is outside the range $0 \leq x \leq 1$.

It is easy to see from the shape of the graph (see Figure 8.11 on the next page) that this must be a maximum, and so the mode is 0.577.

(ii) The median, m, is given by

$$\int_{-\infty}^{m} f(x) \, dx = 0.5$$

> Since $x \geq 0$

$$\Rightarrow \int_{0}^{m} (4x - 4x^3) \, dx = 0.5$$

$$\left[2x^2 - x^4 \right]_{0}^{m} = 0.5$$

155

The Normal distribution

> This equation is a quadratic in m^2. You can solve it using the quadratic formula and then taking the square root of the answer.

$$2m^2 - m^4 = 0.5$$
$$2m^4 - 4m^2 + 1 = 0$$

$m = 0.541$ or 1.307 to 3 decimal places.

$m = \pm 0.541$ or ± 1.307

> Since -0.541 and ± 1.307 are all outside the domain of X, the median is 0.541.

The median is 0.541 (3 s.f.)

> Since 1.307 is outside the domain of X, the median is 0.541.

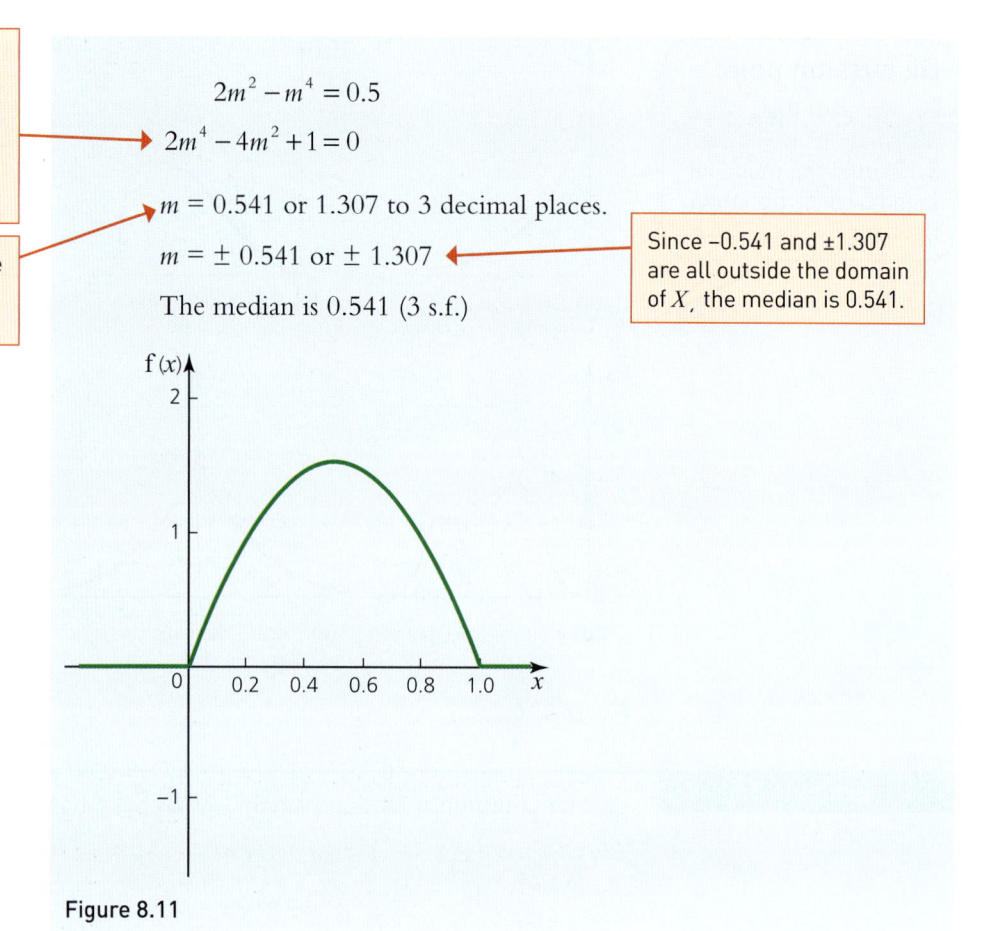

Figure 8.11

3 The Normal distribution

A familiar example of a continuous random variable is provided by the Normal distribution. This distribution is a good model for many naturally occurring continuous random variables, such as the lengths, weights and life spans of living objects. The ideas involved are introduced here and followed up in greater depth in Chapter 10. However, the importance of the Normal distribution in statistics is much more profound than this; in the next section of this chapter it is used in an introduction to confidence intervals and these ideas are also taken further in Chapters 10.

> **Note**
>
> In Chapter 12 of this book, you will also meet two other continuous distributions: the rectangular (uniform) and the exponential.

The probability density function for a Normal distribution with mean μ and standard deviation σ is given by

$$f(x) = \frac{1}{\sigma\sqrt{2\pi}} e^{-\frac{1}{2}\left(\frac{x-\mu}{\sigma}\right)^2}.$$

However it is common to write this in terms of the variable z given by $z = \frac{x-\mu}{\sigma}$. This changes the horizontal scale of the graph from the value of the original variable to the number of standard deviations it is from the mean. It is usual also to use replace the letter f by the Greek letter ϕ so that the p.d.f. is written as

> This process is called **standardising** the variable

> **Note**
> The letter ϕ is the lower case Greek ph. It is called phi and is the nearest equivalent to f in the Greek alphabet. It is also often written φ.

$$\phi(z) = \frac{1}{\sqrt{2\pi}} e^{-\frac{1}{2}z^2}.$$

This gives a symmetrical bell shaped curve.

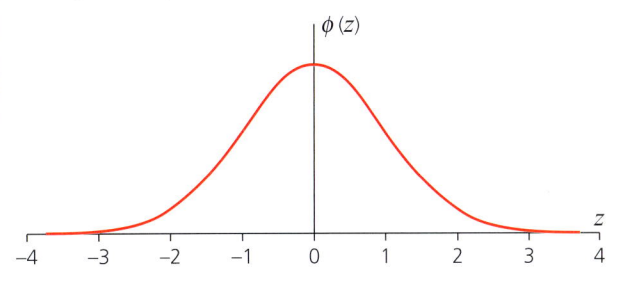

Figure 8.12

In common with other continuous random variables, the area under the graph of the p.d.f. represents a probability and so the area beneath the curve in Figure 8.12 is 1.

So you would expect to find the probability that z lies between, say, -1 and 2 by evaluating the integral $\int_{-1}^{2} \frac{1}{\sqrt{2\pi}} e^{-\frac{1}{2}z^2} \, dz$.

Unfortunately, this function cannot be integrated and so a numerical method has to be used. In Chapter 11, you will use your calculator to do this for you. Alternatively you can use tables of values. However, at this introductory stage, some particular areas are so useful that it is helpful to remember them.

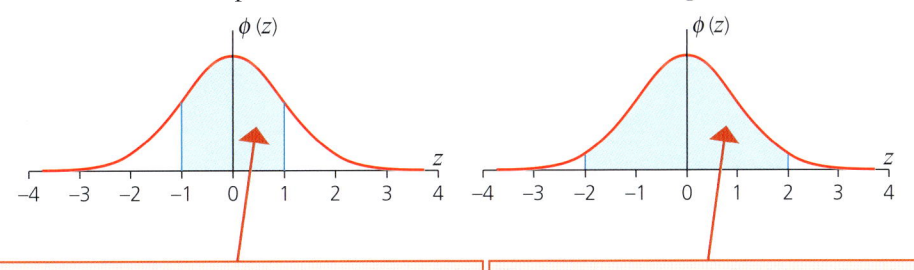

The area between $z = -1$ and $z = +1$ is about 0.68 or 68%

The area between $z = -2$ and $z = +2$ is about 0.95 or 95%

Figure 8.13

It is also helpful to know the values of z for particular areas.

- An area of 90% lies between $z = \pm 1.645$ and so 10% is outside, 5% at each tail.
- An area of 95% lies between $z = \pm 1.960$ and so 5% is outside, 2.5% at each tail.
- An area of 99% lies between $z = \pm 2.576$ and so 1% is outside, 0.5% at each tail.

Example 8.7

A model for the heights of women in a country is that they are Normally distributed with mean 162 cm and standard deviation 6.0 cm.

Use this model to estimate the heights of the middle 90% of women in that country.

Solution

$|z| \leq 1.645$

The heights of the middle 90% of women are within 1.645 standard deviations of the mean.

$162 + 1.645 \times 6.0 = 171.87$

The Normal distribution

$162 - 1.645 \times 6.0 = 152.13$

Given the accuracy of the figures in the model an appropriate estimate is between 152 and 172 cm.

> To the nearest inch, that is between 5 feet 0 inches and 5 feet 8 inches.

Example 8.8

The time Melanie spends on her history assignments may be modelled as Normally distributed with mean 40 minutes and standard deviation 10 minutes. The times taken on assignments may be assumed to be independent.

Find

(i) the probability that a particular assignment takes longer than an hour

(ii) the time in which 95% of all assignments can be completed.

Solution

(i) 1 hour is 60 minutes and $\dfrac{60 - 40}{10} = 2$

So this is 2 standard deviations over the mean.

The probability is the area of the right-hand tail in Figure 8.14. It is 2.5%.

So the probability is 0.025.

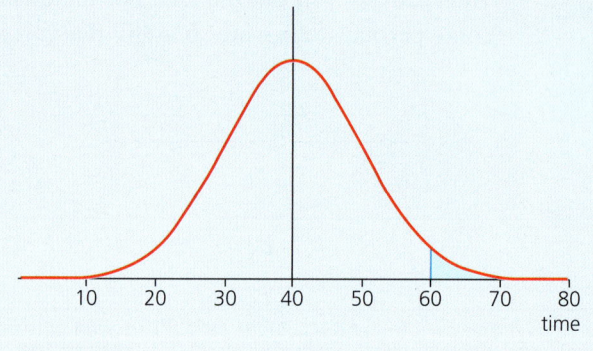

Figure 8.14

(ii) 95% of times correspond to the shaded area in Figure 8.15.

The tail on the right hand side is 5% so the vertical line is 1.645 standard deviations beyond the mean.

$$40 + 1.645 \times 10 = 56.45$$

So the time is about 56½ minutes.

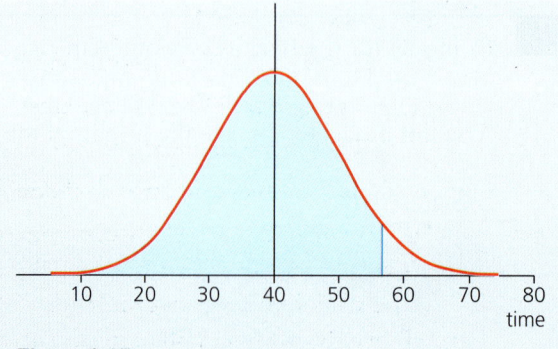

Figure 8.15

Exercise 8.2

① The weights of adult males of a particular type of lizard are Normally distributed with mean 22.4 g and standard deviation 3.2 g. A particular male lizard weighs 30 g.

State whether it is among the heaviest 2.5% of male lizards, giving an appropriate calculation to justify your answer.

② The lengths of young eels of a particular type at a certain age are Normally distributed. 5% of the young eels are less than 12.2 cm long and 5% are more than 20.4 cm long. Find the mean and standard deviation of their lengths, giving your answers to the nearest 0.1 cm.

③ The times for a particular journey are Normally distributed with mean 65 minutes and standard deviation 7.5 minutes. Approximately what percentage of journeys takes less than 50 minutes?

④ The random variable X has a Normal distribution with mean 10 and standard deviation 2. The reading a from this distribution lies within the highest 0.5% of values. Which one of the following statements is definitely true, to 2 decimal places?

(A) $a \leqslant 6.71$ (B) $6.71 \leqslant a \leqslant 13.29$ (C) $a \leqslant 15.15$ (D) $a \geqslant 15.15$

⑤ Find the probabilities represented by the shaded regions of these Normal curves.

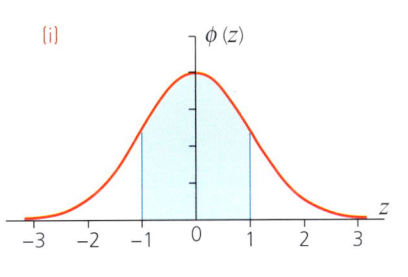

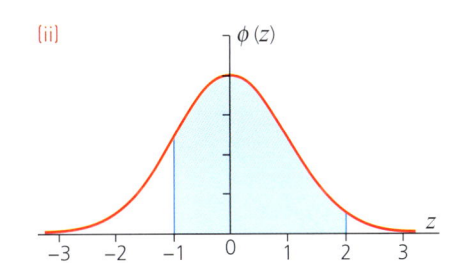

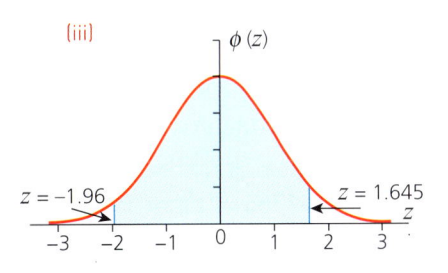

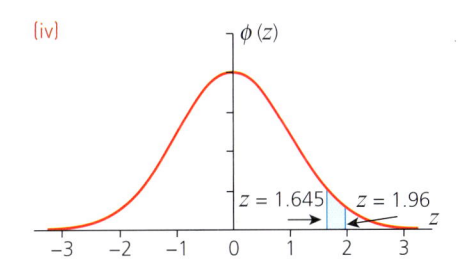

(i) [graph with shaded region between $z=-1$ and $z=1$]

(ii) [graph with shaded region $z \leqslant 0$]

(iii) [graph with shaded region between $z=-1.96$ and $z=1.645$]

(iv) [graph with shaded region between $z=1.645$ and $z=1.96$]

Figure 8.16

⑥ The mean weight of the contents of a jar of jam produced in a factory is 353 g with standard deviation 8 g. Assume that the weight of the jars is Normally distributed.

(i) Find d so that the interval $(353-d, 353+d)$ contains 99% of the weights.

A sample of 50 jars is now taken.

(ii) What is the standard error of the mean here?

(iii) Find a 90% symmetric confidence interval for the mean weight.

⑦ Sally is a fruit farmer. Her trees produce apples with weights that are Normally distributed with mean 90 g and standard deviation 12 g. She sells those with weights between 78 g and 114 g to a supermarket. Does Sally sell over 80% of her apples to the supermarket?

The Normal distribution

⑧ The graph shows the curve $y = \phi(x)$ for a Normal distribution with standard deviation 5.

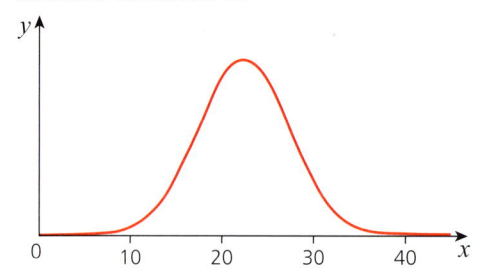

Figure 8.17

(i) Estimate the mean of the distribution.

(ii) Hence, using the equation of the probability density function of a Normal distribution, obtain an estimate of the greatest value of y.

(iii) Write down the area between the curve and the x-axis.

⑨ Large number observations are made of a random variable which has a Normal distribution with mean 50 and standard deviation 10. For each of the following statements say, with reasons, whether it is TRUE or FALSE.

(i) About 95% of the observations will be less than 66.45.

(ii) About 95% of the observations will be greater than 33.55.

(iii) About 95% of the observations will be between 33.55 and 66.45.

(iv) About 5% of the observations will be less than 30.4 or greater than 69.6.

⑩ An intelligence test is designed to produce scores which have a Normal distribution with mean 100 and standard deviation 15.

(i) A girl is selected at random and takes the test. What is the probability that her score is over 130?

(ii) Another girl is selected at random and takes the test. What is the probability that her score is over 130?

(iii) Two more girls are selected at random and take the test. What is the probability that both their scores are over 130?

(iv) Ten boys are selected at random and take the test. What is the probability that all ten of them score over 130?

⑪ In this question four distributions are described. In each case explain how you know that it is not Normal.

(i) The distribution of the total scores when two ordinary dice are thrown.

(ii) The distribution of the annual income in £ of working age people in the UK.

(iii) The distribution of the lengths of the lives of a particular species of animal, given that the mean is 12.4 years and the standard deviation is 8.3 years.

(iv) The distribution of the probability of a continuous random variable X; a and $2a$ are two particular values that X may take.

$P(X = a) = P(X = 2a); P(X = a) > P(X = x)$ for all values of x other than a and $2a$.

⑫ *X* and *Y* are continuous random variables and both are Normally distributed. *X* has mean 60 and standard deviation 20. *Y* has mean 80 and standard deviation 10. One observation is made of each of *X* and *Y*.

Which of the observations is more likely to be

(i) less than 70?

(ii) greater than 100?

(iii) greater than 110?

⑬ The probability density function of a continuous random variable, *X*, is

$f(x) = k(4 - x^2)$ where *k* is a positive constant.

It is valid for all values of *x* for which $f(x) \geq 0$.

(i) State the possible values of *X* and find the value of *k*.

(ii) Find the mean and standard deviation of *X*.

The graph below illustrates the probability density function of the Normal distribution with mean 0 and standard deviation 1.

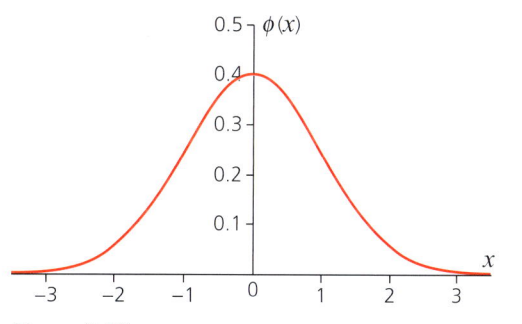

Figure 8.18

(iii) Make a neat copy of this Normal curve and then draw the curve *y* = f(*x*) on the same graph paper.

(iv) Compare the means of the two curves, their standard deviations and the area between them and the *x*-axis.

4 The distribution of sample means

While the Normal distribution often provides a useful model, its importance goes far beyond that.

A common situation in statistics is that you have taken a sample from a population and you use the mean of the sample as an estimate of the population mean.

Imagine that you take a sample of 20 harvest mice, weigh each one and find that their mean mass is 7.24 g. You might then use this figure to estimate that the mean mass of harvest mice in general is 7.24 g, that is, that the population mean is 7.24 g.

The distribution of sample means

The question that then arises is 'How accurate is that estimate?'

To answer that question you need two other pieces of information.

- What is the standard deviation of the population?
- Can you assume that the masses of harvest mice are Normally distributed?

Suppose that the standard deviation is known from previous observations (it is 1.1 g) and it is indeed reasonable to assume that the masses are Normally distributed. In these circumstances, the following really powerful result can be used.

When samples of size n are drawn from a Normal population with mean μ and standard deviation σ, the distribution of the sample means is itself Normal, with mean μ and standard deviation

$$\frac{\sigma}{\sqrt{n}}$$

Thus the standard deviation of the distribution of the sample means is smaller than that of individuals. This should not be very surprising. You expect results to 'average out'. You can see this by looking at the graphs of the population and the sample means.

> **Note**
>
> The quantity $\frac{\sigma}{\sqrt{n}}$ is called the standard error of the mean.

Distribution of the sample means $N\left(\mu, \frac{\sigma^2}{n}\right)$

The Normal distribution of individual items; it has mean μ and standard deviation σ.

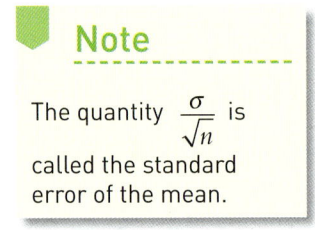

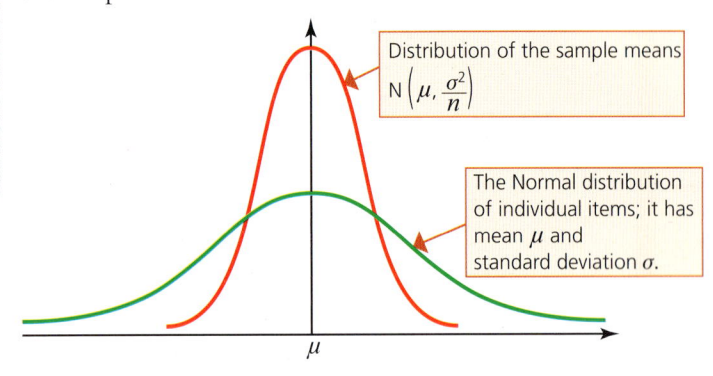

Figure 8.19

So for 95% of samples the sample mean, $\bar{x}$, will lie within the interval $\mu \pm 1.960 \times \frac{\sigma}{\sqrt{n}}$.

This can be rearranged to say that in 95% of cases the population mean lies between $\bar{x} - 1.960 \times \frac{\sigma}{\sqrt{n}}$ and $\bar{x} + 1.960 \times \frac{\sigma}{\sqrt{n}}$.

In the case of the harvest mice, $\bar{x} = 7.24$, $\sigma = 1.1$ and $n = 20$ and so

$$\bar{x} - 1.960 \times \frac{\sigma}{\sqrt{n}} \qquad \text{and} \qquad \bar{x} + 1.960 \times \frac{\sigma}{\sqrt{n}}$$

$$= 7.24 - 1.960 \times \frac{1.1}{\sqrt{20}} \qquad = 7.24 + 1.960 \times \frac{1.1}{\sqrt{20}}$$

$$= 6.757\ldots \qquad = 7.722\ldots$$

This gives an interval of 6.76 to 7.72.

In 95% of cases, an interval calculated in this way will contain the population mean, μ.

Such an interval is called **a 95% confidence interval**. Such intervals are covered in greater detail in Chapter 10.

In the same way, the interval from $\bar{x} - 1.645 \times \frac{\sigma}{\sqrt{n}}$ to $\bar{x} + 1.645 \times \frac{\sigma}{\sqrt{n}}$ is the 90% confidence interval.

For the 99% confidence interval, the figure 2.576 is used.

This calculation of the confidence interval depended on already knowing the standard deviation, something that often seems quite unlikely. In Chapter 10, you will meet a technique for overcoming this difficulty when the sample size is small.

However, if you have a large sample (at least 30), then you can work out the standard deviation of your sample (usually denoted by s) and use it as a reasonable estimate of the population standard deviation, σ.

Example 8.9

A company has two sites some distance apart and people often have to drive from one to the other. It is known from past experience that measurements of the journey time, t minutes, are Normally distributed with standard deviation 10 minutes and it is believed that the mean time is 160 minutes.

(i) Assuming that the mean journey time is indeed 160 minutes, estimate the percentage of journeys that should take at least 3 hours.

The company suspects that the mean journey is no longer 160 minutes. They time a sample of 20 drivers; in total they take 3510 minutes.

(ii) Obtain a 95% confidence interval for the mean journey time.

(iii) How might the company interpret this confidence interval?

Solution

(i) 3 hours is 180 minutes, so it is $\frac{180-160}{10} = 2$ standard deviations beyond the mean. In a Normal distribution 2.5% is at least 1.96 standard deviations above the mean and 2.5% is at least 1.96 standard deviations below the mean. For an estimate, 2 is close enough to 1.96 and so $2\frac{1}{2}\%$ of journeys should take at least 3 hours.

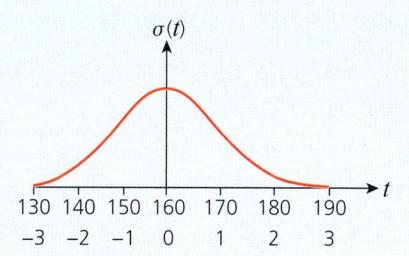

Figure 8.20

(ii) The mean time of the sample is $\bar{t} = \frac{3510}{20} = 175.5$ minutes.

The 95% confidence interval is from $\bar{t} - 1.96\frac{\sigma}{\sqrt{n}}$ to $\bar{t} + 1.96\frac{\sigma}{\sqrt{n}}$ and so from $175.2 - 1.96 \times \frac{10}{\sqrt{20}} = 170.817...$ to $175.2 + 1.96 \times \frac{10}{\sqrt{20}} = 179.582...$ Rounding to the nearest minute gives the 95% confidence interval for the mean time to be 171 to 180 minutes.

(iii) The previous estimate of 160 minutes is well outside the confidence interval and so it must be regarded as unreliable. Maybe with increased traffic journeys have got slower or maybe 160 minutes never was a realistic mean time.

The distribution of sample means

Exercise 8.3

① A random sample of size 10 is taken from a population with a Normal distribution with standard deviation 5.4. The mean of the sample is 14.5. Find a 99% confidence interval for the population mean.

② The members of a family have kept a record of the annual rainfall in their garden over many years. They have found that it is well modelled by a Normal distribution with mean 820 mm and standard deviation 81 mm.

Sam thinks that the rainfall is now increasing, possibly as a result of climate change. These are the readings for the last 10 years.

783   694   1003   817   956   825   877   754   916   943

(i) What percentage of the readings lie within 2 standard deviations of the previous mean annual rainfall of 820 mm?

(ii) Use these figures, and the value of 81 mm for the standard deviation, to obtain a 95% confidence interval for the mean annual rainfall. Give your answer to 3 significant figures.

Does this suggest the rainfall is increasing?

(iii) What percentage of the readings lie within the confidence interval?

③ A long-term study into the weights of new-born full-term babies in a particular region found that they were Normally distributed with the mean 3.54 kg and standard deviation 0.39 kg. A local doctor wonders whether babies in the region are getting heavier and records the birth weights in kg of those born in his hospital one day.

4.02   2.89   3.34   3.21   3.67   3.85   2.97   4.11   3.44

(i) Use these data to obtain a 95% confidence interval for the mean weight of new-born babies in the region.

(ii) What should the doctor conclude?

(iii) Was this a random sample?

④ The weights of a certain type of bird are known to be Normally distributed with standard deviation 12 g.

The weights, in grams, of a random sample of the birds are as follows.

102   110   116   98   84   88   102   106
98   104   107   122   87   97   107   120

(i) Calculate the mean of the sample.

(ii) Find a 90% confidence interval for the mean weight of this type of bird.

⑤ Hamid is a fruit grower. A supermarket asks him to supply pears of a particular type in bags of 100. Hamid decides that, instead of counting them out, he will judge the number of pears in a bag by its weight. The bags are light. So he needs to know the mean weight of that type of pear. He knows from past experience that the distribution of their weights is Normal with standard deviation 8.4 g.

Hamid selects 30 pears at random. Their total weight is 2.46 kg.

(i) Construct a 95% confidence interval for the mean weight of one pear, based on Hamid's sample data.

(ii) What does this tell Hamid about the weights of bags containing 100 pears?

(iii) Hamid then counts 100 pears, puts them in a bag and weighs it. It is 8.45 kg.

Construct a new 95% confidence interval for the mean weight of a pear.

Hamid decides that each bag of pears that he supplies should weigh as nearly as possible 8.5 kg but no less than that. The true mean weight of a pear (which Hamid does not know) is actually 83.3 g.

(iv) Estimate how much money, on average, Hamid saves on a bag of pears by having it weighed. Assume the cost of a pear to Hamid is 25 pence, that counting out 100 pears takes 5 minutes longer than weighing a bag and that he is paying a wage of £8.40 an hour.

⑥ Previous studies have shown that the mean mass of adults of a type of salt water fish is well modelled by the Normal distribution with mean 2.65 kg and standard deviation 0.43 kg, whether male or female.

(i) Given that the mass of 2.5% of the fish is less than a kg and that of 2.5% is greater than b kg, find the values of a and b according to this model.

It is suggested that the previous studies are now out of date and that the mean mass of the adult fish has changed, and so a better model would be a Normal distribution with the same standard deviation but a different mean, μ. As part of a new study, a sample of 40 of the fish are caught. Their total mass is 96.4 kg.

(ii) Obtain a 95% confidence interval for μ.

(iii) Compare the width of the confidence interval with that of $[a, b]$ and comment briefly.

(iv) Does the confidence interval suggest a change in the mean mass of the adult fish?

(v) The 40 fish were caught at three locations. Explain why it was impossible to use simple random sampling to select them and comment on the effect this might have had on how the confidence interval should be interpreted.

⑦ A continuous random variable is Normally distributed. The standard deviation, σ, is known but the mean, μ, is not. A random sample of size n is used to construct a 95% confidence interval for μ. The width of this confidence interval is w.

State, in terms of w, the width of the following confidence intervals for μ.

(i) The same sample data are used to construct a 99% confidence interval.

(ii) A different sample of size $5n$ is used to construct a 95% confidence interval.

(iii) It is found that the value of σ that was used was wrong and it should have been 3 times as large. The data from the original sample are used to construct a new 95% confidence interval.

⑧ The mean of a random sample of 10 observations of a random variable X is 27.2. It is known that X is Normally distributed and that the standard deviation of X is 2.9.

(i) Show that a 95% confidence interval for the mean μ of X is 25.40 to 29.00.

Another sample of size 10 is taken and this time the 95% confidence interval for μ is 27.5 to 31.1.

(ii) The two samples are now combined to make a single sample of size 20. Find a 95% confidence interval for μ based on this sample.

The distribution of sample means

9. It is known that the life span of a type of rodent is Normally distributed with standard deviation 24 days. Six of the rodents are kept in a laboratory. The numbers of days for which they live are

   320   386   340   14   375   305

   (i) Find the mean life span of these 6 rodents.

   (ii) Use your answer to (i) to obtain a 95% confidence interval for the life span of the rodents. Give your answer to the nearest day.

   (iii) Give two reasons why this may not be a very good guide to the mean life span of the rodents generally.

   (iv) Suggest a way in which the data could be used to obtain a more reliable 95% confidence interval, and find this interval.

10. Mac is the editor of a car magazine. He wants to find out how long, on average, readers keep their cars before selling them. He thinks the time, T years, may be getting shorter and wants to obtain a confidence interval for the present mean value of T, μ years.

    He carries out a small pilot survey, based on a random sample of 15 people and obtains a 95% confidence interval of $\mu = 2.32 \pm 0.45$ or $1.87 < \mu < 2.77$.

    (i) State one assumption that Mac must make for the calculation of the confidence interval to be valid.

    (ii) In the calculation, Mac assumes that the standard deviation of T had not changed from its previous known value, denoted by σ years. Calculate the value of σ.

    (iii) The last known value of μ was 2.8. Mac says, 'Since this is outside the confidence interval, I can definitely say that the mean time has decreased.' Criticise this statement.

    (iv) Determine the minimum size of sample that Mac would need for the width of the 95% confidence interval to be no more than 0.2 years.

11. A continuous random variable, R, is known to be Normally distributed; the value of σ, the standard deviation, is known but that of the mean, μ, is not known.

    Using data from a random sample of size n, a 90% confidence interval for μ is found to be 62.4 to 70.8.

    (i) Find the mean of the sample.

    (ii) The quantity $\frac{\sigma}{\sqrt{n}}$ is known as the standard error.

    Calculate the value of the standard error in this case.

    (iii) Obtain a 99% confidence interval for μ.

    (iv) Given that the value of σ is 14.0, find the size of the sample.

KEY POINTS

1. **A continuous random variable**
   If X is a continuous random variable with probability density function $f(x)$
   - $\int_{-\infty}^{\infty} f(x)\,dx = 1$
   - $f(x) \geq 0$ for all x
   - $P(c \leq x \leq d) = \int_{c}^{d} f(x)\,dx$
   - $E(X) = \int_{-\infty}^{\infty} x f(x)\,dx$
   - $\text{Var}(X) = \int_{-\infty}^{\infty} x^2 f(x)\,dx - \left[E(X)\right]^2$
   - The mode of X is the value of X for which $f(x)$ is greatest.

2. The Normal distribution with mean μ and standard deviation σ is denoted by $N(\mu, \sigma^2)$.

3. This may be given in standardised form by using the transformation
$$z = \frac{x - \mu}{\sigma}$$

4. In the standardised form, $N(0, 1)$, the mean is 0, the standard deviation and variance both 1.

5. The standardised Normal curve is given by
$$\phi(z) = \frac{1}{\sqrt{2\pi}} e^{-\frac{1}{2}z^2}$$

6. Probabilities may be found directly from a calculator by entering the mean, standard deviation and lower and upper limits. Alternatively, the area to the left of the value z in the diagram below, representing the probability of a value less than z, is denoted by $\Phi(z)$ and can be found using tables.

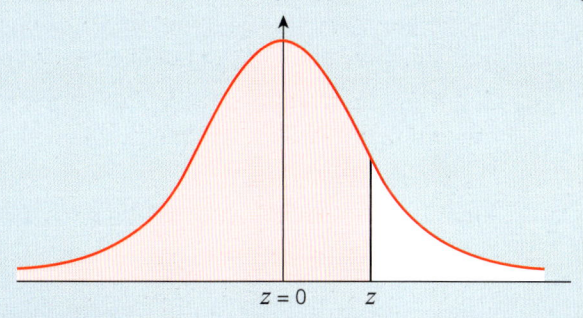

Figure 8.21

7. When the population standard deviation, σ, is known and the distribution is Normal, confidence intervals for μ are found using the Normal distribution.

8. Two-sided confidence intervals based on the Normal distribution are given by
$\bar{x} - k\dfrac{\sigma}{\sqrt{n}}$ to $\bar{x} + k\dfrac{\sigma}{\sqrt{n}}$.

9. The value of k for any confidence level can be found using Normal distribution tables.

Table 8.2

Confidence level	k
90%	1.645
95%	1.960
99%	2.576

The distribution of sample means

LEARNING OUTCOMES

When you have completed this chapter you should:
- be able to use a simple continuous random variable as a model
- understand the meaning of a p.d.f. and be able to use one to find probabilities
- know and use the properties of a p.d.f.
- be able to sketch the graph of a p.d.f.
- be able to find the mean and variance from a given p.d.f.
- be able to use the Normal distribution as a model, and to calculate and use probabilities from a Normal distribution
- know the meaning of the term confidence interval for a parameter and associated language
- understand the factors which affect the width of a confidence interval

Practice questions: set 2

① At a weather station, daily records are kept of the proportion of daylight hours for which the Sun is visible. (So a value of 0.7 on a particular day means that the Sun was visible for 70% of the daylight hours.) For a randomly chosen day in the spring months (March, April and May), this proportion, X, is modelled by the following probability density function (p.d.f.).

$$f(x) = k(x^2 - 0.8x + 0.3) \qquad 0 \leq x \leq 1$$

(i) Show that $k = \dfrac{30}{7}$. [2 marks]

(ii) Sketch the p.d.f. Explain what its shape indicates about the proportion of daylight hours for which the sun is visible. [3 marks]

(iii) Find the expectation and variance of X. [3 marks]

② In an investigation of small business development in England, researchers are examining whether there is any association between the geographical area where such a business is located and the lifespan of the business. A random sample of records has been obtained from a national database. The geographical areas are classified very broadly as South-East, Midlands, North and 'Rest'. Lifespans are classified as short, medium and long. The table shows the frequencies obtained in the sample; row and column totals and the grand total are also shown.

Table 1

Geographical area	Short	Medium	Long	Row totals
South-east	140	72	56	268
Midlands	104	53	45	202
North	71	51	48	170
Rest	57	48	59	164
Column totals	372	224	208	804

Examine at the 1% level of significance whether or not there is any association between geographical area and lifespan, stating carefully the null and alternative hypotheses you are testing. Report briefly on your conclusions.

[8 marks]

③ A fair five sided spinner has faces labelled 1, 2, 3, 4, 5. Martin plays a game in which he gains or loses money according to the number that the spinner comes to rest on when it is spun. He wins £5 if it lands on a 1, loses £2 if it lands on a 2, 3 or 4 and neither gains nor loses if it lands on a 5. Let X represent the amount 'won' each time the spinner is spun.

(i) Complete the following probability distribution for X.

Table 2

r	−2	0	
$P(X = r)$			

[2 marks]

169

Practice questions: set 2

    (ii) Find E(X) and Var(X). [4 marks]

    (iii) How much less would the player have to pay, when the die lands on the face marked 2, so that he would break even in the long run? [2 marks]

4. A boy is watching vehicles travelling along a motorway. All the vehicles he counts are either cars or lorries; the number of each may be modelled by two independent Poisson distributions. The mean number of cars per minute is 8.3 and the mean number of lorries per minute is 4.7.

    (i) For a given period of one minute, find the probability that he sees

        (a) exactly seven cars [1 mark]

        (b) at least three lorries [1 mark]

    (ii) Calculate the probability that he sees a total of exactly ten vehicles in a given one-minute period. [4 marks]

    (iii) Find the probability that he observes fewer than eight vehicles in a given period of 30 seconds. [3 marks]

5. LCD display panels consist of a very large number, typically many millions, of pixels. A very small proportion of pixels will be faulty. Let X denote the number of faulty pixels on a newly manufactured LCD panel of a particular size and type.

    (i) State two assumptions required to justify modelling X using a Poisson distribution. [2 marks]

You are now given that the required assumptions hold and that the average number of faulty pixels per panel at the time of manufacture is 1.2.

    (ii) Find the probability that a newly manufactured panel has (a) no faulty pixels, (b) fewer than 4 faulty pixels. [2 marks]

Newly manufactured panels are checked before sale, and those with 4 or more faulty pixels are not sold. Let Y be the number of faulty pixels on a panel that is sold.

    (iii) Show that P($Y = 0$) = 0.3117 correct to 4 decimal places. [1 mark]

    (iv) Copy and complete the table for the distribution of Y.

Table 3

r	0	1	2	
P ($Y = r$)	0.3117			

[3 marks]

    (v) Calculate the mean and standard deviation of Y. [4 marks]

    (vi) A quality controller suspects the average number of faulty pixels for these LCDs is more than 1.2. The next 15 panels are checked, and they contain 35 faulty pixels. Carrying out a check at the 1% level, is there evidence to back up the controller's claim? [6 marks]

    (vii) What would be the probability of a Type I error in this test? [1 mark]

(6) In a court of law, a defendant is put on trial for a crime. The defendant may or may not be guilty of the crime. The defendant may be or may not be convicted of committing the crime by the court. Let events be defined as follows.

G is the event that the defendant is guilty of the crime.

C is the event that the defendant is convicted of the crime.

(i) State what the events $C \mid G$ and $C \cap G$ are, making clear the distinction between them. [2 marks]

In trials for a particular type of fraud, it is estimated that 90% of defendants are actually guilty of committing the crime. Of those who are guilty, $\frac{4}{5}$ are convicted. Of those who are not guilty, 1 in 20 are convicted.

(ii) Find the probability that, for a randomly chosen defendant, the trial reaches the wrong conclusion. [3 marks]

(iii) Find the probability that a randomly chosen defendant who is convicted is actually guilty of the crime. [3 marks]

[60 marks]

9 Continuous random variables 2

> Whenever a large sample of chaotic elements are taken in hand and marshalled in the order of their magnitude, an unsuspected and most beautiful form of regularity proves to have been latent all along.
>
> Sir Francis Galton

Discussion point
The picture shows runners in a large entry marathon race.
What would you expect the distribution of their finishing times to look like?

1 The expectation and variance of a function of X

There are times when one random variable is a function of another random variable. For example:

- as part of an experiment, you are measuring temperatures in Celsius but then need to convert them to Fahrenheit: $F = 1.8C + 32$
- you are measuring the lengths of the sides of square pieces of material and deducing their areas: $A = L^2$
- you are estimating the ages, A years, of hedgerows by counting the number, n, of types of shrubs and trees in 30 m lengths: $A = 100n - 50$.

In fact, in any situation where you are entering the value of a random variable into a formula, the outcome will be another random variable which is a function of the one you entered. Under these circumstances, you may need to find the expectation and variance of such a function of a random variable.

For a discrete random variable, X, the expectation of a function $g[X]$ is given by:

$$E(g[X]) = \sum g[x_i] p_i$$
$$\text{Var}(g[X]) = \sum (g[x_i])^2 p_i - \{E(g[X])\}^2$$

The equivalent result for a continuous random variable, X, with p.d.f. $f(x)$ is:

$$E(g[X]) = \int_{\substack{\text{All} \\ \text{values} \\ \text{of } x}} g[x] f(x) \, dx$$

$$\text{Var}(g[X]) = \int_{\substack{\text{All} \\ \text{values} \\ \text{of } x}} (g[x])^2 f(x) \, dx - \{E(g[X])\}^2$$

An important special case is when $g(X)$ is a linear function of X, for example when you need to find $E(5X + 2)$ or $\text{Var}(5X + 2)$. In this case, you can use the helpful results $E(aX + b) = aE(X) + b$, $\text{Var}(aX + b) = a^2 \text{Var}(X)$

which are true for all distributions.

Example 9.1

The continuous random variable X has p.d.f. $f(x)$ given by:

$$f(x) = \begin{cases} \dfrac{x}{50} & \text{for } 0 < x \leq 10 \\ 0 & \text{otherwise.} \end{cases}$$

(This random variable was used to model response times in Example 8.4.)

(i) Find $E(3X + 4)$.

(ii) Find $3E(X) + 4$.

(iii) Find $\text{Var}(3X + 4)$.

(iv) Verify that $\text{Var}(3X + 4) = 3^2 \text{Var}(X)$.

The expectation and variance of a function of X

> Here you are using
> $$E(g[X]) = \int_{\text{All values of } x} g[x]f(x)\,dx$$

Solution

(i) $E(3X+4) = \int_0^{10} (3x+4)\dfrac{x}{50}\,dx$

$= \int_0^{10} \dfrac{1}{50}(3x^2+4x)\,dx$

$= \left[\dfrac{x^3}{50} + \dfrac{x^2}{25}\right]_0^{10}$

$= 20 + 4$

$= 24$

(ii) $3E(X) + 4 = 3\int_0^{10} x\dfrac{x}{50}\,dx + 4$

$= \left[\dfrac{3}{150}x^3\right]_0^{10} + 4$

$= 20 + 4$

$= 24$

Notice here that $E(3X+4) = 24 = 3E(X) + 4$.

> **Note**
> You have of course already met these results for discrete random variables in Chapter 5.

(iii) To find $\text{Var}(3X+4)$, use

$$\text{Var}(g[X]) = \int [g(x)]^2 f(x)\,dx - \{E(g[X])\}^2$$

with $g(x) = 3X + 4$.

$\text{Var}(3X+4) = \int_0^{10} (3x+4)^2 \dfrac{1}{50}x\,dx - 24^2$

$= \int_0^{10} \dfrac{1}{50}(9x^3 + 24x^2 + 16x)\,dx - 576$

$= \dfrac{1}{50}\left[\dfrac{9x^4}{4} + 8x^3 + 8x^2\right]_0^{10} - 576$

$= 50$

> **Note**
> The result $\text{Var}(aX) = a^2\text{Var}(X)$ should not surprise you. It follows from the fact that if the standard deviation of a set of data is k, then the standard deviation of the set formed by multiplying all the data by a positive constant, a, is ak. That is,
>
> standard deviation(aX)
> = $a \times$ standard deviation(X)
>
> Since variance
> = [standard deviation]^2
> then Var(aX)
> = [standard deviation(aX)]^2
> = [$a \times$ standard deviation(X)]^2
> = a^2[standard deviation(X)]^2
> = a^2 Var(X).

(iv) $\text{Var}(X) = E(X^2) - [E(X)]^2$

$E(X^2) = \int_0^{10} x^2 \dfrac{1}{50}x\,dx$ and $E(X) = \int_0^{10} x\dfrac{1}{50}x\,dx$

$E(X^2) = \int_0^{10} \dfrac{1}{50}x^3\,dx$ and $E(X) = \int_0^{10} \dfrac{1}{50}x^2\,dx$

$E(X^2) = \left[\dfrac{1}{200}x^4\right]_0^{10}$ and $E(X) = \left[\dfrac{1}{150}x^3\right]_0^{10}$

$E(X^2) = 50$ and $E(X) = 6.\dot{6}$

so $\text{Var}(X) = 50 - 6.\dot{6}^2 = 5.\dot{5}$

and $3^2\text{Var}(X) = 9 \times 5.\dot{5} = 50$

From part (iii), $\text{Var}(3X+4) = 50$

So $\text{Var}(3X+4) = 3^2\,\text{Var}(X)$, as required.

Example 9.2

The continuous random variable X has p.d.f. $f(x)$ given by

$$f(x) = \begin{cases} \dfrac{3}{125}x^2 & \text{for } 0 \leq x \leq 5 \\ 0 & \text{otherwise.} \end{cases}$$

Find

(i) $E(X)$ (ii) $\text{Var}(X)$ (iii) $E(7X-3)$ (iv) $\text{Var}(7X-3)$.

Solution

(i) $$E(X) = \int_{-\infty}^{\infty} x f(x)\,dx$$
$$= \int_0^5 x \frac{3}{125} x^2 \, dx$$
$$= \left[\frac{3}{500} x^4 \right]_0^5$$
$$= 3.75$$

(ii) $$\text{Var}(X) = \int_{-\infty}^{\infty} x^2 f(x)\,dx - [E(X)]^2$$
$$= \int_0^5 x^2 \frac{3}{125} x^2 \, dx - 3.75^2$$
$$= \left[\frac{3}{625} x^5 \right]_0^5 - 14.0625$$
$$= 15 - 14.0625$$
$$= 0.9375$$

(iii) $$E(7X-3) = 7E(X) - 3$$
$$= 7 \times 3.75 - 3$$
$$= 23.25$$

(iv) $$\text{Var}(7X-3) = 7^2 \text{Var}(X)$$
$$= 49 \times 0.9375$$
$$= 45.9 \ (3 \text{ s.f.})$$

General results

This example illustrates a number of general results for random variables, continuous or discrete.

$E(c) = c$ $\qquad\qquad$ $\text{Var}(c) = 0$

$E(aX) = aE(X)$ $\qquad\qquad$ $\text{Var}(aX) = a^2\text{Var}(X)$

$E(aX + b) = aE(X) + b$ $\qquad\qquad$ $\text{Var}(aX + b) = a^2\text{Var}(X)$

$E[g(X) \pm h(X)] = E[g(X)] \pm E[h(X)]$

where a, b and c are constants and $g(X)$ and $h(X)$ are functions of X.

The expectation and variance of a function of X

In Chapter 5, you met results for the expectation and variance of linear combinations of discrete independent random variables, X and Y.

$$E(aX \pm bY) = aE(X) \pm bE(Y) \text{ and } Var(aX \pm bY) = a^2 Var(X) + b^2 E(Y)$$

The same results hold if the variables are continuous, but they must still be independent.

Example 9.3

The continuous random variable X has p.d.f (x) given by

$$f(x) = \begin{cases} ax^3 & \text{for } 0 \leq x \leq 2 \\ 0 & \text{otherwise.} \end{cases}$$

Find

(i) a (ii) $E(2x^3 + x)$ (iii) $Var(2x^3 + x)$

Solution

(i) $\int_0^2 ax^3 \, dx = 1 \Rightarrow a = \dfrac{1}{4}$

(ii) $E(2X^3 + X) = \int_0^2 \dfrac{1}{4}x^3(2x^3 + x) \, dx = \dfrac{376}{35} = 10.7 \, (3\,\text{s.f.})$

(iii) $Var(2X^3 + X) = E((2X^3 + X)^2) - (E(2X^3 + X))^2$

$E((2X^3 + X)^2) = E(4X^6 + 4X^4 + X^2)$

$= \int_0^2 \dfrac{1}{4}x^3(4x^6 + 4x^4 + x^2) \, dx = \dfrac{2056}{15} = 137.1 \, (4\,\text{s.f.})$

$Var(2X^3 + X) = \dfrac{2056}{15} - \left(\dfrac{376}{35}\right)^2 = 21.7 \, (3\,\text{s.f.})$

There are occasions where your random variable is most effectively modelled by a discrete distribution for some of the time, and by a continuous distribution at others.

Example 9.4

The time, t minutes, that you wait to be served at the check-out in a supermarket is modelled by

0.2   for $t = 0$ (discrete)

and

$f(t) = -0.016t + 0.16$ for $0 < t \leq 10$ (continuous).

(i) Explain why this might indeed be a good model for the waiting time at a checkout.

(ii) Show that $\sum p_i + \int_0^{10} f(t) \, dt = 1$. Explain this result.

(iii) Find the mean waiting time.

(iv) Are there any weaknesses of this model?

Solution

(i) The discrete part of the model deals with the possibility that the check-out may be immediately available when you arrive. The continuous part describes the time you might have to wait if there are one or more people already using or waiting for the checkout. With this model the maximum amount of time you can expect to wait is 10 minutes.

(ii) $\sum p_i = 0.2$, $\int_0^{10} f(t)\,dt = \int_0^{10} -0.016t + 0.16\,dt = \left[0.16t - 0.016\dfrac{t^2}{2}\right]_0^{10} = 0.8$.

Thus $\sum p_i + \int_0^{10} f(t)\,dt = 1$. This means that you are guaranteed to achieve some value for t, where $0 \leq t \leq 10$, in your wait.

(iii) The mean wait will be given by $\sum p_i t_i + \int_0^{10} t f(t)\,dt$.

$\sum p_i t_i = 0.2 \times 0 = 0$, $\int_0^{10} t f(t)\,dt = \int_0^{10} t(-0.016t + 0.16)\,dt$

$= \left[0.08t^2 - 0.016\dfrac{t^3}{3}\right]_0^{10} = 2.66....$

So the mean waiting time is about 2 minutes 40 seconds.

(iv) You know if queues are exceptional it is possible to wait for longer than 10 minutes at a checkout. On the other hand, a supermarket may have the policy that if a queue develops, another checkout is opened, so the second part of the model may not be accurate.

Exercise 9.1

1. A continuous random variable X has the p.d.f.:

$$f(x) = \begin{cases} k & \text{for } 0 \leq x \leq 5 \\ 0 & \text{otherwise.} \end{cases}$$

(i) Find the value of k.
(ii) Sketch the graph of $f(x)$.
(iii) Find $E(X)$.
(iv) Find $E(4X - 3)$ and show that your answer is the same as $4E(X) - 3$.

2. The continuous random variable X has p.d.f.

$$f(x) = \begin{cases} 4x^3 & \text{for } 0 \leq x \leq 1 \\ 0 & \text{otherwise.} \end{cases}$$

(i) Find $E(X)$.
(ii) Find $E(X^2)$.
(iii) Find $Var(X)$.
(iv) Verify that $E(5X + 1) = 5E(X) + 1$.

The expectation and variance of a function of X

③ A discrete random variable W has the following distribution.

Table 9.1

x	1	2	3	4	5	6
$P(W = w)$	0.1	0.2	0.1	0.2	0.1	0.3

Find the mean and variance of

(i) $W + 7$

(ii) $6W - 5$

④ The random variable X is the number of heads obtained when four unbiased coins are tossed. Construct the probability distribution for X and find

(i) $E(X)$

(ii) $Var(X)$

(iii) $Var(3X + 4)$.

⑤ An unbiased six-sided die is thrown.

(i) Find the expectation and variance of the score on the die.

(ii) The die is thrown twice. Find the expectation and variance of the total score.

(iii) The die is thrown twice. Find the expectation and variance of the differences in the two scores.

(iv) The die is thrown ten times. Find the expectation and variance of the total score.

⑥ The number of kilograms of metal extracted from 10 kg of ore from a certain mine is modelled by a continuous random variable X with probability density function f(x), where

$$f(x) = \begin{cases} cx(2-x)^2 & \text{for } 0 \leq x \leq 2 \\ 0 & \text{otherwise,} \end{cases}$$

where c is a constant.

Show that c is $\frac{3}{4}$ and find the mean and variance of X.

The cost of extracting the metal from 10 kg of ore is £10x. Find the expected cost of extracting the metal from 10 kg of ore.

⑦ A continuous random variable Y has p.d.f.

$$f(y) = \begin{cases} \frac{2}{9}y(3-y) & \text{for } 0 \leq y \leq 3 \\ 0 & \text{otherwise.} \end{cases}$$

(i) Find $E(Y)$.

(ii) Find $E(Y^2)$.

(iii) Evaluate $E(Y^2) = [E(Y)]^2$.

(iv) Find $E(2Y^2 + 3Y + 4)$.

(v) Find $\int_0^3 (y - E(Y))^2 f(y) \, dy$.

Why is the answer the same as that for part (iii)?

⑧ A continuous random variable X has p.d.f. $f(x)$, where

$$f(x) = \begin{cases} 12x^2(1-x) & \text{for } 0 \leq x \leq 1 \\ 0 & \text{otherwise.} \end{cases}$$

(i) Find μ, the mean of X.

(ii) Find $E(6X - 7)$ and show that your answer is the same as $6E(X) - 7$.

(iii) Find the standard deviation of X.

(iv) What is the probability that a randomly selected value of X lies within one standard deviation of μ?

⑨ The continuous random variable X has probability density function

$$f(x) = \begin{cases} \dfrac{3}{1024}x(x-8)^2 & 0 \leq x \leq 8. \\ 0 & \text{otherwise.} \end{cases}$$

A sketch of $f(x)$ is shown in the diagram.

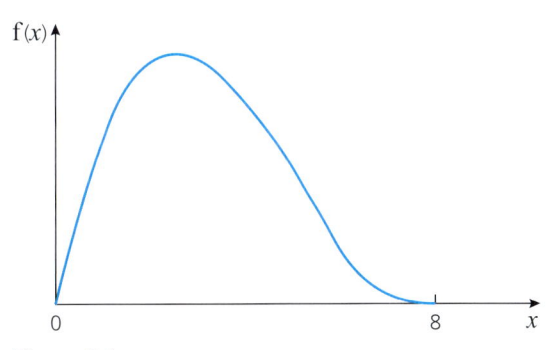

Figure 9.1

(i) Find $E(X)$ and show that $\text{Var}(X) = 2.56$.

The times, in minutes, taken by a doctor to see her patients are modelled by the continuous random variable $T = X + 2$.

(ii) Sketch the distribution of T and describe in words what this model implies about the lengths of the doctor's appointments. [MEI]

⑩ Dean catches a bus from a bus station to work each day. The bus may be waiting at the stop when he arrives. He models the probabilities for various waiting time t in minutes for him to board his bus after arriving at the stop as follows;

0.3 for $t = 0$,

$0.1 - \dfrac{t}{140}$ for $0 < t \leq 14$

(i) Show that the total probability across all waiting times is 1.

(ii) Find the mean time he takes to board his bus.

⑪ The continuous random variable X has p.d.f.

$$f(x) = \begin{cases} \dfrac{2}{25}(7 - x) & \text{for } 2 \leq x \leq 7 \\ 0 & \text{otherwise.} \end{cases}$$

The function $g(X)$ is defined by $g(x) = x^2 + x$.

(i) Find $E(X)$.

(ii) Find $E[g(X)]$.

The expectation and variance of a function of X

(iii) Find $E(X^2)$ and hence find $3E(X^2) + 4E(X) + 7$.

(iv) Use your answers to parts (ii) and (iii) to verify that
$E[g(X)] = 3E(X^2) + 4E(X) + 7$.

(v) Find $\text{Var}(X)$, $\text{Var}(X^2)$ and $\text{Var}(g(X))$.

(vi) Given that $\text{Var}(g(X)) = 1107.6$ show that $\text{Var}(g(X))$ does not equal $9\text{Var}(X^2) + 16\text{Var}(X)$.

12 A continuous random variable has probability density function f defined by

$$f(x) = \begin{cases} kx(6-x) & \text{for } 0 \leq x \leq 6 \\ 0 & \text{otherwise.} \end{cases}$$

Evaluate k and the mean of the distribution.

A particle moves along a straight line in such a way that during the first six seconds of its motion its displacement at time t seconds is s m, where $s = 2(t+1)$.

The particle is observed at time t seconds, where t denotes a random value from a distribution whose probability density function is the function f defined above. Calculate the probability that at the time of observation the displacement of the particle is less than 5 m.

13 Every day, I travel to and from work on the local shuttle bus, which runs every 10 minutes. The time I have to wait for the bus is modelled by the random variable T, which has a uniform (rectangular) distribution on the interval $[0, 10]$.

(i) Write down the probability density function for T, and state its mean and variance.

The *total* time I have to wait for a bus, going to and coming from work, is modelled by the random variable X whose probability density function is given by

$$f(x) = \begin{cases} 0.01x & \text{for } 0 \leq x \leq 10 \\ 0.01(20-x) & \text{for } 10 < x \leq 20 \\ 0 & \text{otherwise.} \end{cases}$$

(ii) Sketch the graph of the probability density function for X.

(iii) State $E(X)$ and use integration to find $\text{Var}(X)$.

The times I wait for the bus when going to work and coming home from work are represented by independent random variables T_1 and T_2, respectively, so that $X = T_1 + T_2$.

(iv) Find $P(X \geq 14)$. Give a reason why you would expect $P(X \geq 14)$ to be greater than $P(T_1 \geq 7) \times P(T_2 \geq 7)$. [MEI]

14 The continuous random variable X has p.d.f.

$$f(x) = \begin{cases} \dfrac{6+2x}{7} & \text{for } 0 \leq x \leq 1 \\ 0 & \text{otherwise.} \end{cases}$$

The function $g(x)$ is $x^2 + x$

(i) Find $E(X)$, $E(X^2)$, $E(X^3)$ and $E(X^4)$.

(ii) What is $\text{Var}(X)$?

(iii) Find $E(g(X))$ and $\text{Var}(g(X))$.
Comment on your findings.

⑮ Anna is a piano teacher who regularly takes a cab from her home to one of the many local houses where her piano students live. Cabs all charge the same.

Anna finds that the probability density function of her journey cost p in pounds is:

$$\begin{cases} 0 & 0 \leq p < 5 \\ 0.4 & p = 5 \\ ap - 10a & 5 < p < 10 \\ 0 & 10 \leq p \end{cases}$$

where a is negative.

(i) Sketch the p.d.f. of Anna's cost, given that $5a < 0.4$.

(ii) Find a.

(iii) Find the mean and variance of the amount Anna pays.

2 The cumulative distribution function

500 enter community half-marathon

There was a record entry for this year's Community half-marathon, including several famous names who were treating it as a training run in preparation for the London marathon. Overall winner was Reuben Mhango in 1 hour 4 minutes and 2 seconds; the first woman home was 37-year-old Lynn Barber in 1 hour 20 minutes exactly. There were many fun runners but everybody completed the course within 4 hours.

Record numbers, but no record times this year

£150 prize to be won

Mike Harrison, chair of the Half Committee, says: 'This year we restricted entries to 500 but this meant disappointing many people. Next year we intend to allow everybody to run and expect a much bigger entry. In order to allow us to marshall the event properly we need a statistical model to predict the flow of runners, and particularly their finishing times. We are offering a prize of £150 for the best such model submitted.'

Time (hours)	Finished (%)
1¼	3
1½	15
1¾	33
2	49
2¼	57
2½	75
3	91
3½	99
4	100

The cumulative distribution function

An entrant for the competition proposed a model in which a runner's time, X hours, is a continuous random variable with p.d.f.

$$f(x) = \begin{cases} \frac{4}{27}(x-1)(4-x)^2 & 1 \leqslant x \leqslant 4 \\ 0 & \text{otherwise.} \end{cases}$$

According to this model, the mode is at 2 hours, and everybody finishes in between 1 hour and 4 hours; see Figure 9.2.

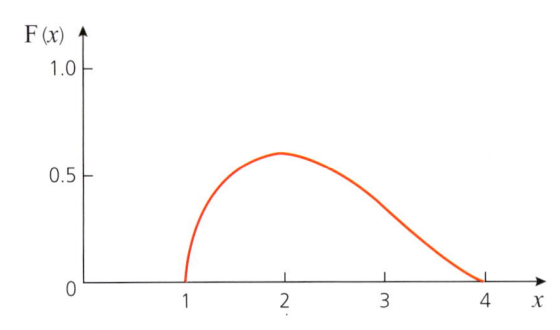

Figure 9.2

How does this model compare with the figures you were given for the actual race?

Those figures gave the **cumulative distribution**, the total numbers (expressed as percentages) of runners who had finished by certain times. To obtain the equivalent figures from the model, you want to find an expression for $P(X \leqslant x)$. The function giving $P(X \leqslant x)$ is called the **cumulative distribution function** (c.d.f.), and it is usually denoted by $F(x)$. The best method of obtaining the cumulative distribution function is to use indefinite integration.

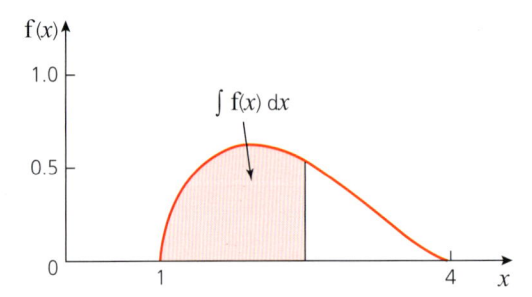

Figure 9.3

In this model, the proportion finishing by time t hours is given by

$$\int_1^t f(x)\,dx$$

$$= \int \frac{4}{27}(x-1)(4-x)^2\,dx$$

$$= \frac{4}{27} \int (x^3 - 9x^2 + 24x - 16)\,dx$$

$$= \frac{4}{27}\left(\frac{1}{4}x^4 - 3x^3 + 12x^2 - 16x\right) + c$$

$$= \frac{1}{27}X^4 - \frac{4}{9}X^3 + \frac{16}{9}X^2 - \frac{64}{27}X + c$$

> No runners finish in less than 1 hour, so if x is less than 1, the probability of a runner finishing in less than x hours is 0.

> All runners finish in less than 4 hours, so if x is greater than 4, the probability of a runner finishing in less than x hours is 1.

> You would not be correct to write down an expression like
> $$F(x) = \int_1^x \frac{4}{27}(x-1)(4-x)^2 \, dx$$
> This is INCORRECT since x would then be both a limit of the integral and the variable used within it.
>
> To overcome this problem, a dummy variable, say t, so that $F(x)$ is now written,
> $$F(x) = \int_1^x \frac{4}{27}(u-1)(4-u)^2 \, du$$
> This is CORRECT.

But $P(X \le 1) = 0$, so $F(1) = 0$ and you can use this to find the value of c:

$$\frac{1}{27} - \frac{4}{9} + \frac{16}{27} - \frac{64}{27} + c = 0$$

$$\Rightarrow c = 1$$

$$F(X) = \begin{cases} 0 & \text{for } X < 1 \\ \frac{1}{27}X^4 - \frac{4}{9}X^3 + \frac{16}{9}X^2 - \frac{64}{27}X + 1 & \text{for } 1 \le X \le 4 \\ 1 & \text{for } X > 4. \end{cases}$$

It is possible to use definite integration, but this causes a problem as you cannot use the same letter for both a limit of the integral and as the variable of integration. So you would have to change the variable of integration, which is a **dummy variable** as it does not appear in the final answer, to a different letter. To find the proportions of runners finishing by any time, substitute that value for x; so when $x = 2$.

$$F(2) = \frac{1}{27} \times 2^4 - \frac{4}{9} \times 2^3 + \frac{16}{9} \times 2^2 - \frac{64}{27} \times 2 + 1$$

$$= 0.41 \text{ to two decimal places.}$$

Here is the complete table, with all the values worked out.

Table 9.2

Time (hours)	Model	Runners
1.00	0.00	0.00
1.25	0.04	0.03
1.50	0.13	0.15
1.75	0.26	0.33
2.00	0.41	0.49
2.25	0.55	0.57
2.50	0.69	0.75
3.00	0.89	0.91
3.50	0.98	0.99
4.00	1.00	1.00

Notice the distinctive shape of the curves of these functions (Figure 9.4), sometimes called an **ogive**.

> **Discussion point**
>
> Do you think that this model is worth the £150 prize? If you were on the organising committee what more might you look for in a model?

The cumulative distribution function

> **Note**
> You have probably met this shape already when drawing cumulative frequency curves.

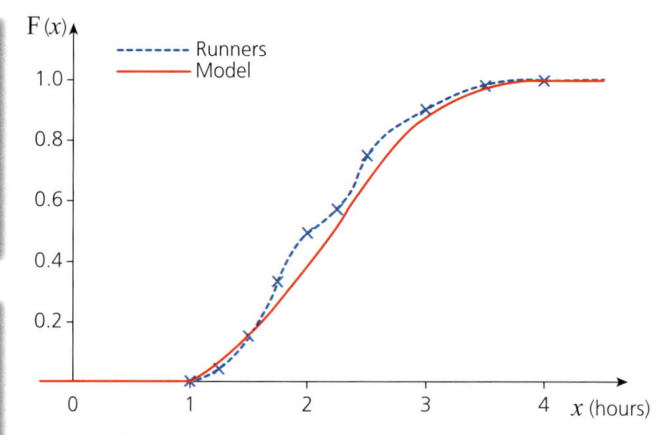

Figure 9.4

> **Note**
> These graphs illustrate the probability density function of a function that can take a limited range of values. The lower limit is a and the upper limit is b. You could look at it in a different way and say, for example, that the lower limit is 0; in that case the two graphs would have line segments along the x-axis joining 0 to a.
>
> Some distributions, for example the Normal distribution, have no limits and so the range of possible values is from $-\infty$ to $+\infty$.

Properties of the cumulative distribution function, F(x)

The graphs, Figure 9.5, show the probability density function f(x) and the cumulative distribution function F(x) of a typical continuous random variable X. You will see that the values of the random variable always lie between a and b.

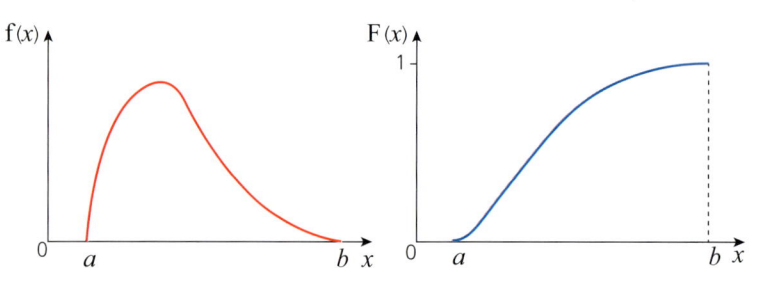

Figure 9.5

These graphs illustrate a number of general results for cumulative distribution functions.

> **Notes**
> 1. Notice the use of lower and upper case letters here. The probability density function is denoted by the lower case f, whereas the cumulative distribution function is given the upper case F.
> 2. The term cumulative distribution function is often abbreviated to c.d.f.

1. $F(x) = 0$ for $x \leq a$, the lower limit of x.

    The probability of X taking a value less than or equal to a is zero; the value of X must be greater than or equal to a.

2. $F(x) = 1$ for $x \geq b$, the upper limit of x. X cannot take values greater than b.

3. $P(c \leq X \leq d) = F(d) - F(c)$

    $P(c \leq X \leq d) = P(X \leq d) - P(X \leq c)$

    This is very useful when finding probabilities from a p.d.f. or a c.d.f.

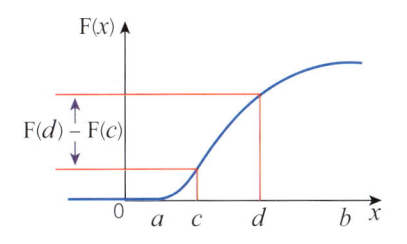

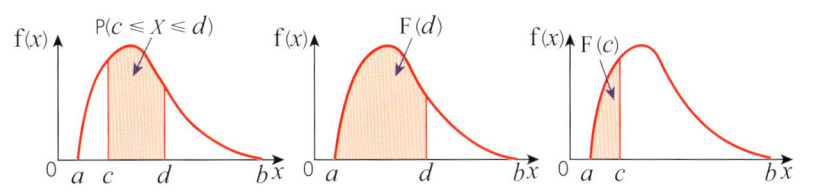

Figure 9.6

4   The median, m, satisfies the equation $F(m) = 0.5$.
    $P(X \leq m) = 0.5$ by definition of the median.

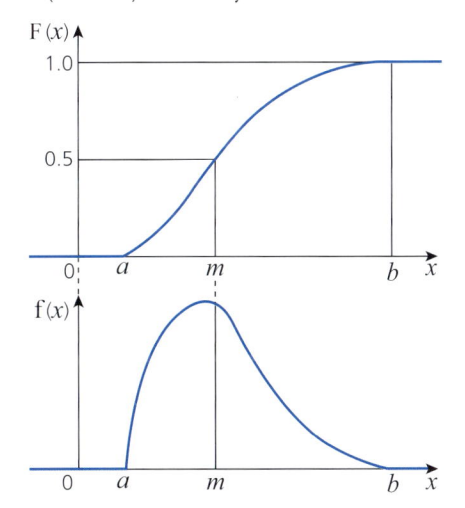

Figure 9.7

5   $f(x) = \dfrac{d}{dx} F(x) = F'(x)$

    Since you integrate $f(x)$ to obtain $F(x)$, the reverse must also be true: differentiating $F(x)$ gives $f(x)$.

6   $F(x)$ is a continuous function: the graph of $y = F(x)$ has no gaps.

Example 9.5

A machine saws planks of wood to a nominal length. The continuous random variable X represents the positive size of the error in millimetres of the actual length of a plank coming off the machine. The variable X has p.d.f. $f(x)$, where

$$f(x) = \begin{cases} \dfrac{10-x}{50} & \text{for } 0 \leq x \leq 10 \\ 0 & \text{otherwise.} \end{cases}$$

(i)   Sketch $f(x)$.

(ii) Find the cumulative distribution function $F(x)$.

(iii) Sketch $F(x)$ for $0 \leq x \leq 10$.

The cumulative distribution function

(iv) Find $P(2 \leq X \leq 7)$.

(v) Find the median value of X.

A customer refuses to accept planks for which the error is greater than 8 mm.

(vi) What percentage of planks will he reject?

Solution

(i)

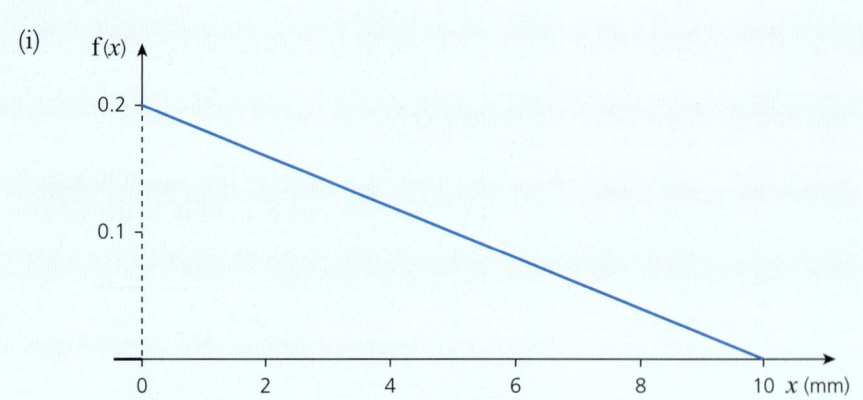

Figure 9.8

(ii) $F(x) = \int_0^x \frac{(10-u)}{50} du$

$= \frac{1}{50}\left[10u - \frac{u^2}{2}\right]_0^x$

$= \frac{1}{5}x - \frac{1}{100}x^2$

The full definition of $F(x)$ is:

$$F(x) = \begin{cases} 0 & \text{for } x < 10 \\ \frac{1}{5}x - \frac{1}{100}x^2 & \text{for } 0 \leq x \leq 10 \\ 1 & \text{for } x > 10. \end{cases}$$

(iii) The graph $F(x)$ is shown in Figure 9.9.

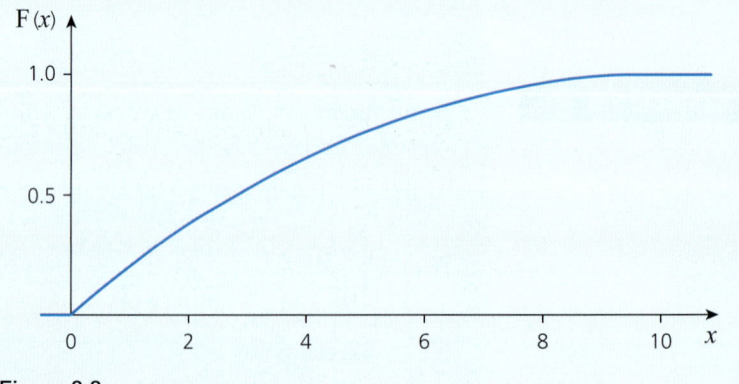

Figure 9.9

(iv) $\quad P(2 \leq X \leq 7) = F(7) - F(2)$
$$= \left[\frac{7}{5} - \frac{49}{100}\right] - \left[\frac{2}{5} - \frac{4}{100}\right]$$
$$= 0.91 - 0.36$$
$$= 0.55.$$

(v) The median value of X is found by solving the equation

$$F(m) = 0.5$$

$$\frac{1}{5}m - \frac{1}{100}m^2 = 0.5.$$

This is rearranged to give

$$m^2 - 20m + 50 = 0$$

$$m = \frac{20 \pm \sqrt{20^2 - 4 \times 50}}{2}$$

$m = 2.93$ (or 17.07, which is outside the domain for X).

The median error is 2.93 mm.

(vi) The customer rejects those planks for which $8 \leq X \leq 10$.
$P(8 \leq X \leq 10) = F(10) - F(8)$
$$= 1 - 0.96$$

so 4% of planks are rejected.

Example 9.6

The p.d.f. of a continuous random variable X is given by:

$$f(x) = \begin{cases} \dfrac{x}{24} & \text{for } 0 \leq x \leq 4 \\ \dfrac{(12-x)}{48} & \text{for } 4 \leq x \leq 12 \\ 0 & \text{otherwise.} \end{cases}$$

(i) Sketch $f(x)$.

(ii) Find the cumulative distribution function $F(x)$.

(iii) Sketch $F(x)$.

Solution

(i) The graph of $f(x)$ is shown in Figure 9.10

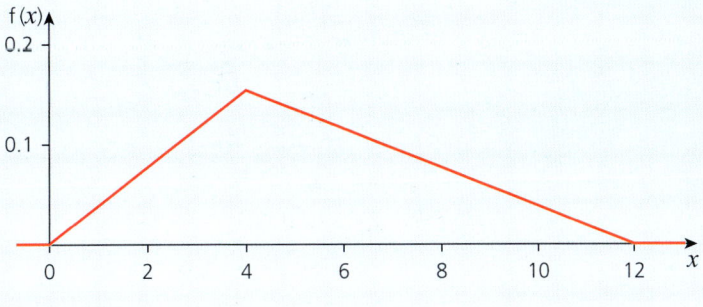

Figure 9.10

The cumulative distribution function

(ii) For $0 \leq x \leq 4$, $F(x) = \int \frac{x}{24} dx$

$$= \frac{x^2}{48} + c$$

$P(X \leq 0) = 0$ so $F(0) = 0$

$\Rightarrow \quad c = 0$

$\Rightarrow \quad F(4) = \frac{1}{3}$ \quad (★)

F(4) must take the same value in both formulae.

For $4 \leq x \leq 12$, $F(x) = \int \frac{12-x}{48} dx$

$$= \frac{x}{4} - \frac{x^2}{96} + c'$$

$F(4) = \frac{1}{3}$ from (★)

$\Rightarrow \quad \frac{4}{4} - \frac{16}{96} + c' = \frac{1}{3} \Rightarrow \quad c' = -\frac{1}{2}$

So the full definition of $F(x)$ is

$$F(x) = \begin{cases} 0 & \text{for } x < 0, \\ \dfrac{x^2}{48} & \text{for } 0 \leq x \leq 4, \\ \dfrac{x}{4} - \dfrac{x^2}{96} - \dfrac{1}{2} & \text{for } 4 \leq x \leq 12, \\ 1 & \text{for } x > 12. \end{cases}$$

Check that this gives $F(12) = 1$ in both formulae.

(iii) The graph of $F(x)$ is shown in Figure 9.11.

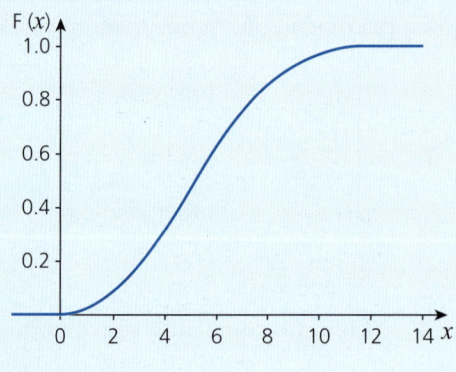

Figure 9.11

Example 9.7

The continuous random variable X has cumulative distribution function $F(x)$ given by:

$$F(x) = \begin{cases} 0 & \text{for } x < 2 \\ \dfrac{x^2}{32} - \dfrac{1}{8} & \text{for } 2 \leq x \leq 6 \\ 1 & \text{for } x > 6. \end{cases}$$

Find the p.d.f. $f(x)$.

Solution

$$f(x) = \frac{d}{dx}F(x)$$

$$f(x) = \begin{cases} \frac{d}{dx}F(x) = 0 & \text{for } x < 2 \\ \frac{d}{dx}F(x) = \frac{x}{16} & \text{for } 2 \leq x \leq 6 \\ \frac{d}{dx}F(x) = 0 & \text{for } x > 6. \end{cases}$$

Exercise 9.2

① The continuous random variable X has p.d.f. $f(x)$ where

$$f(x) = \begin{cases} 0.2 & \text{for } 0 \leq x \leq 5 \\ 0 & \text{otherwise.} \end{cases}$$

(i) Find $E(X)$.

(ii) Find the cumulative distribution function, $F(x)$.

(iii) Find $P(0 \leq x \leq 2)$ using

 (a) $F(x)$

 (b) $f(x)$

and show that your answer is the same by each method.

② The continuous random variable X has p.d.f. $f(x)$, where

$$f(x) = \begin{cases} \frac{1}{8}x & \text{for } 0 \leq x \leq 4 \\ 0 & \text{otherwise.} \end{cases}$$

Find

(i) $E(X)$

(ii) $\text{Var}(X)$

(iii) the median value of X.

③ The continuous random variable T has p.d.f. defined by

$$f(t) = \begin{cases} \dfrac{6-t}{18} & \text{for } 0 \leq t \leq 6 \\ 0 & \text{otherwise.} \end{cases}$$

Find

(i) $E(T)$

(ii) $\text{Var}(T)$

(iii) the median value of T.

④ The continuous random variable U has p.d.f. $f(u)$

where $f(u) = \begin{cases} ku & \text{for } 5 \leq u \leq 8 \\ 0 & \text{otherwise.} \end{cases}$

(i) Find the value of k.

(ii) Sketch $f(u)$.

(iii) Find $F(u)$.

(iv) Sketch the graph of $F(u)$.

The cumulative distribution function

5. A continuous random variable X has p.d.f. $f(x)$
   where $f(x) = \begin{cases} cx^2 & \text{for } 1 \leq x \leq 4 \\ 0 & \text{otherwise} \end{cases}$

   (i) Find the value of c.
   (ii) Find $F(x)$.
   (iii) Find the median of X.
   (iv) Find the mode of X.

6. The continuous random variable X has p.d.f. $f(x)$ given by
   $$f(x) = \begin{cases} \dfrac{k}{(x+1)^4} & \text{for } x \geq 0 \\ 0 & \text{otherwise} \end{cases}$$
   where k is a constant.

   (i) Show that $k = 3$, and find the cumulative distribution function.
   (ii) Find also the value of x such that $P(X < x) = \dfrac{7}{8}$.

7. The continuous random variable X has c.d.f. given by
   $$F(x) = \begin{cases} 0 & \text{for } x < 0 \\ 2x - x^2 & \text{for } 0 \leq x \leq 1 \\ 1 & \text{for } x > 1. \end{cases}$$

   (i) Find $P(X > 0.5)$.
   (ii) Find the value of q such that $P(X < q) = \dfrac{1}{4}$.
   (iii) Find the p.d.f. $f(x)$ of X, and sketch its graph.

8. The continuous random variable X has p.d.f. $f(x)$ given by
   $$f(x) = \begin{cases} k(9 - x^2) & \text{for } 0 \leq x \leq 3 \\ 0 & \text{otherwise} \end{cases}$$
   where k is a constant.

   Show that $k = \dfrac{1}{18}$ and find the values of $E(X)$ and $Var(X)$.

   Find the cumulative distribution function for X, and verify by calculation that the median value of X is between 1.04 and 1.05.

9. A random variable X has p.d.f. $f(x)$ where
   $$f(x) = \begin{cases} 12x^2(1 - x) & \text{for } 0 \leq x \leq 1 \\ 0 & \text{otherwise.} \end{cases}$$

   Find μ, the mean of X, and show that σ, the standard deviation of X, is $\dfrac{1}{5}$.
   Show that $F(x)$, the probability that $X \leq x$ satisfies
   $$F(x) = \begin{cases} 0 & \text{for } x < 0 \\ 4x^3 - 3x^4 & \text{for } 0 \leq x \leq 1 \\ 1 & \text{for } x > 1. \end{cases}$$

   Use this result to show that $P(|X - \mu| < \sigma) = 0.64$. [MEI]

   What would this probability be if, instead, X were Normally distributed?

10. The temperature in degrees Celsius in a refrigerator which is operating properly has probability density function given by

$$f(t) = \begin{cases} kt^2(12-t) & 0 < t < 12 \\ 0 & \text{otherwise.} \end{cases}$$

(i) Show that the value of k is $\dfrac{1}{1728}$.

(ii) Find the cumulative distribution function F(t).

(iii) Show, by substitution, that the median temperature is about 7.37 °C.

(iv) The temperature in a refrigerator is too high if it is over 10 °C. Find the probability that this occurs. [MEI]

⑪ A random variable X has p.d.f. f(x), where

$$f(x) = \begin{cases} k \sin 2x & \text{for } 0 \leqslant x \leqslant \dfrac{\pi}{2} \\ 0 & \text{otherwise.} \end{cases}$$

By integration find, in terms of x and the constant k, an expression for the cumulative distribution function of X for $0 \leqslant x \leqslant \dfrac{\pi}{2}$.

Hence show that $k = 1$ and find the probability that $X < \dfrac{\pi}{8}$. [MEI]

⑫ A firm has a large number of employees. The distance in miles they have to travel each day from home to work can be modelled by a continuous random variable X whose cumulative distribution function is given by

$$F(x) = \begin{cases} 0 & \text{for } x < 1 \\ k\left(1 - \dfrac{1}{x}\right) & \text{for } 1 \leqslant x \leqslant b \\ 1 & \text{for } x > b \end{cases}$$

where b represents the farthest distance anybody lives from work.

The diagram below shows a sketch of this cumulative distribution function.

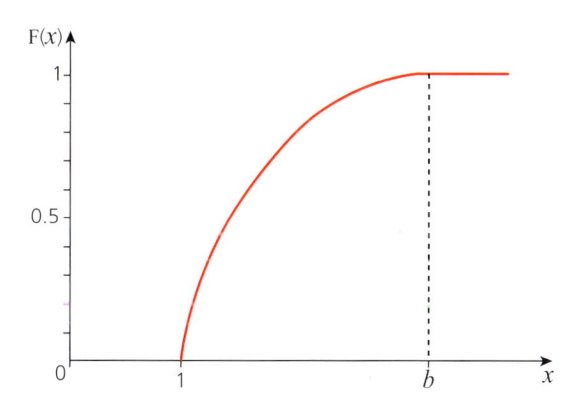

Figure 9.12

A survey suggests that $b = 5$. Use this parameter for parts (i) to (iv).

(i) Show that $k = 1.25$.

(ii) Write down and solve an equation to find the median distance travelled to work.

(iii) Find the probability that an employee lives within half a mile of the median.

(iv) Derive the probability density function for X and illustrate it with a sketch.

(v) Show that, for any value of b greater than 1, the median distance travelled does not exceed 2. [MEI]

The cumulative distribution function

⑬ The continuous random variable Y has p.d.f. $f(y)$ defined by

$$f(y) = \begin{cases} 12y^2(1-y) & \text{for } 0 \leq y \leq 1 \\ 0 & \text{otherwise.} \end{cases}$$

(i) Find $E(Y)$.

(ii) Find $\text{Var}(Y)$.

(iii) Show that, to 2 decimal places, the median value of Y is 0.61.

⑭ The continuous random variable X has p.d.f. $f(x)$ defined by

$$f(x) = \begin{cases} \frac{2}{9}x(3-x) & \text{for } 0 \leq x \leq 3 \\ 0 & \text{otherwise.} \end{cases}$$

(i) Find $E(X)$.

(ii) Find $\text{Var}(X)$.

(iii) Find the mode of X.

(iv) Find the median value of X.

(v) Draw a sketch graph of $f(x)$ and comment on your answers to parts (i), (iii) and (iv) in the light of what it shows you.

⑮ The function $f(x) = \begin{cases} k(3+x) & \text{for } 0 \leq x \leq 2 \\ 0 & \text{otherwise.} \end{cases}$

is the probability density function of the random variable X.

(i) Show that $k = \frac{1}{8}$.

(ii) Find the mean and variance of X.

(iii) Find the probability that a randomly selected value of X lies between 1 and 2.

⑯ The marks of candidates in an examination are modelled by the continuous random variable X with p.d.f.

$$f(x) = \begin{cases} kx(x-50)^2(100-x) & \text{for } 0 \leq x \leq 100 \\ 0 & \text{otherwise.} \end{cases}$$

(i) Find the value of k.

(ii) Sketch the graph of $f(x)$.

(iii) Describe the shape of the graph and give an explanation of how such a graph might occur, in terms of the examination and the candidates.

(iv) Is it permissible to model a mark, which is a discrete variable going up in steps of 1, by a continuous random variable like X, as defined in this question?

⑰ The municipal tourism officer at a Mediterranean resort on the Costa Del Sol wishes to model the amount of sunshine per day during the holiday season. She denotes by X the number of hours of sunshine per day between 8 am and 8 pm and she suggests the following probability density function for X:

$$f(x) = \begin{cases} k\left[(x-3)^2 + 4\right] & \text{for } 0 \leq x \leq 12 \\ 0 & \text{otherwise.} \end{cases}$$

(i) Show that $k = \frac{1}{300}$ and sketch the graph of the p.d.f. $f(x)$.

(ii) Assuming that the model is accurate, find the mean and standard deviation of the number of hours of sunshine per day. Find also the probability of there being more than eight hours of sunshine on a randomly chosen day.

(iii) Obtain a cubic equation for m, the median number of hours of sunshine, and verify that m is about 9.74 to 2 decimal places.

18. The continuous random variable X has p.d.f. f(x) defined by

$$f(x) = \begin{cases} \dfrac{a}{x} & \text{for } 1 \leq x \leq 2 \\ 0 & \text{otherwise.} \end{cases}$$

(i) Find the value of a.

(ii) Sketch the graph of f(x).

(iii) Find the mean and variance of X.

(iv) Find the proportion of values of X between 1.5 and 2.

(v) Find the median value of X.

19. An examination is taken by a large number of candidates. The marks scored are modelled by the continuous random variable X with probability density function

$$f(x) = kx^3(120 - x) \qquad 0 \leq x \leq 100.$$

(You should assume throughout this question that marks are on a continuous scale. Hence there is no need to consider **continuity corrections** which you will meet in Chapter 10.)

(i) Sketch the graph of this probability density function. What does the model suggest about the abilities of the candidates in relation to this examination?

(ii) Show that $k = 10^{-9}$.

(iii) The pass mark is set at 50. Find what proportion of candidates fail the examination.

(iv) The top 20% of candidates are awarded a distinction. Determine whether a mark of 90 is sufficient for a distinction. Find the least whole number mark which is sufficient for a distinction. [MEI]

20. A continuous random variable X has probability density function f(x). The probability that $X \leq x$ is given by the function F(x).

Explain why F'(x) = f(x).

A rod of length $2a$ is broken into two parts at a point whose position is random. State the form of the probability distribution of the length of the smaller part, and state also the mean value of this length.

Two equal rods, each of length $2a$, are broken into two parts at points whose positions are random. X is the length of the shortest of the four parts thus obtained. Find the probability, F(x), that $X \leq x$, where $0 < x \leq a$.

Hence, or otherwise, show that the probability density function of X is given by

$$f(x) = \begin{cases} \dfrac{2(a-x)}{a^2} & \text{for } 0 < x \leq a \\ 0 & \text{for } x \leq 0, x > a. \end{cases}$$

Show that the mean value of X is $\dfrac{1}{3}a$.

Write down the mean value of the sum of the two smaller parts and show that the mean values of the four parts are in the proportions $1 : 2 : 4 : 5$. [MEI]

The cumulative distribution function

㉑ (i) Explain the significance of the results:

(a) $\displaystyle\int_{-\infty}^{\infty} \frac{1}{\sqrt{2\pi}} e^{-\frac{1}{2}z^2}\, dz = 1$ (b) $\displaystyle\int_{-\infty}^{\infty} \frac{1}{\sqrt{2\pi}} z e^{-\frac{1}{2}z^2}\, dz = 0$

The random variable Y is given by $Y = Z^2$ (where Z is the standardised Normal variable).

(ii) Using the results in part (i), find

(a) $E(Y)$ (b) $\text{Var}(Y)$.

(You will need to use integration by parts.)

KEY POINTS

1. **A function of a continuous random variable**
   If $g[X]$ is a function of X then
   - $E\big[g(X)\big] = \displaystyle\int g(x) f(x)\, dx$
   - $\text{Var}\big[g(X)\big] = \displaystyle\int [g(x)]^2 f(x)\, dx - \big[E[g(X)]\big]^2$

2. **A linear combination of continuous random variables**
   - $E(aX \pm bY) = aE(X) \pm bE(Y)$

   and for independent X and Y
   - $\text{Var}(aX \pm bY) = a^2 \text{Var}(X) + b^2 \text{Var}(Y)$

3. **The cumulative distribution function**
   - $F(x) = \displaystyle\int_a^x f(u)\, du$ where the constant a is the lower limit of X.
   - $f(x) = \dfrac{d}{dx} F(x)$
   - For the median, m, $F(m) = 0.5$

LEARNING OUTCOMES

When you have completed this chapter, you should:

▶ know and be able to use the results for the expectation and variance of a linear combination of independent continuous random variables

▶ understand the meaning of a c.d.f. and be able to obtain one from a given p.d.f.

▶ be able to sketch a c.d.f.

▶ be able to obtain a p.d.f. from a given c.d.f.

▶ use a c.d.f. to calculate the median and other percentiles.

▶ be able to use the Normal distribution as a model, and to calculate and use probabilities from a Normal distribution

▶ know the meaning of the term confidence interval for a parameter and associated language

▶ understand the factors which affect the width of a confidence interval

10 Confidence intervals using the Normal and *t*-distributions

To approach zero defects, you must have statistical control of processes.

David Wilson

Florence is an Airedale terrier. People say that she is exceptionally heavy for a female. She weighs 26 kg.

It is true that the majority of female Airedale terriers do weigh quite a lot less than this, but how rare is it for a female to weigh this much? To answer that question you need to know the distribution of weights of female Airedale terriers. Of course, the distribution is continuous, so if you know the probability density function for this distribution, you could work out the probability of a weight which is at least 26 kg.

> ❗ In mechanics and physics the word 'weight' is used exclusively to mean the force of gravity on a body and the units of weight are those of force, such as newton. The word 'mass' is used to denote the amount of material in a body, with units such as kilogram, tonne and pound.
>
> In everyday use the term 'weight' is often used where 'mass' would be used in mechanics.
>
> In statistics the data used often come from everyday contexts or from other subjects. Consequently it is very often the case that the word 'weight' is used to describe what would be called 'mass' in mechanics. Since statistics is a practical subject, using data to solve problems from a wide variety of contexts, this practice is accepted in this book. So the terms weight and mass are used interchangeably and should be interpreted according to the situation.

Note

As you saw in Chapter 8 for a continuous random variable such as this, the probability that a dog's weight is exactly 26 kg is zero. Instead, you need to specify a range of values, in this case at least 26 kg.

Confidence intervals using the Normal and t-distributions

Like many other naturally occurring variables, the weights of female Airedale terriers may be modelled by a Normal distribution, shown in Figure 10.1. You will see that this has a distinctive bell-shaped curve and is symmetrical about its middle. The curve is continuous as weight is a continuous variable.

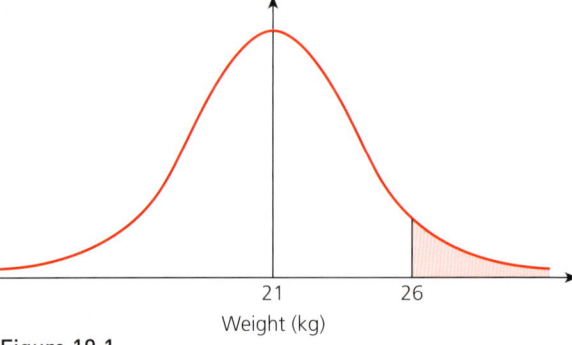

Figure 10.1

Before you can start to find this area, you must know the mean and standard deviation of the distribution, in this case, roughly 21 kg and 2.5 kg, respectively.

You can find the probability of a weight which is at least 26 kg directly from your calculator. You need to enter the mean, standard deviation and lower and upper limits.

This probability is 0.02275, so roughly 2.3% of female Airedale terriers will weigh at least 26 kg.

> **Note**
> The mean μ and standard deviation σ (or variance σ^2), are the two parameters used to define the distribution. Once you know their values, you know everything there is to know about the distribution.

> In this case, the lower limit is 26 kg and the upper limit is infinite. Of course, you cannot enter infinity into your calculator, so instead you have to enter a very large positive number for the upper limit.

> **Note**
> Note that this is a model so the probability that you have calculated is unlikely to be exactly correct.
> - The distribution of the weights is unlikely to be exactly Normal.
> - The mean and standard deviation are not exactly 21 kg and 2.5 kg, respectively.

Notation

- The mean of a population is denoted by μ.
- The standard deviation is denoted by σ and the variance by σ^2.
- The curve (or p.d.f.) for the Normal distribution with mean μ and standard deviation σ (i.e. variance σ^2) is given by the function $\phi(x)$, where

$$\phi(x) = \frac{1}{\sigma\sqrt{2\pi}} e^{-\frac{1}{2}\left(\frac{x-\mu}{\sigma}\right)^2}$$

- The notation $X \sim N(\mu, \sigma^2)$ is used to describe this distribution.
- The number of standard deviations the value of a variable x is beyond the mean, μ, is denoted by the letter z.
- So $z = \dfrac{x - \mu}{\sigma}$. This is called standardised form.
- So the p.d.f. for the standardised Normal distribution, $Z \sim N(0,1)$, is

$$\phi(z) = \frac{1}{\sqrt{2\pi}} e^{-\frac{z^2}{2}}$$

- The function $\Phi(z)$ gives the area under the Normal distribution curve to the left of the value z. So $\phi(1)$ is the shaded area in Figure 10.2. It is the cumulative distribution function. The total area under the curve is 1, and the area given by $\Phi(z)$ represents the probability of a value smaller than z.

> **Note**
> Be careful using the notation $X \sim N(\mu, \sigma^2)$. The notation uses the variance not the standard deviation. So you need to square root the second value to find the standard deviation.

USING ICT

In the past, values of $\Phi(z)$ were found from tables but advances in technology have made these tables no longer necessary.

> **Note**
>
> In the example at the start of this chapter, Florence's weight is 26 kg. The mean is 21 kg and the standard deviation is 2.5 kg.
> So $x = 26$, $\mu = 21$ and $\sigma = 2.5$, and $z = \dfrac{26 - 21}{2.5} = 2$.
> Florence's weight is 5 kg above the mean, and that is 2 standard deviations above the mean.

Notice the scale for the *z* values; it is in standard deviations from the mean.

Notice how lower case letters, *x* and *z*, are used to indicate particular values of the random variables, whereas upper case letters, *X* and *Z*, are used to describe or name those variables.

The shaded area is $\Phi(1)$

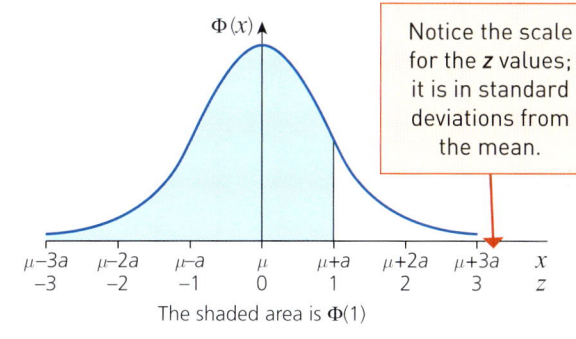

Figure 10.2

- So $P(Z < z) = \Phi(z) = \dfrac{1}{\sqrt{2\pi}} \displaystyle\int_{-\infty}^{z} e^{-\frac{1}{2}u^2} \, du$.
- Unfortunately, the integration cannot be carried out analytically and so there is no neat expression for $\Phi(z)$. Instead, the integration can be performed numerically and, as you have seen, you can find the values directly from a calculator, both for the standardised Normal distribution and for $N(\mu, \sigma^2)$.
- The area to the right of *z* is $1 - \Phi(z)$.

> **Note**
>
> In the example of Florence, the Airedale terrier, you calculated
> $P(Z > 2) = 1 - P(Z < 2)$.
> $P(Z < 2) = \Phi(2)$ so the probability which you calculated is $1 - \Phi(2)$.

Example 10.1

The volume of cola in a can is modelled by a Normal distribution with mean 332 ml and standard deviation 4 ml.

(i) Find the probability that a can contains
  (a) at least 330 ml
  (b) less than 340 ml
  (c) between 325 ml and 335 ml.

(ii) 95% of cans contain at least *a* ml of cola. Find the value of *a*.

Solution

(i) You need to enter the mean and standard deviation into your calculator and then the lower and upper limits.

  (a) Lower limit 300, upper limit e.g. 1000

  P(at least 330 ml) = 0.6914

  (b) Lower limit e.g. 0, upper limit 340

  P(less than 340 ml) = 0.9772

  (c) Lower limit 325, upper limit 335

  P(between 325 ml and 335 ml) = 0.7333

> **⚠ A word of caution**
>
> The symbols for phi Φ, ϕ (or φ) look very alike and are easily confused.
>
> - Φ is used for the cumulative distribution and is the symbol you will often use.
> - ϕ and φ are used for the equation of the actual curve; you won't actually need to use them in this book.
>
> These symbols are the Greek letter phi. Φ is upper case and ϕ is lower case.

The sums and differences of Normal variables

> The inverse Normal function on your calculator gives $P(X \leq x)$ for $X \sim N(\mu, \sigma^2)$.

(ii) You can use your calculator to work out the value of a. You know that 95% of cans contain at least a ml. Therefore 5% of cans contain less than a ml. You need to use the inverse Normal function (often labelled invNormal on a calculator). You enter the mean and standard deviation and then the maximum probability, which in this case is 5% or 0.05.

Using your calculator gives $a = 325.42$.

You can, instead, use the table of percentage points of the Normal distribution.

USING ICT

In these calculations 1000 is typical of numbers that are many standard deviations above the mean and 0 is typical of those that are many standard deviations below the mean.

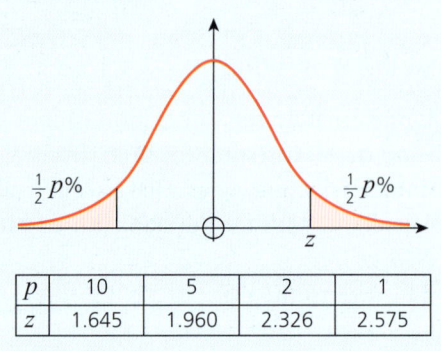

p	10	5	2	1
z	1.645	1.960	2.326	2.575

Figure 10.3

You know that 5% of cans contain less than a ml. The left-hand tail which is labelled $\frac{1}{2}p\%$ is therefore 5%. Thus $p = 10\%$. The z-value for this is 1.645. However, you need the lower tail and so the z-value which you need is actually -1.645.

The standardised value $z = \dfrac{x - \mu}{\sigma}$

$$\Rightarrow -1.645 = \frac{x - 332}{4}$$

$$\Rightarrow x = 332 + 4 \times (-1.645) = 325.42$$

1 The sums and differences of Normal variables

In Chapter 5, you were given general results for discrete random variables. These results are also true for continuous random variables, as you saw in Chapter 8. Here are some of these results.

For any two random variables X_1 and X_2

- $E(X_1 + X_2) = E(X_1) + E(X_2)$
- $E(X_1 - X_2) = E(X_1) - E(X_2)$

If the variables X_1 and X_2 are independent then

- $Var(X_1 + X_2) = Var(X_1) + Var(X_2)$
- $Var(X_1 - X_2) = Var(X_1) + Var(X_2)$

If the variables X_1 and X_2 are Normally distributed, then the distributions of $(X_1 + X_2)$ and $(X_1 - X_2)$ are also Normal. The means of these distributions are $E(X_1) + E(X_2)$ and $E(X_1) - E(X_2)$.

You must, however, be careful when you come to their variances, since you may only use the result that $\text{Var}(X_1 \pm X_2) = \text{Var}(X_1) + \text{Var}(X_2)$ to find the variances of these distributions if the variables X_1 and X_2 are independent.

This is the situation in the next two examples.

Example 10.2

Robert Fisher, a keen chess player, visits his local club most days. The total time taken to drive to the club and back is modelled by a Normal variable with mean 25 minutes and standard deviation 3 minutes. The time spent at the chess club is also modelled by a Normal variable with mean 120 minutes and standard deviation 10 minutes. Find the probability that on a certain evening Mr Fisher is away from home for more than 2½ hours.

Solution

$E(X_1 + X_2) = E(X_1) + E(X_2)$
$= 25 + 120 = 145$
$\text{Var}(X_1 + X_2) = \text{Var}(X_1) + \text{Var}(X_2) = 3^2 + 10^2 = 109$,
so the standard deviation of $(X_1 + X_2) = \sqrt{109}$.
It is NOT 3 + 10.

Let the random variable $X_1 \sim N(25, 3^2)$ represent the driving time, and the random variable $X_2 \sim N(120, 10^2)$ represent the time spent at the chess club.

Then the random variable T, where $T = X_1 + X_2 \sim N\left(145, \left(\sqrt{109}\right)^2\right)$, represents his total time away.

You can use your calculator to find the probability that Mr Fisher is away for more than 2½ hours (150 minutes).

Alternatively it is given by

$$P(T > 150) = 1 - \Phi\left(\frac{150 - 145}{\sqrt{109}}\right)$$
$$= 1 - \Phi(0.479)$$
$$= 0.316$$

Note

You need to assume that X_1 and X_2 are independent. For instance, in Example 10.2, the time to drive to and from the chess club does not affect the time spent at the club. This assumption seems reasonable.

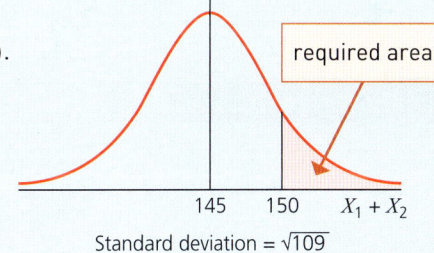

Figure 10.4

Standard deviation = $\sqrt{109}$

Example 10.3

In the manufacture of a bridge made entirely from wood, circular pegs have to fit into circular holes. The diameters of the pegs are Normally distributed with mean 1.60 cm and standard deviation 0.01 cm, while the diameters of the holes are Normally distributed with mean 1.65 cm and standard deviation of 0.02 cm. What is the probability that a randomly chosen peg will not fit into a randomly chosen hole?

Solution

Let the random variable X be the diameter of a hole:

$X \sim N(1.65, 0.02^2) = N(1.65, 0.0004)$.

Let the random variable Y be the diameter of a peg:

$Y \sim N(1.60, 0.01^2) = N(1.6, 0.0001)$.

The sums and differences of Normal variables

Let $F = X - Y$. F represents the gap remaining between the peg and the hole and so the sign of F determines whether or not a peg will fit in a hole.

$E(F) = E(X) - E(Y) = 1.65 - 1.60 = 0.05$

$Var(F) = Var(X) + Var(Y) = 0.0004 + 0.0001 = 0.0005$

$F \sim N(0.05, 0.0005)$

If, for any combination of peg and hole, the value of F is negative, then the peg will not fit into the hole.

You can use your calculator to find the probability that the peg will not fit into the hole, $P(F < 0)$.

The probability that $F < 0$ is given by

$$\Phi\left(\frac{0 - 0.05}{\sqrt{0.0005}}\right) = \Phi(-2.326)$$

$= 1 - 0.9873$

$= 0.0127$

> Note that $Var(X_1 - X_2) = Var(X_1) + Var(X_2)$ and not as you might at first imagine $Var(X_1) - Var(X_2)$.

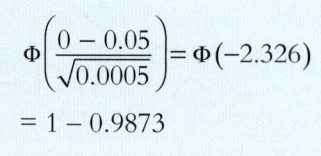

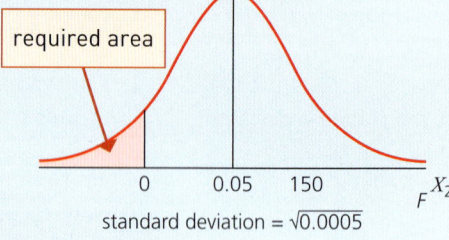

Figure 10.5

Exercise 10.1

① The menu at a cafe is shown below.

Table 10.1

Main course		Dessert	
Fish and chips	£3	Ice cream	£1
Bacon and eggs	£3.50	Apple pie	£1.50
Pizza	£4	Sponge pudding	£2
Steak and chips	£5.50		

The owner of the cafe says that all the main-course dishes sell equally well, as do all the desserts, and that customers' choice of dessert is not influenced by the main course they have just eaten.

The variable M denotes the cost of the items for the main course, in pounds, and the variable D the cost of the items for the dessert. The variable T denotes the total cost of a two-course meal: $T = M + D$.

(i) Find the mean and variance of M.

(ii) Find the mean and variance of D.

(iii) List all the possible two-course meals, giving the price for each one.

(iv) Use your answer to part (iii) to find the mean and variance of T.

(v) Hence verify that for these figures

mean (T) = mean (M) + mean (D)

and

variance (T) = variance (M) + variance (D).

② X_1 and X_2 are independent random variables with distributions N(50, 16) and N(40, 9), respectively. Write down the distributions of

　(i)　$X_1 + X_2$　　(ii)　$X_1 - X_2$　　(iii)　$X_2 - X_1$.

③ The random variable X has a Normal distribution with mean 20 and standard deviation 5. Find

　(i)　$P(X < 25)$　　(ii)　$P(X > 28)$　　(iii)　$P(12 \leq X \leq 24)$.

④ The weights in grams of a variety of apple can be modelled as Normally distributed with mean 124 and standard deviation 15. Find the probability that the weight of a randomly selected apple will be

　(i)　less than 100 g　　(ii)　at least 120 g　　(iii)　between 110 and 140 grams.

⑤ In a vending machine, the capacity of cups is Normally distributed, with mean 200 cm³ and standard deviation 4 cm³. The volume of coffee discharged per cup is Normally distributed, with mean 190 cm³ and standard deviation 5 cm³. Find the percentage of drinks which overflow.

⑥ A play is enjoying a long run at a theatre. It is found that the performance time may be modelled as a Normal variable with mean 130 minutes and standard deviation 3 minutes, and that the length of the intermission in the middle of the performance may be modelled by a Normal variable with mean 15 minutes and standard deviation 5 minutes. Find the probability that the performance is completed in less than 140 minutes.

⑦ On a distant island the heights of adult men and women may both be taken to be Normally distributed, with means 173 cm and 165 cm and standard deviations 10 cm and 8 cm, respectively.

　(i)　Find the probability that a randomly chosen woman is taller than a randomly chosen man.

　(ii)　Do you think that this is equivalent to the probability that a married woman is taller than her husband?

⑧ The lifetimes of a certain brand of refrigerator are approximately Normally distributed, with mean 2000 days and standard deviation 250 days.

Mrs Chudasama and Mr Poole each buy one on the same date.

What is the probability that Mr Poole's refrigerator is still working one year after Mrs Chudasama's refrigerator has broken down?

⑨ A random sample of size 2 is chosen from a Normal distribution N(100, 10). Find the probability that

　(i)　the sum of the sample numbers exceeds 225

　(ii)　the first observation is at least 12 more than the second observation.

⑩ An examination has a mean mark of 80 and a standard deviation of 12. The marks are assumed to be Normally distributed.

　(i)　Find the probability that a randomly selected candidate scores a mark between 75 and 85 inclusive (note that you will need to include a continuity correction in your calculation).

　(ii)　The bottom 5% of candidates are to be given extra help. Find the maximum mark required for extra help to be given.

　(iii)　Three candidates are selected at random. Find the probability that at least one of them is given extra help (you should assume that the examination is taken by a very large group of candidates).

⑪ Scores on an IQ test are modelled by the Normal distribution with mean 100 and standard deviation 15. The scores are reported to the nearest integer.
  (i) Find the probability that a person chosen at random scores
      (a) exactly 105   (b) more than 110.
  (ii) Only people with IQs in the top 2.5% are admitted to the organisation *BRAIN*. What is the minimum score for admission?
  (iii) Find the probability that, in a random sample of 20 people, exactly 6 score more than 110.
  (iv) Find the probability that, in a random sample of 200 people, at least 60 score more than 110.

2 More than two independent random variables

The results in Section 9.1 may be generalised to give the mean and variance of the sums and differences of n random variables, $X_1, X_2, \ldots, X_n$.

$$E(X_1 \pm X_2 \pm \cdots \pm X_n) = E(X_1) \pm E(X_2) \pm \cdots \pm E(X_n)$$

and, provided $X_1, X_2, \ldots, X_n$ are independent,

$$\text{Var}(X_1 \pm X_2 \pm \cdots \pm X_n) = \text{Var}(X_1) + \text{Var}(X_2) + \cdots + \text{Var}(X_n).$$

If $X_1, X_2, \ldots, X_n$ is a set of Normally distributed variables, then the distribution of $(X_1 \pm X_2 \pm \cdots \pm X_n)$ is also Normal.

Example 10.4

The mass, X, of a suitcase at an airport is modelled as being Normally distributed, with mean 15 kg and standard deviation 3 kg. Find the probability that a random sample of ten suitcases weighs more than 154 kg.

Solution

The mass X of one suitcase is given by $X \sim N(15, 9)$.

Then the mass of each of the ten suitcases has the distribution of X; call them $X_1, X_2, \ldots, X_{10}$.

Let the random variable T be the total weight of ten suitcases.

$$T = X_1 + X_2 + \cdots + X_{10}.$$

$$E(T) = E(X_1) + E(X_2) + \cdots + E(X_{10})$$
$$= 15 + 15 + \cdots + 15$$
$$= 150$$

Similarly

$$\text{Var}(T) = \text{Var}(X_1) + \text{Var}(X_2) + \cdots + \text{Var}(X_{10})$$
$$= 9 + 9 + \cdots + 9$$
$$= 90$$

So $T \sim N(150, 90)$

The probability that T exceeds 154 is given by

$$1 - \Phi\left(\frac{154-150}{\sqrt{90}}\right)$$
$$= 1 - \Phi(0.422)$$
$$= 1 - 0.6635$$
$$= 0.3365.$$

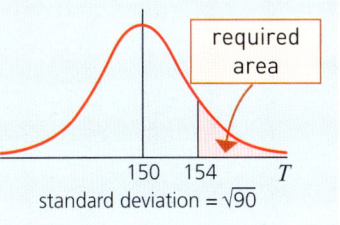

Figure 10.6

Example 10.5

The running times of the four members of a $4 \times 400\,\text{m}$ relay race may all be taken to be Normally distributed, as follows.

Table 10.2

Member	Mean time (s)	Standard deviation (s)
Adil	52	1
Brian	53	1
Colin	55	1.5
Dexter	51	0.5

Making the assumptions that no time is lost during changeovers and that the runners' times are independent, find the probability that the team finishes the race in less than 3 minutes 28 seconds.

Solution

Let the total time be T.

$$E(T) = 52 + 53 + 55 + 51 = 211$$
$$\text{Var}(T) = 1^2 + 1^2 + 1.5^2 + 0.5^2$$
$$= 1 + 1 + 2.25 + 0.25 = 4.5$$

So $T \sim N(211, 4.5)$.

The probability of a total time of less than 3 minutes 28 seconds (208 seconds) is given by

$$\Phi\left(\frac{208-211}{\sqrt{4.5}}\right) = \Phi(-1.414)$$
$$= 1 - 0.9213$$
$$= 0.0787$$

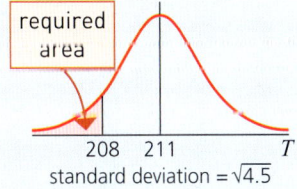

Figure 10.7

Example 10.6

A machine produces sheets of paper the thicknesses of which are Normally distributed with mean 0.1 mm and standard deviation 0.006 mm.

(i) State the distribution of the total thickness of eight randomly selected sheets of paper.

(ii) Single sheets of paper are folded three times (to give eight thicknesses). State the distribution of the total thickness.

More than two independent random variables

Solution

Denote the thickness of one sheet (in mm) by the random variable W, and the total thickness of eight sheets by T.

(i) *Eight separate sheets*

In this situation $T = W_1 + W_2 + W_3 + W_4 + W_5 + W_6 + W_7 + W_8$

where $W_1, W_2, \ldots, W_8$ are eight independent observations of the variable W. The distribution of W is Normal with mean 0.1 and variance 0.006^2.

So the distribution of T is Normal with

mean $= 0.1 + 0.1 + \cdots + 0.1 = 8 \times 0.1 = 0.8$

variance $= 0.006^2 + 0.006^2 + \cdots + 0.006^2 = 8 \times 0.006^2$

$= 0.000\,288$

standard deviation $= \sqrt{0.000288} = 0.016970$

The distribution is $N(0.8, 0.017^2)$.

(ii) *Eight thicknesses of the same sheet*

In this situation $T = W_1 + W_2 + W_3 + W_4 + W_5 + W_6 + W_7 + W_8 = 8W_1$

where W_1 is a single observation of the variable W.

So the distribution of T is Normal with

mean $= 8 \times E(W) = 0.8$

variance $= 8^2 \times \text{Var}(W) = 8^2 \times 0.006^2 = 0.002304$

standard deviation $= \sqrt{0.002304} = 0.048$

The distribution is $N(0.8, 0.048^2)$.

> ❗ Notice that, in both cases, the mean thickness is the same but for the folded paper the variance is greater. Why is this?

Exercise 10.2

① The random variable Y is Normally distributed with mean μ and variance σ^2.

Write down the distribution of

(i) $5Y$ (ii) the sum of five independent observations of Y.

② The distributions of two independent random variables X and Y are $N(10, 5)$ and $N(20, 10)$, respectively.

Find the distributions of

(i) $X + Y$ (ii) $10X$ (iii) $3X + 4Y$.

③ A random sample of 15 items is chosen from a Normal population with mean, 30 and variance, 9. Find the probability that the sum of the variables in the sample is less than 440.

④ A company manufactures floor tiles of mean length 20 cm with standard deviation 0.2 cm. Assuming that the distribution of the lengths of the tiles is Normal, find the probability that, when 12 randomly selected floor tiles are laid in a row, their total length exceeds 241 cm.

⑤ The masses of Christmas cakes produced at a bakery are independent and may be modelled as being Normally distributed with mean 4 kg and standard deviation 100 g. Find the probability that a set of eight Christmas cakes has a total mass between 32.3 kg and 32.7 kg.

⑥ The distributions of four independent random variables X_1, X_2, X_3 and X_4 are N(7, 9), N(8, 16), N(9, 4) and N(10, 1), respectively.

Find the distributions of

(i) $X_1 + X_2 + X_3 + X_4$ (ii) $X_1 + X_2 - X_3 - X_4$ (iii) $X_1 + X_2 + X_3$.

⑦ The distributions of X and Y are N(100, 25) and N(110, 36), and X and Y are independent. Find

(i) the probability that $8X + 2Y < 1000$

(ii) the probability that $8X - 2Y > 600$.

⑧ The distributions of the independent random variables A, B and C are N(35, 9), N(30, 8) and N(35, 9). Write down the distributions of

(i) $A + B + C$ (ii) $5A + 4B$ (iii) $A + 2B + 3C$ (iv) $4A - B - 5C$.

⑨ The distributions of the independent random variables X and Y are N(60, 4) and N(90, 9). Find the probability that

(i) $X - Y < -35$ (ii) $3X + 5Y > 638$ (iii) $3X > 2Y$.

⑩ Given that $X_1 \sim$ N(600, 400) and $X_2 \sim$ N(1000, 900) and that X_1 and X_2 are independent, write down the distributions of

(i) $4X_1 + 5X_2$

(ii) $7X_1 - 3X_2$

(iii) $aX_1 + bX_2$, where a and b are constants.

⑪ The quantity of fuel used by a coach on a return trip of 200 km is modelled as a Normal variable with mean 45 litres and standard deviation 1.5 litres.

(i) Find the probability that in nine return journeys the coach uses between 400 and 406 litres of fuel.

(ii) Find the volume of fuel which is 95% certain to be sufficient to cover the total fuel requirements for two return journeys.

⑫ Assume that the mass of men and women may be taken to be Normally distributed, men with mean 75 kg and standard deviation 4 kg, and women with mean 65 kg and standard deviation 3 kg.

At a village fair, tug-of-war teams consisting of either five men or six women are chosen at random. The competition is then run on a knock out basis, with teams drawn out of a hat. If in the first round a women's team is drawn against a men's team, what is the probability that the women's team is the heavier?

State any assumptions you have made and explain how they can be justified.

⑬ Jim Longlegs is an athlete whose specialist event is the triple jump. This is made up of a *hop*, a *step* and a *jump*. Over a season, the lengths of the *hop*, *step* and *jump* sections, denoted by H, S and J, respectively, are measured, from which the following models are proposed:

$H \sim$ N(5.5, 0.52), $S \sim$ N(5.1, 0.62), $J \sim$ N(6.2, 0.82)

where all distances are in metres. Assume that H, S and J are independent.

(i) In what proportion of his triple jumps will Jim's total distance exceed 18 metres?

The distribution of the sample mean

(ii) In six successive independent attempts, what is the probability that at least one total distance will exceed 18 m?

(iii) What total distance will Jim exceed 95% of the time?

(iv) Find the probability that, in Jim's next triple jump, his step will be greater than his hop. [MEI]

14. The mass of pamphlets are Normally distributed with mean 40 g and standard deviation 2 g. What is the distribution of the total mass of

(i) a random sample of two pamphlets?

(ii) a random sample of n pamphlets?

Pamphlets are stacked in piles nominally containing 25. To save time, the following method of counting is used. A pile of pamphlets is weighed and is accepted (i.e. assumed to contain 25 pamphlets) if its mass lies between 980 g and 1020 g. Assuming that each pile is a random sample, determine, to three decimal places, the probabilities that

(iii) a pile actually containing 24 pamphlets will be accepted

(iv) a pile actually containing 25 pamphlets will be rejected.

Justify the choice of the limits as 980 g and 1020 g. [MEI]

15. Bricks of a certain type are meant to be 65 mm in height, but, in fact, their heights are Normally distributed with mean 64.4 mm and standard deviation 1.4 mm. A warehouse keeps a large stock of these bricks, stored on shelves. The bricks are stacked one on top of another. The heights of the bricks may be regarded as statistically independent.

(i) Find the probability that an individual brick has height greater than 65 mm.

(ii) Find the probability that the height of a stack of six bricks is greater than 390 mm.

(iii) Find the vertical gap required between shelves to ensure that, with probability 0.99, there is room for a stack of six bricks.

(iv) The vertical gap between shelves is Normally distributed with a mean of 400 mm and standard deviation 7 mm. Find the probability that such a gap has room for a stack of six bricks.

(v) A workman buys ten bricks which can be considered to be a random sample from all the bricks in the warehouse. Find the probability that the average height of these bricks is between 64.8 mm and 65.2 mm. [MEI]

3 The distribution of the sample mean

In many practical situations you do not know the true value of the mean of a variable that you are investigating, that is, the parent population mean (usually just called the **population mean**). Indeed, that may be one of the things you are trying to establish.

In such cases, you will usually take a random sample, $x_1, x_2, \ldots, x_n$, of size n from the population and work out the sample mean $\bar{x}$, given by

$$\bar{x} = \frac{x_1 + x_2 + \cdots + x_n}{n}$$

to use as an estimate for the true population mean μ.

How accurate is this estimate likely to be and how does its reliability vary with n, the sample size?

Each of the sample values $x_1, x_2, \ldots, x_n$ can be thought of as a value of an independent random variable $X_1, X_2, \ldots, X_n$. The variables $X_1, X_2, \ldots, X_n$ have the same distribution as the population and so $E(X_1) = \mu$, $\mathrm{Var}(X_1) = \sigma^2$, etc.

So the sample mean is a value of the random variable $\bar{X}$ given by

$$\bar{X} = \frac{1}{n}(X_1 + X_2 + \cdots + X_n)$$

$$= \frac{1}{n}X_1 + \frac{1}{n}X_2 + \cdots + \frac{1}{n}X_n$$

and so

$$E(\bar{X}) = \frac{1}{n}E(X_1) + \frac{1}{n}E(X_2) + \cdots + \frac{1}{n}E(X_n)$$

$$= \frac{1}{n}\mu + \frac{1}{n}\mu + \cdots + \frac{1}{n}\mu$$

$$= n\left(\frac{1}{n}\mu\right)$$

$$= \mu, \text{ the population mean.}$$

Further, using the fact that $X_1, X_2, \ldots, X_n$ are independent,

$$\mathrm{Var}(\bar{X}) = \mathrm{Var}\left(\frac{X_1}{n}\right) + \mathrm{Var}\left(\frac{X_2}{n}\right) + \cdots + \mathrm{Var}\left(\frac{X_n}{n}\right)$$

$$= \frac{1}{n^2}\mathrm{Var}(X_1) + \frac{1}{n^2}\mathrm{Var}(X_2) + \cdots + \frac{1}{n^2}\mathrm{Var}(X_n)$$

$$= \frac{1}{n^2}\sigma^2 + \frac{1}{n^2}\sigma^2 + \cdots + \frac{1}{n^2}\sigma^2$$

$$= n\left(\frac{1}{n^2}\sigma^2\right)$$

$$= \frac{\sigma^2}{n}$$

Thus the distribution of the means of samples of size n, drawn from a parent population with mean μ and variance σ^2, has mean μ and variance $\frac{\sigma^2}{n}$. The distribution of the sample means is called the **sampling distribution of the means**, or often just the **sampling distribution**.

If the parent distribution is $N(\mu, \sigma^2)$, then the sampling distribution will be $N = \left(\mu, \frac{\sigma^2}{n}\right)$.

> **Note**
>
> The derivation has required no assumptions about the distribution of the parent population, other than that μ and σ are finite. If, in fact, the parent distribution is Normal, then the distribution of the sample means will also be Normal, whatever the size of n.
>
> If the parent population is not Normal, the distribution of the sample means will still be approximately Normal, and will be more accurately so for larger values of n.
>
> This result is called the central limit theorem and will be developed after Example 10.9.
>
> The derivation does require that the sample items are independent (otherwise the result for $\mathrm{Var}(\bar{X})$ would not have been valid).

The distribution of the sample mean

Notice that $(\bar{X}) = \dfrac{\sigma^2}{n}$ means that as *n* increases the variance of the sample mean decreases. In other words, the value obtained for $(\bar{X})$ from a large sample is more reliable as an estimate for μ than one obtained from a smaller sample. This result, simple though it is, lies at the heart of statistics: it says that you are likely to get more accurate results if you take a larger sample.

The standard deviation of sample means of size *n* is $\dfrac{\sigma}{\sqrt{n}}$ and this is called the **standard error of the mean**, or often just the **standard error**. It gives a measure of the degree of accuracy of $(\bar{X})$ as an estimate for μ.

Example 10.7

The discrete random variable *X* has a probability distribution as shown.

Table 10.3

X	1	2	3
Probability	0.5	0.4	0.1

A random sample of size 2 is chosen, with replacement after each selection.

(i) Find μ and σ^2.

(ii) Verify that $E(\bar{X}) = \mu$ and $\text{Var}(\bar{X}) = \dfrac{\sigma^2}{2}$

Solution

(i) $\mu = E(X) = 1 \times 0.5 + 2 \times 0.4 + 3 \times 0.1$

$= 1.6$

$E(X^2) = 1^2 \times 0.5 + 2^2 \times 0.4 + 3^2 \times 0.1$

$= 3$

$\sigma^2 = \text{Var}(X) = E(X^2) - [E(X)]^2$

$= 3 - 1.6^2 = 0.44$

(ii) The table below lists all the possible samples of size 2, their means and probabilities.

Table 10.4

Sample	1,1	1,2	1,3	2,1	2,2	2,3	3,1	3,2	3,3
Mean	1	1.5	2	1.5	2	2.5	2	2.5	3
Probability	0.25	0.2	0.05	0.2	0.16	0.04	0.05	0.04	0.01

This gives the following probability distribution of the sample mean.

> For example P(1, 2) = 0.5 × 0.4 = 0.2

Table 10.5

X	1	1.5	2	2.5	3
Probability	0.25	0.4	0.26	0.08	0.01

Using this table gives

$E(X) = 1 \times 0.25 + 1.5 \times 0.4 + 2 \times 0.26 + 2.5 \times 0.08 + 3 \times 0.01$

$= 1.6 = \mu$, as required.

$$E(X^2) = 1^2 \times 0.25 + 1.5^2 \times 0.4 + 2^2 \times 0.26 + 2.5^2 \times 0.08 + 3^2 \times 0.01$$
$$= 2.78$$
$$\text{Var}(X) = E(X^2) - [E(X)]^2$$
$$= 2.78 - (1.6)^2$$
$$= 0.22$$
$$= \frac{0.44}{2} = \frac{\sigma^2}{2} \text{ as required.}$$

EXTENSION

The central limit theorem

This theorem is fundamental to much of statistics and so it is worth pausing to make sure you understand just what it is saying.

It deals with the distribution of the sample mean. This is called the **sampling distribution of the mean**. There are three aspects to it.

1 The expected value of the sample mean is μ, the population mean of the original distribution. That is not a particularly surprising result but it is extremely important. For samples of size n drawn from a distribution with mean μ and finite variance σ^2, the distribution of the sample mean is approximately $N\left(\mu, \frac{\sigma^2}{n}\right)$ for sufficiently large n.

2 The standard deviation of the sample mean is $\frac{\sigma}{\sqrt{n}}$. This is often called the **standard error of the mean**. Within a sample, you would expect some values above the population mean, others below it, so that overall the deviations would tend to cancel each other out, and the larger the sample the more this would be the case. Consequently, the standard deviation of the sample means is smaller than that of individual items, by a factor of $\sqrt{n}$.

3 The distribution of the sample mean is approximately Normal.
This last point is the most surprising part of the theorem. Even if the underlying parent distribution is not Normal, the distribution of the mean of samples of a particular size drawn from it is approximately Normal. The larger the sample size, n, the closer this distribution is to the Normal. For any given value of n, the sampling distribution will be closest to Normal when the parent distribution is not unlike the Normal.
In many cases, the value of n does not need to be particularly large. For most parent distributions, you can rely on the distribution of the sample mean being Normal if n is 20 or more.

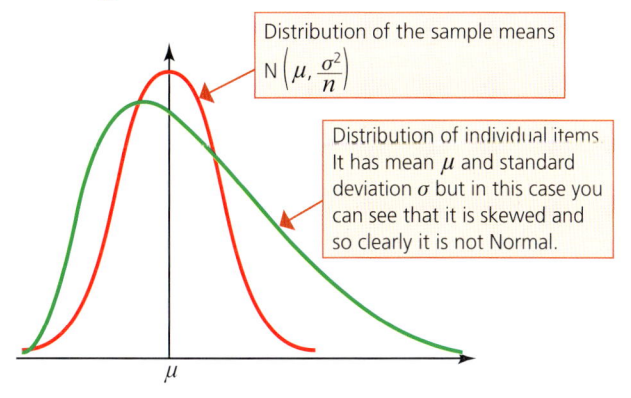

Figure 10.8

The distribution of the sample mean

Example 10.8

It is known that the mean length of a species of fish is 40.5 cm with standard deviation 3.2.

(i) A random sample of five fish is taken. Explain why you cannot find the probability that the mean of this sample is at least 40.

(ii) A random sample of 50 fish is taken. Calculate an estimate of the probability that the mean of this sample is at least 40.

(iii) If the lengths of individual fish could only be measured to the nearest 1 cm, make a new estimate of the probability calculated in part (ii).

Solution

(i) Because you are told nothing about the distribution of the parent population (the distribution of the length of this species of fish), you cannot carry out any probability calculations.

(ii) Although you do not know the distribution of the parent population, the sample size of 50 is large enough to apply the central limit theorem. This states that for a large sample, the distribution of the sample mean is approximately Normal. The distribution is therefore $N(40.5, \frac{3.2^2}{50})$. Using a calculator P(sample mean ≥ 40) = 0.8654.

> Distribution of the sample means is $N\left(\mu, \frac{\sigma^2}{n}\right)$ and you are given that $\mu = 40.5$ and $\sigma = 3.2$

(iii) If the lengths are only measured to the nearest 1 cm, then the sample mean can only take values ... 39.96, 39.98, 40.00, 40.02, 40.04 ... You therefore need to calculate P(sample mean > 39.99) rather than P(sample mean > 40). Using a calculator P(sample mean > 39.99) = 0.8701.

> For example, if all except one of the fish were 40 cm long and the last was 41 cm long the sample mean would be 40.02. If instead the last was 39 cm long the sample mean would be 39.98.

Note

This is an example of a continuity correction which you met earlier in the chapter. As you can see, it requires some careful thought to work out the value needed, particularly when it involves a sample mean.

Exercise 10.3

① The random variable X is Normally distributed with mean 30 and variance 4. Write down the distribution of a random sample of

(i) 2   (ii) 10   (iii) 100

observations of X.

② The random variable X is has mean 200 and standard deviation of 30. Write down if possible the approximate distribution of a random sample of

(i) 10   (ii) 30   (iii) 100

observations of X.

If you cannot write down the distribution, explain why you cannot.

③ At a men's hairdresser, haircuts take an average of 18 minutes with standard deviation 3 minutes. Find the distribution of the total time taken for 30 haircuts at the hairdresser. State any assumption which you make.

④ A random sample of 40 items is chosen from a population with mean 60 and variance 25. Find the probability that the mean of the sample is less than 59.

⑤ A company manufactures paving slabs of mean length 45.5 cm with standard deviation 0.5 cm. Find the probability that the mean length of a random sample of 100 slabs is at least 45.4 cm.

⑥ In a certain city, the heights of women have mean 164 cm and standard deviation 8.5 cm.

(i) Find the probability that the mean height of a random sample of 50 women will be within 1 cm of the mean.

(ii) Find the sample size required so that the probability that a random sample of this size will be within 0.5 cm of the mean is the same as your answer to part (i).

⑦ A random sample of n items is chosen from a population with mean 200 and standard deviation 15. You are given that n is large. The probability that the sample mean is greater than 201 is 0.2755 to 4 significant figures. Find the value of n.

⑧ Wooden sleepers for use in landscape gardening are available in two lengths 1.2 m and 1.8 m. The smaller ones actually have mean length 1.23 m with standard deviation 0.05 m. The larger ones have mean length 1.84 m with standard deviation 0.10 m. Find the probability that:

(i) 30 of the smaller sleepers have mean length less than 1.22 m

(ii) 40 of the longer sleepers have mean length more than 1.85 m.

(iii) The mean length of 45 smaller sleepers is greater than two thirds of the mean length of 30 longer sleepers.

The perfect apple grower

From our farming correspondent, Tom Smith

Fruit grower, Angie Fallon, believes that, after years of trials, she has developed trees that will produce the perfect supermarket apple. 'There are two requirements', Angie told me, 'The average weight of an apple should be 100 grams and they should all be nearly the same size. I have measured hundreds of mine and the standard deviation is a mere 5 grams.'

Angie invited me to take any ten apples off the shelf and weigh them for myself. It was quite uncanny; they were all so close to the magic 100 g: 98, 107, 105, 98, 100, 99, 104, 93, ..., 105, 103.

Discussion point

What can you conclude from the weights of the reporter's sample of ten apples?

Before going any further, it is appropriate to question whether the reporter's sample was random. Angie invited him to 'take any ten apples off the shelf'. That is not necessarily the same as taking any ten off the tree. The apples on the shelf could all have been specially selected to impress the reporter. So what follows is based on the assumption that Angie has been honest and the ten apples really do constitute a random sample.

The theory of confidence intervals

The sample mean is

$$\bar{x} = \frac{98 + 107 + 105 + 98 + 100 + 99 + 104 + 93 + 105 + 103}{10} = 101.2$$

To assess the sample, you need to know something about the distribution of the sample mean and also about the spread of the data. The usual measure of spread is the standard deviation, σ; in the article you are told that $\sigma = 5$.

You would estimate the population mean to be the same as the sample mean, namely 101.2.

You can express this by saying that you estimate μ to lie within a range of values, an interval, centred on 101.2:

101.2 − a bit < μ < 101.2 + a bit.

Such an interval is called a **confidence interval**.

Imagine that you take a large number of samples and use a formula to work out such an interval for each of them. Sometimes the true population mean will be in your confidence interval and sometimes it will not be. If in the long term you catch the true population mean in 90% of your intervals, the confidence interval is called a 90% confidence interval. Other percentages are also used and the confidence intervals are named accordingly.

The width of the interval is clearly twice the 'bit'.

Finding a confidence interval involves a fairly simple calculation but the reasoning behind it is somewhat subtle and requires clear thinking. It is explained in the next section.

> **Discussion point**
> What does that tell you about the population mean, μ?

> **Note**
> Commonly used confidence intervals are 90%, 95% and 99%.

> **Note**
> A word of advice: read through this section twice, lightly first time and then more thoroughly when you have tried a few questions. That will help you to gain a good understanding of the meaning of confidence intervals.

4 The theory of confidence intervals

To understand confidence intervals you need to look not at the particular sample whose mean you have just found, but at the parent population from which it was drawn. For the data on Angie Fallon's apples this does not look very promising. All you know about it is its standard deviation σ (in this case, 5). You do not know its mean, μ, which you are trying to estimate, or even its shape.

For our purposes now, we will assume that the parent distribution is Normal, $N(\mu, \sigma^2)$. That means that the sample mean is also distributed Normally, with mean μ and with standard deviation $\frac{\sigma}{\sqrt{n}}$.

In Figure 10.9, the central 90% region has been shaded leaving the two 5% tails, corresponding to z-values of ± 1.645, unshaded. So if you take a large number of samples, all of size n, and work out the sample mean $\overline{X}$ for each one, you would expect that in 90% of cases the value of $\overline{X}$ would lie in the shaded region between A and B.

> **USING ICT**
>
> The value 1.645 is the 95% point of the cumulative Normal distribution, $\Phi(z)$. You can find this from your calculator or from a table of percentage points of the Normal distribution.

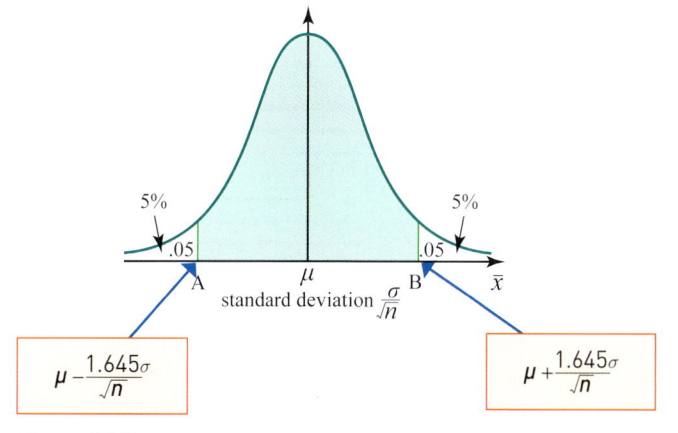

Figure 10.9

For such a value of $\bar{X}$ to be in the shaded region.

- it must be to the right of A: $\bar{x} > \mu - 1.645 \dfrac{\sigma}{\sqrt{n}}$

- it must be to the left of B: $\bar{x} < \mu + 1.645 \dfrac{\sigma}{\sqrt{n}}$

Putting these two inequalities together gives the result that, in 90% of cases,

$$\bar{x} - 1.645 \dfrac{\sigma}{\sqrt{n}} \text{ and } \bar{x} + 1.645 \dfrac{\sigma}{\sqrt{n}},$$

and this is the 90% confidence interval for μ.

The boundaries of this interval, $\bar{x} - 1.645 \dfrac{\sigma}{\sqrt{n}}$ and $\bar{x} + 1.645 \dfrac{\sigma}{\sqrt{n}}$, are called the 90% **confidence limits** and 90% is the **confidence level**. If you want a different confidence level, you use a different z value from 1.645.

This number is often denoted by k; commonly used values are:

Table 10.6

Confidence level	k
90%	1.645
95%	1.96
99%	2.58

> **USING ICT**
>
> You can find all of these values of k from your calculator or from a table of percentage points of the Normal distribution.

and the confidence interval is given by

$$\bar{x} - k \dfrac{\sigma}{\sqrt{n}} \text{ to } \bar{x} + k \dfrac{\sigma}{\sqrt{n}}.$$

The P% confidence interval for the mean is an interval constructed from sample data in such a way that P% of such intervals will include the true population mean. Figure 10.10 shows a number of confidence intervals constructed from different samples, one of which fails to catch the population mean.

The theory of confidence intervals

> **Note**
>
> Notice that this is a two-sided symmetrical confidence interval for the mean, μ. Confidence intervals do not need to be symmetrical and can be one-sided. The term confidence interval is a general one, applying not just to the mean but to other population parameters, like variance and skewness, as well. All those cases, however, are outside the scope of this book.

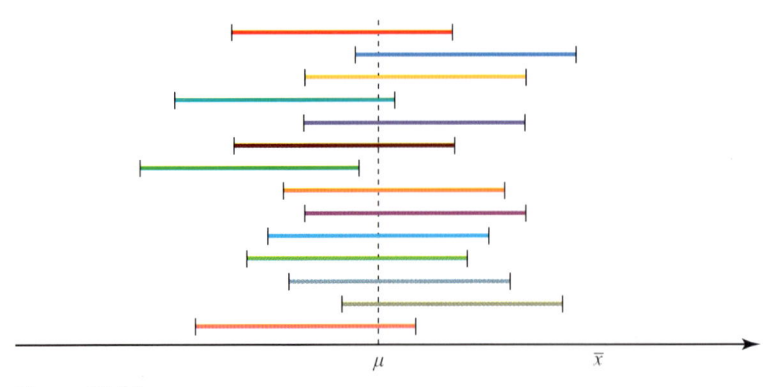

Figure 10.10

In the case of the data on the Angie Fallon's apples,

$\bar{x} = 101.2$, $\quad \sigma = 5$, $\quad n = 10$

and so the 90% confidence interval is

$$101.2 - 1.645 \times \frac{5}{\sqrt{10}} \text{ to } 101.2 + 1.645 \times \frac{5}{\sqrt{10}}$$

98.6 to 103.8.

Since this interval includes 100, this suggests that Angie's claim that the mean weight of her apples is 100 grams may be correct.

USING ICT

Statistical software

You can use statistical software to find a confidence interval.

In order for the software to find the interval, you need to input the values of the sample mean, the variance, the value of n and the confidence level. Here is a typical output using the data on Angie Fallon's apples.

Table 10.7

Z Estimate of a Mean	
Confidence Level	0.90

	Sample
Mean	101.2
σ	5
n	10

	Result
Mean	101.2
σ	5
SE	1.5811
N	10
Lower Limit	98.6
Upper Limit	103.8
Interval	101.2 ± 2.60

> **USING ICT**
>
> The software gives the interval as 101.2 ± 2.60 as well as giving the lower and upper limit.

Known and estimated standard deviation

Notice that you can only use this procedure if you already know the value of the standard deviation of the parent population, σ. In this example, Angie Fallon said that she knew from hundreds of measurements of her apples, that its value is 5.

It is more often the situation that you do not know the population standard deviation or variance, and have to estimate it from your sample data. If that is the case, the procedure is different in that you use the *t*-distribution rather than the Normal distribution, provided that the parent population is Normally distributed, and this results in different values of *k*. The use of the *t*-distribution will be developed later in this chapter.

However, if the sample is large, for example over 50, confidence intervals worked out using the Normal distribution will be reasonably accurate even though the standard deviation used is an estimate from the sample. So it is quite acceptable to use the Normal distribution for large samples whether the standard deviation is known or not.

How large a sample do you need?

You are now in a position to start to answer the question of how large a sample needs to be. The answer, as you will see in Example 10.2, depends on the precision you require, and the confidence level you are prepared to accept.

Example 10.9

A trading standards officer is investigating complaints that a coal merchant is giving short measure. Each sack should contain 25 kg but some variation will inevitably occur because of the size of the lumps of coal; the officer knows from experience that the standard deviation should be 1.5 kg.

The officer plans to take, secretly, a random sample of *n* sacks, find the total weight of the coal inside them and thereby estimate the mean weight of the coal per sack. He wants to present this figure correct to the nearest kilogram with 95% confidence. What value of *n* should he choose?

> **Note**
>
> This example illustrates that a larger sample size leads to a narrower confidence interval. In fact three things affect the width of the confidence interval; sample size, confidence level and population variability. Increasing the sample size results in a decrease in the width of the confidence interval. Increasing the confidence level and/ or population variability results in an increase in the width of the confidence interval.

Solution

Let's assume that the distribution of the weight of the merchant's sacks is distributed Normally, $N(\mu, \sigma^2)$, where we will estimate μ with $\bar{x}$.

The 95% confidence interval for the mean is given by

$$\bar{x} - \frac{1.96\sigma}{\sqrt{n}} \text{ to } \bar{x} + \frac{1.96\sigma}{\sqrt{n}}$$

and so, since $\sigma = 1.5$, the inspector's requirement is that

$$\frac{1.96 \times 1.5}{\sqrt{n}} \leq 0.5$$

The officer wants the mean weight to be correct to the nearest kg, so ± 0.5 kg.

$$\Rightarrow \frac{1.96 \times 1.5}{0.5} \leq \sqrt{n}$$

$$\Rightarrow n \geq 34.57$$

So the inspector needs to take at least 35 sacks.

The theory of confidence intervals

Large samples

Given that the width of a confidence interval decreases with sample size, why is it not standard practice to take very large samples?

The answer is that the cost and time involved has to be balanced against the quality of information produced. Because the width of a confidence interval depends on $\frac{1}{\sqrt{n}}$ and not on $\frac{1}{n}$, increasing the sample size does not produce a proportional reduction in the width of the interval. You have, for example, to increase the sample size by a factor of 4 to halve the width of the interval. In the previous example the inspector had to weigh 35 sacks of coal to achieve a class interval of $2 \times 0.5 = 1$ kg with 95% confidence. That is already quite a daunting task; does the benefit from reducing the interval to 0.5 kg justify the time, cost and trouble involved in weighing another 105 sacks?

> **Discussion point**
> At other times your interest may be in whether the mean is less than a particular value and so you want a one-sided confidence interval with an upper bound. Think of a situation where such a confidence interval is appropriate.

Asymmetrical confidence intervals

The confidence interval $\left(\bar{x} - \frac{1.96\sigma}{\sqrt{n}}, \bar{x} + \frac{1.96\sigma}{\sqrt{n}}\right)$ is clearly a symmetrical one, with $\bar{x}$ at its centre. There are confidence intervals, however, that are not symmetrical.

One-sided confidence intervals

Sometimes when you are estimating the mean of a population your main interest is in whether it is greater than a particular value. So you are interested in its lower bound, but are not concerned about its upper bound. In such a case, a one-sided confidence interval is appropriate, as in the next example.

Example 10.10

A fruit farmer sells a large quantity of apples to a supermarket each year. It is agreed that on average the apples should weigh at least 80 g. The farmer knows from long experience that the weights of apples picked on any day are Normally distributed with standard deviation 10 g. One day the farmer picks a sample of 40 apples at random; their total weight is 3.3 kg.

Obtain a one-sided 95% confidence interval for the mean weight of an apple on that day.

What advice would you give the farmer?

Solution

Let W be the weight of an apple, so $W \sim N(\mu, 100)$.

The variable denoting the mean weight of a sample of size n is denoted by $\overline{W}$. The distribution of $\overline{W}$ is given by $\overline{W} \sim N\left(\mu, \frac{100}{40}\right)$.

A particular value of this mean weight is denoted by $\bar{w}$. In this case, $\bar{w} = \frac{3300}{40} = 82.5$.

In 95% of cases the population mean, μ, lies between $\bar{w} - 1.645 \times \frac{\sigma}{\sqrt{n}}$ and ∞. This is the one-sided confidence interval (l, ∞).

In this case, $l = 82.5 - 1.645 \times \frac{10}{\sqrt{40}} = 79.9$.

So the 95% one-sided confidence interval for the mean weight of an apple on this day is (79.9, ∞)

The lower bound of this confidence interval is 79.9 g which is less than 80 g, so it would be safer for the farmer to wait another day or two for the apples to grow a little heavier.

Exercise 10.4

① Weights in grams of eight bags of sugar are as follows.

1023   1016   1027   1014   1023   1029   1022   1018

It is known that the weights of such bags of sugar are Normally distributed with standard deviation 5.5 grams.

(i) Find the sample mean.

(ii) Write down the standard error.

(iii) Show that a 90% confidence interval for the mean weights of bags of sugar is 1018.3 to 1024.7.

② A delivery company has a fleet of 120 lorries. The company manager wishes to switch from conventional diesel fuel to a blend of biodiesel fuel. Before switching, he decides to check whether using biodiesel will affect the fuel consumption of the lorries. He selects 8 lorries and checks their fuel consumption using conventional diesel and then again using biodiesel. The results, measured in litres per 100 km, are as follows.

Table 10.8

Lorry	A	B	C	D	E	F	G	H
Conventional diesel	36.5	34.4	28.6	25.0	27.8	31.9	33.6	38.7
Biodiesel	38.7	36.0	29.2	25.3	27.8	32.6	33.9	39.3

The manager knows from previous data that fuel consumption is Normally distributed with standard deviation 4.61 litres per 100 km.

(i) Assuming that the standard deviation for biodiesel lorries is also 4.61, show the standard deviation of the difference in fuel consumption between lorries using each type of fuel is 6.520 to 3 decimal places.

(ii) Using the value found in part (i) for the population standard deviation of the differences, calculate 90% confidence limits for the mean difference in fuel consumption.

(iii) Does the confidence interval that you have calculated suggest that there is any difference between fuel consumption using each type of fuel?

[MEI]

③ The management of a large chain of shops has introduced an incentive bonus scheme. A statistician who works for the chain wonders whether the scheme has made any difference to the level of absenteeism among its workforce. In order to investigate this, the statistician measures the percentage of working days lost before and after its introduction for each of a random sample of 60 shops. You can assume that the percentage of working days lost is Normally distributed.

For each shop, the difference d is calculated as:

absentee rate before incentive scheme − absentee rate after incentive scheme.

She then finds:

- the mean of d: $\bar{d} = 0.436$
- the standard deviation of d: $s = 1.150$

(i) Find a 99% confidence interval for the mean value of d.

(ii) Do you think that the scheme has made any difference to the rate?

[MEI]

4. A biologist studying a colony of beetles selects and weighs a random sample of 20 adult males. She knows that, because of natural variability, the weights of such beetles are Normally distributed with standard deviation 0.2 g. Their weights, in grams, are as follows.

5.2 5.4 4.9 5.0 4.8 5.7 5.2 5.2 5.4 5.1
5.6 5.0 5.2 5.1 5.3 5.2 5.1 5.3 5.2 5.2

(i) Find the mean weight of the beetles in this sample.

(ii) Find 95% confidence limits for the mean weight of such beetles.

5. An aptitude test for deep-sea divers has been designed to produce scores which are approximately Normally distributed on a scale from 0 to 100 with standard deviation 25. The scores from a random sample of people taking the test were as follows.

23 35 89 35 12 45 60 78 34 66

(i) Find the mean score of the people in this sample.

(ii) Construct a 90% confidence interval for the mean score of people taking the test.

(iii) Construct a 99% confidence interval for the mean score of people taking the test. Compare this confidence interval with the 90% confidence interval.

6. In a large city the distribution of incomes per family has a standard deviation of £5200. You may assume that the distribution of incomes is Normal.

(i) For a random sample of 400 families, what is the probability that the sample mean income per family is within £500 of the actual mean income per family?

(ii) Given that the sample mean income was, in fact, £8300, calculate a 95% confidence interval for the actual mean income per family. [MEI]

7. An archaeologist discovers a short manuscript in an ancient language which he recognises but cannot read. There are 30 words in the manuscript and they contain a total of 198 letters. There are two written versions of the language. In the *early* form of the language, the mean word length is 6.2 letters with standard deviation 2.5; in the *late* form, certain words were given prefixes, raising the mean length to 7.6 letters but leaving the standard deviation unaltered. The archaeologist hopes the manuscript will help him to date the site. You may assume that word length is Normally distributed.

(i) Construct a 95% confidence interval for the mean word length of the language.

(ii) What advice would you give the archaeologist?

8. The distribution of measurements of thicknesses of a random sample of yarns produced in a textile mill is shown in the following table. You may assume that the distribution of thicknesses is Normal.

Table 10.9

Yarn thickness in microns (mid-interval value)	Frequency
72.5	6
77.5	18
82.5	32
87.5	57
92.5	102
97.5	51
102.5	25
107.5	9

Illustrate these data on a histogram. Estimate, to 2 decimal places, the mean and standard deviation of yarn thickness.

Hence estimate the standard error of the mean to 2 decimal places, and use it to determine approximate symmetrical 95% confidence limits, giving your answer to 1 decimal place. [MEI]

9. An online bookseller believes he needs to sell books at an average of at least £2.50 each to break even. The prices of books can be assumed to be approximately Normally distributed, with a standard deviation of 94 pence. On one day the book-seller sells 125 books (this sample may be assumed to be random). The total sum they sell for is £328. Find a 95% one-sided confidence interval for the mean price of a book on that day in the form (k,∞) where k is to be determined, and interpret the result.

10. The manager of a supermarket is investigating the queuing situation at the check-outs. At busy periods, customers usually have to queue for some time to reach a check-out and then a further amount of time to be served.

    (i) At an initial stage of the investigation, the time Q, in minutes, spent queuing to reach a check-out is modelled by a random variable having mean 5.6 and standard deviation 3.8. Similarly, the time R, in minutes, spent being served is modelled by a random variable having mean 1.8 and standard deviation 1.4. It is assumed that Q and R are independent. The total time for a customer to pass through the system is $Q + R$. Find the mean and standard deviation of $Q + R$.

    100 customers, selected at random, are timed passing through the system. Their times, t minutes, are summarised by
    $$\Sigma t = 764, \Sigma t^2 = 12\,248.$$
    You may assume that the distribution of the sample mean time is approximately Normal.

    (ii) Estimate the mean and variance of the underlying population and hence comment informally on the adequacy of the model for $Q + R$ in part (i).

    (iii) Provide a 90% confidence interval for the mean of the underlying population.

    (iv) Explain why the confidence interval calculated in part (iii) is only approximate. Give two reasons why, with sample of size 100, the approximation is good. [MEI]

11. In an investigation concerning acid rain, a large number of specimens of rain water were collected at different times over a wide area. These may be considered as a large random sample. They were analysed for acidity and the readings for a standard measure of acidity are summarised by

number of specimens = 75, $\Sigma x = 282.6$, $\Sigma x^2 = 1096.42$.

You may assume that the distribution of the sample mean for the acidity is approximately Normal.

(i) Estimate the mean and variance of the underlying population.

(ii) Provide a 90% two-sided confidence interval for the population mean acidity of the rain water.

(iii) Explain carefully the interpretation of the interval in part (ii).

Now let $X_1, X_2, \ldots, X_n$ represent a random sample from a distribution with mean μ and variance σ^2, where n is large. Let $\bar{X} = \frac{1}{n}\Sigma X_i$ and let $V = \frac{1}{n-1}\Sigma(X_i - \bar{X})^2$

(iv) State the approximate distribution of $\dfrac{\bar{X} - \mu}{\frac{\sigma}{\sqrt{n}}}$

(v) Suppose that σ^2 is unknown and is estimated by v, where v is the value of V as calculated from observations on the X_i. Explain whether the approximation in part (iv) is still good when σ is replaced by $\sqrt{v}$. [MEI]

⑫ A solicitor is analysing the cost in terms of time of writing legal letters. In the course of a month, 209 letters are sent from the solicitor's practice (this may be taken as a random sample), and the total time taken to write these letters is measured to be 163 hours, 43 minutes. The time spent on writing each letter can be regarded as a random variable that is Normally distributed, and the standard deviation of the times is known to be 15 minutes. Find a 90% one-sided confidence interval for the mean time taken to write a letter in the form $(0, k)$ where k is to be found.

5 Interpreting sample data using the *t*-distribution

Students find new bat

Two students on an island-hopping holiday in the Seychelles have found their way into the textbooks. On one of the small islands they discovered a small colony of a previously unknown fruit bat.

'On one of the islands', is all that Shakila Mahdavan, 20, would say about its location. 'We don't want the general public disturbing the bats or worse still catching them for specimens', she explained.

The other member of the duo, Alison Evans, showed scores of photographs of the bats, as well as pages of measurements that they had gently made on the few they had caught before releasing them back into their natural habitat.

At a mystery location, students have pushed forward the frontiers of science

The measurements referred to in the article include the weights (in g) of eight bats which were identified as adult males.

156   132   160   142   145   138   151   144

From these figures, the team want to estimate the mean weight of an adult male bat, and 95% confidence limits for their figure.

It is clear from the newspaper report that these are the only measurements available. All that is known about the parent population is what can be inferred from these eight measurements. You know neither the mean nor the standard deviation of the parent population, but you can estimate both.

The mean is estimated to be the same as the sample mean:

$$\frac{156+132+160+142+145+138+151+144}{8}=146.$$

When it comes to estimating the standard deviation, start by finding the sample variance

$$s^2 = \frac{S_{xx}}{n-1} = \sum_i \frac{(x_i - \bar{x})^2}{(n-1)}$$

and then take the square root to find the standard deviation, s.

The use of $(n-1)$ as divisor illustrates the important concept of degrees of freedom.

The deviations of the eight numbers are as follows.

156 − 146 = 10
132 − 146 = −14
160 − 146 = 14
142 − 146 = −4
145 − 146 = −1
138 − 146 = −8
151 − 146 = −5
144 − 146 = −2

These eight deviations are not independent: they must add up to zero because of the way the mean is calculated. This means that when you have worked out the first seven deviations, it is inevitable that the final one has the value it does (in this case −2). Only seven values of the deviation are independent, and, in general, only $(n-1)$ out of the n deviations from the sample mean are independent.

Consequently, there are $n-1$ **free variables** in this situation. The number of free variables within a system is called the **degrees of freedom** and denoted by v.

So the sample variance is worked out using divisor $(n-1)$. The resulting value is very useful because it is an **unbiased estimate of the parent population variance**.

> **Note**
> The deviation is the difference (+ or −) of the value from the mean. In this example the mean is 146.

> **Note**
> You need to know the degrees of freedom in many situations where you are calculating confidence intervals or conducting hypothesis tests. You may recall meeting the idea in earlier chapters.

> **Note**
> A particular value of the sample variance is denoted by s^2, while the associated random variable by S^2.

Interpreting sample data using the *t*-distribution

In the case of the bats, the estimated population variance is

$$s^2 = \frac{(100 + 196 + 196 + 16 + 1 + 64 + 25 + 4)}{7} = 86$$

> The numbers on the top line, 100, 196 and so on, are the squares of the deviations.

and the corresponding value of the standard deviation is $s = \sqrt{86} = 9.27$.

Calculating the confidence intervals

Returning to the problem of estimating the mean weight of the bats, you now know that:

$$\bar{x} = 146, \quad s^2 = 86, \quad s = 9.27 \text{ and } \upsilon = 8 - 1 = 7.$$

Before starting on further calculations, there are some important and related points to notice.

1 This is a small sample. It would have been much better if they had managed to catch and weigh more than eight bats.
2 The true parent standard deviation, σ, is unknown.
3 It is reasonable here to assume the parent distribution is Normal. This means you can use the *t*-distribution, approximating the value of σ from your sample with the sample standard deviation s.

The *t*-distribution looks very like the Normal distribution, and, indeed, for large values of υ is little different from it. The larger the value of υ, the closer the *t*-distribution is to the Normal. Figure 10.11 shows the Normal distribution and *t*-distributions $\upsilon = 2$ and $\upsilon = 10$.

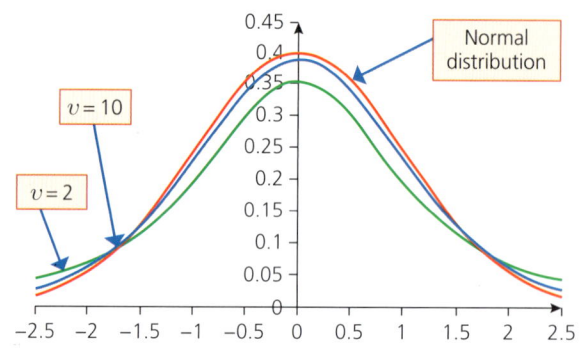

Figure 10.11

Historical note

William S. Gosset was born in Canterbury in 1876. After studying both mathematics and chemistry at Oxford, he joined the Guinness breweries in Dublin as a scientist. He found that an immense amount of statistical data was available, relating the brewing methods and the quality of the ingredients, particularly barley and hops, to the finished product. Much of this data took the form of samples, and Gosset developed techniques to handle them, including the discovery of the *t*-distribution. Gosset published his work under the pseudonym 'Student' and so the *t* test is often called Student's *t* test.

Gosset's name has frequently been misspelt as Gossett (with a double *t*), giving rise to puns about the *t*-distribution.

Confidence intervals using the *t*-distribution are constructed in much the same way as those using the Normal, with the confidence limits given by:

$$\bar{x} \pm k \frac{s}{\sqrt{n}}$$

where the values of *k* are found from a spread sheet or from tables. For instance, to find the value of *K* at the 5% significance level with 7 degrees of freedom, you can use the formula provided by your spread sheet, for example $= \text{T·INV·2T}(0.05, 7)$.

> 2T means that we are using the two-tailed *t*-distribution

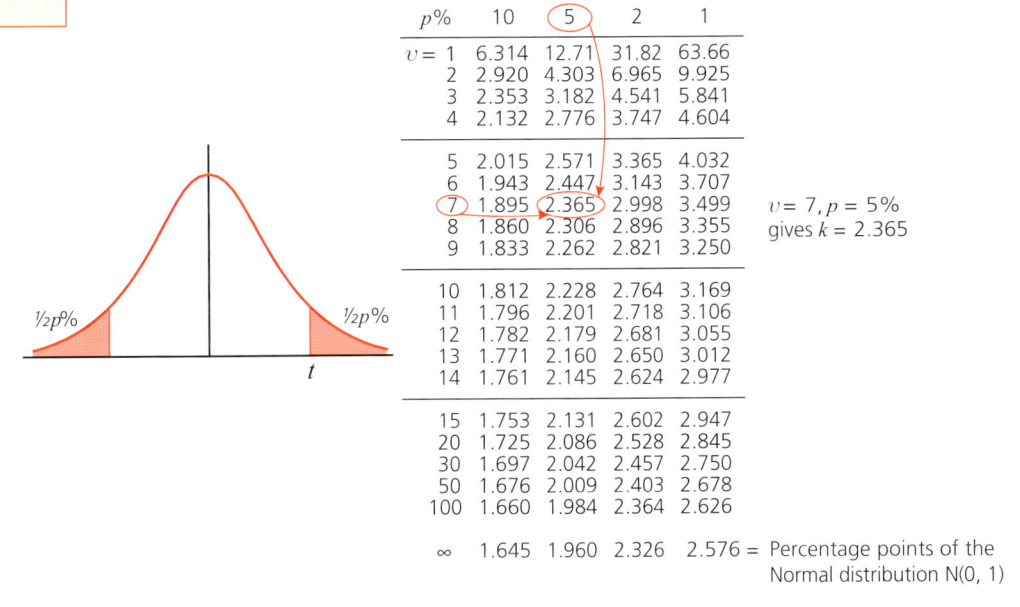

p%	10	5	2	1
v = 1	6.314	12.71	31.82	63.66
2	2.920	4.303	6.965	9.925
3	2.353	3.182	4.541	5.841
4	2.132	2.776	3.747	4.604
5	2.015	2.571	3.365	4.032
6	1.943	2.447	3.143	3.707
7	1.895	2.365	2.998	3.499
8	1.860	2.306	2.896	3.355
9	1.833	2.262	2.821	3.250
10	1.812	2.228	2.764	3.169
11	1.796	2.201	2.718	3.106
12	1.782	2.179	2.681	3.055
13	1.771	2.160	2.650	3.012
14	1.761	2.145	2.624	2.977
15	1.753	2.131	2.602	2.947
20	1.725	2.086	2.528	2.845
30	1.697	2.042	2.457	2.750
50	1.676	2.009	2.403	2.678
100	1.660	1.984	2.364	2.626
∞	1.645	1.960	2.326	2.576

$v = 7, p = 5\%$ gives $k = 2.365$

∞ row = Percentage points of the Normal distribution N(0, 1)

Figure 10.12

To construct a 95% confidence interval for the mean weight of the bats, you look under $p = 5\%$ and $v = 7$, to get $k = 2.365$; see Figure 10.13. This gives a 95% confidence interval of

$$146 - 2.365 \times \frac{9.27}{\sqrt{8}} \text{ to } 146 + 2.365 \times \frac{9.27}{\sqrt{8}}$$

138.2 to 153.8.

Another bat expert suggests that these bats are not, in fact, a new species, but from a known species. The average weight of adult males of this species is 160 grams. However, because the maximum value in the confidence interval is less than 160, in fact, only 153.8, this suggests that the expert may not be correct. Even if you use a 99% confidence interval, the upper limit is $146 + 3.499 \times \frac{9.27}{\sqrt{8}} = 157.5$. Therefore, it seems very unlikely that these bats are of the same species, based simply on their weights.

Interpreting sample data using the *t*-distribution

Example 10.11

A bus company is about to start a scheduled service between two towns some distance apart. Before deciding on an appropriate timetable, they do nine trial runs to see how long the journey takes. The times, in minutes, are:

89 92 95 94 88 90 92 93 91

(i) Use these data to set up a 95% confidence interval for the mean journey time. You should assume that the journey times are Normally distributed.

The company regards its main competition as the railway service, which takes 95 minutes.

(ii) Does your confidence interval provide evidence that the journey time by bus is different from that by train?

Solution

(i) For the given data,

$n = 9,$ $\quad v = 9 - 1 = 8,$ $\quad \bar{x} = 91.56,$ $\quad s = 2.297.$

For a 95% confidence interval, with $v = 8$, $k = 2.306$ (from tables). The confidence limits are given by

$$\bar{x} \pm k \frac{s}{\sqrt{n}} = 91.56 \pm 2.306 \times \frac{2.297}{\sqrt{9}}.$$

So the 95% confidence interval for μ is 89.79 to 93.33.

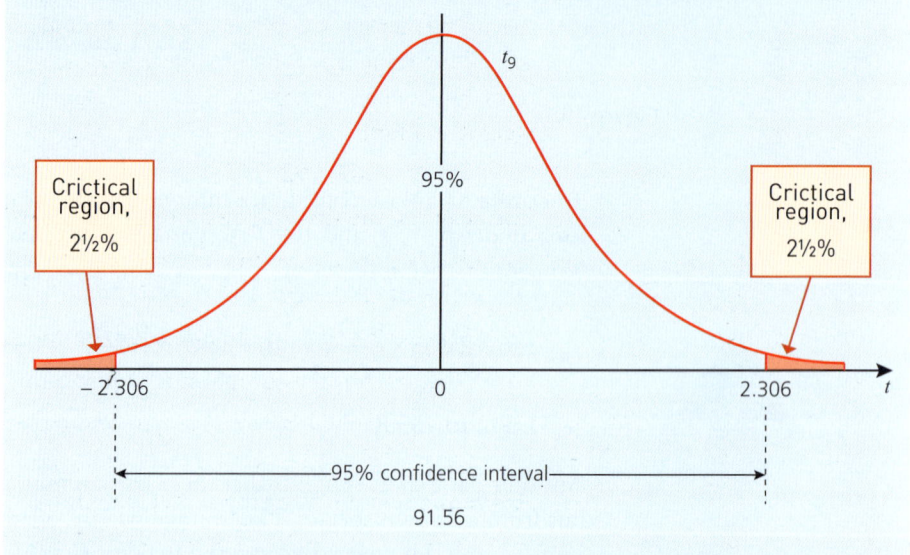

[Figure showing t_9 distribution with critical regions of 2½% at -2.306 and 2.306, 95% confidence interval centred at 91.56]

$$91.56 - 2.306 \times \frac{2.297}{\sqrt{9}} = 89.79 \qquad 91.56 + 2.306 \times \frac{2.297}{\sqrt{9}} = 93.33$$

Figure 10.13

(ii) The confidence interval does not contain 95 minutes (the time taken by the train). Therefore there is sufficient evidence to suggest that the journey time by bus is different from that by train, and that it is, in fact, less.

Exercise 10.5

① The mean of a random sample of seven observations of a Normally distributed random variable X is 132.6. Based on these seven observations, an unbiased estimate of the parent population variance s^2 is 148.84.

(i) Explain why an estimate of the standard error is given by 4.61.

(ii) Show that a 95% confidence interval for the mean μ of X is 121.3 to 143.9.

② The weights in grams of six beetles of a particular species are as follows

12.3   9.7   11.8   10.1   11.2   12.4

You may assume that the distribution of the weights is Normal.

(i) Calculate the sample mean and show that an estimate of the sample variance is 1.291.

(ii) Show that a 90% confidence interval for the mean μ of X is 10.32 to 12.18.

③ An aptitude test for entrance to university is designed to produce scores which may be modelled by the Normal distribution. In early testing, 15 students from the appropriate age group are given the test. Their scores (out of 500) are as follows.

321   445   219   378   317   407   289   345
276   463   265   165   340   298   315

(i) Use these data to estimate the mean and standard deviation to be expected for students taking this test.

(ii) Construct a 95% confidence interval for the mean.

④ A fruit farmer has a large number of almond trees, all of the same variety and of the same age. One year, he wishes to estimate the mean yield of his trees. He collects all the almonds from eight trees and records the following weights (in kg).

36   53   78   67   92   77   59   66

You may assume that the distribution of the weights is Normal.

(i) Use these data to estimate the mean and standard deviation of the yields of all the farmer's trees.

(ii) Construct a 95% confidence interval for the mean yield.

(iii) What statistical assumption is required for your procedure to be valid?

(iv) How might you select a sample of eight trees from those growing in a large field?

⑤ A forensic scientist is trying to decide whether a man accused of fraud could have written a particular letter. As part of the investigation, she looks at the lengths of sentences used in the letter. She finds them to have the following numbers of words.

17   18   25   14   18   16   14   16   16   21   25   19

(i) Use these data to estimate the mean and standard deviation of the lengths of sentences used by the letter writer.

(ii) Construct a 90% confidence interval for the mean length of the letter writer's sentences.

(iii) What assumptions have you made to obtain your answer?

(iv) A sample of sentences written by the accused has mean length 26 words. Does this mean he is in the clear?

Interpreting sample data using the *t*-distribution

⑥ A tyre company is trying out a new tread pattern which it is hoped will result in the tyres giving greater distance. In a pilot experiment, 12 tyres are tested; the mileages (×1000 miles) at which they are condemned are as follows.

65 63 71 78 65 69 59 81 72 66 63 62

(i) Construct a 95% confidence interval for the mean distance that a tyre travels before being condemned.

(ii) What assumptions, statistical and practical, are required for your answer to part (i) to be valid?

⑦ A history student wishes to estimate the life expectancy of people in Lincolnshire villages around 1750. She looks at the parish registers for five villages at that time and writes down the ages of the first ten people buried after the start of 1750. Those less than one year old were recorded as 0. The data were as follows.

Table 10.10

2	6	72	0	0	18	45	91	6	2
0	12	56	4	25	1	1	5	0	7
8	65	12	63	2	76	70	0	1	0
9	15	3	49	54	0	2	71	6	8
6	0	67	55	2	0	1	54	1	5

(i) Use these data to estimate the mean life expectancy at that time.

(ii) Explain why it is not possible to use these data to construct a confidence interval for the mean life expectancy.

(iii) Is a confidence interval a useful measure in this situation anyway?

A friend tells the student that she could construct a confidence interval for the mean life expectancy of those who survive childhood (age ⩾ 15).

(iv) Construct a 95% confidence interval for the mean life expectancy of this group, and comment on whether you think your procedure is valid.

⑧ A large fishing-boat made a catch of 500 mackerel from a shoal. The total mass of the catch was 320 kg. The standard deviation of the mass of individual mackerel is known to be 0.06 kg.

(i) Find a 99% confidence interval for the mean mass of a mackerel in the shoal.

An individual fisherman caught ten mackerel from the same shoal. These had masses (in kg) of

1.04 0.94 0.92 0.85 0.85 0.70 0.68 0.62 0.61 0.59

(ii) From these data only, use your calculator to estimate the mean and standard deviation of the masses of mackerel in the shoal.

(iii) Assuming that the masses of mackerel are Normally distributed, use your results from part (ii) to find another 99% confidence interval for the mean mass of a mackerel in the shoal.

(iv) Give two statistical reasons why you would use the first limits you calculated in preference to the second limits.

⑨ A youth club has a large number of members (referred to as the **population** in the remainder of the question). In order to find the distribution of weekly allowances of the members, a random sample of ten is questioned.

(i) Describe a method of producing the random sample.

Such a random sample produced the following weekly allowances:

£5.20, £4.40, £3.00, £2.00, £3.30,

£7.50, £5.00, £6.50, £4.80, £5.70

(ii) Estimate the population mean and variance.

(iii) Find a 95% confidence interval for the population mean. State any assumptions on which your method is based.

(iv) Explain how the width of the confidence interval may be reduced. Assuming the same variance as in part (ii) what must the sample size be to reduce the width to £2?

10 A tax inspector is carrying out an audit survey of firms located in a certain city.

From the list of all N such firms, a random sample of size n is selected for detailed study.

(i) Define what is meant by a random sample.

(ii) Explain why a sample, even though random, might nevertheless be biased, explaining also the meaning of the word 'biased' in this context.

(iii) For a random sample of size $n = 14$, the values of a particular financial indicator are found to be

8.6   9.1   9.3   8.2   8.9   9.2   9.9   9.2   9.4   8.7   9.1   10.2   9.2   9.1.

Obtain a two-sided 99% confidence interval for the mean value of this indicator in the underlying population. State any required assumption and explain carefully the interpretation of the interval. [MEI]

11 An aggregate material used for road building contains gravel and stones. The average size of the stones is supposed to be 55 mm. Each batch of this material is checked to ensure that the stones are of the correct size. For each batch, a random sample of eight stones is selected and a 95% confidence interval is found for the size of the stones.

(i) Explain why it would not be sensible to simply discard a batch if the confidence interval does not contain 55 mm.

(ii) Suggest what should be done instead if the confidence interval for a particular batch does not contain 55 mm.

For a particular batch, the eight observations are:

46.21   51.67   48.60   47.34   50.93   49.60   60.97   55.17

12 An experiment to determine the acceleration due to gravity, g m s^{-2}, involves measuring the time, T seconds, taken by a pendulum of length l m to perform complete swings. T is regarded as a random variable.

Thirty measurements are made on T, and they are summarised by

$$\Sigma t = 59.8, \quad \Sigma t^2 = 119.7.$$

You may assume that the distribution of the times is Normal.

(i) Construct a two-sided 98% confidence interval for μ, the mean value of T.

(ii) Determine the corresponding range of values of g, using the formula

$$g = \frac{4\pi^2}{\mu^2}$$

Interpreting sample data using the *t*-distribution

(iii) This result for *g* is not precise enough, so a longer series of measurements of *T* is made. Assuming that the sample mean and standard deviation remain about the same, how many measurements will be required in total to halve the width of the 98% confidence interval for μ? What will be the corresponding effect on the range of values for *g*? [MEI]

KEY POINTS

1. The Normal distribution may be used to approximate suitable discrete variables but continuity corrections are then required.
2. For two random variables *X* and *Y*, whether independent or not, and constants *a* and *b*,
   - $E(X \pm Y) = E(X) \pm E(Y)$
   - $E(aX + bY) = aE(X) + bE(Y)$

   and, if *X* and *Y* are independent,
   - $Var(X \pm Y) = Var(X) + Var(Y)$
   - $Var(aX + bY) = a^2 Var(X) + b^2 Var(Y)$.
3. For a set of *n* random variables $X_1, X_2, ..., X_n$
   - $E(X_1 \pm X_2 \pm \cdots \pm X_n) = E(X_1) \pm E(X_2) \pm \cdots \pm E(X_n)$

   and, if the variables are independent,
   - $Var(X_1 \pm X_2 \pm \cdots \pm X_n) = Var(X_1) + Var(X_2) + \cdots + Var(X_n)$.
4. If random variables are Normally distributed, then so are the sums, differences and other linear combinations of them.
5. For samples of size *n* drawn from an infinite (or large) population with mean μ and variance σ^2, or for sampling with replacement
   - $E(\bar{X}) = \mu$
   - $Var(\bar{X}) = \dfrac{\sigma^2}{n}$
   - The standard deviation of the sample mean is $\dfrac{\sigma}{\sqrt{n}}$ called the standard error of the mean or just the standard error.
6. When the population standard deviation, σ, is not known and is estimated as being the sample standard deviation, *s*, and the distribution is Normal, confidence intervals for μ are found using the *t*-distribution.
7. Two-sided confidence intervals for μ based on the *t*-distribution are given by

   $$\bar{x} - k\frac{s}{\sqrt{n}} \text{ to } \bar{x} + k\frac{s}{\sqrt{n}}.$$

8. The value of *k* for any confidence level can be found using *t*-distribution tables.
9. The value of *s* can be found using the formula

   $$s^2 = \frac{S_{xx}}{n-1} = \sum_i \frac{(x_i - \bar{x})^2}{(n-1)}.$$

EXTENSION

10. For samples of size *n* drawn from a distribution with mean μ and variance σ^2, the distribution of the sample mean is approximately $N\left(\mu, \dfrac{\sigma^2}{n}\right)$ for sufficiently large *n*.
    This is the central limit theorem.

Chapter 10: Confidence intervals using the Normal and *t*-distributions

LEARNING OUTCOMES

When you have completed this chapter you should:

- be able to use linear combinations of independent Normal random variables in solving problems
- be able to find the mean of any linear combination of random variables and the variance of any linear combination of independent random variables
- understand that the sample mean is a random variable with a probability distribution
- be able to calculate and interpret the standard error of the mean
- know that if the underlying distribution is Normal, then the sample mean is Normally distributed
- be able to construct and interpret a confidence interval for a single population mean using the Normal or *t*-distributions and know when it is appropriate to do so
- interpret confidence intervals given by software
- use a confidence interval for a population parameter to make a decision about a hypothesised value of that parameter.

EXTENSION

- understand how and when the central limit theorem may be applied to the distribution of sample means and use this result in probability calculations, using a continuity correction where appropriate
- be able to apply the central limit theorem to the sum of identically distributed independent random variables.

11 Hypothesis tests and their power

Every experiment may be said to exist only to give the facts a chance of disproving the null hypothesis.

R. A. Fisher

Herring gulls getting heavier?

In the last few years, the numbers of herring gulls living on roofs in towns has been increasing. It is known that in the past, before the advent of scavenging, the mean weight of adult female herring gulls was 1015 grams, with standard deviation 110 grams. Many of the gulls scavenge food discarded by patrons of takeaway restaurants. A reporter for a local paper says that as a result of the 'easy pickings' from these restaurants, the herring gulls in the town where she lives are heavier now than they were in the past, before they discovered free takeaway food. She enlists the help of an ornithologist to capture and weigh ten adult female herring gulls in the town, before releasing them so that they can continue to take advantage of the free food.

The weights of the ten birds measured in grams are

1050   1145   1205   985   1015   1100   890   940   1290   1080

You have already met several hypothesis tests: for the binomial distribution, for the Poisson parameter and for the chi squared test. This chapter starts with tests for the mean of a Normal distribution and then goes on to the power of a hypothesis test.

1 Hypotheses for a test for a mean

The null hypothesis is always:

- $H_0: \mu = a$, where a is the specified 'original' value of the mean. In other words, a is the mean if nothing has changed.

The alternative hypothesis has one of three forms.

- $H_1: \mu \neq a$ ← This is two-tailed
- $H_1: \mu < a$
- $H_1: \mu > a$ ← These are one-tailed

Hypothesis testing on a sample mean using the Normal distribution

You can carry out a hypothesis test based on the Normal distribution to investigate whether it is likely that the scavenging herring gulls are heavier than herring gulls used to be. Two requirements for this test to be valid are that:

- the population from which the sample is drawn has normal distribution (as the sample size is too small for the central limit theorem to apply).
- the sample is representative of the population; this is usually ensured by having a random sample.

To use the Normal distribution, you also have to know the standard deviation of the parent population. You do not know this for the scavenging herring gulls, but you do know that in the past it was 110 g. You have to assume that it is still 110 g.

To carry out the test, you to decide the significance level; in this case 5% is chosen. You also need to state the null and alternative hypotheses; the alternative hypothesis will tell you whether it is a one- or two-tailed test. In this case,

Null hypothesis. $H_0: \mu = 1015$

Alternative hypothesis: $H_1: \mu > 1015$

Significance level: 5%

Test: one-tailed.

There are three slightly different methods used to carry out a hypothesis test based on the Normal distribution. They all use the fact that the distribution of sample means is given by

$$\overline{X} \sim N\left(\mu, \frac{\sigma^2}{n}\right).$$

Start by calculating the sample mean.

> Since the weight of a herring gull is a naturally occurring variable, it is reasonable to assume its distribution is Normal

> You have no information about how the sample was collected but it is reasonable to assume that it was random

Note

The significance level is the probability of rejecting the null hypothesis when it is actually true. This is called a **Type I error**.

Accepting the null hypothesis when it is false is called a **Type II error**.

Note

You are investigating whether the weights of herring gulls have increased. The test is therefore one-tailed because the alternative hypothesis is $\mu > 1015$ and so is one sided.

If you had instead been investigating whether the weights of herring gulls had changed, then it would have been a two-tailed test and the alternative hypothesis would have been $\mu \neq 1015$.

Hypotheses for a test for a mean

$$\left(\frac{1050+1145+1205+985+1015+1100+890+940+1290+1080}{10}\right)$$
$$=\frac{10700}{10}=1070$$

> **Note**
> For a one-tailed test rather than the symbol ± in the critical values, you either have + or − according to whether you are interested in the upper or lower tail.

Method 1: Using critical regions

Since the distribution of sample means is $N\left(\mu, \frac{\sigma^2}{n}\right)$, critical values for a test on the sample mean are given by

$$\mu \pm k \times \frac{\sigma}{\sqrt{n}}.$$

In this case, if H_0 is true: $\mu = 1015$; $\sigma = 110$; $n = 10$.
The test is one-tailed, for $\mu > 1015$, so only the right-hand tail applies.
k is the critical value for the standardised value, z.

> Make sure that you know how to get this value from your calculator
>
> For some calculators, you may need to calculate 1 − 0.05 = 0.95

Using the inverse Normal function on a calculator, the value of k is 1.645.

For a one-tailed test at the 5% significance level, the critical value is
$1015 + 1.645 \times \frac{110}{\sqrt{10}} = 1072.2$, as shown in the diagram below.

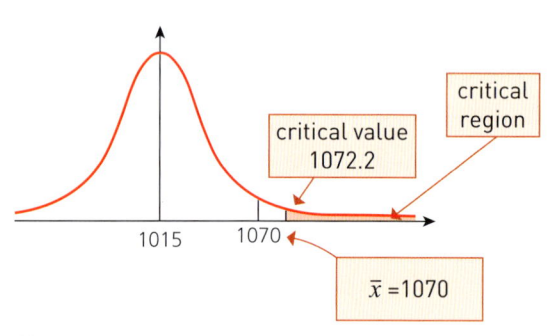

[Diagram: Normal distribution curve with mean 1015, critical value 1072.2 at 1070, critical region shaded to the right, $\bar{x} = 1070$]

Figure 11.1

However, the sample mean $\bar{x} = 1070$, and $1070 < 1072.2$.

Therefore the sample mean lies outside the critical region and so there is insufficient evidence to reject the null hypothesis.

> This does not mean that the null hypothesis is definitely true but that there is not enough evidence to show that it is false.

There is insufficient evidence to suggest that the mean weight of scavenging gulls is greater than before the advent of scavenging.

Method 2: Using probabilities

The distribution of sample means, $\bar{x}$, is $N\left(\mu, \frac{\sigma^2}{n}\right)$.

According to the null hypothesis, $\mu = 1015$ and it is known that $\sigma = 110$ and $n = 10$.

So this distribution is $N\left(1015, \frac{110^2}{10}\right)$, see the diagram on the next page.

Note

In this example, the value of *n* is 10, but if our assumption that the parent population is Normal is justified, we could carry out this test with any positive value of *n*, even *n* = 1.

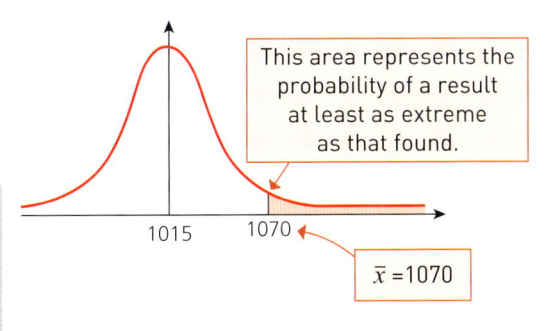

Figure 11.2

The probability of the mean, $\bar{X}$, of a randomly chosen sample being greater than the value found, i.e. 1070, is given by

$$P(\bar{X} \geq 1070) = 1 - \phi\left(\frac{1070 - 1015}{\frac{110}{\sqrt{10}}}\right)$$

$$= 1 - \phi(1.581)$$
$$= 1 - 0.9431$$
$$= 0.0569.$$

0.05 is the significance level

Since 0.0569 > 0.05, there is insufficient evidence to reject the null hypothesis.

There is insufficient evidence to suggest that the mean weight of scavenging gulls is greater than before the advent of scavenging.

Method 3: Using the test statistics (or critical ratios)

Note

The calculated probability is often called the *p*-value.

If the *p*-value is smaller than the significance level, then you reject H_0 and accept H_1. Otherwise, as in this case, you do not reject H_0.

The *test statistic* (or *critical ratio*) is given by $z = \left(\frac{\bar{x} - \mu}{\frac{\sigma}{\sqrt{n}}}\right)$

In this case, $z = \left(\frac{1070 - 1015}{\frac{110}{\sqrt{10}}}\right) = 1.581.$

This is the value of *k* in Method 1

This is now compared with the critical value for *z*, in this case, *z* = 1.645.

Since 1.581 < 1.645, H_0 is not rejected. There is insufficient evidence to reject the null hypothesis.

There is insufficient evidence to suggest that the mean weight of scavenging gulls is greater than before the advent of scavenging.

🖥 USING ICT

Statistical software

You can use statistical software to do all of the calculations for this test. In order for the software to process the test, you need to input the following information:

- the population mean if H_0 is true
- the form of the alternative hypothesis (<, > or ≠)
- the population standard deviation
- the sample mean
- the sample size.

Hypotheses for a test for a mean

! You need to be careful when interpreting the *p*-value. In many tests, like this one, rejecting the null hypothesis, H$_0$, means that you have found an interesting result, expressed as the alternative hypothesis, H$_1$; it is sometimes summarised as 'The test is significant'. So a *p*-value that is less than the significance level might be seen as desirable.

By contrast, with some other tests (like goodness of fit), the 'interesting' result is given by the null hypothesis. In such tests, a *p*-value that is higher than the significance value can be seen as 'desirable'.

Notes

1. A hypothesis test should be formulated before the data are collected and not after. In this case, the reporter thought that the gulls might be larger and so data was collected to test this hypothesis. If sample data had led the reporter to form a hypothesis, then a new set of data would have been required in order to carry out a suitable test.
2. If the data were not collected properly, any test carried out on them may be worthless. So if the herring gulls did not form a random sample from the population, then the test would be invalid.

Figure 11.3 shows the output for the test on the previous page.

	A	B	C
1	Z Test of a mean		
2			
3	Null hypothesis	1015	
4	Alternative hypothesis	>	
5	Mean	1070	
6	σ	110	
7	n	10	
8			
9	Mean	1070	
10	σ	110	
11	SE	34.7851	
12	n	10	
13	z	1.5811	
14	p	0.0569	
15			

INPUTS → rows 3–7
Standard error → row 11
Test statistic → row 13
p-value → row 14
OUTPUTS → rows 9–14

Figure 11.3

You can see that the output from the software gives both the *p*-value of 0.0569 and the test statistic of 1.5811.

Hypothesis testing on a sample mean using the *t*-distribution

In Chapter 10, you met the *t*-distribution. This is the distribution of a sample mean when the parent population is Normally distributed but the standard deviation of the parent population is unknown and has to be estimated using the sample standard deviation, *s*. In addition to finding a confidence interval, you can also carry out a hypothesis test based on the *t*-distribution.

Example 11.1

Tests are being carried out on a new drug designed to relieve the symptoms of the common cold. One of the tests is to investigate whether the drug has any effect on the number of hours that people sleep.

The drug is given in tablet form one evening to a random sample of 16 people who have colds. The number of hours they sleep may be assumed to be Normally distributed and is recorded as follows.

| 8.1 | 6.7 | 3.3 | 7.2 | 8.1 | 9.2 | 6.0 | 7.4 |
| 6.4 | 6.9 | 7.0 | 7.8 | 6.7 | 7.2 | 7.6 | 7.9 |

There is also a large control group of people who have colds but are not given the drug. The mean number of hours they sleep is 6.6.

(i) Use these data to set up a 95% confidence interval for the mean length of time somebody with a cold sleeps after taking the tablet.

(ii) Carry out a test, at the 1% significance level, of the hypothesis that the new drug has an effect on the number of hours a person sleeps.

ACTIVITY 11.1
Use **Methods 1 and 2** to carry out the test. You should of course come to the same conclusion.

Solution

(i) For the given data, $n = 16$, $v = 16 - 1 = 15$, $\bar{x} = 7.094$, $s = 1.276$.

For a 95% confidence interval, with $v = 15$, $k = 2.131$ (from tables).

The confidence limits are given by $\bar{x} \pm k \dfrac{s}{\sqrt{n}} = 7.094 \pm 2.131 \times \dfrac{1.276}{\sqrt{16}}$,

So the 95% confidence interval for μ is 6.41 to 7.77.

Note
The critical value in this case is negative since you are carrying out a lower tail test. You can either give the comparison as shown above $-0.838 > -1.282$ or use the absolute values (moduli) in which case the comparison would be $|-0.838| < |-1.282|$. You should **not** compare -0.838 with $+1.282$.

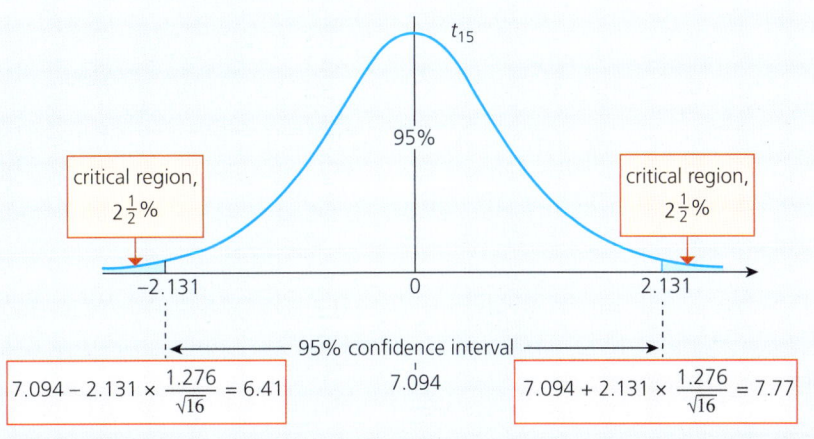

t_{15}

95%

critical region, $2\tfrac{1}{2}\%$ — -2.131 0 2.131 — critical region, $2\tfrac{1}{2}\%$

$7.094 - 2.131 \times \dfrac{1.276}{\sqrt{16}} = 6.41$ ← 95% confidence interval → $7.094 + 2.131 \times \dfrac{1.276}{\sqrt{16}} = 7.77$

7.094

Figure 11.4

(ii) H_0: there is no change in the mean number of hours sleep. $\mu = 6.6$
H_1: there is a change in the mean number of hours sleep. $\mu \neq 6.6$
Two-tailed test at the 1% significance level.

For this sample, $n = 16$, $v = 16 - 1 = 15$, $\bar{x} = 7.094$, $s = 1.276$.

The critical value for t, for $v = 15$, at the 1% significance level, is found from tables to be 2.947.

The test statistic $t = \left(\dfrac{\bar{x} - \mu}{\frac{s}{\sqrt{n}}}\right) = \left(\dfrac{7.094 - 6.6}{\frac{1.276}{\sqrt{16}}}\right) = 1.55$.

This is to be compared with 2.947, the critical value, for the 1% significance level.

Since $1.55 < 2.947$, there is no reason at the 1% significance level to reject the null hypothesis.

There is insufficient evidence to suggest that the mean number of hours sleep is different when people take the drug.

USING ICT

Using a spreadsheet

You can use a spreadsheet (see Figure 11.5) to do all of the calculations for this test using the following steps:

1. Enter the data (in this case into cells B2 to B17)
2. Use the spreadsheet functions provided by your spreadsheet, for example = AVERAGE and = STDEV to find the mean and sample standard deviation.
3. Calculate the t value using the formula = (B18-6.6)/(B19/SQRT(16))

Hypotheses for a test for a mean

4 Use the spreadsheet function provided by your spreadsheet, for example
   = T.INV.2T(0.01,15) to calculate the critical value.
5 You can also find the *p*-value using the spreadsheet function provided by your
   spreadsheet, for example = T.DIST.2T(1.5482,15)

	A	B
1		Data
2		8.1
3		6.7
4		3.3
5		7.2
6		8.1
7		9.2
8		6.0
9		7.4
10		6.4
11		6.9
12		7.0
13		7.8
14		6.7
15		7.2
16		7.6
17		7.9
18	Mean	7.0938
19	Sample sd	1.2757
20	n	16
21	*t* value	1.5482
22	Critical t	2.9467
23	*p*- value	0.1424

In this case, the values of $\bar{x}$ and s are given in cells B18 and B19.

Figure 11.5

Exercise 11.1

① Bags of flour are supposed to weigh at least 1.5 kg. Sampling is carried out at the factory where the bags are filled to check that the bags are not underweight. On a particular day, the sample mean of a random sample of 40 bags is 1.4972 kg with sample standard deviation 0.009 kg. A hypothesis test is carried out at the 1% significance level to check whether the bags are satisfactory.

   (i)   Explain why you do not need to know the distribution of the parent population in order to carry out the test.
   (ii) Write down suitable null and alternative hypotheses.
   (iii) Find the standard error of the mean.
   (iv) Calculate the test statistic.
   (v)   Write down the critical value.
   (vi) Explain whether the null hypothesis should be rejected.

② The spreadsheet on the following page shows the output for a *t* test to investigate the hypotheses

   $H_0: \mu = 180$ and $H_1: \mu \neq 180$.

   (i) State whether the test is one-tailed or two-tailed and use the 'Critical t' in cell B13 to find the significance level of the test.
   (ii) State the result of the test relating it to the content of cells B12 and B13.

(iii) State the result of the test, this time relating it to the content of cell B14.

	A	B
1		Data
2		172.24
3		198.79
4		167.81
5		192.23
6		183.81
7		178.49
8		183.27
9	Mean	182.37
10	Sample sd	10.80
11	n	7
12	t value	0.8796
13	Critical t	2.3646
14	p-value	0.4082

Figure 11.6

③ A farmer grows onions. The weight in kilograms of the variety of onions which he usually grows is Normally distributed with mean 0.155 and variance 0.005. He is trying out a new variety, which he hopes will yield a higher mean weight. In order to test this, he takes a random sample of 25 onions of the new variety and finds that their total weight is 4.77 kg. You should assume that the weight in kilograms of the new variety is Normally distributed with variance 0.005.

(i) Write down suitable null and alternative hypotheses for the test in terms of μ. State the meaning of μ in this case.

(ii) Carry out the test at the 1% level. [MEI]

④ It is known that the diameter of marigold flowers is Normally distributed with mean 47 mm and standard deviation 8.5 mm. A certain fertiliser is expected to cause flowers to have a larger mean diameter, but without affecting the standard deviation. A large number of marigolds are grown using this fertiliser. The diameters of a random sample of ten of the flowers are measured and the mean diameter is found to be 49.2 mm. Carry out a hypothesis test at the 5% significance level to check whether flowers grown with this fertiliser appear to be larger on average. [MEI]

⑤ Freeze drying is often used in the production of coffee. For best results, the drying rate (measured in suitable units) should be 72.0. It is thought that the drying rate in a particular batch may be higher than this. In order to test this, a sample of 12 observations was selected and the drying rates were as follows.

75 73 81 88 75 79 69 91 82 76 73 72

(i) Carry out a test at the 0.5% significance level to determine whether the drying rates in this batch are greater than the ideal. State clearly your null and alternative hypotheses and your conclusion.

(ii) What assumptions are required for your answer to part (i) to be valid?

⑥ A fisherman claims that pollack are not as big as they used to be. 'They used to average three quarters of a kilogram each', he says. When challenged to prove his point, he catches 20 pollack from the same shoal. Their masses (in kg) are as follows.

0.65   0.68   0.77   0.71   0.67   0.75   0.69   0.72   0.73   0.69

0.70   0.70   0.72   0.76   0.73   0.78   0.75   0.69   0.70   0.71

Hypotheses for a test for a mean

(i) State the null and alternative hypotheses for a test to investigate whether the fisherman's claim is true.

(ii) Carry out the test at the 5% significance level and state the conclusion.

(iii) State any assumptions underlying your procedure and comment on their validity.

7 At a bottling plant, wine bottles are filled automatically by a machine. The bottles are meant to hold 75 cl. Under-filling leads to contravention of regulations and complaints from customers. Over-filling prevents the bottles being sealed securely.

The contents of ten bottles are carefully measured and found to be as follows, in centilitres.

75.6   76.2   74.3   74.8   75.3   76.3   75.9   74.2   75.6   76.7

(i) State appropriate null and alternative hypotheses for the usual t test for examining whether the bottles are being filled correctly.

(ii) State the conditions necessary for correct application of this test.

(iii) Carry out the test, using a 5% significance level. [MEI]

8 Sugar is automatically packed by a machine into bags of nominal weight 1000 g. Due to random fluctuations and the set up of the machine, the weights of bags are, in fact, Normally distributed with mean 1020 g and standard deviation 25 g. Two bags are selected at random.

(i) Find the probability that the total weight of the two bags is less than 2000 g.

(ii) Find the probability that the weights of the two bags differ by less than 20 g.

Another machine is also in use for packing sugar into bags of nominal weight 1000 g. It is assumed that the distribution of the weights for this machine is also Normal. A random sample of nine bags packed by this machine is found to have the following weights (in grams).

1012   996   984   1005   1008   994   1003   1017   1002

(iii) Test at the 5% level of significance whether it may be assumed that the mean weight for this machine is 1000 g. [MEI]

9 A notional allowance of 9 minutes has been given for the completion of a routine task on a production line. The operatives have complained that it appears usually to be taking slightly longer.

An inspector took a sample of 12 measurements of the time required to undertake this task. The results (in minutes) were as follows.

9.4   8.8   9.3   9.1   9.4   8.9   9.3   9.2   9.6   9.3   9.3   9.1

Stating carefully your null and alternative hypotheses and the assumptions underlying your analysis, test at the 1% level of significance whether the task is indeed taking on average longer than 9 minutes. [MEI]

⑩ Archaeologists have discovered that all skulls found in excavated sites in a certain country belong either to racial Group A or to racial Group B. The mean lengths of skulls from Group A and Group B are 190 mm and 196 mm, respectively. The standard deviation for each group is 8 mm, and skull lengths are distributed Normally and independently.

A new excavation produced 12 skulls of mean length x and there is reason to believe that all these skulls belong to Group A. It is required to test this belief statistically with the null hypothesis (H_0) that all the skulls belong to Group A and the alternative hypothesis (H_1) that all the skulls belong to Group B.

(i) State the distribution of the mean length of 12 skulls when H_0 is true.

(ii) Explain why a test of H_0 versus H_1 should take the form: 'Reject H_0 if $\bar{x} > c$', where c is some critical value.

(iii) Calculate this critical value c to the nearest 0.1 mm when the probability of rejecting H_0 when it is, in fact, true is chosen to be 0.05.

(iv) Perform the test, given that the lengths (in mm) of the 12 skulls are as follows.

204.1 201.1 187.4 196.4 202.5 185.0
192.6 181.6 194.5 183.2 200.3 202.9

[MEI]

2 The power of a test

You have already met the idea of errors in hypothesis testing in Chapters 3 and 6. The ideas are revisited and developed further here.

Example 11.2

A gold coin is used for the toss at a country's football matches but it is suspected of being biased. It is suggested that it shows heads more often than it should.

A test is planned in which the coin is to be tossed 19 times and the results recorded. It is decided to use a 5% significance level; so, if the coin shows heads 14 or more times, it will be declared biased.

(i) If the coin is unbiased, what is the probability of it being declared biased?

(ii) If the coin is biased, with a probability of 0.8 of coming up heads on any throw, what is the probability of it being declared unbiased?

Solution

Both situations can be modelled by the binomial distribution, B(19, p).

(i) If the coin is unbiased, $p = 0.5$. This is the null hypothesis for the test.

The probabilities of outcomes near the critical value of 14 are given to 2 significant figures in Table 11.1.

Table 11.1

Number of heads	⩾13	⩾14	⩾15
Probability	0.084	0.032	0.010

The power of a test

The table shows that the probability of getting 14 or more heads is 0.032.

So the probability of rejecting the true null hypothesis is 0.032.

(ii) Given that $p = 0.8$, the equivalent table is Table 11.2, below.

Table 11.2

Number of heads	$\geqslant 13$	$\geqslant 14$	$\geqslant 15$
Probability	0.93	0.84	0.67

So the probability of rejecting the null hypothesis is 0.84

and

the probability of accepting the false null hypothesis is $1 - 0.84 = 0.16$

> When this is written as a conditional probability statement it is
> $P(X \leqslant 13 \mid p = 0.8) = 0.16$

The two parts of this example illustrate the two types of error that can occur in a hypothesis test.

- In part (i) a true null hypothesis is rejected and this is a Type I error.
- In part (ii) a false null hypothesis is accepted and this is a Type II error.

The circumstances under which these errors occur are shown below.

Table 11.3

		Decision Accept H_0	Decision Reject H_0
Reality	The null hypothesis, H_0, is true	Correct decision	H_0 wrongly rejected Type I error
Reality	The null hypothesis, H_0, is false	H_0 wrongly accepted Type II error	Correct decision

Type I errors

The probability of a Type I error is represented by the size of the critical region. In tests involving continuous random variables this is the same as the significance level of the test. However, if the distribution is discrete, the critical region is often less than the significance level. The example above used the binomial distribution and the least number of heads in the critical region was 14, corresponding to a probability of 0.032 or 3.2%; this is the nearest probability to the significance level of 5% but below it.

So the probability of a Type I error is either equal to the significance level of the test or slightly less than it.

Type II errors

In the previous example you could work out the probability of a Type II error because the value of p was given; it was 0.8. Without similar information you can't work out the probability of a Type II error and this is often the case. Indeed finding out about the population parameter, in this case p, is the object of the test so it is often not possible to calculate the probability of a Type II error. However, that does not mean such errors do not occur.

The power of a test

The power of a test is a measure of its ability to obtain the correct result by failing to accept a false null hypothesis. It is given by

Power = 1 − Probability of a Type II error.

What does the power tell you? If the alternative hypothesis, H_1, is true, then there are consequences for your data which you hope to pick up. The power of the test tells you how likely it is that you will do so, and so how powerful the test is. With this in mind you can see that as the sample size increases, the test becomes more powerful. When you ask questions like 'What is the smallest sample size that I need to have a good chance of detecting an effect in the population?', this is really a question about the power of your test.

Using the notation of conditional probability

Using the conditional probability symbol | for 'given that' allows you to write the probabilities more formally.

$$P(\text{Type I error}) = P(\text{Rejecting } H_0 \mid H_0 \text{ is true})$$

$$P \text{ Type II error} = P(\text{Accepting } H_0 \mid H_0 \text{ is false})$$

The power of a test is clearly linked to these, although it is not the probability of an error but of a success. It can be written as

$$\text{Power of a test} = P(\text{Rejecting } H_0 \mid H_0 \text{ is false})$$

and so it follows that

$$\text{Power of a test}$$
$$= 1 - P(\text{Accepting } H_0 \mid H_0 \text{ is false}) = 1 - P(\text{Type II error})$$

So as the power of a test increases, the probability of a Type II error decreases, and vice versa.

Example 11.3

It is known that 60% of the moths of a certain species are red; the rest are yellow.

A biologist finds a new colony of these moths and observes that more of them seem to be red than she would expect. She designs an experiment in which she will catch 10 moths at random, observe their colour and then release them. She will then carry out a hypothesis test using a 5% significance level.

(i) State the null and alternative hypotheses for this test.

(ii) Find the rejection region.

(iii) Find the probability of a Type I error.

(iv) If in fact the proportion of red moths is 80%, find the probability that the test will result in a Type II error. Hence write down the power of the test

The power of a test

Solution

(i) Let p be the probability that a randomly selected moth is red.

Null hypothesis: $H_0: p = 0.6$ The proportion of red moths in this colony is 60%.

Alternative hypothesis: $H_1: p > 0.6$ The proportion of red moths is greater than 60%.

(ii) Assuming H_0 is true, you can calculate the following probabilities for the 10 moths in the sample.

All 10 moths are red: $(0.6)^{10} = 0.0060...$

9 are red and 1 yellow: $^{10}C_1 \times (0.6)^9 \times 0.4 = 0.0403...$

8 are red and 2 yellow: $^{10}C_2 \times (0.6)^8 \times (0.4)^2 = 0.1209...$

There is no need to go any further.

The probability that there are nine or ten red moths is

$$0.0403... + 0.0060... = 0.0463...$$

and this is less than the 5% significance level.

The probability that there are eight, nine or ten red moths is

$$0.1209... + 0.0403... + 0.0060... = 0.167...$$

and this is greater than 5%.

So the rejection region for this test is 9 or 10 red moths.

(iii) A Type I error occurs when a true null hypothesis is rejected.

In this case if H_0 is true, and so $p = 0.6$, the probability of it being rejected because a particular sample has 9 or 10 red moths has already been worked out to be 0.0463... in part (ii). When rounded to 3 significant figures, this gives 0.0464.

So the probability of a Type I error is 0.0464 (to 3 s.f.).

(iv) If the proportion of red moths is 80%, the correct result from the test would be for the null hypothesis to be rejected in favour of the alternative hypothesis. The probability of this happening is

$$^{10}C_1 \times (0.8)^9 \times 0.2 + (0.8)^{10} = 0.376 \text{ (to 3 s.f.)}$$

A Type II error occurs when this result does not occur.

So in this situation the probability of a Type II error is $1 - 0.376 = 0.624$. The power of the test $= 1 - 0.624 = 0.376$

Example 11.4

A die is known to be biased in favour of a 6. One gamer believes that $p = P(6) = 0.2$ while another believes that $p = 0.4$. The die is rolled 10 times and the number of times it comes up 6 is recorded.

A hypothesis test is then carried out at the 5% significance level with the null hypothesis that $p = 0.2$.

(i) Find the critical region.

(ii) Find the probability of a Type I error.

(iii) Given that the correct value of p is 0.4, find the probability of a Type II error and the power of the test.

(iv) How could the test be improved?

Solution

Use X to denote the number of sixes thrown.

Assuming H_0 to be true, $X \sim B(10, 0.2)$.

(i) $P(X \leqslant 3) = 0.879... \Rightarrow P(X \geqslant 4) = 0.121...$ so 4 is not in the critical region

$P(X \leqslant 4) = 0.967... \Rightarrow P(X \geqslant 5) = 0.033...$ so 5 is not in the critical region

> The significance level is 5% and 0.121 > 5% but 0.033 < 5%.

So the critical region is $X \geqslant 5$.

(ii) The probability of a Type I error is 0.033.

> This is the probability that the value of X lies in the critical region.

(iii) Given that $p = 0.4$, the null hypothesis is false.

So a Type II error occurs if H_0 is accepted.

This happens if $X \leqslant 4$.

For $p = 0.4$, $P(X \leqslant 4) = 0.633$

So the probability of a Type II error is 0.633.

The power of the test is $1 - 0.633 = 0.367$

(iv) Rolling the die more times would make the test more powerful.

The hypothesis test in the next example is based on the Poisson distribution.

Example 11.5

A popular website believes they receive 25 visitors a minute between the hours of 9 am and 5 pm each day. To test this hypothesis they count the number of visitors during a randomly selected minute.

There are 34 visitors.

(i) Carry out the test at the 5% significance level.

(ii) Draw a diagram to illustrate the probability distribution and the critical region if the mean is 25.

The power of a test

> Since the visits are likely to occur singly, independently, and at a uniform rate, it is reasonable to assume that the Poisson distribution is a good model.

Solution

The situation is modelled by the Poisson distribution Po(25).

(i) H_0: The mean number per minute is 25, $\lambda = 25$

H_1: The mean number per minute is not 25, $\lambda \neq 25$

Two-tailed test

Significance level: 5%

Since it is a two-tailed test the critical region should be 2.5% or slightly less for each tail.

The observed value is 34.

Using a calculator gives the probability of a value of 34 or greater to be 0.04978...

Since $0.04978 > 0.025$, the observed value is not in the critical region.

There is not sufficient evidence to reject the null hypothesis.

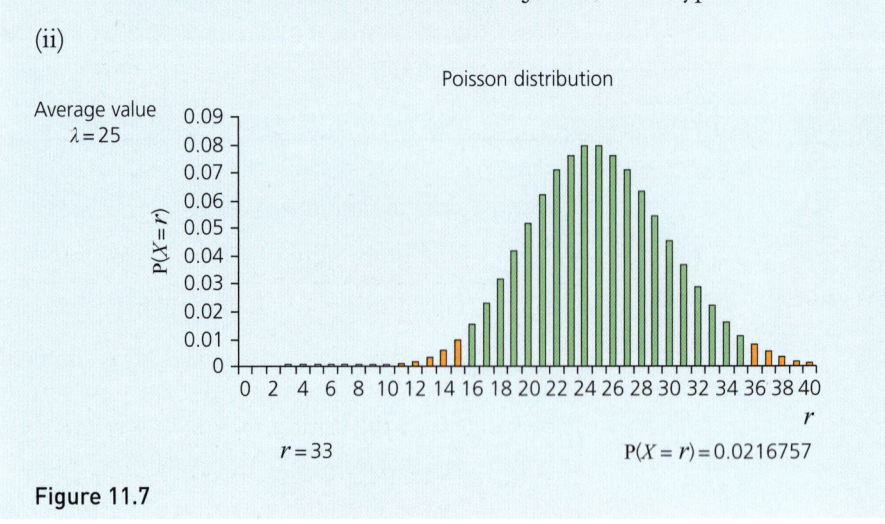

(ii)

[Poisson distribution bar chart with Average value $\lambda = 25$, showing $P(X = r)$ on vertical axis from 0 to 0.09, and r on horizontal axis from 0 to 40. $r = 33$, $P(X = r) = 0.0216757$]

Figure 11.7

It is possible to make Type I and Type II errors in exactly the same way as for a test based on the binomial distribution.

> The ... tells you that this number is truncated, and that you are expected to be working with the full number on your calculator.

The critical regions are $X \leq 15$ with probability 0.02229...

and $X \geq 36$ with probability 0.02245...

So the probability of a Type I error is $0.02229... + 0.02245... = 0.04475...$

or 4.48% (to 3 s.f.).

> Notice that this is slightly less than the significance level of 5%.

Suppose that the true value of the mean is 30 so the null hypothesis is false.

A Type II error occurs if H_0 is accepted. This occurs if X is not in the critical region and that means that $16 \leq X \leq 35$.

Using a calculator gives

$P(X \leq 15) = 0.00194...$

$P(X \leq 35) = 0.84261...$

so $P(16 \leq X \leq 35) = 0.84261... - 0.00194... = 0.840\,67...$

So the probability of a Type II error is 0.841 or 84.1% (to 3 s.f.)
and
the power of the test is $1 - 0.841 = 0.159$

Errors for the Normal distribution

The examples of Type I and Type II errors that you have met so far have been based on hypothesis tests using the binomial and Poisson distributions and so have involved discrete random variables. The same principles apply for tests involving continuous variables, like those based on the Normal distribution.

Suppose you are working with the Normal distribution $N(\mu, \sigma^2)$, where the population variance, σ, is known but the population mean, μ, is not known. Your test statistic is denoted by X.

You are conducting a one-tailed test with

$\qquad$ Null hypothesis, H_0 $\qquad$ $\mu = k$

$\qquad$ Alternative hypothesis, H_1 $\qquad$ $\mu > k$.

The distribution of X is shown in red in Figure 11.8 with the critical region for the significance level of the test shaded yellow. The critical value is marked as c in the diagram.

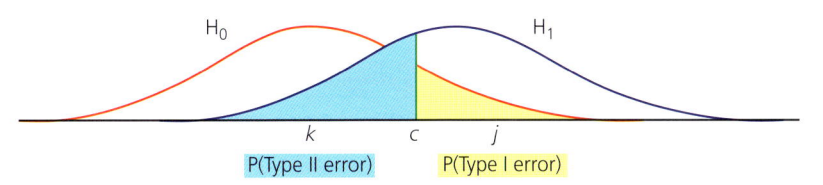

Figure 11.8

If $X \geq c$, it is in the critical region. In that case H_0 is rejected.

If H_0 is in fact true, a Type I error has occurred.

So the probability of a Type I error is given by the area of the yellow region.

If on the other hand, the null hypothesis is false and the alternative hypothesis is true, the value of the population mean has a value j where $j > k$. The distribution is that shown in purple in Figure 11.8.

In this case a Type II error occurs if $X < c$, so that the false null hypothesis is accepted. This is represented by the blue region in Figure 11.8.

Figure 11.8 allows you to see how changing the significance level of the test and the sample size affects the accuracy of the test.

> So if you decrease the significance level, say from 5% to 1%, the probability of a Type I error is decreased and that of a Type II error is increased.

- As you vary the significance level of the test, the value of c will change. If the significance level is increased, say from 5% to 10%, the value of c is decreased. So the area of the yellow region is increased and the area of the blue region is decreased. So the probability of a Type I error is increased and the probability of a Type II error is decreased. And vice versa.
- If you increase the sample size, the two curves in Figure 11.8 will get spikier as the sampling error decreases, and so you will reduce the probabilities of both Type I and Type II errors, and increase the power of the test.

The power of a test

Exercise 11.2

1. At a certain airport 20% of people take longer than an hour to check in. A new computer system is installed, and it is claimed that this will reduce the time to check in. It is decided to accept the claim if, from a random sample of 22 people, the number taking longer than an hour to check in is either 0 or 1.

   (i) Calculate the significance level of the test.

   (ii) State the probability that a Type I error occurs.

   (iii) Calculate the probability that a Type II error occurs if the probability that a person takes longer than an hour to check in is now 0.09.

   [Cambridge International AS and A Level Mathematics 9709, Paper 7 Q4 June 2007]

2. A manufacturer claims that 20% of sugar-coated chocolate beans are red. George suspects that this percentage is actually less than 20% and so he takes a random sample of 15 chocolate beans and performs a hypothesis test with the null hypothesis $p = 0.2$ against the alternative hypothesis $p < 0.2$. He decides to reject the null hypothesis in favour of the alternative hypothesis if there are 0 or 1 red beans in the sample.

   (i) With reference to this situation, explain what is meant by a Type I error.

   (ii) Find the probability of a Type I error in George's test.

   [Cambridge International AS and A Level Mathematics 9709, Paper 7 Q2 November 2005]

3. Ten fair dice are rolled. The number of times that a six occurs is denoted by X.

   (i) State the distribution of X.

   (ii) What is the expected number of sixes?

   (iii) Find $P(X = 1)$.

   (iv) Find $P(X > 2)$.

   (v) Suppose now that each die is suspected of being biased, with probability p of rolling a 6, where p is constant across all dice. The ten dice are rolled and four sixes are thrown. If you carry out a test at the 5% level, is this sufficient evidence to say the dice are biased?

   (vi) If the probability of a 6 on any die is in fact $\frac{1}{4}$, find the power of the test.

4. 350 raisins are put into a mixture which is well stirred and made into 100 small buns. Estimate how many of these buns will

   (i) be without raisins

   (ii) contain five or more raisins.

   In a second batch of 100 buns, exactly one has no raisins in it.

   (iii) Estimate the total number of raisins in the second mixture.

   (iv) A different set of buns have been made to a recipe that also includes randomly distributed raisins. A hypothesis test is carried out on the value of λ, where λ is the mean number of raisins per bun. A random selection of five buns is found to contain a total of 60 raisins.

   If the null hypothesis is that $\lambda = 10$, carry out a two-tailed test at the 10% level.

   (v) If the alternative hypothesis is that $\lambda = 12$, find the probability of a Type I and a Type II error with a one-tailed 5% level test.

   (vi) What is the power of the test?

5. A hypothesis test is to be carried out at the 5% level on a Normally distributed population with standard deviation 2.7. The null hypothesis is $H_0: \mu = 25$, and the alternative hypothesis is $H_1: \mu > 25$. A random sample of size 9 is selected and the sample mean is 26.71.

   (i) Find the standard error of the mean.

   (ii) Calculate the test statistic.

   (iii) Write down the critical value.

   (iv) Explain whether the null hypothesis should be rejected.

   (v) Suppose instead that the alternative hypothesis is $\mu = 27$. What would be the probability of a Type I error? What would be the probability of a Type II error?

   (vi) Find the *p*-value associated with this test.

6. In a certain city it is necessary to pass a driving test in order to be allowed to drive a car. The probability of passing the driving test at the first attempt is 0.36 on average. A particular driving instructor claims that the probability of his pupils passing at the first attempt is higher than 0.36. A random sample of 8 of his pupils showed that 7 passed at the first attempt.

   (i) Carry out an appropriate hypothesis test to test the driving instructor's claim, using a significance level of 5%.

   (ii) In fact, most of this random sample happened to be careful and sensible drivers. State which type of error in the hypothesis test (Type I or Type II) could have been made in these circumstances and find the probability of this type of error when a sample of size 8 is used for the test.

   [Cambridge International AS and A Level Mathematics 9709, Paper 71 Q4 June 2009]

7. A garage uses a particular spare part at an average rate of five per week. Assuming that usage of this spare part follows a Poisson distribution, find the probability that

   (i) exactly five are used in a particular week

   (ii) at least five are used in a particular week

   (iii) exactly ten are used in a two-week period

   (iv) at least ten are used in a two-week period

   (v) exactly five are used in each of two successive weeks.

   (vi) If stocks are replenished weekly, determine the number of spare parts which should be in stock at the beginning of each week to ensure that, on average, the stock will be insufficient on no more than one week in a 52-week year.

   (vii) A different spare part has been required 5 times a day on average, but it is thought this figure might have been reduced. The part is subsequently required 15 times in a randomly chosen five-day week. Carry out a test at the 5% level.

   (viii) If the alternative hypothesis is that the part is required on average 4 times a week, find the probability of a Type I and a Type II error with a one-tailed 5% level test, and the *p*-value of the test.

   (ix) What is the power of the test?

The power of a test

8. The random variable $X \sim B(25, 0.1)$.
   (i) State
      (a) the number of trials
      (b) the probability of success in any trial
      (c) the probability of failure in any trial.
   (ii) Find the probability of at most 4 successes.
   (iii) Find the value of the integer a such that $P(X < a) < 0.99$ and $P(X \leq a) > 0.99$.
   (iv) It is now suspected that $p = 0.2$. A new test is carried out with this as the null hypothesis. There are 6 successes in 25 trials. Find the probabilities of a Type I and a Type II error for this test.

9. In an election, 20% of people support the Progressive Party. A random sample of eight voters is taken.
   (i) Find the probability that at least two of them support the Progressive Party.
   (ii) Find the mean and variance of the number of Progressive Party supporters in the sample.
   (iii) The opposition claim that the value 20% over-estimates the support for the Progressive Party. A sample of n voters is chosen so that the critical region for a 5% level test is $0 \leq X \leq 4$, where X is the number of voters in the sample supporting the Progressive Party. What is the smallest possible value for n?
   (iv) Assuming this is the value of n used, find the p-value for the test.
   (v) If the true proportion of Progressive Party voters is in fact 15%, calculate the probabilities of a Type I and Type II error with this test.

10. A council is investigating the weight of rubbish in domestic dustbins. It has recently started a recycling initiative and wishes to determine whether there has been a reduction in the weight of rubbish. Before the initiative, the mean weight was 33.5 kg. A random sample of 60 domestic dustbins is selected and the weight x kg of rubbish in each bin is recorded. The results are summarised as follows.

    $\Sigma x = 1801.2 \qquad \Sigma x^2 = 56963$

    (i) Carry out a hypothesis test at the 1% level to investigate whether the mean weight has been reduced.
    (ii) If the alternative hypothesis is instead that $\mu = 31$, find the probability of a Type I and of Type II error for this test.
    (iii) What is the power of this test?

11. A calculator is used to generate a random integer R, where $0 \leq R \leq 29$. The calculator is fair; there is an equal chance that each of these values for R will arise. 100 values for R are chosen.
    (i) What is the distribution of X, where X is the number of times 29 is generated?
    (ii) Find $P(10 < R)$ for any single reading.
    (iii) The fairness of the calculator is now questioned, and a bias towards the number 29 is suspected. 100 more random numbers are selected by the calculator, and the number 29 is chosen 7 times. If you carry out a test at the 10% level, what does this suggest?
    (iv) If in fact $P(29) = 0.05$, find the probabilities of a Type I and a Type II error for this test.

12 Joe has a drawer containing a large amount of A4 rough paper of two colours, yellow and cream. 35% of the sheets are yellow. When he sits at his desk, he picks pieces of rough paper as required at random from the drawer. One day he picks 12 sheets in total. If Y is the number of yellow sheets he picks, then

(i) Find the probability that he picks more than 6 yellow sheets.

(ii) Find the probability that he picks exactly 4 yellow sheets.

(iii) Joe wonders if in fact the percentage of yellow paper in the drawer is less than 35%. He takes out 20 sheets at random, and there are 3 yellow sheets in his sample. Carry out a 1% level test to see if Joe's suspicions are justified.

(iv) If the true percentage of yellow sheets is 30%, find the power of the test.

13 A farmer divides his apples into two grades; A (supermarket-ready) and B (other). After long experience, he judges that each year on average 64% of apples are grade A. He samples 20 apples at random.

(i) What is the most likely number of apples in the sample to be grade A?

The next year, he changes the way he fertilises his apple trees, and wonders if that increases the percentage of apples that are grade A. He takes a sample of 50 apples at random, and finds that 36 are of grade A standard.

(ii) Carry out a hypothesis test at a 5% significance level.

(iii) The new percentage of grade A apples is in fact k%. It is also true that the probability of a Type I error here is the same as the probability of a Type II error. Using a calculator, find k to two significant figures.

14 It is claimed that a certain 6-sided die is biased so that it is more likely to show a six than if it was fair. In order to test this claim at the 10% significance level, the die is thrown 10 times and the number of sixes is noted.

(i) Given that the die shows a six on 3 of the 10 throws, carry out the test.

On another occasion the same test is carried out again.

(ii) Find the probability of a Type I error.

(iii) Explain what is meant by a Type II error in this context.

[Cambridge International AS and A Level Mathematics 9709, Paper 71 Q6 November 2010]

The power of a test

EXTENSION

KEY POINTS

1. **Hypothesis test for the mean using a Normal distribution**
   - Sample data may be used to carry out a hypothesis test on the null hypothesis that the population mean has some particular value μ_0, i.e. $H_0: \mu = \mu_0$.
   - The alternative hypothesis takes one of the three forms.
     - $H_1: \mu \neq \mu_0$
     - $H_1: \mu < \mu_0$
     - $H_1: \mu > \mu_0$
   - The test statistic $z = \dfrac{\bar{X} - \mu_0}{\frac{\sigma}{\sqrt{n}}}$ is used.
   - If the sample is large, you can use the sample standard deviation s as an estimate of the population standard deviation σ if the latter is not known.
   - If the sample is large, then using the central limit theorem, you can carry out a test using a Normal distribution even if the distribution of the parent population is not known.

2. **Hypothesis test for the mean using a t-distribution**
   - If the population is Normally distributed but the population standard deviation σ is not known then, whatever the sample size, you can carry out a hypothesis test using a t-distribution.
   - The null hypothesis is the same as for the Normal distribution $H_0: \mu = \mu_0$.
   - You estimate the population standard deviation using the sample standard deviation s.
   - The test statistic $t = \dfrac{\bar{x} - \mu_0}{\frac{s}{\sqrt{n}}}$ is used.

3. **Type I and Type II errors**
   (i) A Type I error with a test occurs when you reject H_0 when it is true.
   (ii) A Type II error with a test occurs when you accept H_0 when it is false.
   The power of a test is the probability that you reject the null hypothesis H_0 when the alternative hypothesis H_1 is true.
   Definitions of the significance level of a test, a critical value, the acceptance region and the critical region for a test are exactly the same as for a binomial hypothesis test (see Key Points on page 68).

LEARNING OUTCOMES

When you have completed this chapter you should be able to:
- carry out a hypothesis test for a single population mean using the Normal or t-distributions and know when it is appropriate to do so
- understand what a Type I error or a Type II error is, and calculate the probability of these events for a test
- understand what is meant by the power of a test
- calculate the probability of a Type I or a Type II error in a Poisson hypothesis test
- understand the meaning of the power of a Poisson hypothesis test.

12 The rectangular and exponential distributions

A theory is a good theory if it satisfies two requirements: it must accurately describe a large class of observations on the basis of a model that contains only a few arbitrary elements, and it must make definite predictions about the results of future observations.

— Stephen Hawking

Discussion point

The picture shows a number of students at a lecture. They all look about the same age. Think of the students in an 11-18 school at a time when education was compulsory to the age of 16 but not beyond. What would you expect the distribution of the students' ages to look like?

The continuous uniform (rectangular) distribution

1 The continuous uniform (rectangular) distribution

Note

It is common to describe distributions by the shapes of the graphs of their p.d.f.s: U-shaped, J-shaped, etc.

You will recall having studied the discrete uniform distribution in Chapter 5. You will now meet the continuous uniform distribution. Since the term uniform distribution can be applied to both discrete and continuous variables, in the continuous case it is often written as uniform (rectangular).

The **continuous uniform (rectangular) distribution** is particularly simple since its p.d.f. is constant over a range of values and zero elsewhere.

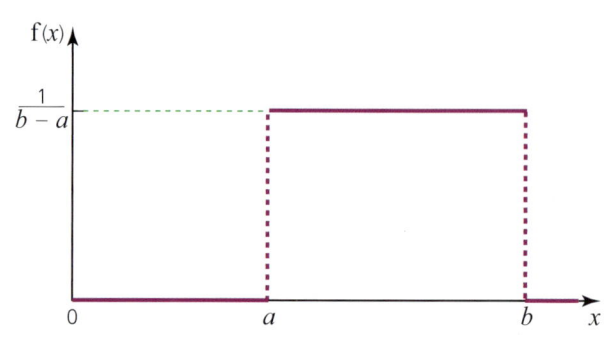

Figure 12.1

In Figure 12.1, X may take values between a and b, and is zero elsewhere. Since the area under the graph must be 1, the height is $\frac{1}{b-a}$.

Example 12.1

A junior gymnastics league is open to children who are at least five years old but have not yet had their ninth birthday. The age, X years, of a member is modelled by the uniform (rectangular) distribution over the range of possible values between five and nine. Age is measured in years and decimal parts of a year, rather than just completed years. Find

(i) the p.d.f. $f(x)$ of X

(ii) $P(6 \leq X \leq 7)$

(iii) $E(X)$

(iv) $Var(X)$

(v) the percentage of the children whose ages are within one standard deviation of the mean.

Solution

(i) The p.d.f. $f(x) = \begin{cases} \frac{1}{9-5} = \frac{1}{4} & \text{for } 5 \leq x < 9 \\ 0 & \text{otherwise.} \end{cases}$

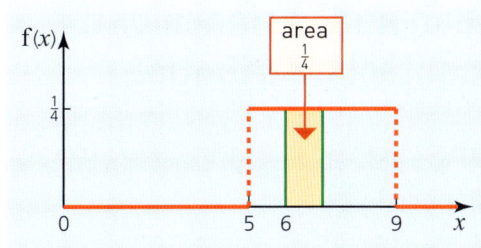

Figure 12.2

(ii) $P(6 \leq X \leq 7) = \frac{1}{4}$ by inspection of the rectangle above.

Alternatively, using integration

$$P(6 \leq X \leq 7) = \int_6^7 f(x)\,dx = \int_6^7 \frac{1}{4}\,dx$$

$$= \left[\frac{x}{4}\right]_6^7$$

$$= \frac{7}{6} - \frac{6}{4}$$

$$= \frac{1}{4}.$$

(iii) By the symmetry of the graph $E(X) = 7$. Alternatively, using integration

$$E(X) = \int_{-\infty}^{\infty} x f(x)\,dx = \int_5^9 \frac{x}{4}\,dx$$

$$= \left[\frac{x^2}{8}\right]_5^9$$

$$= \frac{81}{8} - \frac{25}{8} = 7.$$

$$\mathrm{Var}(X) = \int_{-\infty}^{\infty} x^2 f(x)\,dx - [E(X)]^2 = \int_5^9 \frac{x^2}{4}\,dx - 7^2$$

$$= \left[\frac{x^3}{12}\right]_5^9 - 49$$

$$= \left(\frac{729}{12} - \frac{125}{12}\right) - 49$$

$$= 1.333 \text{ to 3 decimal places.}$$

(v) Standard deviation $\sqrt{\text{variance}} = \sqrt{1.333} = 1.155$.

So the percentage within 1 standard deviation of the mean is

$$\frac{2 \times 1.155}{4} \times 100\% = 57.7\%.$$

> Those within 1 standard deviation of the mean are those whose ages lie between 7 − 1.155 and 7 + 1.155. So the total range of ages is 2 × 1.155.

The continuous uniform (rectangular) distribution

The mean and variance of the uniform (rectangular) distribution

In the previous example the mean and variance of a particular uniform distribution were calculated. This can easily be extended to the general uniform distribution given by:

$$f(x) = \begin{cases} \dfrac{1}{b-a} & \text{for } a \leq x \leq b \\ 0 & \text{otherwise.} \end{cases}$$

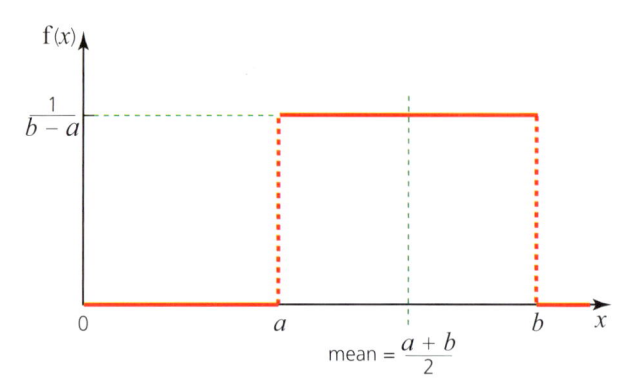

Figure 12.3

Mean: By symmetry the mean $E(X)$ is $\dfrac{a+b}{2}$.

Variance:
$$\text{Var}(X) = \int_{-\infty}^{\infty} x^2 f(x)\,dx - [E(X)]^2$$
$$= \int_{a}^{b} x^2 f(x)\,dx - [E(X)]^2$$
$$= \int_{a}^{b} \frac{x^2}{b-a}\,dx - \left(\frac{a+b}{2}\right)^2$$
$$= \left[\frac{x^3}{3(b-a)}\right]_{a}^{b} - \frac{1}{4}\left(a^2 + 2ab + b^2\right)$$
$$= \frac{b^3 - a^3}{3(b-a)} - \frac{1}{4}\left(a^2 + 2ab + b^2\right)$$
$$= \frac{(b-a)}{3(b-a)}\left(b^2 + ab + a^2\right) - \frac{1}{4}\left(a^2 + 2ab + b^2\right)$$
$$= \frac{1}{12}\left(b^2 - 2ab + a^2\right)$$
$$= \frac{1}{12}(b-a)^2$$

The cumulative distribution function of the uniform (rectangular) distribution

In Chapter 9 you learnt that the cumulative distribution function, F(x), of a continuous random variable, X, with probability density function f(x) is given by

$$F(x) = \int f(x)\,dx.$$

The lower limit of the integral is the lowest value that X can take and the upper limit is x.

So for the general uniform (rectangular) distribution with values between a and b, as shown in Figure 12.3,

F(x) is given by $\int_a^x f(x)\,dx.$

So

$$F(x) = \int_a^x \frac{1}{b-a}\,dx$$

$$\Rightarrow F(x) = \frac{x-a}{b-a} \quad \text{for} \quad a \leq x \leq b.$$

Outside this range of values, F(x) = 0 for $x < a$ and F(x) = 1 for $x > b$.

This is illustrated by the graph in Figure 12.4.

> Strictly, when you write an integral you should not use the same letter to denote the variable and one of the limits. So it would be more correct to write this integral as
> $\int_a^x f(u)\,du$ where u is a dummy variable.

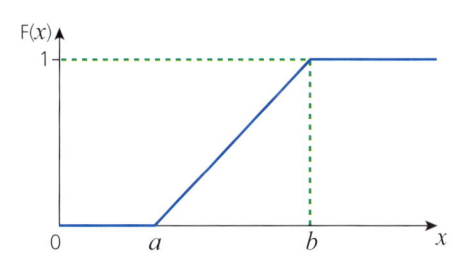

Figure 12.4

Exercise 12.1

1. The random variable X has p.d.f.

$$f(x) = \begin{cases} \dfrac{1}{6} & \text{for } -2 \leq x \leq 4 \\ 0 & \text{otherwise.} \end{cases}$$

   (i)   Sketch the graph of f(x).
   (ii) Find P($X < 2$).
   (iii) Find E(X).
   (iv) Find P($X < 1$).

The continuous uniform (rectangular) distribution

② The graph shows the cumulative distribution function of a continuous random variable, X.

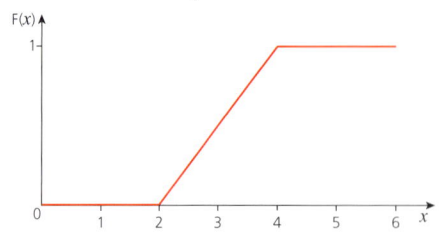

Figure 12.5

  (i) The equation of the sloping line segment is $F(x) = mx + c$.
      Find the values of m and c.
  (ii) Hence find the probability density function, $f(x)$, of X.
  (iii) Describe the distribution of X.
  (iv) Write down
      (a) $P(2 \leqslant X \leqslant 3)$
      (b) $P(3 \leqslant X \leqslant 4)$
      (c) $P(2 \leqslant X \leqslant 3) + P(3 \leqslant X \leqslant 4)$

③ The continuous random variable X has p.d.f. $f(x)$ where
$$f(x) = \begin{cases} 0.2 & \text{for } 0 \leqslant x \leqslant 5 \\ 0 & \text{otherwise.} \end{cases}$$

  (i) Find $E(X)$.
  (ii) Find the cumulative distribution function, $F(x)$.
  (iii) Find $P(0 \leqslant x \leqslant 2)$ using
      (a) $F(x)$ (b) $f(x)$
      and show your answer is the same by each method.

④ A continuous random variable X has a uniform (rectangular) distribution over the interval $(4, 7)$. Find
  (i) the p.d.f. of X
  (ii) $E(X)$
  (iii) $Var(X)$
  (iv) $P(4.1 \leqslant X \leqslant 4.8)$.

⑤ The probability density function of a random variable, X, is
  $f(x) = 0$ for $x < a$,
  $f(x) = c$ for $a \leqslant x \leqslant b$ where c is a constant,
  $f(x) = 0$ for $x > b$.

  Given that $E(X) = 6$ and $Var(X) = 3$, find the values of a, b and c.

⑥ The distribution of the lengths of adult Martian lizards is uniform between 10 cm and 20 cm. There are no adult lizards outside this range.
  (i) Write down the p.d.f. of the lengths of the lizards.
  (ii) Find the mean and variance of the lengths of the lizards.
  (iii) What proportion of the lizards have lengths within
      (a) one standard deviation of the mean
      (b) two standard deviations of the mean?

⑦ A continuous random variable X has the p.d.f.
$$f(x) = \begin{cases} k & \text{for } 0 \leq x \leq 5 \\ 0 & \text{otherwise.} \end{cases}$$

(i) Find the value of k.

(ii) Sketch the graph of $f(x)$.

(iii) Find $E(X)$.

(iv) Find $E(4X - 3)$ and show that your answer is the same as $4E(X) - 3$.

⑧ A toy company sells packets of coloured plastic equilateral triangles. The triangles are actually offcuts from the manufacture of a totally different toy, and the length, X, of one side of a triangle may be modelled as a random variable with a uniform (rectangular) distribution for $2 \leq x \leq 8$.

(i) Find the p.d.f. of X.

(ii) An equilateral triangle of side x has area a. Find the relationship between a and x.

(iii) Find the probability that a randomly selected triangle has area greater than $15\,\text{cm}^2$. (Hint: What does this imply about x?)

(iv) Find the expectation and variance of the area of a triangle.

⑨ The random variable X has a rectangular distribution whose p.d.f. $f(x)$ is given by
$$f(x) = \begin{cases} \dfrac{1}{6} & \text{for } -2 \leq x \leq 4 \\ 0 & \text{otherwise.} \end{cases}$$

Sketch the p.d.f. of X and hence, or otherwise, find the probabilities that

(i) $X \leq 2$

(ii) $|X| \leq 2$

(iii) $|X| \leq x$ for $0 \leq x \leq 2$

(iv) $|X| \leq x$ for $2 \leq x \leq 4$

(v) $|X| \leq x$ for $x > 4$

Hence obtain, and sketch, the p.d.f. of $|X|$. Thus determine the mean of $|X|$.

⑩ The continuous random variable X has the rectangular distribution on the interval $a \leq x \leq b$ where a, b are unknown. Let the expectation and variance of X be μ and σ^2 respectively.

(i) State, in terms of a and b, the values of μ and σ^2.

Now let $\overline{X}$ denote the mean of a random sample of 25 values of X.

(ii) Write down, in terms of a and b, the mean and variance of $\overline{X}$.

In a random sample of 25 values of X the following totals were obtained.

$$\sum x = 1242.5 \qquad \sum x^2 = 61982.89$$

(iii) Use these values to estimate μ and σ^2. Hence estimate a and b.

The exponential distribution

⑪ A computer displays coloured squares of random size. The length of the side of a square is X cm. The random variable X has a rectangular distribution on the interval $1 \leq x \leq 5$, as shown in Figure 12.6.

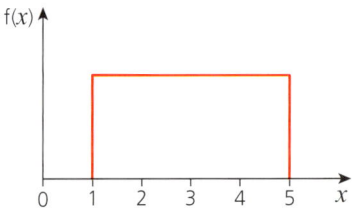

Figure 12.6

(i) Write down the probability density function for X and state its median.

(ii) Find the cumulative distribution function $F(x) = P(X \leq x)$.

The area of a square of side X is denoted by Y.

(iii) Show that the cumulative distribution function for Y is given by
$P(Y \leq y) = \frac{1}{4}(\sqrt{y} - 1)$. Find $g(y)$, the probability density function for Y, and state the interval of values of y for which it applies.

(iv) Find the median area of a square.

(v) Sketch the graph of $g(y)$, and indicate the median and mean on your sketch.

2 The exponential distribution

You open a book, and read until you find the first typo. How many more pages will you have to read before finding the next typo? If you assume that the book's typos are distributed randomly, which seems reasonable, then the distance between typos is a random variable which will in turn have a distribution. This distribution is called **the exponential distribution**.

The exponential distribution is often used to model the waiting times between events such as earthquakes, radioactive emissions, telephone calls, etc.

One condition is essential for the exponential distribution to be used in this way:

- The events occur randomly.

In addition, for the exponential distribution to provide a good model it must also be reasonable to make two assumptions:

- The events occur independently of one another.
- The mean number of events occurring in each interval of the same size is the same.

The same condition and assumptions are required for the Poisson distribution. However, the Poisson distribution is used to model the number of events occurring in a given interval whereas the exponential is used to model the time between events. So while they can be applied to the same events, they are being used in different ways.

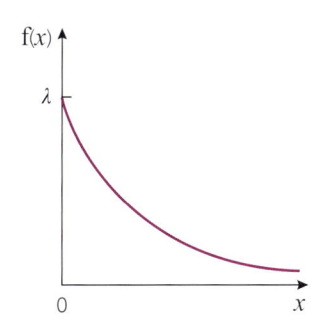

f(x) graph showing exponential decay starting at λ on y-axis.

Figure 12.7

The random variable X has p.d.f. f(x) as shown in Figure 12.7, given by:

$$f(x) = \begin{cases} \lambda e^{-\lambda x} & \text{for } x \geq 0 \\ 0 & \text{otherwise.} \end{cases}$$

where λ is a constant and $\lambda > 0$.

The mean is $\frac{1}{\lambda}$ and the variance is $\frac{1}{\lambda^2}$.

Proof

(i) Show that, for $x \geq 0$, f(x) satisfies the requirements for a p.d.f., that is,
- f(x) ≥ 0 for all x. This is true because both λ and $e^{-\lambda}$ are positive.

and

- $\int_{\text{All values of } x} f(x)\,dx = 1$

> It should not be a surprise to you that the curve of $y = \lambda e^{-\lambda x}$ is above the x-axis because λ is positive, and e raised to any real power is also positive.

The graph in Figure 12.7 shows that f(x) ≥ 0 for all x, and

$$\int_0^\infty e^{-\lambda x}\,dx = \left[-e^{-\lambda x}\right]_0^\infty$$

$$= (0) - (-1)$$

$$= 1, \text{ as required.}$$

(ii) Show that $E(X) = \frac{1}{\lambda}$.

$$E(X) = \int_0^\infty x f(x)\,dx = \int_0^\infty \lambda x e^{-\lambda x}\,dx$$

Integrating by parts gives

$$E(X) = \left[-x e^{-\lambda x}\right]_0^\infty + \int_0^\infty e^{-\lambda x}\,dx$$

$$= 0 - \left[\frac{e^{-\lambda x}}{\lambda}\right]_0^\infty$$

$$= -\left(-\frac{1}{\lambda}\right)$$

$$= \frac{1}{\lambda}, \text{ as required.}$$

The exponential distribution

> **Note**
>
> Since it has been shown in part (ii) that
> $$\int_0^\infty \lambda x e^{-\lambda x}\,dx = \frac{1}{\lambda}$$
> it follows that
> $$2\int_0^\infty x e^{-\lambda x}\,dx = \frac{2}{\lambda^2}$$

(iii) Show that $\operatorname{Var}(X) = \frac{1}{\lambda^2}$.

$$\operatorname{Var}(X) = \int_0^\infty x^2 f(x)\,dx - [E(X)]^2 = \int_0^\infty x^2 \lambda e^{-\lambda x}\,dx - \left(\frac{1}{\lambda}\right)^2$$

Integrating by parts gives

$$\operatorname{Var}(X) = \left[-x^2 e^{-\lambda x}\right]_0^\infty + \int_0^\infty e^{-\lambda x} 2x\,dx - \frac{1}{\lambda^2}$$

$$= 0 + 2\int_0^\infty x e^{-\lambda x}\,dx - \frac{1}{\lambda^2}$$

and so $\operatorname{Var}(X) = \frac{2}{\lambda^2} - \frac{1}{\lambda^2}$

$$= \frac{1}{\lambda^2}, \text{ as required.}$$

The cumulative distribution function for the exponential distribution

You have met the idea of the cumulative distribution function for a random variable above, and it is sensible to ask what the c.d.f. might be for the exponential distribution. Fortunately, since the exponential function is easy to integrate, it is straightforward to provide an answer.

Example 12.2

Find the cumulative distribution function for the random variable X with p.d.f.

$$f(x) = \begin{cases} 5e^{-5x} & \text{for } x \geq 0 \\ 0 & \text{otherwise.} \end{cases}$$

Hence find the probability that $\frac{1}{7} \leq X \leq \frac{1}{3}$, and show this probability on a diagram.

Solution

You can call the c.d.f. $F(t) = \int_0^t 5e^{-5x}\,dx \quad (t \geq 0)$.

Now $\int_0^t 5e^{-5x}\,dx = \left[\frac{5e^{-5x}}{-5}\right]_0^t = 1 - e^{-5t}$

and so $P\left(\frac{1}{7} \leq X \leq \frac{1}{3}\right) = (1 - e^{-\frac{5}{3}}) - (1 - e^{-\frac{5}{7}})$

$$= e^{-\frac{5}{7}} - e^{-\frac{5}{3}} = 0.301 \text{ (3 s.f.)}$$

Figure 12.8

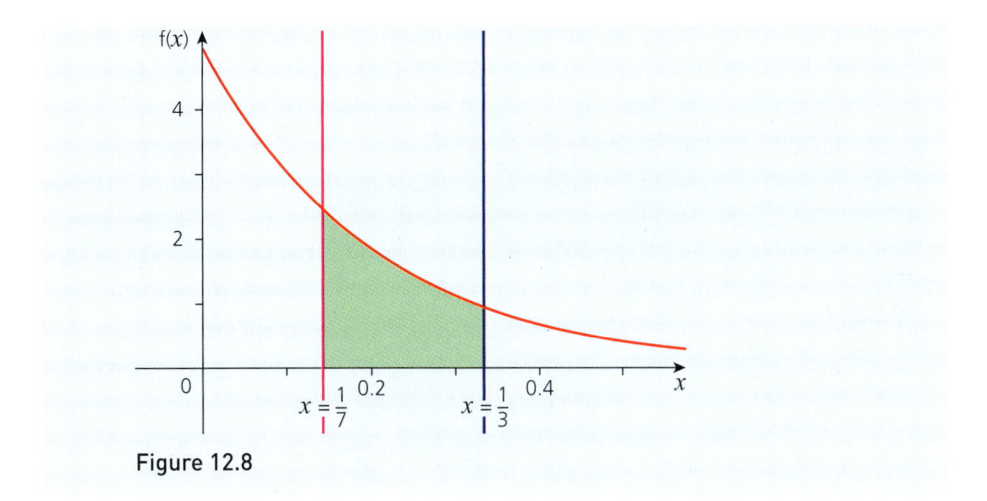

In general, the c.d.f. for the exponential distribution with parameter λ is

$$F(t) = 1 - e^{-\lambda t} \text{ for } 0 \leq t < \infty.$$

Exercise 12.2

① The graph shows the probability density function, f(x), of a random variable with an exponential distribution with parameter λ.

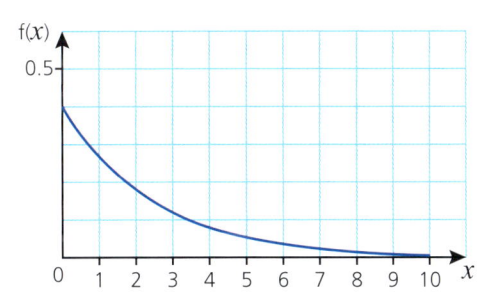

Figure 12.9

(i) Find the value of λ.

(ii) Find the equation of the cumulative distribution function, F(x).

② The random variable X has the exponential distribution with parameter $\lambda = \frac{1}{7}$.

(i) Find $P(1 \leq X \leq 5)$.

(ii) Given that $P(0.5 \leq X \leq a) = P(1 \leq X \leq 5)$, find a.

③ A city bus route passes through several congested road junctions. The delay, in minutes, at each such road junction is modelled by a random variable X having p.d.f.

$$f(x) = \begin{cases} \frac{1}{2} e^{-\frac{x}{2}} & x \geq 0 \\ 0 & x < 0. \end{cases}$$

(i) Find the probability that the delay at a junction exceeds 2 minutes.

(ii) Find the expected delay and the standard deviation of delay at a junction.

④ The continuous random variable X has p.d.f. f(x) defined by

$$f(x) = \begin{cases} ae^{-kx} & \text{for } x \geq 0 \\ 0 & \text{otherwise.} \end{cases}$$

The exponential distribution

Find, in terms of k,

(i) a

(ii) $E(X)$

(iii) $Var(X)$

(iv) the median value of X.

(v) There are many situations where this random variable might be used as a model. Describe one such situation. [MEI]

⑤ A statistician is also a keen cyclist. He believes that the distance which he cycles between punctures may be modelled by the random variable, X km, with p.d.f. $f(x)$ given by

$$f(x) = \begin{cases} 0.005e^{-0.005x} & \text{for } x > 0 \\ 0 & \text{otherwise.} \end{cases}$$

(i) Find the mean distance he cycles between punctures.

(ii) He has just repaired one puncture. What is the probability that he will travel at least 500 km before having another one?

(iii) He has just repaired one puncture. What is the probability that he will travel less than 30 km before having another one?

On one occasion he starts a race with new tyres but then has a puncture after 30 km. When he starts again, he has another puncture after k km. He says that according to his model the combined probability of first a puncture within 30 km and then one within k km is 0.005.

(iv) What is the value of k?

⑥ The graph shows the cumulative distribution function of an exponential distribution with parameter λ.

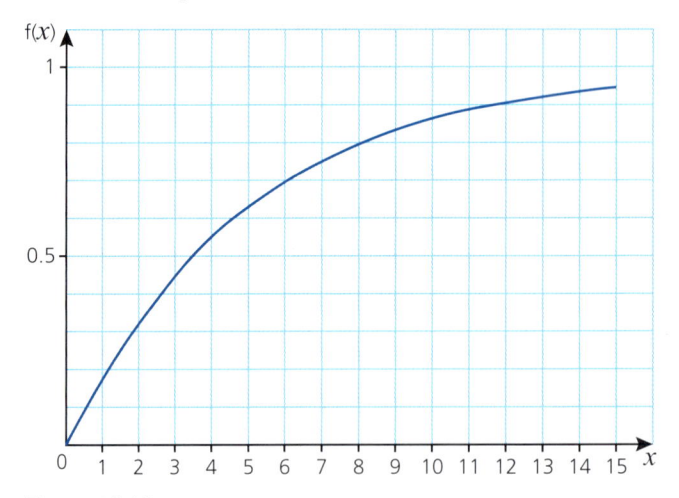

Figure 12.10

(i) By selecting a suitable point on the graph, find the value of λ correct to 2 significant figures.

(ii) Write down the mean and variance of the distribution.

(iii) Find the value of x for which $F(x) = 0.975$.

How many standard deviations is this beyond the mean?

What is the equivalent figure for a Normal distribution?

7 The random variable X has the rectangular distribution on the interval $[a,1]$, where a is negative.

The random variable Y has the exponential distribution with probability density function

$f(y) = \lambda e^{-\lambda y}$ for $y \geq 0$.

Given that X and Y have the same expectation and the same variance, find the values of a and λ.

8 The probability density function for the life x of a motor car sparking plug is given by

$f(x) = \theta e^{-\theta x} \quad (x \geq 0)$,

x measured in units of 1000 miles. What is the probability that a single sparking plug will last more that 10 000 miles if the average life is 5000 miles?

A car has four plugs in use and they are all of the same age. What is the probability that 3 of them will need replacing before 15 000 miles after they were installed?

9 A company specialises in extinguishing oil fires. For much of the time its personnel have no work to do but have to be available to travel anywhere at a moment's notice. The company reckons its overhead costs are £10 000 per day, whether they have work or not.

The company models the waiting time, t days, between jobs by the exponential distribution

$f(t) = \dfrac{1}{100} e^{-\tfrac{t}{100}}$.

(i) Find the mean time that they wait between jobs.

(ii) Find the probability that they go for one year or more between jobs.

(iii) Find the number of days, x, within which they have a 95% probability of getting another job.

When they work, they take an average of 20 days to put out a fire. They aim to make enough profit during that time to be able to meet their costs for the next x days, so that there is a probability of 0.95 that they will have another job before the profit from the last one has run out.

(iv) How much should they charge per day when on a job?

(v) What is their expectation of profit per day?

10 Engineers at a factory are investigating models for the life-length of a particular component. They consider using the random variable X, which has probability density function $f(x) = 3e^{-3x}$ for $x \geq 0$.

(i) Show that the cumulative distribution function for X is $1 - e^{-3x}$.

(ii) Show that the mean value of X is 0.23, correct to 2 decimal places.

(iii) Write down an expression for $P(X > t)$ where $t > 0$. Hence show that the conditional probability $P(X > a + b \mid X > a)$ is equal to $P(X > b)$ for any a and b greater than zero.

(iv) Explain why the result in part(iii) suggests that X is unlikely to be a fully satisfactory model.

The exponential distribution

KEY POINTS

1 The uniform (rectangular) distribution over the interval (a, b)
   - $f(x) = \dfrac{1}{b-a}$
   - $E(x) = \dfrac{1}{2}(a+b)$
   - $\text{Var}(X) = \dfrac{(b-a)^2}{12}$
   - $F(x) = \dfrac{x-a}{b-a}$

2 The exponential distribution
   - $f(x) = \lambda e^{-\lambda x}$ for $x \geq 0$
   - $E(X) = \dfrac{1}{\lambda}$
   - $\text{Var}(X) = \dfrac{1}{\lambda^2}$
   - $F(x) = 1 - e^{-\lambda x}$

LEARNING OUTCOMES

When you have completed this chapter you should be able to:
- understand when a uniform rectangular distribution is likely to be a good model
- use the p.d.f. for a uniform rectangular distribution
- use the formulae for the mean and variance of a uniform rectangular distribution
- understand when an exponential distribution is likely to arise, in particular to model the waiting time between Poisson events
- use the p.d.f. for an exponential distribution
- use the formulae for the mean and variance of an exponential distribution
- Calculate and use the c.d.f. for an exponential distribution

Practice questions: set 3

① A website allows people to give approval ratings to restaurants by moving a slider on a scale from 0 to 10.

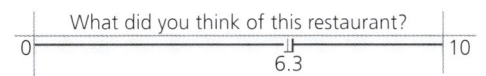

| What did you think of this restaurant? |
| 0 —————————— 6.3 —————————— 10 |

Figure 1

From having eaten there, I think that Paulo's Pizza Parlour should get an average rating of 5, and I want to test that hypothesis. The 10 most recent scores for Paulo's Pizza Parlour on the website are as follows.

3.3   2.2   0.0   4.6   2.8   9.9   8.7   4.9   4.3   8.2

(i) Assuming that the underlying distribution of the scores is approximately Normal once rogue scores are eliminated, carry out a t-test on the data at the 10% level to evaluate whether the mean score is 5 or not. [5 marks]

(ii) Do you think this assumption is valid? [1 mark]

② A rail commuter suspects that the train he travels to work by arrives late regularly. On five such journeys, he noted the times, T minutes, by which the train was late. The data were summarised by

$$\Sigma t = 11.8, \quad \Sigma t^2 = 65.3.$$

(i) Find the mean and standard deviation of the data, and use them to find a and b, the lower and upper limits for the 90% confidence interval for μ, the mean time by which the train is late. State clearly two important assumptions you need to make. [6 marks]

(ii) The commuter interprets the result in part (i) as 'the probability that μ lies between a and b is 0.9'. Comment on this interpretation. [2 marks]

(iii) Use your result in part (i) to comment on whether the commuter's suspicions are justified. [1 mark]

(iv) The railway management notes the value of T on a further 40 occasions. State, with reasons, how you might expect its confidence interval for μ to differ from the one calculated in part (i). [1 mark] [MEI]

③ Over a long period, it has been found that the time that it takes for an underground train to complete a particular journey is 18.6 minutes. New signalling equipment is introduced which might affect the journey time. The times t taken for a random sample of 30 journeys after the change are summarised as follows.

$$\Sigma t = 548.0 \qquad \Sigma t^2 = 10055$$

(i) Carry out a test at the 10% significance level using the Normal distribution to investigate whether there has been any change in journey time since the introduction of the new signalling equipment. You should use an estimate of the population standard deviation. [5 marks]

(ii) It is suggested that, because the sample size is only 30, the estimate of population standard deviation may not be very reliable. Carry out an alternative test and state an assumption necessary for this test. [4 marks]

Practice questions: set 3

④ The time, T minutes, between customer arrivals at a country store, from Monday to Friday, can be modelled, for $t \geq 0$, by the probability density function f(t) defined by illustrating these probabilities on a sketch of the graph of f(t).

$$f(t) = 0.1\, e^{-0.1t}$$

(i) Find the probability that the time between arrivals is
   (a) less than 5 minutes [1 mark]
   (b) more than 15 minutes. [1 mark]

(ii) Obtain the cumulative distribution function for T. Hence find the median time between arrivals.

The time, X minutes, between customer arrivals at the country store on Saturdays can be modelled by the probability density function g(x) defined by g(x) = $\lambda e^{-\lambda t}$ where λ is a positive constant. [3 marks]

(iii) On Saturdays, the probability of the time between customer arrivals exceeding 5 minutes is 0.4. Estimate the value of λ. [3 marks]

⑤ The random variable X has a uniform (rectangular) distribution over the interval (–2, 5). Find

(i) the p.d.f. of X [2 marks]
(ii) $E(X)$ [1 mark]
(iii) $Var(X)$ [2 marks]
(iv) P(X is positive). [1 mark]

⑥ A certain type of low energy light bulb is claimed to have a lifetime L of 8000 hours, with standard deviation 600 hours. A random sample of 25 bulbs is selected. Assuming that the claim is true and that L is distributed Normally:

(i) write down the standard error of the sample mean [1 mark]
(ii) find the probability that the sample mean is greater than 7800 hours. [2 marks]
(iii) The mean is measured and found to be 7750 hours. Comment on this result. [2 marks]
(iv) It is now suspected that the population mean lifetime of the bulb is less than 7800 hours. A fresh random sample of 25 bulbs is taken, and the sample mean lifetime this time is 7500 hours. Carry out a hypothesis test at the 1% level (you can assume that the standard deviation is as before). [5 marks]
(v) What would the probability of a Type I error be here? [1 mark]

Suppose now that the population mean lifetime is in fact 7600 hours.

(vi) What would the probability of a Type II error be for this test? [1 mark]
(vii) What would the power of the test be? [1 mark]

⑦ The wages department of a large company models the incomes of the employees by the continuous random variable X with cumulative distribution function

$$F(x) = 1 - \left(\frac{3}{x}\right)^4 \quad x \geq 3 \text{ and } 0 \text{ otherwise}$$

where X is measured in an arbitrary currency unit. (X is said to have a Pareto distribution.)

(i) Find the median income. Find also the smallest income of an employee in the top 10% of incomes. [3 marks]

(ii) Find the probability density function of X and hence show that the mean income is 4. [3 marks]

(iii) Find the probability that a randomly chosen employee earns more than the mean income. [2 marks] [MEI]

[60 marks]

Answers

Chapter 1

Discussion point, page 1
Statistics often points the way to new knowledge, for example the health dangers in smoking. In Carlyle's time much of the statistics that you will meet in this book had not yet been discovered. There were no calculators or computers, making it almost impossible to analyse data sets of any size. So what could be achieved was distinctly limited.

Discussion point, page 4
- Are the data relevant to the problem? In an investigation into accidents involving cyclists, collecting data on accidents involving pedestrians would be of no use.
- Are the data unbiased? In an investigation into average earnings, taking a sample consisting only of householders would give a biased sample.
- Is there any danger that the act of collection will distort the data? When measuring the temperature of very small objects, the temperature probe might itself heat up or cool down the object.
- Is the person collecting the data suitable? In a survey into the incidence of drug use, a policeman would not be a suitable person to carry out interviews with individuals since people who use drugs would be unlikely to give truthful answers and so the sample obtained would not be representative.
- Is the sample of a suitable size? In an opinion poll for an election, a sample of size 500 is too small to give a reliable result.
- Is a suitable sampling procedure being followed? In an investigation into the weight of individual carrots from a large crop in a field, sampling 50 carrots form the edge of the field would not be appropriate as those at the edge of the field might grow larger or smaller than in the middle of the field.

Discussion point, page 10

Same	They are illustrating the same data	
Different	**Labels**	
	Frequency chart	The vertical scale is labelled 'Frequency'
	Histogram	The vertical scale is labelled 'Frequency density'
	Scales on the vertical axes	
	Frequency chart	The vertical scale is the frequency
	Histogram	The vertical scale is such that the areas of the bars represent frequency. The frequency density is Trains per minute
	Class intervals	
	Frequency chart	The class intervals are all the same, 5 minutes
	Histogram	The class intervals are not all the same; some are 5 minutes, others 10 minutes and one is 40 minutes.

Exercise 1.1

1. (i) E.g. Members who attend may be of a particular type.
      E.g. Absent members cannot be included.
   (ii) 156, 248, 73, 181
2. (i) Either 19th or 20th
   (ii) $Q_2 = 30$, $Q_1 = 19.5$, $Q_3 = 41$
   (iii) $1.5 \times$ IQR $= 32.25$; $19.5 - 32.25 < 0$ so no low outliers; $41 + 32.25 = 73.24$ so 80 and 89 are both outliers.
   (iv) Positively skewed.
   (v) No. There is no reason to believe it would be representative. (As European countries tend to be affluent it is unlikely to be representative.)
3. (i) Opportunity
   (ii) The total number of children is 43 and there were 20 mothers. $\frac{43}{20} = 2.15$
   (iii)
   - The sample is not representative of all women because all the women are mothers; those who have had no children have been excluded.
   - The answer 0 looks like a mistake and needs to be investigated.
   - The word 'exactly' should not be used. At best it is an estimate.
   - Debbie has given her answer to 3 significant figures which implies an unrealistic level of accuracy.
4. Mean = 1540 (3 s.f.), standard deviation = 81.2 (3 s.f.)
5. $\sum x = 1560$ (3 s.f.), $\sum x^2 = 84500$ (3 s.f.)
6. (i) Quota
   (ii)
   - Opinion is almost equally divided for and against.
   - There is a strong difference of opinion between men and women with most men against the scheme and most women in favour.
   - Most adults have made up their minds but many young people don't know.
   (iii) Proportional stratified.
7. (i) The population size appears to be cyclic with period 16 years.
   (ii) 2007 and 2015
   (iii) (a) The population is decreasing sharply.
         (b) The population is steady at about 330 000 animals.
   (iv) A systematic sample is very unsuitable for data with a cyclic pattern. It may select items at about the same points in the cycle and so give misleading information.
8. (i) Cluster
   (ii) The total number of the birds is unknown.
   (iii) $\frac{887}{734} = 1.21$ (2 d.p.)
   There is considerable variability between the clusters and with only four of them it would be surprising if the mean was very close to the true value.
   (iv) The highest rate is D with 1.613... fledglings per nest.
   The lowest rate is C with 0.362... fledglings per nest.
   These figures suggest outer limits of about 43 000 and 194 000 fledglings.
9. (i) Self-selected or opportunity
   (ii) All pregnant women, or all pregnant women in the UK.
   It may well be that only the fitter women agreed to take part.
   People taking part must be volunteers otherwise it would be unethical.
   (iii) 167
   (iv) (a) 3.0% (b) 6.0% (c) About 9.2%
        (d) The categories are not exhaustive as there are others which are not counted in (e.g. day 276).
10. (i) 0.667, 1.25
    (ii) Mean is reduced by 13.3%, standard deviation by 21.52%
    (iii) 0.56% (iv) 51

Chapter 2

Discussion point, page 20

1. There is a negative association (or correlation) between life expectancy and birth rate. This is a situation where correlation does not imply causation. Neither directly causes the other but there are other factors that influence both, such as the level of economic development in a country.
2.
   - The life expectancy in that country
   - The average age of mothers and fathers when they have their first child
   - The number of children that people have

Discussion point, page 25

All the diagrams seem to show outliers. There is some evidence of positive correlation in the top right-hand diagram and negative correlation in the bottom right-hand diagram once outliers have been removed.

Exercise 2.1

1. (i) 0.8   (ii) −1   (iii) 0
2. (i) $H_0: \rho = 0, H_1: \rho > 0$ (ii) Accept H_1
3. (i) $H_0: \rho = 0$ (Jamila), $H_1: \rho > 0$ (coach)
   (ii) Accept H_0; there is not enough evidence to reject H_0. r needs to be > 0.4973 to reject H_0 at the 5% significance level.
4. (i) Although these data items are a little way from the rest of the data, the sample is very small and with more data it could be that the distribution is bivariate Normal.
   (ii) $H_0: \rho = 0, H_1: \rho > 0$
   Accept H_0; there is not enough evidence to reject H_0. r needs to be > 0.7155 to reject H_0 at the 1% significance level.
5. (i) $H_0: \rho = 0, H_1: \rho > 0$
   (ii) $0.015 < 0.05$ so reject H_0. There is sufficient evidence to suggest that there is positive correlation between chess grade and bridge grade.
6. (i) $H_0: \rho = 0, H_1: \rho > 0$
   (ii) Accept H_1; there is very strong positive correlation.
7. $H_0: \rho = 0, H_1: \rho > 0$; $r = 0.901$; Andrew
8. (i) $H_0: \rho = 0, H_1: \rho \neq 0$. 5% sig. level
   (ii) Accept H_1
   (iii)

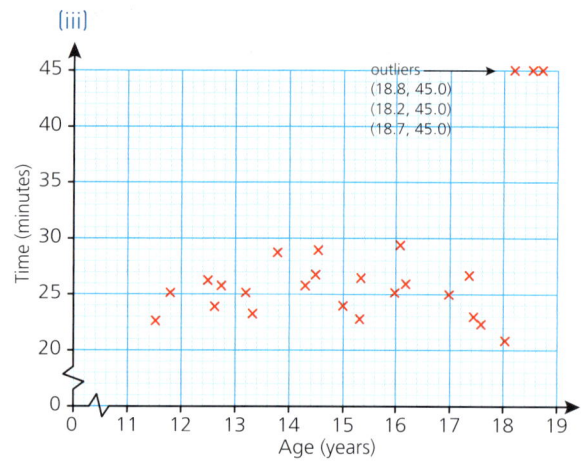

   Outliers: (18.8, 45), (18.2, 45), (18.7, 45), it seems as though these girls stopped for a rest.

   (iv) The scatter diagram should have been drawn first and the outliers investigated before calculating the product moment correlation coefficient. With the three outliers removed, $r = -0.1612$, accept H_0.
9. (i) $H_0: \rho = 0, H_1: \rho > 0$; $0.3377 < 0.5214$ so accept H_0.
   (ii) It reduces the value of the product moment correlation coefficient. It should be included, unless there is any reason to suppose it is an error, as it is as valid as any other point.
10. (i)

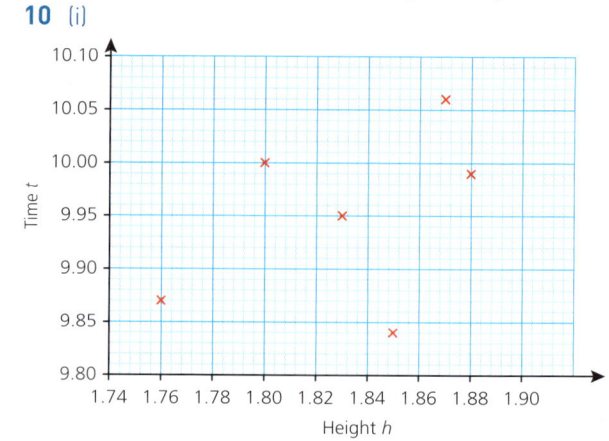

    (ii) $H_0: \rho = 0, H_1: \rho > 0$;
    $0.4386 < 0.7293$ so accept H_0; there is not sufficient evidence to reject H_0.

    (iii)

    | Rank h | 2 | 3 | 5 | 6 | 4 | 1 |
    | Rank t | 5 | 3 | 6 | 4 | 1 | 2 |

    (iv) 0.3143
    (v) the correlation coefficient for the ranked data is quite a bit lower than for the unranked. This is probably because ranking loses information.

Exercise 2.2

1. H_0: no association between judges' scores,
   H_1: positive association between judges' scores.
   $r_s = 0.6667 > 0.6429$ accept H_1 at 5% significance level. There is positive association between judges' scores.
2. (i) These results are on the face of it surprising! The value of r is fairly large and positive, suggesting the coach is right, while the value for r_s is negative, suggesting he is wrong.
   (ii) Testing at the 5% level. For r, $H_0: \rho = 0$, $H_1: \rho > 0$, critical value is 0.729, accept H_1. For r_s, H_0: no association, H_1: positive association, critical value is 0.886, accept H_0.
   (iii) Product moment correlation coefficient is more suitable here because it takes into account the magnitude of the variables.
3. (i) Positive sign indicates possible positive correlation.
   (ii) H_0: no association between time and quality, H_1: some association between time and quality. Accept H_1; there is some association between time taken and quality of work.

4 (i) $H_0: \rho = 0, H_1: \rho > 0$, $0.680 > 0.6694$ so accept H_1.
 (ii) The two correlation coefficients measure different quantities. The product moment correlation coefficient measures linear correlation using the actual data values. Spearman's coefficient measures rank correlation using the data ranks. Mr Smith ought to have used Spearman's coefficient.

5 (i) H_0: no association between January and July temperatures, H_1: positive association between January and July temperatures. Accept H_0
 (ii) It is more appropriate to use the product moment correlation coefficient since it utilises the actual data values.

6 (i) H_0: no association between level of community charge and approval rating. H_1: some association between level of community charge and approval rating.
 (ii) $0.0279 < 0.05$ so reject H_0. There is sufficient evidence to suggest that there is some association between level of community charge and approval rating.

7 (i) H_0: no association between amount of additive and weight of marrow, H_1: positive association between amount of additive and weight of marrow. The alternative hypothesis is one-sided because the additive is claimed to enhance growth.
 (ii) $0.612 > 0.5636$ so reject H_0. There appears to be positive association between amount of additive and weight of marrow.
 (iii) This does not change the rankings so does not affect the conclusions.

8 (i) H_0: no association between expenditure and score, H_1: positive association between expenditure and score. $0.5035 > 0.1608$ so accept H_0. There is insufficient evidence to suggest positive association between expenditure and score.
 (ii) If $r_s = 0.15$ for the whole population then there is an association but it is weak.

9 (i) H_0: no association between prosperity and death rate, H_1: positive association between prosperity and death rate. $0.952 > 0.4637$ so reject H_0. There is insufficient evidence to suggest positive association between prosperity and death rate.
 (ii) It is not justified; a strong association exists but this does not imply that poverty causes a higher death rate.
 (iii) Death rates depend on age distributions, for example an area with many old people will have a higher death rate.

10 There is significant correlation at the 5% level in all three cases. There are outliers in (i) contraceptives, (ii) contraceptives and (iii) nuclear power.

11 (i) $H_0: \rho = 0, H_1: \rho \neq 0$; two-tailed test is used because the analyst does not specify a positive or a negative correlation.
 (ii) 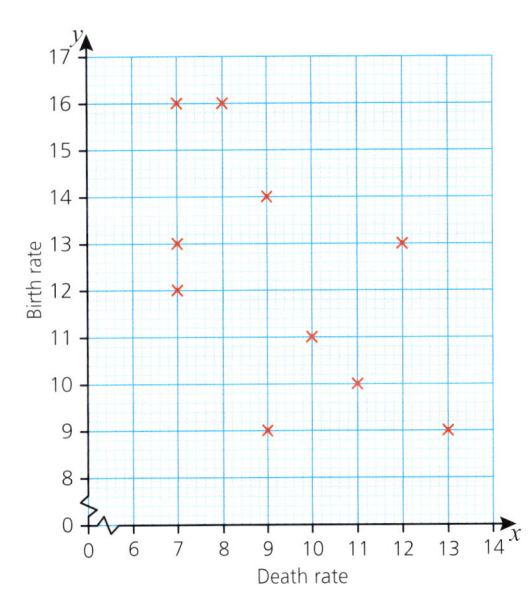
 (iii) Since $-0.574 > -0.6319$, accept H_0; the death rates and birth rates are not correlated.
 (iv) There is weak negative correlation between death rates and birth rates.
 (v) No, the additional evidence shows that H_0 should be rejected.

12 (i)

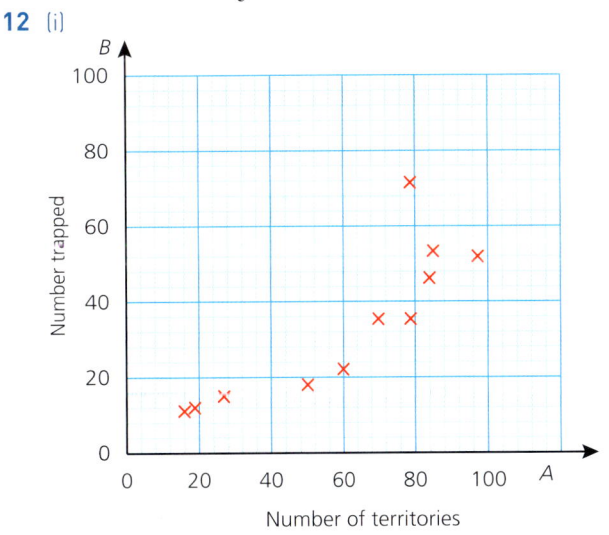

(ii) H_0: no association between the results of the two surveys, H_1: some association between the results of the two surveys. c.v. = 0.6182, 0.916 > 0.6182 so reject H_0, generally, the greater the number of territories recorded, the greater the number trapped.

(iii) It would be less appropriate; the data do not seem to conform to a linear pattern and there is no real evidence of an elliptical scatter.

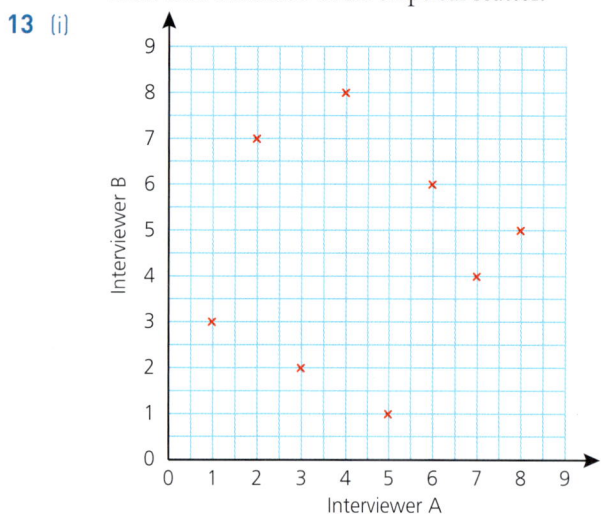

13 (i)

(ii) Because the data are ranked.

Chapter 3

Discussion point, page 48

On average, you would expect $0.25 \times 50 = 12.5$ questions.

Exercise 3.1

1 (i) B(10, 0.5) (ii) 0.2051 (iii) 0.6230
2 (i) 6 (ii) 0.0634 (iii) 0.9095
3 (i) 3.501×10^{-5} (ii) 28 560 (iii) £3.77
4 (i) 0.8178 (ii) 0.8504 (iii) 0.6689
  (iv) Because in part (ii) you can put 0 in first and 8 in second, 1 and 7, … whereas in (iii) you can only have 4 and 4
5 (i) 0.2637 (ii) 0.6328 (iii) 16.25 times
6 (i) 0.0301 (ii) 0.0445

Exercise 3.2

1 0.1275   Accept H_0
2 0.0547 > 5%   Accept H_0
3 H_0: probability that the toast lands butter-side down = 0.5
   H_1 probability that toast lands butter-side down > 0.5
   0.240   Accept H_0

4 0.048   Reject H_0
   There is evidence that the complaints are justified at the 5% significance level, though Mr McTaggart might object that the candidates were not chosen randomly.
5 0.104   Accept H_0
   Insufficient evidence at the 5% significance level that the machine needs servicing.
6 (i) 2; s.d = 1.844
   (ii) P(2 defectives in 10) = 0.302
        In 50 samples of 10, the expected number of samples with two defectives is 15.1, which agrees well with the observed 15.
   (iii) H_0: P(mug defective) = 0.2
         H_1: P(mug defective) < 0.2
         n = 20. P(0 or 1 defective mug) = 0.0692
         Accept H_0 since 0.0692 > 5%
         It is not reasonable to assume that the proportion of defective mugs has been reduced.
   (iv) Opposite conclusion since 0.0692 < 10%
7 (i) 0.590 (ii) 0.044 (iii) 0.0000729
   (iv) 0.0292
   (v) H_0: P(long question right) = 0.5
       H_1: P(long question right) > 0.5
   (vi) No

Discussion point, page 61

$X \leqslant 4$

Exercise 3.3

1 (i) Let p = P(business operates no smoking policy), H_0: p = 0.7, H_1: p < 0.7
  (ii) $k \leqslant 10$ (iii) $k \leqslant 1$
  (iv) For 19 businesses, P(H_0 rejected) = 0.1855
       For 4 businesses, P(H_0 rejected) = 0.1265
       The 19 business test is preferable because it gives a greater probability of rejecting H_0 when it should be rejected.
2 (i) 0.430 (ii) 0.9619 (iii) 0.0046
  (iv) H_0: p = 0.9, H_1: p < 0.9
  (v) n = 17; P(X ≤ 13) = 0.0826 > 5%
      not sufficient evidence to reject H_0
  (vi) Critical region is $X \leqslant 12$, since P(X ≤ 12) = 0.0221

3 (i) (a) 0.2344 (b) 0.8906
  (ii) Let p = P(blackbird is male)
       $H_0: p = 0.5$, $H_1: p > 0.5$
  (iii) Result is significant at the 5% significance level. Critical region is $X \geq 12$.
  (iv) You would be more reluctant to accept H_1. Although H_0 is still $p = 0.5$, the sampling method is likely to give a non-random sample.
4 (i) (a) 0.0991 (b) 0.1391
  (ii) Let p = P(seed germinates)
       $H_0: p = 0.8$, $H_1: p > 0.8$, since a higher germination rate is suspected.
  (iii) Critical region is $X \geq 17$, since $P(X \geq 17) = 0.0991 < 10\%$ but $P(X \geq 16) = 0.2713 > 10\%$
  (iv) (a) When $p = 0.8$ he reaches the wrong conclusion if he rejects H_0, i.e. if $X \geq 17$, with probability 0.0991.
       (b) When $p = 0.82$ he reaches the wrong conclusion if he fails to reject H_0, i.e. if $X \leq 16$, with probability $1 - 0.1391 = 0.8609$

Exercise 3.4

1 $P(X \leq 7) = 0.1316 > 5\%$ Accept H_0
2 $H_0: p = 0.5$, $H_1: p \neq 0.5$,
   $P(X \leq 13 | p = 0.5) = 0.0622 > 2.5\%$, Accept H_0
3 $P(X \geq 9) = 0.0730 > 2.5\%$ Accept H_0
4 $P(X \geq 10) = 0.0193 < 5\%$ Reject H_0, but data not independent
5 $P(X \geq 6) = 0.1018 > 5\%$ Accept H_0
6 $P(X \leq 1) = 0.0395$
   (i) $0.0395 < 5\%$ Reject H_0
   (ii) $0.0395 > 2.5\%$ Accept H_0
7 ≤ 1 or > 9 males
8 ≤ 1 or > 8 correct
9 Critical region is ≤ 3 or ≥ 12 letter Zs
10 (i) 20 (ii) 0.0623 (iii) Complaint justified

Chapter 4

Discussion point, page 70

$P(Y \cap C)$ = Probability tests positive and has the condition = 0.20.

$P(Y \cap C')$ = Probability tests positive and does not have the condition = 0.15.

$P(Y' \cap C)$ = Probability tests negative and has the condition = 0.05.

$P(Y' \cap C')$ = Probability tests negative and does not have the condition = 0.60.

Discussion point, page 71

The four numbers in the body of the table occur at the ends of the branches of the trees. Those in the margins do not appear.

The final answers would be the same, although the tree would look different.

Discussion point, page 73

When DNA is collected, the probability of two people having the same DNA profile is very small, but not zero. If only a partial DNA sample has been collected from a crime scene, then this probability could be rather larger. Let us suppose that the probability of two different people having the same partial profile as that found at a crime scene in London is only 1 in one million. The population of London is roughly 9 million. So there will be approximately 9 people who share this profile. So without any other evidence, the probability that the sample comes from a person who has this DNA profile is $\frac{1}{9}$.

Exercise 4.1

1 (i) 0.33 (ii) 0.385 (iii) 0.2
2 (i) 0.24 (ii) 0.44 (iii) 0.136
3 (i) $P(W) \times P(C) = 0.20 \times 0.17 = 0.034 \neq P(W \cap C) = 0.06$ so not independent
  (ii)

  Venn diagram: W and C overlapping circles with 0.14, 0.06, 0.11, and 0.69 outside.

  (iii) 0.353
  (iv) Children are more likely than adults to be able to speak Welsh.
4 (i) 0.033 (ii) 0.545
5 (i) 0.05329 (ii) 0.0650 (iii) 0.9350
  (iv) It has a high false positive rate so it is not very effective unless combined with further testing.
6 (i) 0.07 (ii) 0.0476
7 0.6087
8 (i) 0.01465 (ii) 0.662
9 (i) 0.025 (ii) 0.4
10 (i) 0.1825 (ii) 0.8

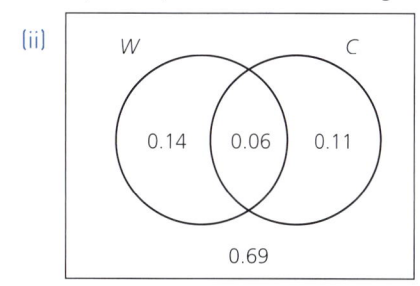

Practice questions: set 1 (page 78)

1. (i) Proportional stratified
   (ii) Writing the names on sheets of paper and drawing them from a hat.
   Listing and numbering the three groups and then using random numbers to make the selections.
   (iii) Not all samples can be selected, for example one with 20 shops.
   (iv) £407 000
   (v) There are major differences within two of the groups; these need to be understood and addressed in the stratifies sampling.

2. (i) 0.0417 (ii) 0.0592 (iii) 0.0834
   (iv) 0.1184
   (v) $H_0: p = 0.5$, $H_1: p \neq 0.5$, under H_0 $P(X \leq 1)$ = 0.1875 > 2.5%, so accept H_0, there is not sufficient evidence to say the procedure gives men and women an unequal chance.

3. (i) Vertical sections through the weight on age scatter diagram show similar means (except perhaps for the very oldest patients). Spread is greatest for younger patients because there are more with very high weight. Vertical sections through the height on age scatter diagram show decreasing means from the twenties onwards. The spread decreases too.
   (ii) Using the raw data, the mean weight is about 74 kg so accept 69–79 kg.
   Using the raw data, the mean height is about 162 cm so accept 159–165 cm.
   Mean height (about 5'4") strongly suggests that these are women.
   Mean weight (just over 11 stone) sounds a little high for women, but it is consistent with recent figures in the United States.
   (iii) The scatter diagrams for weight and age and for height and age show negative correlation. Height and weight will be positively correlated, so 0.31.
   (iv) There is no suggestion that these individuals form a random sample. They may differ from the population in having a condition that has brought them to the clinic for treatment.

4. (i) Simple random samples
   (ii) A $\bar{x} = 81.52$, $s = 10.02$,
   B $\bar{x} = 77.71$, $s = 10.16$,
   C $\bar{x} = 80.75$, $s = 10.27$
   Statistical variability
   (iii) Overall $\bar{x} = 79.88$, $s = 10.20$. Should be more accurate with the larger total sample size.

5. (i) (A) $0.6^2 \times 0.4 = 0.144$
      (B) $0.6^6 = 0.0467$
      (C) $0.6^6 \times (1 - 0.6^6) = 0.0445$
      (D) 0.311
   (ii) $H_0: p = 0.4$, $H_1: p < 0.4$. $P(X \leq 2) = 0.083$ under H_0, which is greater than 0.05, so you do not have sufficient evidence to reject H_0: you cannot reject the idea that $p = 0.4$.

6. (i) These values look like clear errors (or outliers). It seems likely that the students concerned have measured the length of one arm.
   (ii) The correlation shows that increases in height are closely associated with increases in arm length, but it does not show that they are approximately equal. The same correlation could apply if height was equal to 0.8 × arm length, for example.
   (iii) The gradient (1.017) shows that a 1 cm increase in arm span is, on average, associated with just over a 1 cm increase in height. This supports the hypothesis.
   However, the intercept (−3.989) indicates that the regression line does not pass through the origin. This casts some doubt on the hypothesis.
   The gradient and intercept would vary from sample to sample so these two figures might be not significantly different from 1 and 0.

Chapter 5

Exercise 5.1

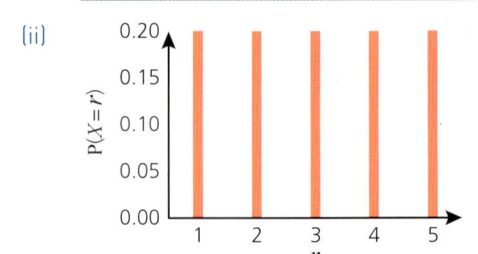

1. (i)
r	1	2	3	4	5
P(X = r)	0.2	0.2	0.2	0.2	0.2

   (ii) [bar chart showing P(X=r) = 0.2 for r = 1, 2, 3, 4, 5]

274

(iii) (a) 0.6 (b) 0.4 (c) 0

2 (i)

r	1	2	3	4
P(X = r)	k	2k	3k	4k

(ii) $k = 0.1$

(iii) (a) 0.4 (b) 0.6

3 (i)

r	3	4	5	6	7	8	9
P(X = r)	$\frac{1}{27}$	$\frac{1}{9}$	$\frac{2}{9}$	$\frac{7}{27}$	$\frac{2}{9}$	$\frac{1}{9}$	$\frac{1}{27}$

(ii)

Symmetrical

(iii) (a) $\frac{10}{27}$ (b) $\frac{14}{27}$ (c) $\frac{10}{27}$

4 (i)

r	0	1	2	3	4
P(Y = r)	$\frac{1}{5}$	$\frac{8}{25}$	$\frac{6}{25}$	$\frac{4}{25}$	$\frac{2}{25}$

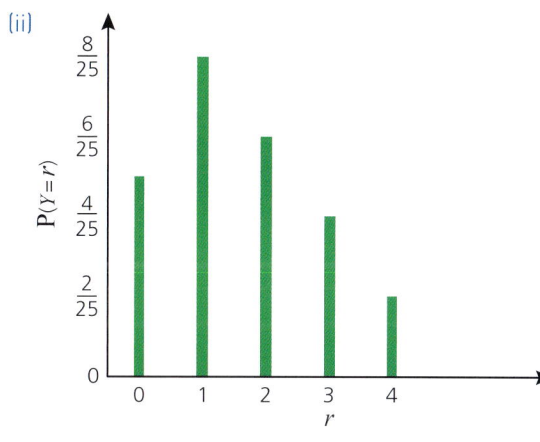

(ii)

Positive skewed

(iii) (a) $\frac{13}{25}$ (b) $\frac{13}{25}$

5 (i)

r	1	2	3	4	5	6	8	9	10	12	15	16	18	20	24	25	30	36
P(X = r)	$\frac{1}{36}$	$\frac{1}{18}$	$\frac{1}{18}$	$\frac{1}{12}$	$\frac{1}{18}$	$\frac{1}{9}$	$\frac{1}{18}$	$\frac{1}{36}$	$\frac{1}{18}$	$\frac{1}{9}$	$\frac{1}{18}$	$\frac{1}{36}$	$\frac{1}{18}$	$\frac{1}{18}$	$\frac{1}{18}$	$\frac{1}{36}$	$\frac{1}{18}$	$\frac{1}{36}$

(ii) $\frac{3}{4}$

6 (i) $k = \frac{2}{7}$

r	2	3	4	5
P(X = r)	$\frac{1}{7}$	$\frac{3}{14}$	$\frac{2}{7}$	$\frac{5}{14}$

(ii) (a) $\frac{27}{98}$ (b) $\frac{71}{196}$

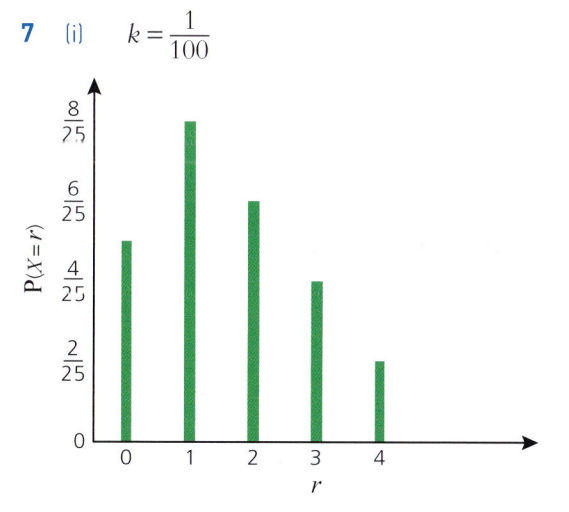

7 (i) $k = \frac{1}{100}$

8 (i)

r	0	1	2	3	4
$P(X=r)$	$\frac{1}{16}$	$\frac{1}{4}$	$\frac{3}{8}$	$\frac{1}{4}$	$\frac{1}{16}$

(ii) Symmetrical

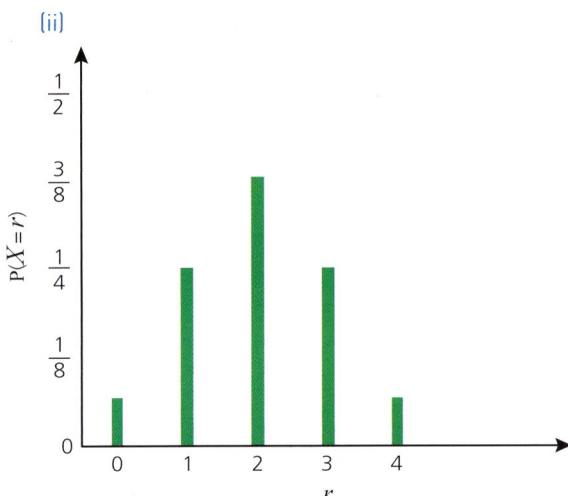

(iii) $\frac{5}{16}$

(iv) Greater because you cannot have equal numbers of heads and tails, so the probability of more heads than tails will be equal to the probability of less heads than tails and both will be equal to $\frac{1}{2}$.

9 (i) $k = 0.014$

r	0	1	2	3	4	5
$P(X=r)$	$\frac{3}{10}$	$\frac{49}{250}$	$\frac{49}{250}$	$\frac{21}{125}$	$\frac{14}{125}$	$\frac{7}{250}$

(ii) $\frac{1}{25}$

10 (i) $a = 0.1$ (ii) $k = \frac{32}{31}$

(iii)

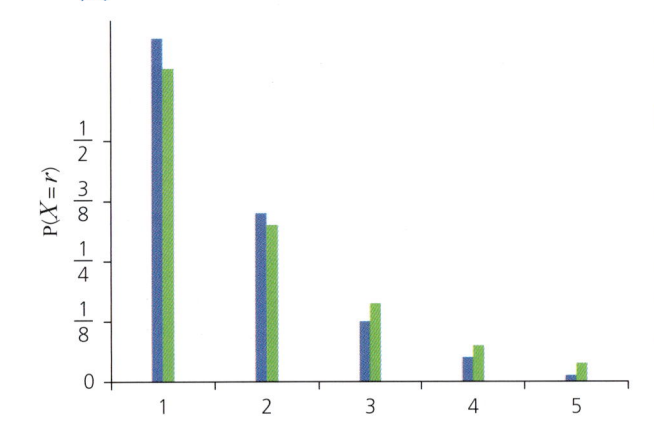

Note: actual values in blue, model in green.
The model is fairly good although it suggests that there are rather fewer cars with 1 or 2 people and rather more with 3, 4 or 5 people.
Highly positively skewed

11 (i)

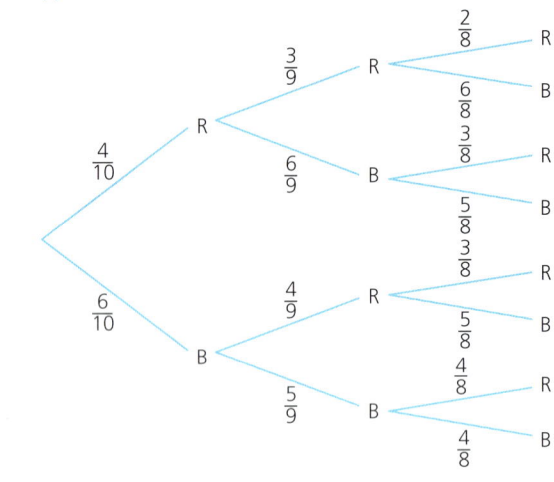

(ii)

r	0	1	2	3
$P(X=r)$	$\frac{1}{30}$	$\frac{3}{10}$	$\frac{1}{2}$	$\frac{1}{6}$

Discussion point, page 87

By comparing the mean scores in each competition (and perhaps also the standard deviation to get an idea of variation).

Discussion point, page 89

The mean score after the relaxation session is 1.855 as compared with 1.49 before, which suggests that the relaxation session has helped the archers to achieve higher scores. The variance after the relaxation session is 2.084 as compared with 1.97 before, which suggests that the relaxation session has made very little difference to the variation in performance.

Discussion point, page 90

The first method is preferable if the mean is not a round number, since in that case all of the values $(r - \mu)$ will be decimals resulting in a lot of work in the calculations. However, if the mean is a round number the second method may be a little quicker than the first.

Exercise 5.2

1 $E(X) = 3$; Because the distribution is symmetrical so take the mid-range value.

2 Mean = 3.2, Variance = 3.26

	A	B	C	D
1	r	$P(X=r)$	$r \times P(X=r)$	$r^2 \times P(X=r)$
2	1	0.20	0.20	0.20
3	2	0.30	0.60	1.20
4	3	0.10	0.30	0.90
5	4	0.05	0.20	0.80
6	5	0.20	1.00	5.00
7	6	0.15	0.90	5.40
8	SUM	1.00	3.20	13.50

3 (i) $E(X) = 3.125$ (ii) $P(X < 3.125) = 0.5625$

5 (i) $p = 0.8$

r	4	5
$P(Y=r)$	0.8	0.2

(ii)

r	50	100
$P(Y=r)$	0.4	0.6

6 (i) $E(Y) = 1.944$; $Var(Y) = 2.052$

(ii) (a) $\frac{5}{9}$ (b) $\frac{1}{18}$

7 (i) $E(X) = 1.5$ (ii) $Var(X) = 0.75$
(iii) $E(Y) = 5, Var(Y) = 2.5$

8 (i)

r	−5	0	2
$P(X=r)$	0.25	0.25	0.5

(ii) $E(X) = -0.25, Var(X) = 8.188$; Negative expectation means a loss
(iii) £1 less

9 (i) $P(X = 1) = 0.4 \times 0.85 + 0.6 \times 0.1$

(ii)

r	1	2	3	4
$P(X=r)$	0.4	0.3	0.21	0.09

(iii) $E(X) = 1.99, Var(X) = 0.97$

10 (i) $p = 0.3, q = 0.4$

r	3	4	5
$P(X=r)$	0.3	0.4	0.3

(ii)

r	20	50	100
$P(Y=r)$	0.7	0.2	0.1

11 (i)

x	1	2	3	4	5	6
$P(X=x)$	$\frac{1}{36}$	$\frac{3}{36}$	$\frac{5}{36}$	$\frac{7}{36}$	$\frac{9}{36}$	$\frac{11}{36}$

(ii) negatively skewed

(iii) mode is 6, mean is $161/36 = 4.47$ (3 s.f.), median = 5

12 (i)

r	$P(X=r)$
0	0.03
1	0.10
2	0.13
3	0.16
4	0.18
5	0.17
6	0.12
7	0.09
8	0.02

(ii) $E(X) = 3.92, Var(X) = 3.83$ (to 3 s.f.)

(iii) $k = \frac{1}{84}$

(iv) $E(X) = 4, Var(X) = 3$

(v) The expectations are almost the same and the theoretical variance is only slightly less than the experimental variance, so the model is quite good.

Exercise 5.3

1 (i) $\frac{1}{3}$ (ii) $\frac{5}{9}$

2 (i) $\frac{1}{2}$

(ii) $E(X) = 3.5$ (iii) $Var(X) = 1.25$

3 (i) $E(X) = 3.5, Var(X) = \frac{35}{12}$

(ii) $E(X) = 17.5, Var(X) = \frac{175}{12}$

4 $E(X) = 10, Var(X) = 4$

5 (i) $E(X) = 2, Var(X) = \frac{2}{3}$

(ii) $E(Y) = 20, Var(Y) = \frac{200}{3}$

(iii) $E(Z) = 20, Var(Z) = \frac{20}{3}$

(iv) Means are equal but variance of Y is larger because it is $10^2 \times Var(X)$ rather than $10 \times Var(X)$

Exercise 5.4

1 (i) (a) $E(X) = 3.1$ (b) $Var(X) = 1.29$
2 (i) (a) $E(X) = 0.7$ (b) $Var(X) = 0.61$
3 (i) $E(A + B + C) = 90, Var(A + B + C) = 23$
(ii) $E(5A + 4B) = 295, Var(5A + 4B) = 353$
(iii) $E(A + 2B + 3C) = 170$, $Var(A + 2B + 3C) = 95$

(iv) $E(4A - B - 5C) = -15$, $\text{Var}(4A - B - 5C) = 302$

5 (i) $E(2X) = 6$ (ii) $\text{Var}(3X) = 6.75$

6 (i)

r	1	2	3	4	5	6
P(X = r)	$\frac{11}{36}$	$\frac{1}{4}$	$\frac{7}{36}$	$\frac{5}{36}$	$\frac{1}{12}$	$\frac{1}{36}$

(ii) $E(X) = 73.2p$ $\text{Var}(X) = 1232$

(iii) Make money since cost £1 and average winnings 73.2p.

7 (i) (a) $E(X) = 2.3$ (b) $E(Y) = 1.3$
    (c) $\text{Var}(X) = 0.81$ (d) $\text{Var}(Y) = 0.61$

(ii)

r	1	2	3	4	5	6
P(Z = r)	0.04	0.14	0.28	0.31	0.18	0.05

(iii) (a) $E(Z) = 3.6 = 2.3 + 1.3$
     (b) $\text{Var}(Z) = 1.42 = 0.81 + 0.61$

(iv)

r	−1	0	1	2	3	4
P(W = r)	0.1	0.26	0.31	0.22	0.09	0.02

(v) (a) $E(W) = 1 = 2.3 - 1.3$
    (b) $\text{Var}(W) = 1.42 = 0.81 + 0.61$

8 $E(\text{Amount}) = 65$ $\text{Var}(\text{Amount}) = 591.7$

9 (i) $E(X) = 1$ $\text{Var}(X) = 0.5$
(ii) $E(10X - 5) = 5$ $\text{Var}(10X - 5) = 50$
(iii) $E(50 \text{ obs of } X) = 50$ $\text{Var}(50 \text{ obs of } X) = 25$
(iv) $E(50X) = E(50 \text{ obs of } X) = 50$
but $\text{Var}(50X) = 1250 = 50 \times \text{Var}(50 \text{ obs of } X)$
(v) $E(X^3) = 2.5$ $\text{Var}(X^3) = 10.25$

10 (i) $E(X) = 1.05$ $\text{Var}(X) = 0.6475$

(ii)

r	0	1	2	3	4
P(Y = r)	0	0.1	0.7	0.2	0

(iii) $E(Y) = 2.1$

(iv) Because X_1 and X_2 are not independent.

11 $E(3X^2 - 4) = 3E(X^2) - 4$, $\text{Var}(3X^2 - 4) = 9\text{Var}(X^2)$

$E(X^2) = \frac{13}{12}$, $\text{Var}(X^2) = \frac{197}{576}$, so

(i) $-\frac{3}{4} = -0.75$ (ii) $\frac{197}{64} = 3.08$

Chapter 6

Discussion point, page 112

(i) Births would need to occur independently of one another and at a constant average rate throughout the day.

(ii) The 'independence' condition would seem to be reasonable. There is some evidence that more births occur in the morning than at other times of the day.

(iii) This is a complex question and there are many issues to consider. They include:
- Does the expected number of births differ from one month to another?
- For how long is each bed needed?
- How many births are likely to take place at home?
- Is the expected number of births in Avonford likely to change much during the period for which the decisions are being made?
- What happens if there are too few beds, or too many beds?

You may well be able to think of other issues.

Exercise 6.1

1 (i) 0.266   (ii) 0.826

2 (i) 0.2237   (ii) 0.1847   (iii) 0.4012

3 X may be modelled by a Poisson distribution when cars arrive singly and independently and at a known overall average rate; 0.4416

4 (i) 0.058   (ii) 0.099

5 (i) 25   (ii) 75   (iii) 112   (iv) 288
Errors occur randomly and independently.

6 (i) Aeroplanes land at Heathrow at an almost constant rate (zero at some times of the night), so the event 'an aeroplane lands' is not a random event.

(ii) Foxes may well occur in pairs, in which case the events would not be independent. (The fact that some regions of area 1 km² will be less popular for foxes than others may be an issue but it is at least partially dealt with by choosing the region randomly.)

(iii) Bookings are likely not to be independent of one another, as there may be groups requiring more than one table.

(iv) This should be well modelled by a Poisson distribution (although it would be necessary to assume that the rate of emission was not so high that the total mass was likely to be substantially reduced during a period of 1 minute – i.e. that the half-life of substance is substantially larger than 1 minute).

7 (i) The mean is much greater than the variance therefore X does not have a Poisson distribution.

(ii) Yes, because now the values of the mean and variance are similar.
(iii) 0.012
8 (i) $X \sim \text{Po}(1)$ (ii) 0.0144 (iii) 0.187
(iv) $H_0: \lambda = 20$, $H_1: \lambda > 20$, $P(X \geq 30 | \lambda = 20) = 0.0218 < 5\%$, reject H_0

Exercise 6.2
1 (i) 0.0906 (ii) 8
(iii) 0.0916; This is very similar to the binomial probability.
2 (i) $\lambda = 5$
(ii)

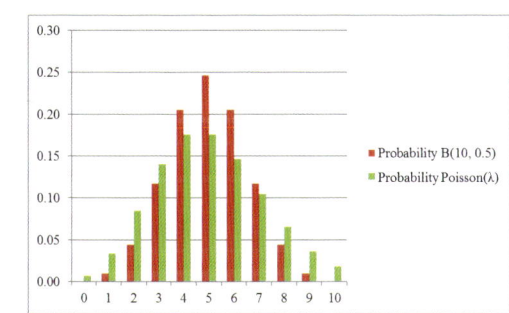

(iii) The probabilities in the chart showing B(10, 0.5) and Poisson(5) are not very similar at all for each value of X and so the Poisson distribution (λ) is a not good approximation to the B(10, 0.5) distribution.
(iv) $\mu = 5$
(v) The probabilities in the chart showing B(100, 0.05) and Poisson(5) are very similar for each value of X. The probabilities in the chart showing B(10, 0.5) and Poisson(5) are not very similar at all for each value of X. This is to be expected because in the former case n is large and p is small whereas in the latter case n is small and p is not small.
3 (i) 0.7153 (ii) 0.7149
(iii) Because if n is large and p is small then a Poisson distribution with mean np is a good approximation to a binomial distribution.
4 (i) 0.102 (ii) 0.3586 (iii) 0.2545
5 (i) 0.175 (ii) 0.973 (iii) 0.031
(iv) 0.125 (v) 0.248
6 (i) (a) 0.180 (b) 0.264 (c) 0.916
(ii) 0.296
(iii) 0.05
7 (i) 0.135 (ii) 0.5947 (iii) 0.125
8 (i) 0.233 (ii) 0.123 (iii) 0.262
9 (i) (a) 0.007 (b) 0.034 (c) 0.084
(ii) $T \sim \text{Poisson}(5.0)$
10 (i) 0.531 (ii) 0.065 (iii) 0.159

11 (i) (a) 0.257 (b) 0.223 (c) 0.168
(ii) 0.340
12 (i) 0.161 (ii) 0.554 (iii) 10
(iv) 0.016 (v) 0.119

Chapter 7

Discussion point, page 125
They should ideally choose a random sample of customers. However, this will be difficult, so they could instead ask, for example, 1 in every 10 customers to fill in a questionnaire. They should do this over a period so that they sample customers who are watching different types of films.

Discussion points, page 134
- the expected frequencies
  The first figure in each cell in the table
- the contributions to the X^2 statistic
  The second figure in each cell in the table
- the degrees of freedom
  Next to df below the table
- the value of the X^2 statistic
  Next to X^2 below the table
- the p-value for the test
  Next to p below the table

The observed frequencies which is the third figure in each cell in the table.

Exercise 7.1
1 (i) Walk 78, Cycle 66, Bus 113, Car 73, Age 13 172, Age 16 158
(iv) No, because, for instance, younger students might be less likely to be allowed by their parents to cycle.

2 (i)

	Pass	Fail
Less than 10 hours	21.31	9.69
At least 10 hours	33.69	15.31

(ii)

	Pass	Fail
Less than 10 hours	2.86	6.29
At least 10 hours	1.81	3.98

3 $X^2 = 35.87$
   $v = 12$
   Reject H_0 at 5% level or above; association
4 $X^2 = 2.886$
   $v = 1$
   Accept H_0 at 5% level or below; independent
5 $X^2 = 0.955$
   $v = 1$
   Accept H_0 at 10% level or below; no association
6 $X^2 = 7.137$
   $v = 4$
   Accept H_0 at 10% level or below; independent
7 $X^2 = 10.38$
   $v = 1$
   Reject H_0 at 1% level (c.v. = 6.635): related
8 $X^2 = 13.27$
   $v = 6$
   Reject at 2.5% level or above: not independent
9 $X^2 = 11.354$
   $v = 4$
   Reject H_0 at 5% level (c.v. = 9.488): association.
   The cells with the largest value of $\frac{(f_o - f_e)^2}{f_e}$ are medium/induction and long/induction so medium and long service seem to be associated, respectively, with more than and fewer than expected employees with induction-only training.
10 $v = 9$
   Reject H_0 at 5% level (c.v. = 16.92): association
   Considering the values of $\frac{(f_o - f_e)^2}{f_e}$ for each cell, shows that rural areas seem to be associated with more reasonable and excellent and less poor or good air quality than expected.
11 (i)   Some of the expected frequencies may be less than 5.
   (ii) H_0: no association, H_1: association
   (iii) $X^2 = 1.445$, $v = 2$, c.v. = 5.991. Accept H_0 not enough evidence to suggest association.
   (iv) Best to combine small and large businesses as these have more similarities than any other group.
         H_0: no association, H_1: association
         $X^2 = 0.0384$, $v = 1$, c.v. = 3.841. Accept H_0 not enough evidence to suggest association.
12 (i)   4.136, 5.091
   (ii) Because some of the expected frequencies are less than 5.
   (iii) Combine 'Under 20' and '20–39' and combine '40–59' and '60 or over'.

(iv) H_0: no association, H_1: association. $X^2 = 13.22$, $v = 2$, c.v. = 5.991. Reject H_0 there is enough evidence to suggest association.

(v)
Contribution to test statistic	Pop	Classical	Jazz
Under 40	4.060	0.077	3.375
40 and over	3.086	0.058	2.565

The values of 4.06 and 3.09 show that under 40s have a strong positive association with pop, whereas 40 and over have a strong negative association with pop. The values of 3.37 and 2.56 show that under 40s have a strong negative association with jazz, whereas 40 and over have a strong positive association with jazz. The observed frequencies for classical are much as expected.

Chapter 8

Discussion point, page 143

It is reasonable since the wave heights are not predictable.

Exercise 8.1

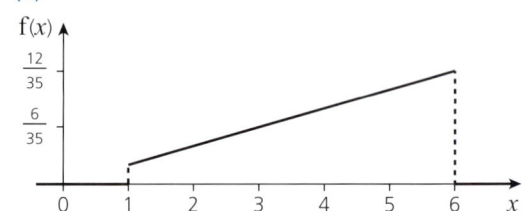

1 (i) $k = \frac{2}{35}$
   (ii)
   (iii) $\frac{11}{35}$ (iv) $\frac{1}{7}$
2 (i) $k = \frac{1}{12}$
   (ii)
   (iii) 0.207

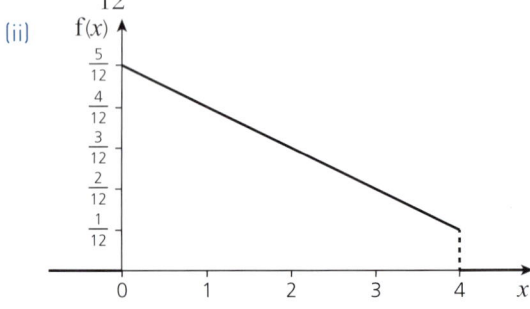

3 (i) $c = \frac{1}{8}$

(ii) [graph: f(x) rectangular, height 1/8 from x=-3 to x=5]

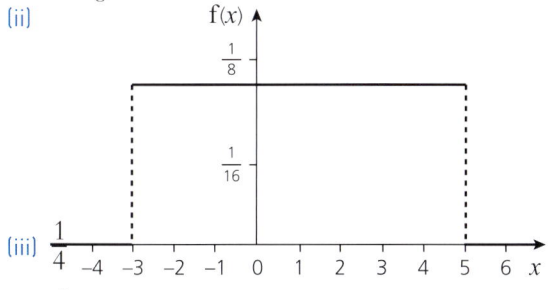

(iii) $\frac{1}{4}$

(iv) $\frac{3}{8}$

4 (i) $k = \frac{1}{4}$

(ii) [graph: f(x) triangular, peak 1/2 at x=2, from 0 to 4]

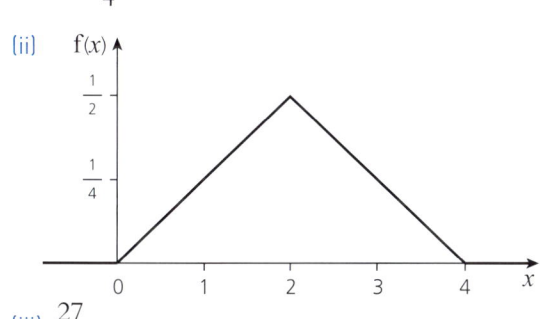

(iii) $\frac{27}{32}$

5 (i) $a = \frac{4}{81}$

(ii) [graph: f(x) increasing curve from 0 to 3]

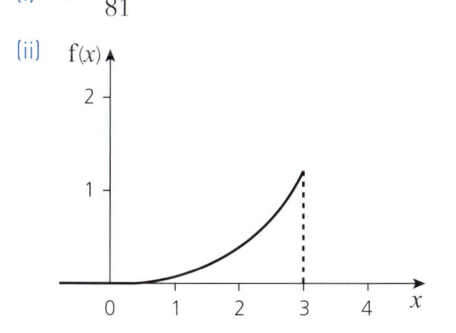

(iii) $\frac{16}{81}$

6 (i) $k = 0.048$

(ii) [graph: f(x) parabolic, peak 0.3 around x=3.5, from 1 to 6]

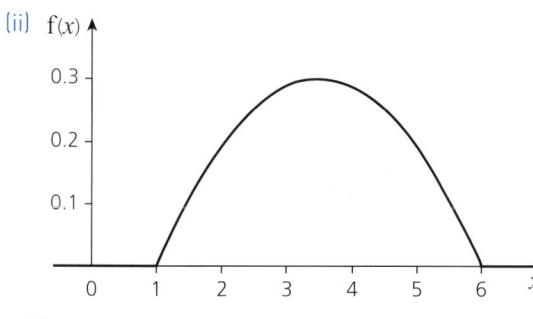

(iii) 0.248

7 (i) $a = \frac{5}{12}$

(ii) [graph: f(x) with bump from 1 to 2 reaching 3/12, rectangle at 5/12 from 2 to 4]

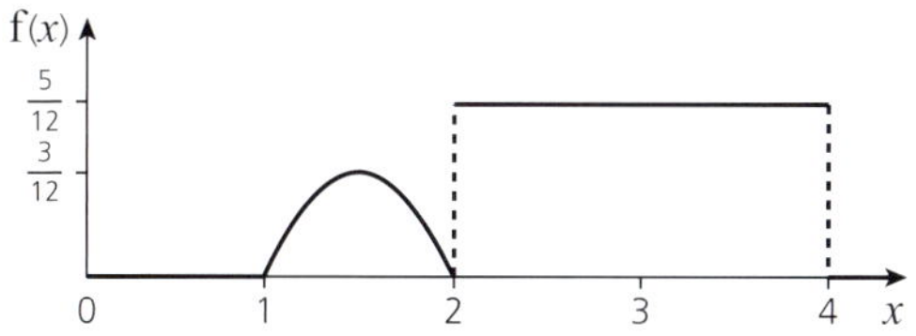

(iii) 0.292   (iv) $\frac{7}{12}$

8 (i) $k = \frac{2}{9}$ (ii) 0.067

9 (i) $k = \frac{1}{100}$

(ii) [graph: f(x) linear decreasing from 0.2 at x=0 to 0 at x=10, Length of stay (hours)]

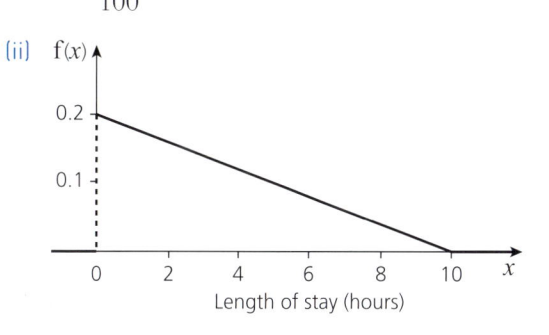

(iii) 19, 17, 28, 36   (iv) Yes

(v) Further information needed about the group 4–10 hours. It is possible that many of these stay all day so are part of a different distribution.

10 (i) $a = 100$ (ii) 0.045

(iii) 0.36

11 (i) 0, 0.1, 0.21, 0.12, 0.05, 0.02, 0

(ii) 0.1, 0.31, 0.33, 0.17, 0.07, 0.02

(iii) $k = \frac{1}{1728}$

(iv) 0.132, 0.275, 0.280, 0.201, 0.095, 0.016

(v) Model quite good. Both positively skewed.

Discussion point, page 155

b, c, d, e

Exercise 8.2

1 Yes, $30 > 22.4 + 1.96 \times 3.2$

2 16.3 cm, 2.5 cm

3 2.5%

4 D

5 (i) 0.68   (ii) 0.815   (iii) 0.925   (iv) 0.025

6 (i) $d = 20.6$ (3. s.f.)

(ii) 1.13 (3 s.f.)

(iii) (339.8, 366.2)

7 Yes, she sells 81.5%.

8 (i) 22.5   (ii) 0.080 (to 2 s.f.)

(iii) 1

9 (i) T   (ii) T   (iii) F   (iv) T

10 (i) 0.025   (ii) 0.025   (iii) 0.000 625

(iv) $0.025^{10} = 9.5 \times 10^{-17}$ (to 2 s.f.)

11 (i) The distribution is discrete and not continuous
(ii) The distribution is positively skewed by some people having very high incomes so it is not symmetrical
(iii) The minimum length of life is 0 years and this is only 1.49 standard deviations below the mean. The distribution cannot be Normal because the left hand side is truncated.
(iv) This distribution is bimodal.

12 (i) X (ii) Both the same (iii) X

13 (i) Possible values are from -2 to $+2$, $k = \dfrac{3}{32}$
(ii) Mean = 0, standard deviation = 0.894
(iii)

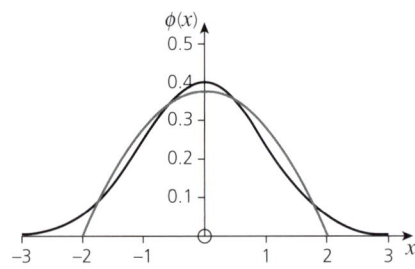

(iv) Means both 0, sd of X (0.894) < sd of Normal curve (1), both areas are 1.

Exercise 8.3

1 10.1 to 18.9 (to 3 s.f.)

2 (i) 90%
(ii) 807 to 907. The long-term mean of 820 is inside the confidence interval so there is no evidence that the rainfall is increasing.
(iii) 30%

3 (i) 3.25 kg to 3.75 kg (to 3 s.f.)
(ii) There has been no change.
(iii) It was not random and so may not be representative. It was an opportunity sample.

4 (i) 103 g (ii) 98 g to 108 g (to nearest gram)

5 (i) 79.0 g to 85.0 g (to 3 s.f.)
(ii) 95% of the bags will weigh between 7.9 kg and 8.5 kg
(iii) 82.9 g to 86.1 g (to 3 s.f.) (v) 20 p

6 (i) $a = 1.81$, $b = 3.49$ (to 3 s.f.)
(ii) 2.28 to 2.54 (to 3 s.f.)
(iii) The confidence interval is 0.267 (to 3 s.f.). The width of $[a, b]$ is 1.69 (to 3 s.f.). The confidence interval is smaller by a factor of $\sqrt{40}$.
(iv) The previous value of the mean is well outside the confidence interval so it looks as though there may well have been a change.

(v) There is no list of fish from which to make a random selection (ie no sampling frame) as would be required in simple random sampling.
The method used makes it more likely that the sample was biased and so the confidence interval should be treated with caution.

7 (i) $1.314w$ (ii) $0.447w$ (iii) $3w$

8 (ii) 26.98 to 29.52 (to 4 s.f.)

9 (i) 290 (ii) 271 to 309
(iii) The life spans of rodents kept in a laboratory may not be typical of those of the species generally. There is an outlier in the data. One of the rodents died very young.
(iv) Excluding the outlier gives a confidence interval of 324 to 366 days.

10 (i) T is Normally distributed.
(ii) 0.90 (to 2 s.f.)
(iii) Only 95% of 95% confidence intervals are expected to include the true, but unknown, population mean. So it could be that that this is one of the other 5%. Mac is wrong to use the word 'definitely'.
(iv) 80

11 (i) 66.6 (ii) 2.553...
(iii) 60.0 to 73.2 (to 3 s.f.) (iv) 30

Practice questions: set 2 (page 169)

1 (ii)

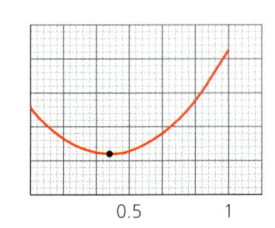

Low and high proportions are more common than middling proportions. That is, days tend to be mostly sunny or mostly cloudy rather than mixed.
(iii) $E(X) = 4/7$. $Var(X) = 3/7 - (4/7)2 = 5/49$.

2 H_0: no association, H_1: association
$X^2 = 19.79$, c.v. = 16.81
Reject H_0, seems to be association
SE and Midlands have more short and fewer long lifespans than expected; 'rest' has fewer short and more long lifespans than expected.

3 (i)

r	-2	0	5
$P(X = r)$	0.6	0.2	0.2

(ii) $E(X) = -0.2$ $Var(X) = 7.36$
(iii) Pay 0.33 pounds less, so pay £1.67.

4 (i) (a) 0.134   (b) 0.848
   (ii) 0.086   (iii) 0.673
5 (i) Faulty pixels occur independently of one another and at a uniform average rate.
   (ii) (a) 0.3012   (b) 0.9662
   (iii) $P(Y = 0) = 0.3012 / 0.9662 = 0.3117$
   (iv) $P(Y = 1) = 0.3741$, $P(Y = 2) = 0.2244$, $P(Y = 3) = 0.0898$
   (v) $E(Y) = 1.092$
       $E(Y^2) = 2.0798$ $Var(Y) = 0.8867$
       $SD(Y) = 0.9417$
   (vi) $H_0: \lambda = 18$, $H_1: \lambda > 18$, $P(X \geq 35 | \lambda = 18) = 0.0002 < 1\%$, reject H_0
   (vii) P(Type I error) = P(reject H_0 when $\lambda = 18$) = 0.00594, since the critical region is 30+
6 (i) $C | G$: the defendant is convicted given that the defendant is guilty.
       That is, a defendant who is guilty is convicted.
       $C \cap G$: the defendant is both convicted and guilty.
   (ii) $P(C \cap G') = 0.005$, $P(C' \cap G) = 0.18$, P(wrong conclusion) = 0.185
   (iii) $P(C \cap G) = 0.72$, $P(C \cap G') = 0.005$, $P(C) = 0.725$. $P(G | C) = 0.993$.

Chapter 9

Discussion point, page 172

Its range will be from a little over 2 hours to 5 or 6 hours. There will be a mode at about 3½ hours. It will probably be positively skewed with a tail of slow runners taking a long time.

Exercise 9.1

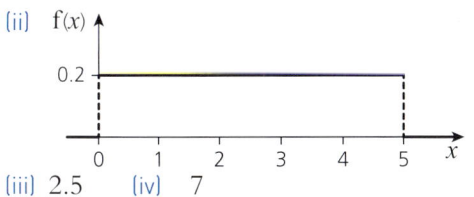

1 (i) $k = 0.2$
   (ii) f(x) graph
   (iii) 2.5   (iv) 7
2 (i) 0.8   (ii) $0.\dot{6}$ (iii) $0.02\dot{6}$
3 (i) 10.9, 3.09   (ii) 18.4, 111.24

4 (i) 2   (ii) 1   (iii) 9
5 (i) E(Score) = 3.5   Var(Score) = 2.917
   (ii) E(Total Score) = 7.0   Var(Total Score) = 5.833
   (iii) E(Difference) = 0   Var(Difference) = 5.833
   (iv) E(Total Score) = 35   Var(Total Score) = 29.17
6 0.8, 0.16, £8
7 (i) 1.5   (ii) 2.7   (iii) 0.45   (iv) 13.9
   (v) 0.45; both are the variance of Y.
8 (i) 0.6   (ii) −3.4   (iii) 0.2
   (iv) 0.64
9 (i) $E(X) = 3.2$
   (ii) p.d.f. graph

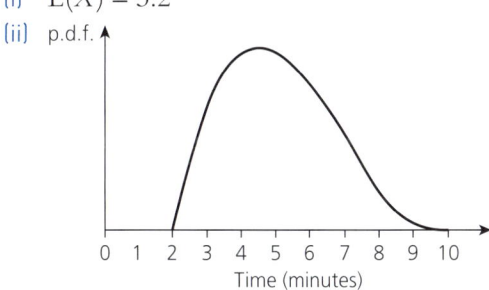

The model implies that all of the doctor's appointments last between 2 and 10 minutes, the mean time being 5.2 minutes and the variance of the distribution being 2.56 minutes².

10 (i) $0.3 + \int_0^{14} 0.1 - \frac{t}{140} dt = 1.$
   (ii) $\int_0^{14} 0.1t - \frac{t^2}{140} dt = 3.2666\ldots$ so Dean waits on average 3.27 (3 s.f.) minutes.

11 (i) $3\frac{2}{3}$ (ii) $66\frac{1}{6}$ (iii) $14\frac{5}{6}$, $66\frac{1}{6}$
   (iv) Both sides = $66\frac{1}{6}$
   (v) $Var(X) = 1.388$ (4 s.f.), $E(X^4) = 311$,
       $Var(X^2) = 90.97$ (4 s.f.),
       $E(X^3) = 65.5$, $E([3X^2 + 4X+7]^2) = 5485\frac{2}{3}$,
       $Var(g(X)) = 1108$ (4 s.f.)

12 $k = \frac{1}{36}$, mean = 3, probability = $\frac{5}{32}$

13 (i) $f(t) = \begin{cases} 0.1 & \text{for } 0 \leq t \leq 10 \\ 0 & \text{otherwise} \end{cases}$
   mean = 5, variance = $8\frac{1}{3}$

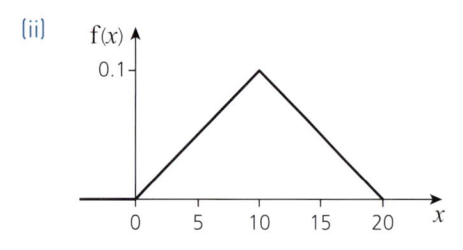

(ii) [graph of f(x): triangular distribution peaking at 0.1 around x=10, from 0 to 20]

(iii) $E(X) = 10$, $Var(X) = 16\frac{2}{3}$

(iv) 0.18; because $T_1 \geq 7$ and $T_2 \geq 7$ is not the only way for $X \geq 14$. The latter inequality also includes other possibilities, such as waiting 9 minutes in the morning and 6 minutes in the evening.

14 (i) $E(X) = \frac{11}{21}$, $E(X^2) = \frac{5}{14}$, $E(X^3) = \frac{19}{70}$,

$E(X^4) = \frac{23}{105}$

(ii) $Var(X) = \frac{73}{882} = 0.0828$

(iii) $E(g(X)) = \frac{37}{42} = 0.881$ (3 s.f.),
$Var(g(X)) = 0.343$ (3 s.f.)
$E(g(X)) = 5E(X^2) - 2E(X) + 1$. You cannot do anything similar with $Var(g(X))$.

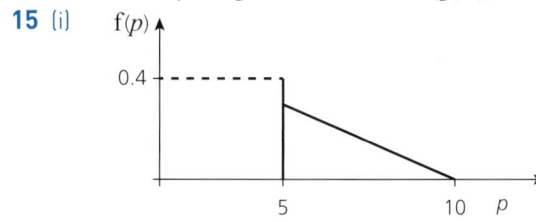

15 (i) [graph of f(p): value 0.4 from 0 to 5, then decreasing linearly to 0 at p=10]

(ii) $\int_5^{10} ax - 10a \, dx = 0.6 \Rightarrow \left[\frac{ax^2}{2} - 10ax\right]_5^{10}$

$= 0.6 \Rightarrow a = -\frac{6}{125}$

(iii) Mean $= \int_5^{10} ap^2 - 10ap \, dp + 0.4 \times 5 = 6$

$Var(P) = E(P^2) - (E(P))^2 = 37.5 - 36 = 1.5$

Discussion point, page 183

£150 is quite a large prize, but probably small in comparison to the total entry fees so it may be worth it if the model is very good. The model should work for any number of runners and should be adjustable if the nature of the entry changes.

Exercise 9.2

1 (i) 2.5

(ii) $F(x) = \begin{cases} 0 & \text{for } x < 0 \\ \dfrac{x}{5} & \text{for } 0 \leq x \leq 5 \\ 1 & \text{for } x > 5 \end{cases}$

(iii) 0.4

2 (i) 2.67   (ii) 0.89   (iii) 2.828

3 (i) 2   (ii) 2   (iii) 1.76

4 (i) $k = \dfrac{2}{39}$

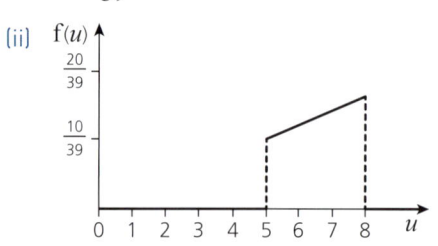

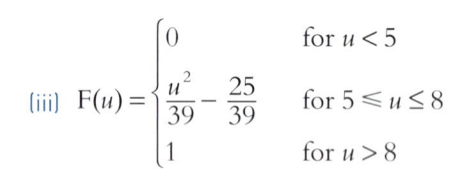

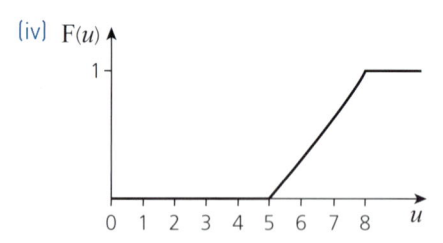

(ii) [graph of f(u): line from (5, 10/39) to (8, 20/39)]

(iii) $F(u) = \begin{cases} 0 & \text{for } u < 5 \\ \dfrac{u^2}{39} - \dfrac{25}{39} & \text{for } 5 \leq u \leq 8 \\ 1 & \text{for } u > 8 \end{cases}$

(iv) [graph of F(u): 0 until u=5, increasing to 1 at u=8, then 1]

5 (i) $c = \dfrac{1}{21}$

(ii) $F(x) = \begin{cases} 0 & \text{for } x < 1 \\ \dfrac{x^3}{63} - \dfrac{1}{63} & \text{for } 1 \leq x \leq 4 \\ 1 & \text{for } x > 4 \end{cases}$

(iii) 3.19   (iv) 4

6 (i) $F(x) = \begin{cases} 0 & \text{for } x < 0 \\ 1 - \dfrac{1}{(1+x)^3} & \text{for } x \geq 0 \end{cases}$

(ii) $x = 1$

7 (i) $\dfrac{1}{4}$ (ii) 0.134

(iii) $f(x) = 2 - 2x$ for $0 \leq x \leq 1$

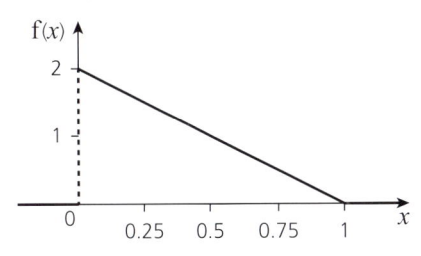

8 $E(X) = \frac{3}{4}$, $Var(X) = \frac{19}{80}$

$F(x) = \begin{cases} 0 & \text{for } x < 0 \\ \frac{3x}{4} - \frac{x^3}{16} & \text{for } 0 \leq x \leq 2 \\ 1 & \text{for } x > 2 \end{cases}$

9 $\frac{3}{5}$, 0.683

10 (ii) $F(t) = \begin{cases} 0 & \text{for } t < 0 \\ \frac{t^3}{432} - \frac{t^4}{6912} & \text{for } 0 \leq t \leq 12 \\ 1 & \text{for } t > 12 \end{cases}$

(iv) 0.132

11 $F(x) = \frac{k}{2} - \frac{k\cos 2x}{2}$; 0.146

12 (ii) $1.25\left(1 - \frac{1}{m}\right) = \frac{1}{2}$ (iii) VV0.495

(iv) $f(x) = \frac{1.25}{x^2}$ for $1 \leq x \leq 5$

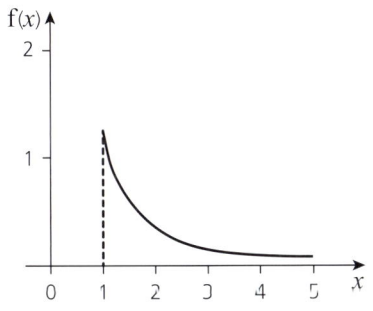

(v) $m = \frac{2b}{b+1}$, which is always less than 2

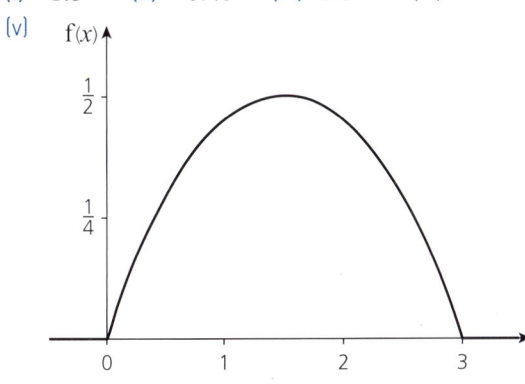

13 (i) 0.6 (ii) 0.04
14 (i) 1.5 (ii) 0.45 (iii) 1.5 (iv) 1.5
(v)

The graph is symmetrical and peaks when $x = 1.5$ thus $E(X)$ = mode of X = median value of X = 1.5.

15 (ii) 1.083, 0.326 (iii) 0.5625
16 (i) $k = 1.2 \times 10^8$
(ii)

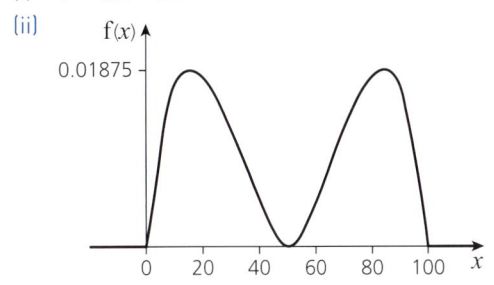

(iii) The distribution is the sum of two smaller distributions, one of moderate candidates and the other of able ones.
(iv) Yes, if the step size is small compared with the standard deviation.

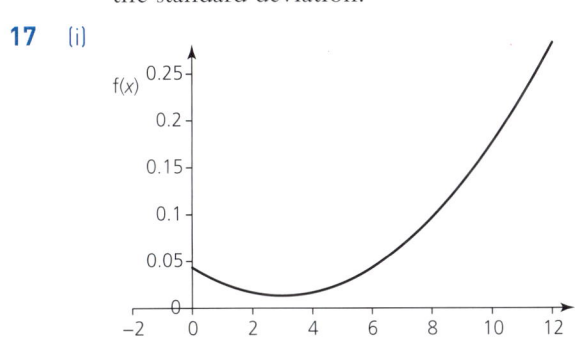

17 (i)

(ii) 8.88, 2.88; 0.724
(iii) $m^3 - 9m^2 + 39m - 450 = 0$

18 (i) $a = 1.443$
(ii)

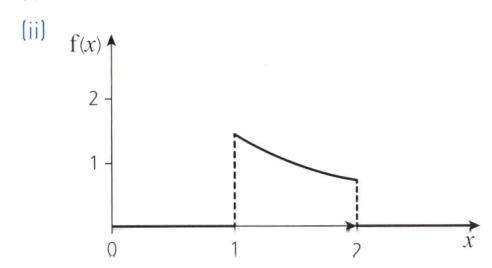

(iii) 1.443, 0.083
(iv) 41.5% (v) 1.414

19 (i)

The model suggests that these candidates were generally of high ability as a large proportion of them scored a high mark.
(iii) 12.5% (iv) No; 91

20 $F(x) = \int f(t)\,dt$ and so $F'(x) = f(x)$.

Uniform distribution with mean value $\frac{a}{2}$.

$F(x) = 1 - \frac{(a-x)^2}{a^2}$ for $0 \leq x \leq a$.

Mean of sum of smaller parts = a

21 (i) (a) Validates p.d.f. form of Z.
      (b) Demonstrates that $E(Z) = 0$.
   (ii) (a) $E(Y) = 1$ (b) $Var(Y) = 2$

Chapter 10

Exercise 10.1

1 (i) 4, 0.875
   (ii) 1.5, 0.167
   (iii)

Main course	Dessert	Price
Fish and chips	Ice cream	£4
Fish and chips	Apple pie	£4.50
Fish and chips	Sponge pudding	£5
Bacon and eggs	Ice cream	£4.50
Bacon and eggs	Apple pie	£5
Bacon and eggs	Sponge pudding	£5.50
Pizza	Ice cream	£5
Pizza	Apple pie	£5.50
Pizza	Sponge pudding	£6
Steak and chips	Ice cream	£6.50
Steak and chips	Apple pie	£7
Steak and chips	Sponge pudding	£7.50

   (iv) Mean of $T = 5.5$, variance $= 1.042$

2 (i) $N(90, 25)$ (ii) $N(10, 25)$
   (iii) $N(-10, 25)$

3 (i) 0.8413   (ii) 0.0548
   (iii) 0.7333

4 (i) 0.0548   (ii) 0.6051
   (iii) 0.6816

5 5.92%

6 0.196

7 (i) 0.266
   (ii) No, people do not choose their spouses at random: the height of a husband and wife may not be independent.

8 0.151

9 (i) 0   (ii) 0.0037

10 (i) 0.3533   (ii) 60
    (iii) Using exact probability of 0.0521 gives 0.1482, using 0.05 gives 0.1426

11 (i) (a) 0.025   (b) 0.242
    (ii) 130   (iii) 0.161   (iv) 0.03559

Exercise 10.2

1 (i) $N(5\mu, 25\sigma^2)$ (ii) $N(5\mu, 5\sigma^2)$

2 (i) $N(30, 15)$ (ii) $N(100, 500)$
   (iii) $N(110, 205)$

3 0.1946

4 0.0745

5 0.1377V

6 (i) $N(34, 30)$ (ii) $N(-4, 30)$
   (iii) $N(24, 29)$

7 (i) 0.316   (ii) 0.316

8 (i) $N(100, 26)$ (ii) $N(295, 353)$
   (iii) $N(200, 122)$ (iv) $N(-65, 377)$

9 (i) 0.0827   (ii) 0.3103   (iii) 0.5

10 (i) $N(7400, 28\,900)$ (ii) $N(1200, 27\,700)$
    (iii) $N(600a + 1000b, 400a^2 + 900b^2)$

11 (i) 0.4546   (ii) 93.491

12 0.9026
Assume weights of participants are independent since told teams were chosen at random.

13 (i) 14%   (ii) 0.6   (iii) 15 m
    (iv) 0.3043

14 (i) $N(80, 8)$ (ii) $N(40n, 4n)$
    (iii) 0.0207   (iv) 0.0456
Choice of limits is ± 2 standard deviations from the mean and so will include 95% of piles that contain 25 pamphlets.

15 (i) 0.3341   (ii) 0.1469
    (iii) 394.38 mm   (iv) 0.9595
    (v) 0.1478

Exercise 10.3

1 (i) $N(60, 8)$ (ii) $N(300, 40)$
   (iii) $N(3000, 400)$

2 (i) Cannot because the distribution of the parent population is unknown
   (ii) $N(6000, 27\,000)$
   (iii) $N(20\,000, 90\,000)$

3 $N(540, 270)$. Assume that the times are independent.

4 0.1030

5 0.9772

6 (i) 0.5945   (ii) 200

7 $n = 80$

8 (i) 0.1367
   (ii) 0.2635
   (iii) 0.5176

Discussion point, page 211

One cannot make any firm conclusions unless it is known that the sample is random.

Discussion point, page 212

It tells you that μ is about 101.2 but it does not tell you what 'about' means, i.e. how close to 101.2 it is reasonable to expect μ to be.

Discussion point, page 216

You may be interested in the time a particular journey takes. You may want to have an upper limit for μ, the population mean time for such a journey, that you know will hold 95% of the time.

Exercise 10.4

1. (i) 1021.5 (ii) 1.94
2. (ii) −3.00 to 4.58
   (iii) No evidence to suggest that there is any difference since the interval contains zero.
3. (ii) 0.054 to 0.818
   (iii) Since the interval does not contain zero, there is evidence to suggest that the absentee rate is less after the introduction of the scheme.
4. (i) 5.205 (ii) 5.117, 5.293
5. (i) 47.7 (ii) 34.7 to 60.7
   (iii) 27.3 to 68.1. This interval is wider than the 90% confidence interval.
6. (i) 0.9456 (ii) £7790–£8810
7. (i) 5.71 to 7.49
   (ii) It is more likely that the short manuscript was written in the early form of the language.
8.

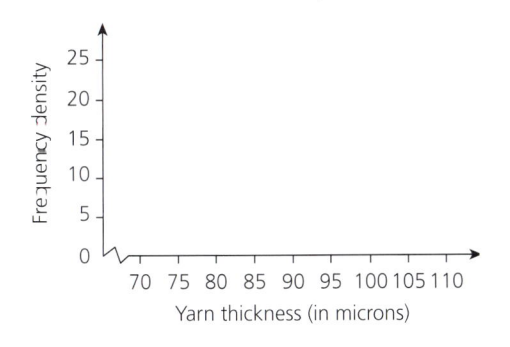

91.32, 7.41; 0.43; 90.5, 92.2

9. A one-sided 95% confidence interval for the mean price of a book is (2.49, ∞). The bookseller is likely to break even.
10. (i) 7.4, 4.05
    (ii) 7.64, 64.758

This suggests that the mean is about right but that the variance is much too small.
   (iii) 6.316 to 8.964
   (iv) The confidence interval is only approximate because the distribution cannot be assumed to be Normal and because σ^2 is not known. The approximation is good because the sample is large enough to suggest that both the central limit theorem would apply, so that $\bar{X}$ can be assumed to be approximately Normal, and that s^2 could be used as an approximation for σ^2 without serious loss of accuracy.
11. (i) 3.768, 0.4268 (ii) 3.644 to 3.892
    (iii) 90% of all such intervals that could arise in repeated sampling will contain the population mean.
    (iv) N(0, 1)
    (v) The sample is large enough to suggest that v could be used as a good approximation for σ^2 without serious loss of accuracy.
12. The required 90% confidence interval is (0, 48.33…) or (0, 48 minutes 20 seconds).

Exercise 10.5

1. (i) $\sqrt{\dfrac{s^2}{n}} = \sqrt{\dfrac{148.84}{7}} = 4.61$
2. (i) 11.25
3. (i) 322.9, 79.54 (ii) 278.8–366.9
4. (i) 66, 17.15 (ii) 51.7–80.3
   (iii) The distribution of the yield of all the fruit farmer's trees is Normal.
   (iv) Number all the trees with different consecutive integers. Copy these integers on to separate pieces of paper; put these in a hat and pick out eight at random. The numbers chosen will identify the trees to be picked for the sample.
5. (i) 18.25, 3.72 (ii) 16.32–20.18
   (iii) The distribution of lengths of sentences written by the accused man is Normal and the text represented by the sample sentences is representative of the general length of sentences he writes.
   (iv) The sample mean lies just outside the particular 90% confidence limits provided by this sample but could well be inside those provided by other samples. Further, it is within the 95% confidence limits. So the evidence is not sufficient to declare him not guilty.

6 (i) 63.6–72.0

(ii) Statistical: the distribution of tyre condemnation mileages is Normal and the 12 tyres tested in the sample are representative of the distribution. Practical: the tyres are tested under genuine working conditions.

7 (i) 21

(ii) The distribution is not Normal.

(iii) No because the confidence interval obtained would be too wide to be meaningful.

(iv) 45.0–66.3; the procedure will be valid provided that the distribution of life expectancies for this group is Normal.

8 (i) 0.633–0.647 (ii) 0.78, 0.160

(iii) 0.616–0.944

(iv) Large sample; no need to assume underlying Normality

9 (i) The method must ensure that each club member has an equal chance of being chosen. Could put names in a hat and select at random or use the random number generator on a calculator.

(ii) Mean = 4.74, $s^2 = 2.74$

(iii) $3.56 < \mu < 5.92$
Background population is Normal.

(iv) By increasing the sample size; 13

10 (i) A random sample is one selected in such a way that all possible samples of the given size are equally likely.

(ii) All samples are possible so a sample of 'unusual' firms might be chosen. 'Biased' here means not representative of the population.

(iii) 8.748–9.552
The population is Normally distributed. 99% of all such intervals that could arise in repeated sample will contain the population mean.

11 (i) Because, on average, the confidence interval will not contain 55 mm in 1 in 20 batches.

(ii) Take a larger sample and construct a confidence interval based on this sample.

12 (i) $t = \dfrac{59.8}{30}$, $s_t^2 = \dfrac{119.7 - 30\left(\dfrac{59.8}{30}\right)^2}{29} = 2.0655$,

$s_t = 1.437$, σ in unknown, so use the t-distrubution, $\nu = 29$.

Limits for CI given by $\dfrac{59.8}{30} \pm \dfrac{2.462 \times 1.437}{\sqrt{30}}$, so CI is (1.347, 2.639).

(ii) Corresponding values for g are 21.8, 5.67.

(iii) 120 measurements will be required. The width of the range for g reduces from about 16 to about 7.

Chapter 11

Exercise 11.1

1 (i) Because the sample is large so the central limit theorem applies.

(ii) $H_0: \mu = 1.5, H_1: \mu < 1.5$

(iii) 0.00142 (iv) −1.968 (v) −2.326

(vi) −1.968 > −2.326 so H_0 should be accepted. There is insufficient evidence to suggest that the bags are underweight.

2 (i) This is the critical value for a 5% two-tailed test.

(ii) 0.8796 < 2.3646 so accept H_0.

(iii) p-value 0.4082 > 0.05 so accept H_0.

3 (i) $H_0: \mu = 0.155; H_1: \mu > 0.155$
Where μ denotes the mean weight in kilograms of the population of onions of the new variety.

(ii) 2.531 > 2.326 so reject H_0. It is reasonable to conclude that the new variety has a higher mean weight.

4 $H_0: \mu = 47, H_1: \mu > 47, 0.8185 < 1.645$ so accept H_0.

5 (i) $H_0: \mu = 72\ H_1: \mu > 72, 3.047 < 3.106$ so accept H_0. There is insufficient evidence to suggest that the batch has a higher than ideal rate.

(ii) Statistical: the distribution of drying rates is Normal and the sample is random.

6 (i) $H_0: \mu = 750\,g, H_1: \mu < 750\,g$

(ii) $t = -4.57$, significant

(iii) The distribution of weights in the shoal is Normal, this may be reasonable. The sample is random; this is certainly not the case since all the pollack came from one shoal. The masses are independent; this may not be true when all the fish are taken from one shoal and so are likely to be of the same age.

7 (i) $H_0: \mu = 75, H_1: \mu \neq 75$

(ii) The population must be Normally distributed and the sample must be random

(iii) $t = 1.836$, not significant

8 (i) 0.1290 (ii) 0.4284

(iii) $t = 0.7026$, not significant

288

9 $H_0: \mu = 9$, $H_1: \mu > 9$; $t = 3.51$, significant
Assume the population is Normally distributed and the sample is random.

10 (i) $N(190, 5\frac{1}{3})$
(ii) The skulls in group B have greater mean lengths and so a one-tailed test is required.
(iii) 193.8
(iv) Sample mean = 194.3 > 193.8 (or 1.809 > 1.645) so reject H_0. There is evidence to support the belief that the skulls belong to group B.

Exercise 11.2

1 (i) P(longer than 1 hour) = p,
$P(X \leq 1 \mid p = 0.2) = 0.0480 = 4.8\%$
(ii) 0.0480
(iii) $P(\text{Accept } H_0 \mid p = 0.09)$
$= P(X \geq 2 \mid p = 0.09) = 0.601$

2 (i) A Type I error here would mean you say that less than 20% of the beans are red when in fact the manufacturer's claim is correct.
(ii) $P(X \leq 1 \mid p = 0.2) = 0.167$

3 (i) $B\left(10, \frac{1}{6}\right)$ (ii) $\frac{5}{3}$ (iii) 0.3230 (iv) 0.2248
(v) $H_0: p = \frac{1}{6}$, $H_1: p \neq \frac{1}{6}$, $P(X \geq 4) = 0.0697 > 0.025$, so insufficient evidence to say the dice are biased.
(vi) power = $P(\text{reject } H_0 \mid p = \frac{1}{4})$
$= P(X \geq 5 \mid p = \frac{1}{4}) = 0.078$

4 (i) 3 (ii) 27.5 (iii) 460
(iv) $P(X \geq 60 \mid \lambda = 50) = 0.0923 > 5\%$, so not significant.
(v) $P(X \geq 63 \mid \lambda = 50) = 0.957$, so critical region is $X \geq 63$.
$P(X \geq 63 \mid \lambda = 50) = 0.0424 = P(\text{Type I error})$.
$P(X \leq 62 \mid \lambda = 60) = 0.634 = P(\text{Type II error})$.
(vi) Power of test = 1 − P(Type II error) = 0.366.

5 (i) 0.9 (ii) 1.9
(iii) 1.645, critical value = 26.48
(iv) 26.71 > 26.48 so H_0 should be rejected.
(v) Critical value = 26.48. $P(X > 26.48 \mid \mu = 25) = 0.05 = P(\text{Type I error})$.
$P(X < 26.48 \mid \mu = 30) = 0.460 \times 10^{-4}$
$= P(\text{Type II error})$.
(vi) 0.0287

6 (i) $H_0: p = 0.36$, $H_1: p > 0.36$,
$P(X \geq 7 \mid p = 0.36) = 0.00429 < 5\%$. Reject H_0
(ii) The likely mistake is to reject H_0 when it is true, which is a Type I error.
Critical region is 6, 7, 8.
$P(X \geq 6 \mid p = 0.36) = 0.0293$

7 (i) 0.175 (ii) 0.560 (iii) $\lambda = 10$ 0.1251
(iv) 0.5421 (v) 0.0308 (vi) 10
(vii) Critical value = 16, $P(X \leq 16 \mid \lambda = 25) = 0.0377$, so the value of 15 is significant; there is evidence to suggest the part is needed less than 5 times a day.
(viii) $P(X \leq 16 \mid \lambda = 25) = 0.0377 = P(\text{Type I error})$.
$P(X \geq 17 \mid \lambda = 20) = 0.779 = P(\text{Type II error})$.
(ix) Power of test = 1 − P(Type II error) = 0.221.

8 (i) (a) 25 (b) 0.1 (c) 0.9
(ii) 0.9020 (iii) $a = 6$
(iv) $H_0: p = 0.1$, $H_1: p = 0.2$, $P(X \geq 6) = 0.0334 > 0.01$, so insufficient evidence to say that $p = 0.2$.
$P(\text{Type I error}) = P(\text{reject } H_0 \mid H_0 \text{ true})$
$= P(X \geq 7 \mid p = 0.1) = 0.00948 \approx 1\%$
$P(\text{Type II error}) = P(\text{accept } H_0 \mid H_0 \text{ false})$
$= P(X \leq 6 \mid p = 0.2) = 0.780$

9 (i) 0.4967
(ii) mean 1.6, variance 1.28
(iii) $n = 44$
(iv) p-value = 0.0440
(v) $P(\text{Type I error}) = P(\text{reject } H_0 \text{ when true})$
$= P(X \leq 4 \mid p = 0.2) = 0.0440$
$P(\text{Type II error}) = P(\text{accept } H_0 \text{ when false}) = P(X \geq 5 \mid p = 0.15) = 0.810$

10 (i) $H_0: \mu = 33.5$, $H_1: \mu < 33.5$, $-3.851 < -2.326$ so reject H_0. There is sufficient evidence to suggest that the mean weight has been reduced.
(ii) critical value is 31.4, P(Type I error) is 0.01, P(Type II error) is 0.329
(iii) power of test = 1 − P(Type II error) = 0.671.

11 (i) $B(100, \frac{1}{30})$ (ii) $\frac{19}{30}$
(iii) $H_0: p = \frac{1}{30}$, $H_1: p > \frac{1}{30}$.
$P(X \geq 7) = 0.050\ldots < 10\%$, so evidence suggests the calculator is biased towards 29.
(iv) P(Type I error) = 0.0501 (3 s.f.), P(Type II error) = 0.766 (3 s.f.)

12 (i) 0.0846   (ii) 0.237
   (iii) $H_0: p = 0.35$, $H_1: p < 0.35$, $P(Y \leq 3) = 0.044 > 1\%$, so not sufficient evidence to suggest the percentage of yellow paper is less than 35%.
   (iv) critical region = $\{0,1\}$. Power = P(reject H_0 when H_0 is false) = 0.00764

13 (i) 13
   (ii) $H_0: p = 0.64$, $H_1: p > 0.64$, $P(X \geq 36) = 0.151... > 5\%$, so there is not sufficient evidence to say that the percentage of A grade apples has increased.
   (iii) critical region = $\{X \geq 38\}$, $P(X \geq 38) = 0.0495 = P(\text{Type I error})$.
      P(Type II error) $= 0.0495 \Rightarrow k = 84$ (2 s.f.)

14 (i) $H_0: p = \frac{1}{6}$, $H_1: p > \frac{1}{6}$, $P(X \geq 3 \mid p = \frac{1}{6}) = 0.225 > 10\%$, so accept H_0
   (ii) P(Type I error) = $P(X \geq 4 \mid p = 1/6) = 0.0697$
   (iii) This would mean saying the die is unbiased when in fact it is.

Chapter 12

Discussion point, page 251

There would be two continuous uniform distributions, one for those aged between 11 and 16, another for those from 16 to 18. The probability density would be higher for the 11 to 16 students.

Exercise 12.1

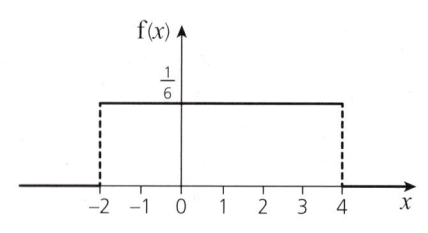

1 (i) [graph of f(x) = 1/6 for −2 ≤ x ≤ 4]
   (ii) $\frac{2}{3}$ (iii) 1   (iv) $\frac{1}{2}$

2 (i) $m = 0.5$, $c = -1$
   (ii) $f(x) = 0$ for $x < 2$, $f(x) = 0.5x - 1$ for $(2 \leq x \leq 4)$, $f(x) = 1$ for $x > 4$
   The distribution is uniform (rectangular).
   (a) $\frac{1}{2}$ (b) $\frac{1}{2}$ (c) 1

3 (i) 2.5
   (ii) $F(x) = \begin{cases} 0 & \text{for } x < 0 \\ \frac{x}{5} & \text{for } 0 \leq x \leq 5 \\ 1 & \text{for } x > 5 \end{cases}$
   (iii) 0.4

4 (i) $f(x) = \frac{1}{3}$ for $4 \leq x \leq 7$
   (ii) 5.5 (iii) $\frac{3}{4}$ (iv) 0.233

5 $3, 9, \frac{1}{6}$

6 (i) $f(x) = \frac{1}{10}$ for $10 \leq x \leq 20$
   (ii) 15, 8.33
   (iii) (a) 57.7% (b) 100%

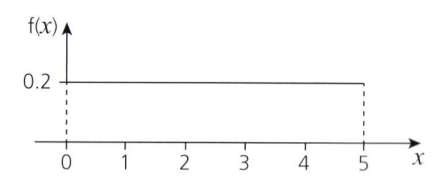

7 (i) $k = 0.2$
   (ii) [graph of f(x) = 0.2 for 0 ≤ x ≤ 5]
   (iii) 2.5 (iv) 7

8 (i) $f(x) = \frac{1}{6}$ for $2 \leq x \leq 8$
   (ii) $a = \frac{\sqrt{3}x^2}{4}$
   (iii) 0.352 (iv) 12.12, 57.6

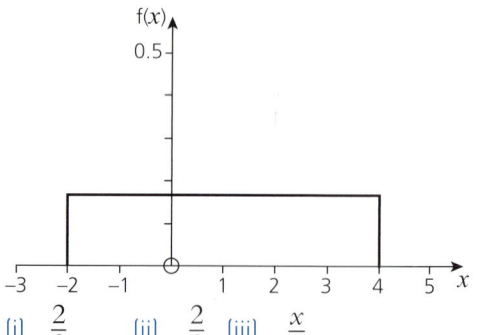

9 [graph of f(x) showing value 0.5 on interval from −2 to 4]
   (i) $\frac{2}{3}$ (ii) $\frac{2}{3}$ (iii) $\frac{x}{3}$
   (iv) $\frac{x+2}{6}$
   (v) 0
   For $x < 0$, $f(x) = 0$
   $0 \leq x \leq 2$, $f(x) = \frac{x}{3}$
   $2 < x \leq 4$, $f(x) = \frac{x}{6}$
   $x > 4$, $f(x) = 0$
   Mean $= \frac{5}{3}$

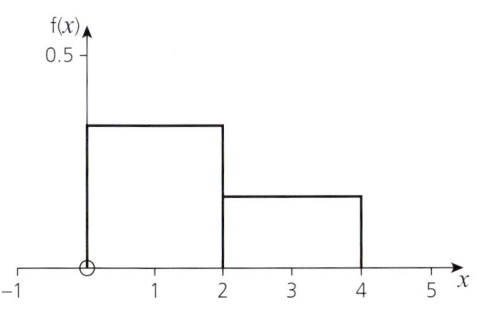

[Graph: f(x) histogram with bars at 0.5 from 1 to 2, and lower bar from 2 to 4; x-axis from -1 to 5]

10 (i) $\mu = \dfrac{b+a}{2}, \sigma^2 = \dfrac{(b-a)^2}{12}$

(ii) $E(\overline{X}) = \dfrac{b+a}{2}, \text{Var}(\overline{X}) = \dfrac{(b-a)^2}{300}$

(iii) Estimate for $\mu = 49.7$, estimate for $\sigma^2 = 9.61$, which gives $a = 44.3$ (3 s.f.), $b = 55.1$ (3 s.f.)

11 (i) p.d.f. is $f(x) = 0.25$ for $1 \leq x \leq 5$, 0 otherwise. Median = 3.

(ii) c.d.f. is $F(x) = 0$ for $x \leq 1$, $\dfrac{x}{4} - \dfrac{1}{4}$ for $1 \leq x \leq 5$, and 1 for $5 \leq x$.

(iii) $P(Y \leq y) = P(X \leq \sqrt{y}) = \dfrac{\sqrt{y}}{4} - \dfrac{1}{4}$.

Differentiating, $g(y) = \dfrac{1}{8\sqrt{y}}$ for $1 \leq y \leq 25$.

(iv) Median = 9

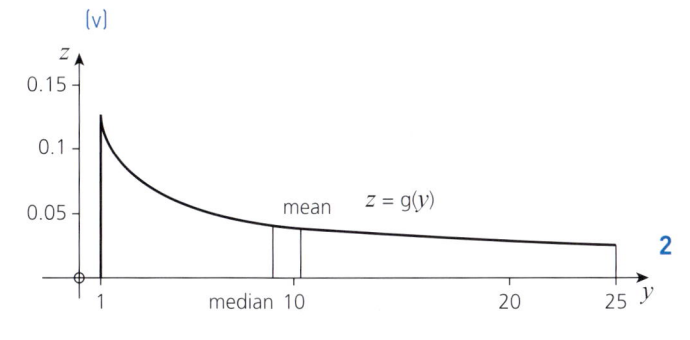

(v) [Graph of $z = g(y)$ with z-axis showing 0.05, 0.1, 0.15 and y-axis from 1 to 25, showing median 10 and mean labels]

Exercise 12.2

1 (i) 0.4 (ii) $F(x) = 1 - e^{-0.4x}$

2 (i) 0.377 (3 s.f.) (ii) 4.14 (3 s.f.)

3 (i) 0.368 (ii) 2 minutes, 2 minutes

4 (i) $a = k$ (ii) $\dfrac{1}{k}$ (iii) $\dfrac{1}{k^2}$ (iv) $\dfrac{\ln 2}{k}$

(v) For example, the lifetime in hours of an electric light bulb.

5 (i) 200 (ii) 0.082 (iii) 0.139

(iv) $k = 7.31$

6 (i) 0.20 (ii) 5, 25 (iii) 18.4..., 2.68, 1.96

7 $\dfrac{a+1}{2} = \dfrac{1}{\lambda}, \dfrac{(1-a)^2}{12} = \dfrac{1}{\lambda^2}$

$\Rightarrow a = \sqrt{3} - 2,$

$\lambda = \dfrac{2}{\sqrt{3}-1}$

8 0.135, 0.171

9 (i) 100 days (ii) 0.026 (iii) 300 days

(iv) £160 000 (v) £16 700

10 (i) $\displaystyle\int_0^x 3e^{-3x}\,dx = \left[-e^{-3x}\right]_0^x = 1 - e^{-3x}$.

(ii) $1 - e^{-3x} = 0.5 \Rightarrow x = 0.23$ (2 s.f.)

(iii) $P(X > t) = e^{-3t} \Rightarrow P(X > a+b \mid X > a)$
$= \dfrac{P(X > a+b)}{P(X > a)} = \dfrac{e^{-3(a+b)}}{e^{-3a}} = e^{-3b} = P(X > b)$

(iv) Suppose a component that still works has been used for T hours. The model suggests that the length of its remaining life is independent of T, which is surely unrealistic.

Practice questions: set 3 (page 265)

1 (i) Omit 0.0, mean = 4.89, sample variance = $\dfrac{328.17 - 9 \times 4.89}{8} = 35.52$ $v = 8$. Critical value is 1.860 and test statistic is 0.0185, so no evidence to reject the hypothesis that the mean score is 5.

(ii) It seems highly unlikely that the distribution of the scores is Normal.

2 (i) Mean = 2.36, standard deviation = 3.06; $a = -0.557, b = 5.277$
Assumptions: journey times are a random sample; distribution of T is Normal.

(ii) Commuter's interpretation is wrong. It should be '90% of such confidence intervals should contain the true mean'.

(iii) Since the confidence interval contains zero, there is insufficient evidence to support the suspicion.

(iv) Confidence interval is likely to be narrow because of lower percentage-point for t value and lower standard error since sample size is large.

3 (i) $H_0: \mu = 18.6$, $H_1: \mu \neq 18.6$, Estimate of population standard deviation = 1.2438, $-1.46 < -1.645$ so accept H_0. There is insufficient evidence to suggest that the mean times have changed.

(ii) Alternative test is *t*-test. Critical value for $v = 29$ not given in tables but for $v = 25$ critical value is 1.725 so using this $-1.908 < -1.725$ so reject H_0. There is sufficient evidence to suggest that the mean times have changed.
Assumption is that the population of journey times is Normally distributed.

4 (i) (a) 0.3935 (b) 0.2231

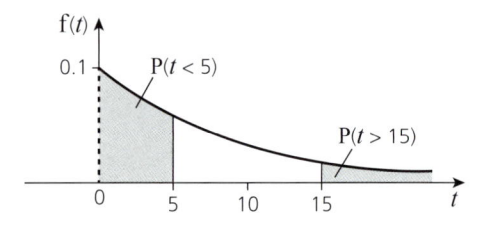

(ii) $F(t) = 1 - e^{-0.1t}$; median = 6.93

(iii) 0.183

5 (i) $f(x) = \dfrac{1}{7}$ for $-2 \leq x \leq 5$

(ii) 1.5 (iii) 4.08 (iv) $\dfrac{5}{7}$

6 (i) 120 (ii) 0.9525

(iii) If the claim is true, the probability of a result as low or lower than this is 0.0000023. This suggests very strongly that the claim is wrong.

(iv) $H_0: \mu = 7800$, $H_1: \mu < 7800$.
$P(\overline{X} < 7500) = 0.0062 < 1\%$ so there is significant evidence that the mean lifetime is less than 7800 hours.

(v) 0.01 (vi) 0.745 (vii) 0.255

7 (i) $M = 3.568$; 5.335

(ii) $f(x) = \begin{cases} \dfrac{324}{x^5} & \text{for } x \geq 3 \\ 0 & \text{otherwise} \end{cases}$

(iii) $\dfrac{81}{256}$

Index

A
alternative hypothesis 53, 231
associations 22
    non-linear 32, 41
    rank correlation 37–8
asymmetrical distributions, hypothesis testing 64–5
averages *see* measures of central tendency

B
bar charts 9
bimodal distributions 7
binomial distribution 49–50, 82
    expectation and variance 91–2
    hypothesis testing 52–4
    link to Poisson distribution 119–20
    using a spreadsheet 50–51
bivariate data 12, 21–2
    interpreting correlation 32
    interpreting scatter diagrams 23–5
    Pearson's product moment correlation coefficient 26–31
    regression lines 25
box plots (box and whiskers diagrams) 8

C
categorical (qualitative) data 8
causation 32
censuses 3
central limit theorem 207, 209–10
central tendency, measures of 11
    discrete random variables 87
    see also mean (expectation); median; mode
chi-squared (χ^2) distribution 128–30
    critical values 130
chi-squared (χ^2) statistic 127–8
    frequency sizes 133
    properties of 131
    using ICT 134–5
    Yate's correction 130–31
class intervals 9, 144
cluster sampling 5
conditional probability 68–9, 240, 241
    notation 69
    screening tests 69–74
confidence intervals 162–3, 212, 224
    asymmetrical 216
    known and estimated standard deviation 215
    one-sided 216–17
    sample size 215–16
    t-distribution 222–3
    theory of 212–14
    two-sided 214
    using ICT 214
confidence levels 213
confidence limits 213
contingency tables 70–71, 126–7
    chi-squared (χ^2) test 127–8, 132–4
continuity corrections 210
continuous random variables 9
    class intervals 144
    cumulative distribution function 181–8
    expectation and variance 151–4
    functions of 173–7
    median 154
    mode 154–6
    probability density 142–3
    probability density functions 143–8
continuous uniform (rectangular) distribution 252–3
    cumulative distribution function 255
    mean and variance 254
controlled variables 22
correlation 22
    interpretation of 32
    interpreting scatter diagrams 23–5
    Pearson's product moment correlation coefficient 26–31
    rank correlation 37–8
critical ratios (test statistics) 233
critical regions 59–61, 232
    and Type I errors 240
critical values 28–30, 59–61, 232, 235
    chi-squared distribution 130
cumulative distribution 182
cumulative distribution functions (c.d.f.s) 181–3
    for the exponential distribution 260–61
    median 184
    properties of 183–8
    of the uniform distribution 255
cumulative frequency curves 10

D
data collection 234
    terminology and notation 3
    see also sampling; sampling techniques
data description 7–9
data displays 9–10
data types 8–9
degrees of freedom 31, 221
    and chi-squared distribution 129
dependent variables 22
deviation from the mean 12
differences of Normal variables 198–204
differences of random variables 99–102
discrete frequency distributions 81–2, 84
discrete random variables 9, 81–2
    expectation and variance 87–91
    functions of 103, 173, 175–7
    linear combinations of 102
    notation and conditions 83–4
    sums and differences of 99–102

Index

discrete uniform distribution 82, 94–5
  expectation and variance 95–7
distributions 7

E

errors, Type I and Type II 55, 114–15, 231, 239–45
  for the Normal distribution 245
exhaustive outcomes 83
expectation (mean)
  of the binomial distribution 91–2
  of continuous random variables 151–4
  of a continuous uniform distribution 253–4
  of discrete random variables 87–91
  of the exponential distribution 259–60
  of functions of random variables 103, 173–7
  general results 98
  of linear combinations of random variables 102
  of a linear function of a random variable 97
  of the Poisson distribution 112
  of sums and differences of Normal variables 198–204
  of sums and differences of random variables 99–102
  of the uniform distribution 95–7
exponential distribution 258–9
  cumulative distribution function 260–61
  mean and variance 259–60
extrapolation 32

F

factorials 109
false positives and false negatives 69–70, 73–4
finite discrete random variables 82
frequency 7
frequency charts 9–10
functions of random variables 103

G

Gosset, William S. 222
grouped data 7
grouping data 9

H

histograms 9–10
hypothesis testing
  one-tailed and two-tailed tests 63–5
  checklist 54
  chi-squared (χ^2) statistic 127–8, 132–4
  critical values and critical regions 59–61
  data collection 234
  definition of terms 53–4
  example 55–7
  null and alternative hypotheses 231
  power of a test 241–5
  procedure 54–5
  significance levels 53–4, 55, 231, 233
  using the binomial distribution 52–3
  using the Normal distribution 231–4
  using Pearson's product moment correlation coefficient 27–31
  using the Poisson distribution 114–15, 243–5
  using Spearman's rank correlation coefficient 39–40
  using the t-distribution 234–6

I

ICT
  binomial distribution 50–51
  chi-squared (χ^2) test 134–5
  confidence intervals 214
  correlation coefficients 30, 40
  hypothesis testing using the Normal distribution 233–4
  hypothesis testing using the t-distribution 235–6
independent events 69
independent variables 22
infinite discrete random variables 82
  Poisson distribution 108–10
interpretation 2
interquartile range 8

L

left and right experiment 61
linear combinations of random variables 102
linear functions of a random variable 97

M

marginal totals 126–7
mass 195
mean (expectation)
  of the binomial distribution 91–2
  of continuous random variables 151–4
  of a continuous uniform distribution 253–4
  of discrete random variables 87–91
  of the exponential distribution 259–60
  of functions of random variables 103, 173–7
  general results 98
  of linear combinations of random variables 102
  of a linear function of a random variable 97
  of the Poisson distribution 112
  of sums and differences of Normal variables 198–204
  of sums and differences of random variables 99–102
  of the uniform distribution 95–7
  see also sample means
measures of central tendency 11
  of discrete random variables 87
  see also mean (expectation); median; mode
median 8
  of continuous random variables 154–6
  of the cumulative distribution function 184

of discrete random variables 87
mind reading experiment 61
mode
    of continuous random variables 154–6
    of discrete random variables 87
modelling 82
    with the Poisson distribution 111–14
multivariate data sets 21
mutually exclusive events 69

N

negative correlation 22, 23
negative skew 7
non-linear association 32, 41
non-parametric tests 41
Normal distribution 156–8, 196–8
    central limit theorem 207, 209–10
    comparison with t-distribution 222
    confidence intervals 212–14, 224
    hypothesis testing on a sample mean 231–4
    notation 196–7
    standardised form 156
    Type I and Type II errors 245
Normal variables, sums and differences of 198–204
notation 3, 131
    for conditional probability 69, 241
    for discrete random variables 83
    for mean and standard deviation 12–13, 19
    for the Normal distribution 196–7
    set notation 70
null hypothesis 53, 231
numerical (quantitative) data 8–9

O

ogive curve 183
one-sided confidence intervals 214, 216–17
one-tailed tests 52–3, 55–7, 63

opportunity sampling 6
outliers 8, 24

P

parent population 3
Pearson, Karl 41
Pearson's product moment correlation coefficient (r) 26
    critical values 28–30
    hypothesis testing 27–31
perfect correlation 22
phi (ϕ, Φ) 197
pie charts 8
Poisson distribution 82, 108–10
    conditions for 110
    expectation and variance 112
    hypothesis testing 114–15, 243–5
    link to binomial distribution 119–20
    modelling with 111–14
    shapes of 111
    sum of two or more distributions 116–18
population correlation coefficient (ρ) 27
population parameters, notation 3
positive correlation 22, 23
positive skew 7
power of a test 241–5
    effect of sample size 245
probabilities, hypothesis testing 232–3
probability density 142–3
probability density functions (p.d.f.s) 143–8
    for a continuous uniform distribution 252–3
    for the exponential distribution 259
    for a Normal distribution 156–8, 196
problem solving cycle 2
    information collection 3–7
    interpretation 2
    problem specification and analysis 2
    processing and representation 7–13
proportional stratified sampling 5

prosecutor's fallacy 72–3
p-values 53–4, 234

Q

qualitative (categorical) data 8
quantitative (numerical) data 8–9
quartiles 8
quota sampling 6

R

random processes 3
random variables 7
range of data 8
rank correlation 37–8, 39–40
    hypothesis testing 39–40
    when to use it 41
ranked data 8
rectangular (continuous uniform) distribution 252–3
    cumulative distribution function 255
    mean and variance 254
recurrence relations 113
regression lines 25
relative frequency 82
representative sampling 4

S

sample means
    distribution of 161–3
    hypothesis testing using the Normal distribution 231–4
    hypothesis testing using the t-distribution 234–6
sample size
    and confidence intervals 215–16
    effect on power of a test 245
sample statistics, notation 3
sampling 4, 211
sampling distribution of the means 206–10
sampling error 3
sampling fractions 3
sampling frames 3
sampling techniques 7
    cluster sampling 5
    opportunity sampling 6
    quota sampling 6
    self-selected sampling 6

simple random sampling 4
stratified sampling 5
systematic sampling 5–6
scatter diagrams 21–2
    interpretation of 23–5
    non-linear association 32, 41
screening tests 69–74
self-selected sampling 6
set notation 70
significance levels 53–4, 231, 233
    choice of 55
    effect on probability of errors 245
simple random sampling 4
skew 7
Smarties experiment 61
Spearman, Charles 41
Spearman's rank correlation coefficient 38
    hypothesis testing 39–40
spread, measures of 11
    standard deviation 11–13
spreadsheets
    binomial distribution 50–51
    chi-squared (χ^2) test 134
standard deviation 11–13
    of continuous random variables 152
    of discrete random variables 89
standard error of the mean 162, 208, 209
standardised form of the Normal distribution 156, 196
stratified sampling 5
summary measures 11
sums of Normal variables 198–204
sums of Poisson distributions 116–18
sums of random variables 99–102
systematic sampling 5–6

T

t-distribution 215, 222–4
    hypothesis testing 234–6
test statistics (critical ratios) 233
    see also chi-squared statistic; t-distribution
tree diagrams 71, 74
two-sided confidence intervals 214
two-tailed tests 63–4
    in asymmetrical distributions 64–5
Type I and Type II errors 55, 114–15, 231, 239–45
    for the Normal distribution 245

U

unbiased estimation of population variance 221–2
uniform distribution *see* continuous uniform (rectangular) distribution; discrete uniform distribution
unimodal distributions 7

V

variables 7
    controlled 22
    dependent and independent 22
    discrete and continuous 9
    see also continuous random variables; discrete random variables; Normal variables
variance 12, 13
    of the binomial distribution 91–2
    of continuous random variables 151–4
    of a continuous uniform distribution 253–4
    of discrete random variables 88–91
    of the exponential distribution 259–60
    of functions of random variables 103, 173–7
    general results 98–9
    of linear combinations of random variables 102
    of a linear function of a random variable 97
    of the Poisson distribution 112
    of sums and differences of Normal variables 198–204
    of sums and differences of random variables 99–102
    unbiased estimates of 221–2
    of the uniform distribution 95–7
vertical line charts 82, 84
    Poisson distribution 111
    uniform (discrete) distribution 95

W

weight 195

Y

Yate's correction
    chi-squared statistic 130–31